T0294263

BARRY &
'THE BOYS'

THE CIA, THE MOB AND AMERICA'S SECRET HISTORY

DANIEL HOPSICKER

THE MADCOW PRESS

Library of Congress Cataloging-in-Publication Data
Daniel Hopsicker, 1951
Barry and The Boys — the CIA, the Mob and America's
secret history / Daniel Hopsicker.
p. cm.
ISBN 0-9706591-7-2
1. Seal, Barry 1939-1986. 2. United States—Politics
and government—. 3. Political corruption—United
States—History-20th century. 4. Narcotics Trafficking 5.
Arkansas/Louisiana-Politics and government I.Title.

Published in the United States by Mad Cow Press LLC

madcownews@gmail.com

Manufactured in the United States of America

10 9 8 7 6 5 4 3

DEDICATION

To Debbie Seal, for her courage and grace.
And to the victims of the longest War ever fought for profit,
the Drug War.

CONTENTS

AFTERWORLD

The supra-national criminal organization which we have been calling "the boys" did not, of course, cease activity with the assassination of one of its most famous members.

We'd like to touch lightly on a few events and scandals since Seal's assassination which can be clearly attributed to this organization: the Venice, Florida aviation activity that preceded the 9.11 attack, the startling discovery that Porter Goss is in the picture on the cover of this book; how Hurricane Katrina revealed what had happened to a man who used to pick up duffel bags dropped from Barry Seal's airplane; and the amazing discovery that the "owners" of a DC9 caught carrying 5.5 tons of cocaine in Mexico in 2006 are names already familiar to those of you who have read this book.

The first is the covert activity in Venice Florida which resulted in the 9.11 attack, the biggest crime in aviation history.

As a result of spending several years writing a book—*this book*—about a life-long CIA pilot who had also been the biggest drug smuggler in American history, we had developed a certain unintended expertise in the many ways in which aviation is used in the pursuit of illegal ends.

And this newly-acquired skill stood us in good stead when we moved to Venice, Florida, home of three of the four terrorist pilots, to investigate what had happened there.

And, briefly, what we learned was this: during the same month that Mohamed Atta arrived to attend his flight school, the *owner* of the flight school had his Lear jet confiscated, on July 25, 2000, on the runway of Orlando Executive Airport, by DEA agents brandishing submachine guns.

They found 43 pounds of heroin on board. You can read all about it in our second book, *Welcome to TERRORLAND*, which can be ordered using the form at the end of this book.

Remind us: What is it, again, that they produce in Afghanistan?

This once again illustrates the central thesis of this book: the importance of narcotics trafficking to the covert intelligence services of the U.S., and all the other countries in the world who like to consider themselves "players."

When you imagine how different America's recent history might have been if this news had come out a week or so after the attack, you can see how tragic it is that we no longer seem to have much of a free press.

A further irony was that Federal court records showed that Wally Hilliard had gotten his Learjet from the same people, at the company called World Jet, who—two decades earlier—provided the Learjet used by Barry Seal.

As we've seen, when the notorious drug smuggling Whittington brothers of Fort Lauderdale, FL. were indicted for smuggling and tax evasion, their prized Learjet had gone to a man soon to become the biggest drug smuggler in American history, Barry Seal.

La plus ca change.... The more things change, the more they stay the same.

We learned the identity of another of the men whose picture is on the front cover of this book. And it could not have come as more of a shock...

Along with the four already identified, whose names became famous and whose lives and careers comprise a large part of America's Secret History, no less a personage than CIA Director Porter Goss appears (see the comparison in the index) in this historic photograph.

In the photograph, he's seated just to the right of Barry Seal. At the time the picture was taken Barry Seal was a young-looking 24-year old. Porter Goss was the same age.

Strangely, Mohamed Atta and the other terrorist hijackers used Porter Goss' Congressional District in Charlotte County as one of their main bases of operations.

We don't think it's a coincidence. It is a fact which virtually shouts out for closer examination.

The product of a patrician Connecticut upbringing, an elite preparatory school and Yale University, Goss entered the high-stakes espionage game being played out between the Florida Keys and the coast of Cuba after the CIA-backed coup against Castro collapsed at the Bay of Pigs.

"During his junior year, he met a CIA recruiter through his ROTC commanders," reported the September 24, 2002 *Orlando Sentinel*, in a story headlined "TERRORISM FIGHT KEEPS REP. GOSS IN POLITICAL FRAY."

"It is true I was in CIA from approximately the late 50's to approximately the early 70's," Goss told antagonist Michael Moore. Goss acknowledged he had recruited and run foreign agents and said he would be uncomfortable traveling to Cuba, but wouldn't say more.

Although the photo was available at the time of his confirmation as head of the CIA, the major media showed no inclination to press Goss on the matter. In fact, the party line rang out everywhere.

"Rep. Porter J. Goss has disclosed precious few details of his CIA employment from roughly 1960 to 1971," reported a profile in the Associated Press. Reuters called him a "mystery man," and said he had been "close-mouthed about his past."

"He worked in Haiti, the Dominican Republic and Mexico-tumultuous countries during that decade of the Cold War," Reuters reported.

During a 2002 interview with the *Washington Post*, Goss joked that he performed photo interpretation and "small-boat handling," which led to "some very interesting moments in the Florida Straits."

"With a prep-school education and a Greek major at Yale, Goss passed up the conventional life to be a CIA spook," reads one typical wire service account.

Actually, the facts lean heavily towards the proposition that with "a prep school education and a Greek major at Yale," Goss's choice to become a CIA spook in the early 60's was an *entirely* conventional one.

The appointment of Porter Goss reveals that what passes for American civic life may in reality be just an elaborate game of Inside Baseball. Goss often found himself paired with fellow Floridian, Democratic Sen. Bob Graham, then the chairman of the Senate Intelligence Committee, and leading the Joint Congressional inquiry into the 9.11 attack.

The two men share another unique distinction, as well. Both men were having breakfast on the morning of September 11th, 2001, with a man who reportedly wired $100,000 to Mohamed Atta.

"When the news [of the attacks on the World Trade Center] came, the two Florida lawmakers who lead the House and Senate intelligence committees were having breakfast with the head of the Pakistani intelligence service."

On a slightly lighter note, another recent development illustrated how dead-on accurate this book's central storyline is: the corruption and drug smuggling in Arkansas during the 1980's.

A year-end recap from New Orleans about Hurricane Katrina on Chris Matthews' *HARDBALL* featured an interview with a local "restaurateur" named Finis Shellnut.

We thought his name looked familiar, but we didn't know why. He's married to Jennifer Flowers, one of Bill Clinton's old tabloid flames. But that wasn't it...

Shellnut on TV was crowing about the blow the disaster had struck to the city's poor people, citing it as an excuse to remake the city in a slightly more upscale image.

Then we read another hurricane interview he'd done, with an accompanying picture showing him drinking a bottle of champagne at an outdoor table...

"Finis Shellnut is wealthy and he isn't hiding it," Germany's *Der Spiegel* reported, "even in the difficult times following the Katrina disaster. The 53-year-old real estate magnate sits in front of one of his buildings in the French Quarter, enjoying a chilled bottle of French champagne... a walking glitz machine, from the diamonds on his Rolex to his gold-framed glasses to the silver cross dangling on his chest under his half-open shirt."

"Shellnut is doing well these days, extremely well. He senses a lot of post-Katrina business coming his way."

"Shellnut wasn't particularly hard-hit by the storm and the flooding in New Orleans. "My real estate is in the city's better neighborhoods," he told Der Spiegel, clearly pleased with himself, "a tree fell down here and there, but otherwise everything's just fine."

He saw the storm as a not-so-undesirable cleanup machine.

"Driving through the city with Shellnut is like going house-hunting with a real estate agent," the magazine reported. "I could get that house for two million, but the one with the park would cost you a little more than that."

"Despite all the chaos and destruction, the storm and the floods came with a silver lining for people like Shellnut. "Most importantly, the hurricane drove poor people and criminals out of the city," he says, "and we hope they don't come back."

Now we remembered where we'd run across his name: in the circle of Barry Seal's drug smuggling buddies in Arkansas. Like that old song from Disneyland: "Its a small world After all... A small small world."

Shellnut may have been responsible for some of the early inaccurate reports from New Orleans stating atrocities were being committed in the days after the hurricane. "Finis Shellnut stuck in French Quarter on phone, surrounded by looters," FOX NEWS reported. Then, a little later: "Finis Shellnut reports looters shot police officer in head."

The atrocities turned out to have no basis in fact, but they may have helped depress real estate prices. That would have made Finis Shellnut real happy.

Shellnut's claim on notoriety came after he was identified as the man who picked up duffel bags filled with cash dropped by Barry Seal at the Triple S Ranch near Hot Springs, Arkansas.

An estimated $9 million per week fell out of the sky.

Shellnut is also the former brother-in-law of Bill Clinton's close personal and political friend, former Asst U.S. Attorney General Webster Hubbell, who went to federal prison for a Whitewater-related conviction.

"A bond trader, that worked for Lasater, was a man by the name of Finis Shellnut," alleged Iran Contra operative Terry Reed in the book *Compromised*. "He was Seth Ward's son-in-law at the time. And Seth Ward owned (whose daughter, was married to Webster Hubbell) a piece of property west of Little Rock called the Triple S Ranch. And that is the ranch in which Seal was jettisoning the large, large... what's called a B-4 bag in the military, a large duffel bag, that can hold about $3 million, complete with radio transmitters so you can locate it."

"That money was being kicked out of Seal's planes onto the Triple S Ranch. And the man that was retrieving the cash was Finis Shellnut and, who worked for Lasater."

In case you were wondering, Finus is pronounced FI-nus, with a long "I" sound, as in "high." For example, His Highness, Finus.

God works in mysterious ways.

Alas, America doesn't.

In America, being connected means never having to say you're sorry.

And, speaking of Seth Ward, here's another connection between the world of *Barry & 'the boys'* and that of our second book: *Welcome to* TERRORLAND: *Mohamed Atta & the 9.11 Cover-up in Florida.* From *Barry & 'the boys'*:

Another client was Truman Arnold, chief money man at the Democratic National Committee for a critical five-month period in 1995 when the DNC was deeply in debt and reeling from its historic 1994 defeat at the polls. Arnold was, interestingly, also one of the select group of people who put Webster Hubbell on the payroll in 1994 between Hubbell's resignation as the Clintons' man at the Justice Department and his subsequent guilty plea to charges that he had defrauded clients and law partners.

Truman Arnold gets around. He also appears in *Welcome to Terrorland*.

And you'll never guess why... Arnold "gave" an airplane to terror flight school owner Wally Hilliard who owned it for a whole year before he had to begin paying for it.

Finally, there is the hugely underreported story of an American-owned DC9 which was caught carrying *5.5 tons* of cocaine in Mexico in April 2006, just as the paperback edition of this book was about to go to the printer.

The plane, which we dubbed "COCAINE ONE," had been owned by a long list of people and companies with whom we were familiar from researching the genealogy of the Beech King Air which was the favorite plane of both Barry Seal and George W. Bush, detailed in the chapter of this book called "The War of 82."

Start with this paragraph about the ownership of the infamous King Air:

> "On paper at least the plane was owned by *a Greyhound Bus Lines subsidiary, Greycas,* which in turn leased it to a mysterious Phoenix firm close to John Singlaub's Enterprise operations named Systems Marketing, Inc, ... [which] then leased it to Continental Desert Properties (a firm owned by Glick.)."

Singlaub's Southern Air Transport owned the C123 used in the Nicaragua sting operation which made Barry Seal famous and was later shot down over Nicaragua with Eugene Hasenfus onboard. This event set off what became known as the Iran-Contra scandal.

Back then, no one knew--or admitted knowing--just who *owned* the company which owned the downed plane, Southern Air Transport.

Government officials were, however, quick to tell reporters it hadn't been the CIA.

Then, long after the Iran Contra scandal had become a fading memory and no one was paying any attention, Southern Air Transport filed for bankruptcy. And the filing revealed that Southern Air Transport had been owned all along by a Phoenix AZ company, Greyhound Leasing.

Greyhound Leasing changed its name to *Finova Capital,* the filing disclosed.

Well, Seal's Beech King Air, which later became George W Bush's, had *also* been owned by *Finova Capital.*

Flash forward to May 2006. While the FAA has been stonewalling requests for the registration history for "Cocaine One" down in Mexico, they did send along the records of its twin, an identical DC9 controlled by the mysterious folks who last owned the unfortunate DC9 with all that coke. Like Cocaine One, this DC9 had also been painted to look like a Dept. of Homeland Security plane.

And its ownership reads like a who's who of CIA aviation front companies. The same companies which were said to have "owned" Barry Seal and George W. Bush's mil-spec King Air are listed as prior "owners" of this plane as well.

Greyhound Leasing and Finova Capital are on the list of prior owners. And one other name too... Ramy Al Batrawi, lieutenant to Saudi billionaire and long-time CIA asset Adnan Khashoggi.

A strange coincidence? Hardly. The airplane clearly belongs to the CIA. Its "ownership" changes as circumstances warrant, from one front company to another.

But the "client" remains the same.

The implication is clear and staggering: the DC9 caught carrying 5.5 tons of cocaine, confiscated in Mexico as it groaned its way northward under a load of 5.5 tons of cocaine, belonged to the CIA.

America's Central Intelligence Agency got caught with 5.5 tons of cocaine.

When CIA Director Porter Goss' resignation was unexpectedly accepted the week after the plane was busted, reporters in Washington dismissed the reasons given by the White House, and professed to be baffled for why Goss was being so suddenly and unceremoniously dumped.

Having a Government Agency caught holding, quite literally, five tons of cocaine can't have pleased the already-embattled President.

Besides, he had John Negroponte to fall back on. Negroponte was U.S. Ambassador to Honduras during the period in the 1980's when it was used as a "trampoline" to bounce planeloads of cocaine from South America on their way north to the lucrative U.S. market. Negroponte not only knew how to make the planes run on time…

He knew how to keep them from being confiscated as well.

Norman Mailer once wrote that the only valid reason for a writer to write is money.

This makes a certain cynical sense. There are easier ways to make a living than stringing words together on a page, especially when the headline we used to advertise *Barry & 'the boys'* on our www.madcowprod.com website turns out to be *too too true*.

"Read a book you're not supposed to."

It is only after five long years of costly and painful litigation that *Barry & 'the boys'* is finally making it to the shelves of your local Barnes & Noble. Now, I *could* wax as bitter as any other obscure writer who thinks he should be hanging out on Oprah.

What was it about the book which made some people work so hard to keep it from coming to light? We'll let you draw your own conclusions.

But we will mention one odd fact: Four best-sellers had already been written about Barry Seal before we moved to Louisiana to do ours.

And all four failed to mention Seal's life-long career as a CIA agent.

Perhaps we should have taken the hint. But we didn't. And we're glad. In the years since *Barry & 'the boys'* was released it has managed to become an underground bestseller…

Still, it hasn't made it into bookstores, which is, after all, the place where they sell *books*.

I have a reason beside Norman Mailer's for writing.

How I found out was when I briefly became significant enough to receive the odd death threat while writing it. Getting a death threat can be wonderful for focusing the mind, and the experience taught me several important lessons.

One is that you can feel relatively safe if what you're doing reveals details about 20-year old covert operations. However, this is decidedly *not* the case if you begin to do what those in the 'trade' refer to as "threatening to compromise current operations."

In between locking all the doors and windows, I stared at my face in the mirror and asked myself more than once why was I doing this. And answering the question actually taught me something important about myself.

With a shock of recognition, I realized that I am a person who wants—at some point before shuffling off this mortal coil—to have some vague idea of what the bloody hell was going on while I was alive.

It doesn't seem too much to ask. Does it?

Daniel Hopsicker
Venice Florida
May 22, 2006

PREFACE

"They wanted the world we got… and we got the world they wanted."

WE ALL KNOW WHERE we were… If you're over 40 you remember where you were and what you were doing when you heard the news. There are moments in life when time freezes, when the clock stops. For my generation, this was that moment.

Thirty years later a generation shocked, horrified, and finally numbed first by JFK's murder and then Martin and Bobby's become hardened; somewhere between Dallas and Vietnam and Watergate and Iran-Contra and whatever that Clinton thing was. Conspiracies might be easier to believe in than our own government… but so what? We all still had to make a living.

But the questions keep coming back. The one I've lived with, and spent two years trying to answer, is this: "Could the assassinations and scandals of the '60s and '70s be somehow related to the cocaine epidemic that swept America during the 1980s? Could the most successful drug smuggler in American history, Barry Seal, have also been involved in the seminal covert operations comprising America's still-secret history? The Kennedy hit, Watergate, and CIA-drug smuggling? In other words, could the "goings-on in Mena, Arkansas" of Barry and 'the boys' about which conspiracy theorists have spun such elaborate gossamer webs… could this have been just the continuation of 'business as usual?'

For me, a three-year long odyssey is ending, a roller coaster ride through the savage heartland of America to find the truth about Adler Berriman 'Barry' Seal, a journey which ended at two separate locations in the French Quarter of Old New Orleans.

The Quarter is America's Casablanca... a scruffy place featuring nightly covert intrigue. Musicians on Bourbon Street still hammer out three-chord blues on old guitars while old dogs lay idly alongside a top hat salted with dollar bills. Old New Orleans is today in the middle stages of Disneyfication; but it can still be seen out of the corners of your eyes: a place of narrow alleyways crowded by overhanging wrought iron balconies, with Ionic pilasters and plaster cornices vying for attention with strangely-plump women with fiery red hair and cat-eyed sunglasses, stuffed into too-tight turquoise dresses.

Here in the heart of the French Quarter one finds—not the beanie babies and Pokemon of middle America—but 'gris-gris' spells, bad 'mojo,' ancient 18th-century skulls, wishing stumps, and black velvet paintings illustrating the lineage's of past voodoo priestesses. New Orleans, sometimes called the least annoying French place on Earth, is where the Saints go 6-and-10.

Our quest ended a block off Bourbon Street, on Royal Street, since the 1830's home to pricey galleries and antique shops. It was here, one recent rainy day, while sipping a café au lait and nibbling a beignet, that we sat waiting for a tall erect man in his early seventies to return from lunch to his antique store across the street, located next to Rothschild's Gallery.

The owner of 'Dixon and Dixon' art and antique store, Dave Dixon, has long been one of Louisiana's most prominent citizens. Known as an intimate of Governors for decades, locally revered as the "father of the Louisiana Superdome," described in the local press most often as 'a French Quarter art dealer,' Dixon, we discovered, was the long-time CIA handler of the most successful drug smuggler in American history, Barry Seal.

You will hear about Mr. Dixon and the world which he and his cohorts have wrought in the pages of this book. His life, and Seal's, truly comprise significant chunks of America's secret history.

But first, so that you might better evaluate what you are about to hear, here is a little about the teller of this tale: two years ago, while heading a production company which produced a business magazine television show airing internationally on NBC, we (the editorial 'we:' there's only one of us) had just set out to do a pilot for a new half-hour show.

Remember *In Search Of,* with Leonard Nimoy? A successful format, we thought, and back in those more innocent Trek-y times there had been no one running around in camouflage uniforms blubbering on and on about the 'New World Order.' So we figured we would update *In Search Of,* for the paranoid '90s.

Alas, the story we chose to feature on our pilot, called "America's most famous unsolved mystery," turned out to be the ultimate sticky wicket. Known as "The Train Deaths," or *The Boys on the Tracks,* the title of Mara Leveritt's excellent recent book (St. Martin's Press) on the case, it involves the murders of two high school seniors in the wrong place at the wrong time who end up being brutally murdered after stumbling onto a "drug drop" in Arkansas in 1987, in a bedroom suburb of Little Rock, an area where neighbors had complained to local sheriffs about low-flying aircraft buzzing over their homes late at night with their lights off.

We arrived in Arkansas as a more-or-less typical example of Los Angeles' Westside liberal mentality. If we gave any thought at all to the hysteria surrounding Bill Clinton at the time (1997), which we didn't, we probably would have told you we assumed it was the result of a successful right-wing Republican propaganda campaign. We learned in Arkansas that we had been both right and wrong: it might be propaganda, but much too much of it also seemed to be all-too-real... the systemic corruption, the intimidation, the fear, and, most importantly, the legendary officially-sanctioned drug smuggling through the small town of Mena.

California may be the place for freeway helicopter pursuits; but we know nothing of drugs raining in duffel bags from the skies on a semi-regular basis, like they do in Arkansas. And California has nothing remotely equivalent to the colorful behavior and criminal exotica which help relieve the tedium of daily life along the humid Gulf Coast.

In the Southeast, from Texas through Louisiana and Arkansas to Florida, life's two biggest rituals may seem to be high school football Friday night and Sunday morning's in church. But, strangely, its also here that the nationwide distribution of narcotics has been a major growth industry for as long as some people can remember.

Like in Louisiana... where the weather permanently hovers between sultry and sweltering, and the lawyers outside Federal courthouse specialize in desultory speculation about whether this or that particular fix "might could" remain in place long enough for this or that politician/miscreant to contact the right people and make the right deal at just the right price.

Or in Arkansas... where "drug drops" in some neighborhoods were endured by the citizenry like they were long lines at the Department of

Motor Vehicles... We heard, from seemingly-solid citizens, whose faces we scrutinized closely and in vain for hints of right-wing Republican fanaticism, that drug drops happened regularly in that otherwise heartbreakingly-unexceptional state.

The citizens of Saline County, where the Train Deaths took place, seem anything but a conspiracy-mongering bunch. They live and work in a bedroom community thirty minutes outside the State Capital of Little Rock with the anonymity of middle class people everywhere. They go to church. They pay their taxes. They mow their lawns. They sew.

The results of our initial investigation became not a half-hour TV pilot but a 2-hour TV documentary about the Train Deaths and their connection to the rampant drug smuggling carried on through Mena, Arkansas helmed by the legendary Barry Seal. Virtually everyone we met in Arkansas had heard about Seal's multibillion dollar cocaine cargo airline operation. And although Barry Seal had been very-publicly assassinated a year before the Train Deaths occurred, his name is so inextricably linked to the subject of drug smuggling in Arkansas that he had immediately became the focus of our attempts to understand what might have taken place there while Bill Clinton was Governor.

During production we went on an unforgettable midnight ride through the Mena airport with Russell Welch, formerly a criminal investigator for the Arkansas State Police. He is a man who was exposed, according to his doctors, to military-grade anthrax because, Welch says, he wouldn't 'turn a blind eye' on the smuggling taking place there. He wouldn't let us film him, or even tape-record his voice that night; even if we *had* been carrying a recorder it would have been rendered useless when he pulled the old trick of cranking the car radio in his Oldsmobile loud, while talking and wheeling around the perimeter of the Interregional Mountain Airport at Mena.

But we caught, clearly, the gist of what he had to say. What has come to be known as the 'Mena Scandal' is not just about things that went on during the 1980s. Apparently, it is also about things that are going on—*right now.*

"See that hangar?" Welch would ask, pointing out this or that building looming in the darkness. "That's owned by..." And he'd launch into an anecdote.

"That's owned by George Reeb, who today owns almost half the airport," he said at one stop on our tour. "When the Arkansas State Police looked into his suspicious activities, we found that he doesn't exist in history past a safe house in Baltimore in 1972."

At another hangar, he said, "That hangar's owned by a guy who smuggled heroin through Laos back in the Seventies."

Again: "That hangar's owned by a guy who just went bankrupt. So what's he do? Flies to Europe for more money. Don't tell me crime doesn't pay!"

Welch pointed out a half dozen lumbering Fokker aircraft parked in a row on the apron. "The DEA's been tracking those planes back and forth to Columbia for a while now."

You get the picture. So did we.

When we had finished our documentary we proudly showed it to our "big dog" Hollywood manager/producer friend, who handles stellar talents like Billy Crystal and Robin Williams. And since only your friends in Hollywood ever give you the bad news straight, we believed him when he told us, sadly, "Your show will not air while Clinton is President."

We believed him, but we didn't stop *trying...* until months later, when a man closing negotiations for the airing of the special had his car deliberately smashed while driving through suburban Los Angeles. A black Chevrolet Suburban with *(natch)* heavily-tinted glass cut him off on Wilshire Boulevard near Los Angeles' Federal Building, stopped in front of him and, oblivious to the heavy noontime traffic, shifted into reverse and rammed back into his small Honda, causing extensive damage and minor injury before escaping onto the 405 freeway.

That weekend the warning was punctuated. His home was ransacked and vandalized, but the only items taken were marketing materials for our show. Left untouched were valuable collections of rare coins and guns.

That *did* get our attention. Our now-incensed friend was busily-pricing weaponry and home surveillance equipment. Fearing injury or worse, we told our friend to cease all efforts on our behalf.

After the dust had settled we decided to write this book.

In November of 1973, while Nixon was still in the White House, an article called "From Dallas to Watergate: The Longest Cover-Up," came out in muckraking *Ramparts* magazine, written by UC Berkeley Professor Peter Dale Scott.

"I believe that a full exposure of the Watergate conspiracy will help us to understand what happened in Dallas and also to understand the covert forces which later mired America in a covert war in Southeast Asia," he wrote. "What links the scandal of Watergate to the assassination in Dallas is the increasingly ominous symbiosis between U.S. intelligence networks and the forces of organized crime."

It is, Scott wrote, no coincidence that most of Watergate's shadow players dwelt in the same conspiratorial world that led to the Bay of Pigs, the assassination plots against Castro involving CIA-mob teamwork, and the gun-and-drug running syndicates formed in pre-revolutionary Cuba and later transplanted to Miami… that had led to, in other words, the JFK assassination.

Barry Seal was an active participant in all of these events, which comprise America's recent secret history. Seal flew guns to Castro in the mountains of Cuba when the CIA was backing him, and then he flew weapons to Castro's CIA Cuban opponents after the Agency had turned on its creation. Seal flew at the Bay of Pigs, flew weapons and got busted in Watergate. Most controversially, he is even alleged to have flown a get-away plane out of Dallas, Texas after the Kennedy Assassination.

And all this *before* he became infamous for importing tons of cocaine—at least $5 billion's worth, by Government estimates—through Mena, Arkansas, in the scandal that's been called the 'scandal behind the scandal' in Iran Contra and Whitewater.

We discovered that it had not been by accident that Barry Seal had found the riches of El Dorado in the covert drug smuggling operation in Mena. He had big boosters and received big help on both the state and federal level. The epic squalor of the events illumined by Seal's life can be almost painful to describe.

The *second* terminus of our journey was at the doorstep of 4507 Magazine Street in New Orleans. There, from behind the screen door of a dark apartment around the back of a dilapidated old rooming house, a man named 'Clay' spoke above the noise from a TV tuned to an ESPN workout show from some sandy beach a million miles away, and confirmed that his was, indeed, the apartment where Lee Harvey Oswald had lived while in New Orleans in 1963… and no, he isn't bothered by many curious sightseers anymore.

We went to Magazine Street to check out a story, first reported by author Ed Haslam while researching Frontline's 1992 documentary on Lee Harvey Oswald, that the rooming house Oswald lived in while in New Orleans had been controlled by Mike McLaney, a Havana casino owner and Meyer Lansky lieutenant, while he was at the same time also running for the CIA a training camp for assassins from which one of the 'shooter teams' in the JFK hit is reputed to have come…. a camp which Lee Oswald had visited.

If Haslam was right, while CIA-sponsored exiles were encamped in the swampy country across Lake Pontchartrain from New Orleans, Lee Harvey Oswald was living in a CIA safe house.

More importantly, Lee Harvey Oswald and Barry Seal had been cadets together in the Louisiana Civil Air Patrol, we will learn, and had even gone to a two-week long CAP summer camp together where both first met their eventual recruiter into what E. Howard Hunt puckishly calls 'clandestine services,' David Ferrie...

It is the central thesis of this book that following Barry Seal's life-long government career in 'clandestine services' leads in a straight line from the killing of a President—Seal's CIA handler Dave Dixon was a 'great good friend' of the only man ever charged with conspiracy to murder President Kennedy, Clay Shaw—to the ruin of the inner cities of this country by the cocaine epidemic of the 1980's, an epidemic fueled in no small part by the billions of dollars' worth of cocaine which Barry Seal's operation imported.

Commenting on the CIA's affair with the Mafia, L.B.J.'s press secretary Bill Moyers said, "Once we decide that anything goes, anything can come home to haunt us."

"If a fool would persist in his folly, he would become wise," wrote poet William Blake. I persisted.... And I may have proved him right.

New Orleans

July 27, 2000

CHAPTER ONE

ALL OUR SECRETS
ARE THE SAME

THIS IS THE STORY of Barry Seal, the biggest drug smuggler in American history, who died in a hail of bullets with George Bush's private phone number in his wallet...

"It looks like a hit," said Baton Rouge Police Chief Wayne Rogillio. "Daredevil pilot, gunrunner, CIA covert operative extraordinaire, and soldier of fortune" are a few of the tags journalists have stuck on Barry Seal.

"They felt from the beginning it was for hire," FBI Special Agent Ed Grimsley stated. "It would appear from the way it happened that it was well-planned and well-executed."

But the most common description of Seal in the press was as "a wealthy, convicted drug smuggler working as a federal informant in hopes of leniency."

"It'll empty a 20-round magazine before the first casing hits the ground," ATF agent Jim Adamcek stated, about the Mac-10 machine gun used in the killing.

Ten years after his death the *Wall Street Journal* gave Barry Seal another 'tag.' They called him "the ghost haunting Whitewater."

Barry Seal, and the 'goings-on in Mena to which he is inextricably linked, have been an issue in three consecutive Presidential elections.

And now a fourth, with allegations re-surfacing of Seal's involvement in a DEA sting in which a group of red-faced federal officials netted a nonplussed George W. Bush, Jr. This is a remarkable testament to the fact that nothing can remain *totally* hidden from the American body politic. But that's not to say that *both* major political parties aren't still giving it the old college try.

This book will tell you why.

Barry Seal was dead, gunned down by two quick bursts from a fully automatic silencer-equipped MAC-10 machine pistol in the most visible assassination in America since John Kennedy's.

The killer had been lurking in the shadow of a garbage dumpster, lying in wait when Seal maneuvered his large white Cadillac into the parking lot at 6 PM and backed into a parking spot.

The shooter approached from the driver's side, firing. Two quick bursts from his machine gun ripped through Seal's head and body.

He saw it coming, and covered his ears with his hands. Then, with his head settled onto the Cadillac's steering column, Barry Seal slipped into history in the soft Baton Rouge twilight of February 19, 1986, dead instantly.

The shooter dashed back into the getaway car and it sped off, forcing a pedestrian to leap out of its path.

A bystander later said he heard the men inside the car laughing.

The newspapers called Seal's killing a "gangland-style murder." But in Webster's dictionary is another word, which more accurately describes what happened. 'Assassination,' reads this definition, is "murder which changes the world." Because when Barry Seal died, taking with him answers to questions that congressional investigators in two major American scandals were never quite able to puzzle out for themselves, it was, indeed, "murder which changes the world."

What Seal could have revealed—had he lived—would have likely changed the course of American politics in the 1988, 1992, and 1996 Presidential elections. But since the death of Barry Seal, very little light has been shed on the dark secrets about America, which he carried to his grave.

"It looked like they were getting rid of people who knew too much about Mena," stated one observer at the time.

A high-rolling mercenary, a rogue pilot, an infamous gun-runner, the chief Mena narcotics trafficker, a fast-talking, self-assured, 300-pound pilot and Special Forces veteran, a notorious drug smuggler, a mystery man, and "the most valuable informant in DEA history"... Barry Seal has been called all of these.

Seal's life was so exciting that Hollywood has already made it into a movie, *Double-Crossed*, starring Dennis Hopper, and his daredevil persona was too big to be contained by just one name.... He was "Ellis McKenzie" to the Colombians, "Thunder Thighs" to his fellow drug pilots, "El Gordo" to Honduran military authorities, and "Bill Elders" to the press... and his life had as many Byzantine turns as his numerous *nom de guerres* attest.

Though he was a contemporary of James Dean, Barry Seal was another kind of American icon; while Dean always played the outsider, the suave Seal was the master of the *inside move*. An American James Bond with his own Lear jet... as American as the crawfish étouffeé in one of Carlos Marcello's New Orleans restaurants, Seal, a close friend of pop singer and fellow Baton Rouge native Johnny Rivers, may even have provided the songwriter the inspiration for his hit *Secret Agent Man.*

And although the name Barry Seal will go down in history in connection with the Arkansas scandals of President Bill Clinton, Arkansas was *not* the place that nurtured him into the swashbuckling figure he became. He grew, instead, from the fertile culture of *Louisiana*, the only place in the Western World where you can get a drive-through daiquiri in a monogrammed 'go-cup.'

Louisiana—run by Mafia Kingfish Carlos Marcello—is where Barry set up his illegal air cargo airline, which someone once dubbed "AirCocaine." And Louisiana, with its overripe culture, reeking slightly of Roman decay, is arguably as far away as you can get and still be considered to be in the United States. More than just the setting for the story of Barry Seal, the state whose license plates boast "Sportsman's Paradise" is a character in the drama in its own right.

"How is it," we asked former *Baton Rouge Advocate* reporter John Semien, who worked the 'Seal' beat there for many years, "that the people of this smallish bayou-infested state have managed to have such a powerful influence on the course of national events?

His answer, when it came, was succinct, poignant, and rendered in the local dialect.

"They eccentric," he stated simply. And so they are.

The dramatic saga of Louisiana native Seal has already been the stuff of numerous bestsellers: *Partners in Power,* by Sally Denton and Roger Morris, *The Secret Life of Bill Clinton* by British journalist Ambrose Evans-

Pritchard, and *Compromised*, by Terry Reed and John Cummings, first to bring an incredulous nation an account of what went on in Mena, Arkansas.

And at least one writer, Arkansas state trooper L. D. Brown, was reportedly paid a tidy sum *not* to write about it, just before the 1996 Presidential election. Which makes it too bad nobody offered to buy and then not publish reporter Danny Casolaro, who was murdered in Martinsburg, West Virginia in 1992, reportedly en route to meeting an informant with evidence of CIA and NSA involvement in drug smuggling through Mena in support of American military operations in Central America.

Well before his slaying in 1986 at the age of 46 Barry Seal's colorful life had made him famous in his native Louisiana. But the events, which gained him *national* recognition, strangely, both occurred *after* his death. In the first President Ronald Reagan went on national television in March of 1986, less than a month after Seal's assassination, to announce that the Sandinistas were involved in the drug trade. Mr. Reagan brandished photos purporting to show a top Sandinista official, Federico Vaughan, loading cocaine onto a plane alongside Seal and Medellin drug lord Pablo Escobar.

Looking visibly angry, Reagan said, "I know every American parent concerned about the drug problem will be outraged to learn that top Nicaraguan (Sandinista) officials are deeply involved in drug trafficking."

Reagan's evidence, though he never cited its source, were photographs taken by Barry Seal from hidden cameras in the back of his "Fat Lady" C-123 military cargo plane, in the Nicaraguan drug sting operation for which he was later called "the most important government informant in DEA history."

The second event that made Barry Seal famous came seven months later. It became the milestone event of the Reagan '80's, the shooting down over Nicaragua of Seal's C-123 military cargo plane, with Eugene Hasenfus on board. The crash cracked open the Iran Contra Scandal and inspired an ambitious burst of emergency damage control by Lt. Colonel Oliver North, who embarked on a three-day shredding spree reportedly designed to remove any trace of the name "Barry Seal" from his files.

Even with North's three-day head start, congressional investigators later discovered in North's remaining notebooks over 500 references to drugs, in just the files North & Co. deigned to declassify for Congress, in the same spirit of *noblesse oblige* shown by the CIA in 1997 when it announced that it was clearing itself, after investigating itself, of allegations of drug smuggling.

Lt. Colonel North's ties with Barry Seal are covered in this book. As former CIA pilot and lawyer Gary Eitel remarked about North, "Going to church doesn't make you a Christian, anymore than going to a carwash makes you a car."

Also covered are the persistent allegations of ties between Seal and former President George Bush, as well as his two sons, Jeb and George W. "We found a drilling rig moored in Mexican waters that served as a safe harbor for drug smuggling," one Southern lawman told us. "When we set up a sting out at Tammiani Airport in South Florida, it was aborted—way higher-up and at the last possible minute—upon discovery that the Bush brothers were flying in on the King Air we were tracking."

But this is not a scandal of any *one* political party. Several of Seal's fleets of smuggling aircraft, we will learn, were owned by a man whose personal attorney was the then head of the Democratic National Committee, Charles Manatt. Small world: Manatt was also the political mentor of the leading Congressional voice calling for an accounting of the CIA's involvement in the drug trade, California Democrat Maxine Waters. And he is today the US Ambassador to the Dominican Republic, whose countrymen, law enforcement sources say, have come to dominate narcotics distribution on the Eastern Seaboard.

It is instead a scandal of what sociologists call "elite deviance," a condition that exists when the elite in a society begin to believe that the rules no longer apply—to *them.*

"Scandal in contemporary U.S. life is an institutionalized sociological phenomenon," states Professor David Simon in *Elite Deviance.* "It is not due primarily to psychopathological variables, but to the institutionalization of elite wrongdoing which has occurred since 1963. Many of the scandals that have occurred in the

U.S. since 1963 are fundamentally interrelated: that is, the same people and institutions have been involved." Barry Seal's life and violent death provide the perfect illustration of this idea.

The 'official story' about Seal, the cornerstone of the Iran Contra cover-up, can be boiled down to a few succinct statements: "Drug smuggler-turned-DEA-informant Barry Seal conducted the most important 'sting' in narcotics enforcement history when he flew to Nicaragua in May and June of 1984."

"The CIA rigged a hidden camera in the plane, enabling him to snap photos of several men, including Pablo Escobar and high-ranking Sandinista official Federico Vaughn, loading cocaine aboard his C-123 military cargo plane. These pictures later resulted in the indictment on narcotics smuggling charges of the Medellin Cartel, Jorge Ochoa and Pablo Escobar."

"In retaliation, Seal was murdered by cartel hit men twenty months later."

This official version of events, we will learn, is a complete lie, scripted and orchestrated at the highest levels of government in Washington D.C. in an operation which swung into high gear before Seal's bullet-ridden corpse had even been delivered to the Baton Rouge morgue.

Why has so much energy been expended to cover up the circumstances of the death of what the *Clinton Chronicles* called just a "sleazy drug smuggler?" The answer lies in the tiny hamlet that has been dubbed the "conspiracy capital of the western world," Mena, Arkansas.

For well over a decade disturbing allegations have dribbled out about a clandestine operation in Mena involving arms sales, drug trafficking, two American Presidents, and all the elements of a fast-paced thriller: daring drug smugglers, gunrunners, duffel bags filled with cash dropping from the sky, murder by ambush, revenge in the dead of night...

It is a scandal to rival any in the history of American politics. In outline it goes like this: Mena, a town in far western Arkansas, was the base for a large, clandestine CIA aviation operation in the 1980s that flew weapons to the Contras in Nicaragua and returned from Central America with drugs which were then distributed throughout the United States, with protection from both the state and federal government.

"Mena Arkansas is just a small town of 5000 or so souls, attached to an international airport bigger than the Little Engine That Could," one waggish law enforcement source told us. "And to top it off, its tucked away in the farthest corner of one of the hardest-to-get-to places in the lower forty-eight contiguous states."

It's as apt a characterization as any for why this small town in the foothills of the Ozarks should have become the center of controversy in both the Iran Contra and Whitewater Presidential scandals. "The greatest story never told," British journalist Ambrose Evans-Pritchard called what happened when someone finally tried to tell it.

In the winter of 1995, Dr. Roger Morris and Sally Denton, veteran investigators with established reputations, sold their detailed and well-documented piece on Barry Seal and Mena to the *Washington Post* for the largest sum paid by that paper's Sunday Outlook section.

These weren't a couple of kooks on the Internet… Morris had worked for the National Security Council at the White House under Nixon, taught at Harvard, and was a Guggenheim Fellow and National Book Award Winner; Denton was a respected author and former head of UPI's investigative unit.

Their story, "The Crimes of Mena," had already passed an excruciatingly-long vetting process overseen by the paper's lawyers, and was cleared to run—*on two full facing pages*—when the *Post* abruptly cancelled it after the galleys had already been set, pulled at the last minute by the paper's executive editor under circumstances that are the very definition of "murky."

As *Post* nemesis Ambrose Evans-Pritchard reported gleefully in his paper the *London Telegraph*, "The article was typeset and scheduled to run. It had the enthusiastic backing of the editors and staff of the Sunday Outlook section, where it was to appear after 11 weeks of soul-searching and debate. Lawyers had gone through the text line by line. Supporting documents had been examined with meticulous care. The artwork and illustrations had been completed. The contract with the authors had been signed. The executive editor of the paper had given his final assent."

"But on Thursday morning the piece was cancelled," continued Evans-Pritchard. "It had been delayed before—so often, in fact, that its non-appearance was becoming the talk of Washington—a cover-up of the biggest scandal in American history."

"Its down to naked politics now," Morris said in the heat of journalistic combat. "We've jumped through every hoop. We've given them everything that they've asked for. They can't say the story's not credible now."

Based on Barry Seal's "own archives of more than 2000 documents" the article, when it finally came out in *Penthouse*, reported that western Arkansas had been a center of international drug smuggling during the 1980's, and the headquarters of perhaps the biggest drug trafficking operation in *history.*

But *Post* Managing Editor Robert Kaiser told reporters that there was really nothing *to* this "non-existent story;" he dismissed it as a reprise of rumors and allegations. "I am confident that it doesn't have any great revelations," he said.

Especially after reading it, others were less confident. Its contents "appear to be absolutely explosive," said one insider.

When the *Washington Post* arbitrarily decided that the discovery of the drug smuggling capital of the century was non-news in America, The

London Telegraph stated with consummate British understatement that the treatment of the article would fuel claims that the *Post* had engaged in "active suppression of the news to protect either Clinton or the CIA or both."

But few Americans get their news from the British press, and by killing the story the *Post* was successful in keeping the scandal out of the mainstream media. Sally Denton and Roger Morris' effort, the initial serious journalistic telling of the story of Barry Seal, then went on to become something of a journalistic *cause célébre*. And just as doubts about the 'lone nut' theory of the Kennedy Assassination first surfaced among the knowledgeable elite, so too, did word of the Mena Scandal, spreading first among the newly-digital cognoscenti with the emergence of the Internet. There, the inconsistencies of the 'official version of events' quickly caught the eye of a jaded public cynical of its government, and prepared to believe it capable of *almost* anything.

But of *drugging* its own citizens? That's a tough pill to swallow. And it would have seemed too bizarre to even contemplate until the CIA-drugs story got what's known in the trade as *legs*... with the publication of Gary Webb's Dark Alliance series in the *San Jose Mercury News*. Webb's series showed how US intelligence had facilitated the distribution, down to the street level, of the flood of narcotics that washed away the infrastructure of America' inner cities in the 1980's. Street-level Drug Kingpins like Freeway Ricky Ross and CIA operatives like Ron Lister instantly became well known.

"You know, this is not something that comes into the daylight easily," Webb told us. "It comes out inch by grudging inch. And with every inch given, the reporters pulling it out from underneath the rug were systematically discredited and criticized."

"I did part of a chapter in *Dark Alliance* about Barry Seal and Mena, because it was so similar to what the drug ring that I was writing about was doing in El Salvador," Webb continued. "One of the things I found fascinating was an FBI report on their 4-year long investigation into the Dan Lasater drug ring."

"I discovered a secret FBI report tucked away in the FBI's own annual report that describes Lasater's organization as a vast, *vast* drug operation that they had uncovered. And I could never figure it out since it doesn't jibe with what happened: the investigation stopped at Lasater, and he got a slap on the wrist, as if he had been dealing maybe just a kilo here or there. But the FBI description is that his was a *monstrous* operation. They don't send Organized Crime Drug Task Forces after businessmen taking a couple of toots now and then. These are major investigations. There's clearly much more to that Mena investigation than we know about."

Gary Webb's curiosity earned him the reward today's newspapers reserve for gutsy investigative reporting on politically sensitive issues. He was ostracized, his follow-up stories went unpublished, and after being transferred and taken off the investigative beat, he left journalism.

A journalist of our acquaintance was recently asked, "What qualities are top newspapers looking for today when hiring?"

He replied, "The ability to stand there with your hair on fire while assuring your readers you can't smell smoke."

Journalism has failed America, and often, on the subject of the drug trade. Barry Seal's death in 1986 was front-page news in major metro centers of the drug trade in the Southeastern United States like Miami, New Orleans, and Baton Rouge, Louisiana. But there was a parrot-like sameness to the coverage, as if every news outlet were reading from the same DEA handout. No attention was paid to the massive inconsistencies in the official version of events, and faster than you can say "lone nut gunman" the Medellin Cartel was blamed for Seal's assassination.

In each journalistic re-telling of his assassination, Barry Seal was the drug smuggler-turned-informant who goes down for ratting out Pablo Escobar and Jorge Ochoa, the top cocaine barons of the Medellin Cartel. Seal, described as "the most important drug informant in U.S. history," is left unprotected by vengeful Louisiana authorities—who don't care that he's been providing crucial testimony in some of the biggest drug prosecutions in DEA history—to be machine-gunned to death outside a half-way house in Baton Rouge by cartel hit-men exacting revenge for breaking the code of silence.

A sample from the *Miami Herald*:

"How did a man described as the most important drug informant in U.S. history find himself alone in a seedy Baton Rouge Louisiana neighborhood? Unarmed, unguarded, a sitting duck for assassins eager to collect the $500,000 bounty on his head?"

John Semien covered the Seal saga better than most from a perch at Barry's hometown *Baton Rouge Advocate*:

"Seal was a trusted courier for cartel leader Jorge Ochoa-Vasquez, who Seal said was pioneering a new cocaine distribution route through Nicaragua with the help of the Sandinistas. The resulting sting operation made drug enforcement history and blew Seal's cover as an undercover informant. A $500,000 contract on Seal's life followed, and Seal was murdered shortly before he was expected to testify about the Nicaraguan sting operation against powerful Colombian drug czars under indictment in Miami."

But even a cursory examination of this story reveals that Seal himself had not shown any nervousness or anxiety about being assassinated by the Medellin cartel. He had even explicitly denied that he had anything to fear from them, just weeks before his death.

The *Miami Herald* reported: "After a bitter argument with federal officials in his home town of Baton Rouge, La. Seal chose to serve out a probationary sentence at a local Salvation Army halfway house instead of enrolling in the federal Witness Protection Program. Seal told the DEA the cartel would never try to kill him for turning informant. "He said it was just business," one DEA agent remembered.

Barry Seal was *not* murdered by the Medellin Cartel, we discovered. And the cover story that Jorge Ochoa, head of the Medellin Cartel, had Seal murdered in a contract killing is a much a Big Lie as anything ever churned out of Nazi propaganda mills during World War II.

Incredibly, on the night Barry Seal was killed three other top lieutenants of the Medellin Cartel were also assassinated: Pablo Ochilla, Pablo Carrera, and the brother-in-law of Jorge Ochoa. The coordinated operation committed murders occurring simultaneously in Miami, Colombia and Baton Rouge.

It's as if in *The Godfather* Robert Duvall, Jimmy Caan, and Al Pacino all get whacked and newspapers the next day pin the blame for the killings on Marlon Brando. Even more incredibly… they've gotten away with it for 13 years. They've made it stick. One intelligence veteran termed it "a classic 'disinfo' campaign."

Though contemporaneous TV news coverage reporting the murder of Barry Seal linked it to this larger drug world slaughter, in the newspaper articles and books that have been written since Seal's murder is always treated as a solitary event.

This is America's secret history. Barry Seal was murdered in an intelligence operation that was the blackest of black ops, an underworld putsch of terrible dimensions, and then completely covered up. And why it's taken fifteen years for the facts to begin to seep out leaves many who have delved into this subject with a nauseous feeling in the pit of the stomach, a queasiness normally associated with those incurably-existential French.

Gary Webb felt it. "I thought it (the CIA drug story) was very depressing, frankly. I mean, my dad was a Marine for 20 years, and I grew up on military bases. And I was a true believer. You can't live that kind of life without believing very strongly in what your father stands for, and what your country stands for… and it sure as shit didn't stand for drug trafficking."

What remains of America's free press isn't the only institution spooked by the immensity of the scandal of Barry Seal's officially-sanctioned drug smuggling. The story frightened poor testosterone-impaired Independent Counsel Kenneth Starr so much he tried to flee to Malibu to take up surfing with Pepperdine law students. His Whitewater inquiry had once raised hopes of getting to the bottom of allegations of government-sanctioned drug smuggling during the 1980's, generating headlines like 'Whitewater Probe to Eye Arkansas Drug Ring."

"Congressional investigators are trying to find out who interfered with the ability of law enforcement to stop the flow of Latin American cocaine into that state (Arkansas)—and why," began one AP story on Starr's investigation.

When Starr's report turned out to be nothing more than a weird All-Monica News-channel, many were entertained by the absurd spectacle of a dim-witted law professor investigating the sex life of a movie star President. But astute observers were left with the uncomfortable feeling that the American people had been left holding the bag on yet *another* 4-year long investigation into corruption in Arkansas which buried the scandal it was supposed to expose, proving only that the best way to cover-up really major corruption in Washington is to appoint a Special Prosecutor.

Why is there still such persistent interest in Barry Seal? Because there is abroad in America today big questions about illicit drugs in America. Who controls and runs this most lucrative trade? Who profits? Anyone in, say, Washington D.C.? It is patently absurd that the vertical integration of one of the largest industries in the world is so studiously ignored in the media.

Had he not been such a larger-than life character Seal's story might not have attracted as much attention. But in the submerged world of covert operations, "Biggie," as he sometimes called himself, was the whale that breached the surface while the tourists in the whale-watching boat had their binoculars pointed in his direction.

The covert side of the American government has grown increasingly important since the early 80s. Said one veteran of American military intelligence, "Barry Seal had, basically, a middle management career in covert operations."

Even so, the exploits of Barry Seal exceed anything this side of a Tom Clancy novel... and it is in large measure a cover-up of *his* activities, and those of the men for whom he worked, which has been at the root of the failure of American democracy in the last two major Presidential scandals, Iran Contra and Whitewater.

Seal's slaying was a crucial first strike in a successful operation that effectively neutralized a key ingredient in any functioning democracy: the truth. It was the opening salvo in a clean-up operation designed to cover the tracks of what has been called the most massive covert operation in this nation's history, Operation Black Eagle. Run in large part out of Mena, Arkansas, it became a network of 5000 people, who made possible the export of arms to Central and South America and the import of drugs from the same places the weapons went.

"It went far beyond a simple operation to finance the 50,000man Contra army," according to retired Navy Lt. Commander Al Martin, who was a participant. "Black Eagle eventually created an intricate web of state-sponsored fraud, as well as trafficking in narcotics and weapons."

Events during Bill Casey's tenure as Director of Central Intelligence lead to several questions never posed by Bob Woodward in his puffball book on Casey, which never once even used the word "cocaine." Did a shadowy group of government officials and intelligence operators turn "Benedict Arnold's" in America's War On Drugs? If so, did the billions in "soft money" generated by Barry Seal's operations and the ones which succeeded it end up subverting the very democracy these operatives were sworn to uphold?

Some may have thought that this sordid chapter in American history ended with Oliver North raising his right hand in front of the hot TV lights at the Iran Contra Congressional hearing, while spectators in the gallery chanted, "Ask about the cocaine smuggling! Ask about the cocaine smuggling!"

But it didn't. The Enterprise lives, generating more dirty cash today than ever. That's the sour reality in the quote from Marine Corps spokesman Lt. Colonel John Shotwell, who said of North, "He could have gone to the moon, and it wouldn't be in the file."

"Barry and 'the Boys'" is the story of some of the things that didn't go into the file.

So if Jorge Ochoa didn't order the assassination, who did?

Just ten days before he died, Barry Seal had threatened, in a typical display of the fearlessness for which he was justly famous, to expose the gun running and drug smuggling that flourished in Mena Arkansas in the early and mid-Eighties.

The man he threatened? Vice President George Bush.

"All three of the guys on trial," states Richard Sharpstein, the Miami attorney for one of the three Colombians convicted in the killing, "all told their attorneys that once they reached the United States their actions were directed by a United States military officer, whom they very quickly figured out was Lieutenant Colonel Oliver North."

"Barry was smuggling drugs for the government," says Homer "Red" Hall, an electronics technician who traveled to Nicaragua with Seal on his CIA sting mission, designed to be a Gulf of Tonkin incident spurring a wider U.S.-Nicaraguan war. "There's no doubt about that. The only thing, Ollie North was trying to cover his tracks from what we were doing down there, working with the Sandinistas. North stepped into something that he tried to back out of, that he wanted to keep quiet."

"I know that we took a load of equipment and a bag-full of money to buy drugs, and I set up all the communications for them (the Sandinistas) so they could talk back and forth, putting in high-frequency radios from E-Systems. We supplied the Sandinistas with communications equipment," Hall said, "and I don't think that's ever come out before."

Said Hall, the only living participant in the Nicaragua "sting" operation who is still alive, "The only person who knew as much as North did about all this was Barry Seal. Barry knew it all. I can't figure any other reason (for his killing)."

Events in Baton Rouge the night of Seal's death have been whispered about by investigators for years. One enduring mystery swirls around the appearance of what local law enforcement officials on the scene nervously referred to as "The Men in Black."

Late the night of Seal's slaying a squad of FBI and other federal agents swooped down in force on the Baton Rouge headquarters of the Louisiana State Police, and confiscated, at virtual gunpoint, material evidence in the case from investigating homicide officers charged by law with preserving it uncompromised for the prosecution of the capital crime of murder.

"It was a 'clean-up' crew pure and simple," said one state lawman who was there.

"The FBI went into the Baton Rouge Police Department and literally and physically seized the contents of the trunk of Barry Seal's Cadillac on the night he died from the Baton Rouge Police. In fact, the Baton Rouge

Police probably would have had to draw their guns to keep possession of that evidence," says New Orleans attorney Sam Dalton, who represented one the three Colombian hit men convicted of Seal's killing.

Through the rules of courtroom discovery, Dalton's investigation gained access to something more valuable than gold: information, enough to glean evidence of a massive cover-up underway before Seal's body had grown cold in the morgue.

"Some of the things that had been in it (the trunk) we didn't get back. But they had missed a few things that indicated just how valuable that trunk was. The Baton Rouge Police should have, by law, done anything necessary to prevent the FBI from confiscating that evidence."

Dalton shrugs. "But they didn't."

When he was murdered Barry Seal had with him three boxes filled with documents that went with him everywhere. *Forbes* magazine senior editor Jim Norman later reported that found among those documents was the encrypted code number of a secret Swiss bank account containing over ten million dollars 'belonging' to then-Secretary of Defense Casper Weinberger.

According to Norman, a co-signatory on the account was a relative of then-Senator Howard Metzenbaum, D-Ohio, "which is why Congress is so squeamish about investigating this stuff. We are talking about bi-partisan payola," Norman said in a letter to the managing editor of Forbes protesting their decision to kill his scoop. "The clear implication is that Casper Weinberger, while Secretary of Defense, was taking kickbacks on drug and arms sales by arms/ drug smuggler Barry Seal."

Police officials who were present the night of Seal's murder still speak softly about what they saw. "Seal's trunk contained compelling and… well, just say—very *very* compelling documents and tapes. Several briefcases, boxes—wherever Seal's Cadillac was, that was where Barry's instant records were," says one Louisiana law enforcement source who spoke to us, though reluctantly. He quickly added, "This is all third-hand, understand."

From the way he stressed *'third-hand'* we knew he was speaking for the record, assuming we were being overheard. And this law enforcement officer had good reason to be wary: his family dog was decapitated and left floating in his backyard pool as a warning not to talk, he told us, a full three months *after* Seal's assassination.

What about Barry Seal made "unauthorized" knowledge of him so sensitive? Behind the curtain of Barry Seal's life—beyond the contra drug smuggling and gun running through Mena, Arkansas for which he became justly famous—lies the story of the *origins* of his career in covert operations. It clearly indicates that Seal participated in many of the signal events in America during the second half of the 20th century…Running guns to Fidel Castro in the mountains of Cuba… flying at the Bay of Pigs invasion… piloting a get-away plane after the assassination of John Fitzgerald Kennedy… flying into the Golden Triangle during America's Secret War in Laos… Barry Seal even had a cameo role in the Watergate Scandal. His career reveals much about the secret history of our life and times—that history, in other words, in which lone gunmen play no role.

Following the thread of Seal's life will lead us back to the very headwaters of this secret history… Miami, before the Bay of Pigs fiasco, the failed operation which introduced so many crucial players in our story: Brigade 2506, the Shooter Teams, Ted Shackley, Howard Hunt, Frank Sturgis, Felix Rodriguez… and George Bush.

Seal was initiated into covert operations in Miami in the early '60's, when guys paid to protect us—*CIA guys*—hobnobbed, schemed, wheeled and dealed with people most Americans assume they're being paid to protect us *against*… 'Made' guys. Mobsters. Organized Crime. Miami was the largest CIA station in the world, until the stink grew so bad in 1965 that the station was disbanded after its fleet of planes was shown to be engaged in drug smuggling.

Then these men, "Barry and 'the boys,'" all go off to Southeast Asia. Laos was where they went; because Laos was where the *money* was. "Barry was not a soldier of fortune or a mercenary—he was a covert operative. It was the 70's when I saw Barry again," says friend 'Red' Hall, delivering a bombshell. "Right after he got caught flying drugs in a 747 out of the Orient during the Vietnam War. He had a lot of government connections; that's a fact."

Needless to say, no official record of this, nor many other events in this story, remains.

Sparking our examination of the mysterious roots of Barry Seal's career was a conversation we had in the sun-drenched Santa Fe, New Mexico study of Roger Morris and Sally Denton, the team who first brought serious national attention to Barry Seal.

We had been exchanging pleasant tidbits of information each of us had gleaned about our common subject, drinking cokes in the warm sun, when they asked us, "What have *you* heard about Barry Seal having flown a get-away plane out of Dallas after the Kennedy assassination?"

We hadn't known that there *was* a getaway plane out of Dallas, we replied. And that was the end of it… for the moment. But we never forgot the *question*. It's not the kind of thing you would.

Then, while doing research in the newspaper morgue in Barry's hometown paper, the *Baton Rouge Advocate*, we struck up a conversation with the morgue librarian. She had a throaty kind of whiskey voice that you don't hear a lot in librarians, and after she grew comfortable with a "Yankee" asking questions, she told us casually, in the sweet-as-pie tone in which some Southern women couch their major revelations, "My ex-husband, who was 'connected,' told me that, too: Barry Seal flew a getaway plane out of Dallas after JFK was killed."

"How long ago?" we demanded. "How long ago did he tell you? When did you hear about this?'

"Hell, she said, "a good 20 years. I've been remarried for ten."

But it wasn't until much later, after we'd heard stories about Barry Seal from his friends and classmates in high school, that we began to realize what we'd sensed all along: it was *true.*

"One Friday evening, while we were in high school, I got a call from Barry, asking if I'd like to fly with him in the morning over to Lacombe, a little town on the north shore across Lake Pontchartrain from New Orleans," said high school chum John Odom, who grew up two blocks from Barry.

"We left about 5.30 A.M. and flew over to the little airport there, and Barry and I get out off the plane and there's this guy sitting in this Hollywood director's chair, dressed all in black… black military fatigues, black boots, and a black beret. And he's got these fake eyebrows, real weird, one eyebrow was turned up at a 45-degree angle, and the other was horizontal."

"I laughed when I saw him, but Barry told me to stay by the plane or he wouldn't let me fly back to Baton Rouge. And he was drilling a bunch of Civil Air Patrol cadets, all carrying the old M1 rifles, standing in formation in front of him."

"His name was David Ferrie. He was a captain in the Louisiana Civil Air Patrol."

Even if you're not a JFK assassination researcher—and we weren't— its no secret that David Ferrie, played by Joe Pesci in Oliver Stone's movie JFK, is on researchers Top Ten List of "People In On the Hit." He was, in fact, under suspicion of involvement in the assassination *less than forty-eight hours* after Kennedy died.

John Odom had watched 17-year old Barry Seal confer with David Ferrie; he saw Ferrie point to the 50-or-so wooden crates staged next to the tarmac. Then, on the way back to Baton Rouge, he said that Barry told him that he was making $400 a week flying "runs" for Ferrie, and that Ferrie was CIA. The crates were weapons and ordinance, according to Seal.

"'How'd you like to make that kind of money?' Seal asked Odom, whose brother is author Richmond Odom. "Our dad only made about $400 *a month* back then, and we weren't poor."

John Odom, according to his brother Richmond, was stunned, and didn't know how to respond. Finally he told Barry, 'I'll think about it.'"

They never discussed it again.

Later, we spoke to a doctor, a medical doctor, but still, a man of science... which means he had a software program on his personal computer which translates dollar amounts from any year into current dollars. And we sat in silence while it did the math for us, and then while it re-calculated it again, because neither one of us could believe the number flickering on his laptop screen.

David Ferrie had been paying young Barry Seal, back in 1957, the equivalent of $2500 *per week.*

The well-known pictures of Barry Seal which the general public has seen include the one popularized in the *Clinton Chronicles* video, where Seal is a rotund and genial man waving to reporters and cameramen as he climbs the granite steps of the Baton Rouge courthouse. In another, he is a 300-pound blood-soaked body draped across the front seat of a Cadillac in the ghoulish crime scene photos taken the night of his death in Baton Rouge.

But the picture of Barry Seal which lingers in our mind is a haunting photo of a 16-year old youth still in high school. In it, Barry is just a scared-looking teen-age boy wearing a paramilitary Civil Air Patrol flight suit, preparing to step onto a US Air Force plane bound for a two-week summer camp of the Louisiana Civil Air Patrol, and turning uncertainly to look back at the family which have come to see him off, seeking in their familiar faces some reassurance.

The young Seal looks like anyone might when leaving home for the first time: nervous, apprehensive, and uncertain. After practicing 'touch and goes' all summer in a tiny Piper Tri-Pacer with the enthusiasm of a high school basketball star practicing free throws, he was bound, that muggy 23rd of July, 1955, for Barksdale Air Force Base in Shreveport.

There, while America basked in the dawn of a Golden Age of Aviation with American planes ruling the skies as British ships had once ruled the oceans, cadet pilot Barry Seal will meet fellow cadet Lee Harvey Oswald. And there both will fall into the orbit of the freakish David Ferrie.

At the tender age of 16, in the flush of optimism that characterized American life in the 1950's, Barry Seal put on a military-style uniform that marked him, somehow, as one of the *chosen,* one of the 'elite.' And the overriding question posed by his extraordinary life and death is was he not—in some fashion—still wearing that uniform when he died?

Something strange went on in the Louisiana Civil Air Patrol of the middle 1950's, something which will lead us onward, a trail of breadcrumbs, if you will, through the signal events of America's secret history in the second half of the 20th Century, from the Bay of Pigs to the Kennedy Assassination to Watergate and then to Mena, Arkansas.

Barry Seal, we will discover, was a contemporary of Lee Harvey Oswald's in the Louisiana Civil Air Patrol, where both young men came under the tutelage of CIA pilot David Ferrie, who was *himself* murdered, we will hear from cops working surveillance on Ferrie when he died, the night before he was to be called to testify before Jim Garrison's grand jury probe of the Kennedy assassination.

While still an impressionable teenager Barry Seal came under the tutelage of a man you wouldn't want your worst enemies' kid to know... David Ferrie, a pedophile, and worse.

When we discovered this, we wondered: had no one known?

Of course they had.

Today Delbert Hahn is a retired FBI agent in Baton Rouge, and an amiable Cleveland Indians fan. But between 1983 and 1985 he was the Special Agent in Charge of the Middle District of Louisiana Organized Crime Drug Task Force investigation into the Barry Seal drug smuggling organization.

"Delbert," we asked, "when you got the Barry Seal folder from the FBI, did it have a bright red flag on it across the top, saying 'started off in high school making a fortune with David Ferrie, 'connected' individual? Check with the desk sergeant?'"

He never knew, he told us bluntly.

What secret is there so big that FBI Special Agents-in-Charge of multi-agency task forces aren't told?

This is a story of something called "elite deviance," a condition sociologists say exists in a society when the elite of that society no longer believe that the rules apply... to *them.*

"You referred to the gentleman Barry worked for, David Ferrie. I knew Barry had some unusual financing because he owned two airplanes by the time he was eighteen," said one of Seal's employees, pilot Joe Hurston.

"I'm going to tell you that there is a lot more to this that meets the eye," this man continued. "I had an airplane that crashed, with seven souls aboard, one of whom was a representative of the US Treasury Department. My aircraft was screwed with, and I'm still very concerned for my family's safety."

This individual, with some obvious concerns, was with Seal when he played his role in the Watergate Scandal, when he was arrested less than two weeks after the bungled burglary by CIA Cubans like Frank Sturgis, with 13,500 pounds of plastic C4 explosives destined for anti-Castro Cubans in Mexico.

"Mena is very real," Hurston concluded, before declining to talk further, at least on the record. "And what did happen back then is tied to that. And you mess with '72, and you're messing with Mena. And Mena is tied right in to current stuff. So there is a strong connection, and you should be aware of it."

"You mean, this is *all* somehow connected?" we asked.

"Touch one, you've touched them all," he stated solemnly. "All these secrets are the same secret."

Ironically, this is the same message we've heard from another part of the forest altogether… academic David Simon in a sociology textbook called *Elite Deviance*. Simon's book is in its 6th edition. So at least some social science types know the score. Leave it to a university professor to dish the news even the raciest tabloid newspapers won't report. Go figure.

What possible connection could there be between Barry Seal and the massive drug smuggling in Mena, Arkansas in the 1980's, and the swirling intrigue in Mexico City in 1963 that preceded the Kennedy assassination?

We couldn't have imagined that there was one—until we saw what we've come to refer to as *"the picture."* It was taken at a nightclub in Mexico City on January 22, 1963, ten months to the day before the Kennedy assassination, and comes complete with the sort of frame nightclub photographers use to create a keepsake. Barry Seal, then a young-looking 24-year old, is seated at a table with a mixed group of apparent Cuban exiles, Italian wise-guys, and square-jawed military-intel types. Who were these guys, we wondered, when we first saw it. What are they doing together in Mexico City?

But when we put out word that we needed to make some ID's, almost immediately a full-fledged disinformation campaign began, designed solely to discredit the photo. First Seal's former brother-in-law, drug pilot Bill Bottoms, claimed it wasn't even a picture of Seal. But that was expected; Bottoms has long been on the Mena "clean-up crew," attempting to dispel what he termed the "Mena Myth."

We took the picture to helicopter pilot Ben Seal, Barry's brother. Before he arrived we showed the photo to his son, Barry's nephew Benjie, also a helicopter pilot. He immediately pointed to the young Barry seated in the picture and exclaimed, "Uncle Barry!" But when Ben Seal entered the room later, not knowing what his son had just confirmed, he denied his brother was in the picture.

Finally we received word from former CIA pilot Tosh Plumlee, who had boasted of his long-time association and friendship with Barry Seal to us in an interview. Now he wanted us to know that he had seen the photo, and that it was not what it appeared to be...

He was himself one of the unidentified participants in the picture, he stated. It had been taken at a party of "Narcs having a little fun after receiving awards from the American DEA in 1976." The Kerry Committee had had this picture during their investigation, he said; it was old news. He even sent us the same photo back, as if he had had it in his possession all this time, with a professionally printed caption across the top reading "DEA men celebrating awards."

But the source of this photograph is what historians call a 'primary' source, the best possible kind, in this case Barry Seal's widow, who had it hidden in a safe when a 7-man team from the State Department arrived in 1995 to comb through her records. No one had been wearing skinny ties, as these men were, in 1976. And of course there was no DEA in 1963.

So some people had gone to some little trouble (the printed caption across the picture) to attempt to pass off a clumsy lie. But why? Suspicions about the sensitive nature of this picture, were confirmed when we met a former military intelligence officer who had known and worked with Barry Seal since 1964, and known *of* him even earlier. When he saw the Mexico City picture, his reaction was instantaneous and shocked.

"Where did you get that picture?" he demanded. "There weren't supposed to be any pictures! Where did this come from?"

His nervousness was explained by the identities of the people seated with Seal in that nightclub in Mexico City in 1963. They are members of the CIA's super-secret assassination squad Operation 40. Seated with Barry Seal around that nightclub table are such later-to-be-infamous figures as professional assassin and CIA agent Felix Rodriguez, who tracked down and killed Che Guevara in Bolivia and whom to this day, we were told, keeps Guevara's *hands* sitting in a jar on his dresser.... And Watergate burglar Frank Sturgis, covering his face with his sport coat.... And William Houston Seymour, the New Orleans representative of the Double-Chek Corporation, a CIA front used to recruit pilots... like Barry Seal.

These are people whose lives and careers are bound up in America's secret history. And Barry Seal was one of them.

No one quibbles about Barry Seal's reputation as the most successful drug smuggler in American history. He was the most famous cocaine buccaneer in an era that abounded with them. He brought over five billion dollars worth of cocaine into the United States—according to the Government's own bean-counters—to fuel the go-go 80's.

Here, then, is Mena's big dirty secret: Barry Seal was no accident. He didn't stumble onto Mena, nor did he just happen to 'luck' into his eventual drug smuggling career. Instead, he was a life-long member of what E. Howard Hunt puckishly refers to as "clandestine services."

But somehow Seal accomplished what is an extremely rare feat in the field of covert operations. Barry Seal became famous. In certain circles, this was not thought to have been, on Mr. Seal's part, a particularly good career move.

But then probably no one in Langley's domestic psy-ops division foresaw that Barry Seal's legend would grow and keep growing, and that during the course of two successive Presidential scandals he would achieve a certain well-deserved folk hero status... not for his drug smuggling, no: for that he deserved to go to jail. But for this poorly hidden fact, the true reason for his assassination: Barry Seal was getting ready to spill the beans...

"Biggie's getting set to talk," he told a family gathering at the last Easter Sunday he ever spent on Earth. "There's gonna be some fireworks, that's for sure."

The story of Barry Seal's life and violent assassination is a thrill-ride into the most secret places in American life, a trip to a place where bad things happen, and nobody cares. After you've been there, no place will look like Kansas anymore—ever again.

This is the story of Barry Seal, the biggest drug smuggler in American history, who died in a hail of bullets with George Bush's private phone number in his wallet.

CHAPTER TWO

FIRST COUSIN TO A BIRD

ON THE 16TH OF JULY in 1955, while Dwight David Eisenhower was President, the Yankees were in first place, and a kid could still look through an issue of Boy's Life without snickering, an American aviation milestone passed into history unnoted in the sultry air of a Louisiana summer.

"See, that was the day Barry Seal got his pilot's license, right on his 16TH birthday," an early flying buddy, Clifford Rice, recalls. "Whatever the headlines of the *Baton Rouge Advocate* newspaper were that evening, if they'd have known what was to come they'd have been about Barry."

Born July 16, 1939, Barry Seal grew up with his two younger siblings Benjy and Wendell in seemingly proto-typical '50's style, in a one-story white frame house in a quiet neighborhood in Baton Rouge on a shady street named Lover's Lane. His father, B.C., was a candy wholesaler; his mother Mary Lou a homemaker. The boys played ball in the yard and worked on souped-up old cars in the garage behind the house.

But Barry's first love was flying. A childhood friend remembers that he would peddle his bicycle over to a local private airport called Ryan's Field just a few miles away, lean on the chain-link fence and watch small planes take off and land. He got hooked on flying; one story goes, when, while still a kid, a barnstorming pilot took him for a ride. With an abundance of natural talent and zeal to fly, he soloed at 15, and was soon making money towing advertising banners.

Maybe it's the influence of the Big Muddy flowing by, but Barry's hometown Baton Rouge has always had a slightly raffish air. Well before the Civil War an old steamer here, fitted up as a wharf-boat and lodging-house, was serving as headquarters for the gamblers that ran the river, who played cards until dawn.

Mark Twain hated the mock castle at Baton Rouge that served as the early capital; but even he praised the magnolia trees, lovely and fragrant with their dense rich foliage and huge snowball blossoms. Today the charm of the antebellum mansions set in groves of tall live oaks and Spanish moss abruptly changes into an industrial expanse. One minute you're driving along the frontage of Tara; the next you see an oil refinery, a pile of steel and sheet metal with octopus arms and bulgy pipes and conveyor belts leaning against the river, where America's Fortune 500 companies churn out the products of daily life, from oil refineries to prescription drugs to the wax coating on milk cartons.

As Louisiana's capital, Baton Rouge has also always had a *dark* side; it's where the back-room deals cut in smoky old New Orleans, its sister city a few bends further down the Mississippi, get ratified into law. Right in the governor's office, Cliff Rice, former chief pilot for the state told us, there was a phone that was a direct line to Carlos Marcello, the Mafia Kingfish himself. Unlike anywhere else in America, the state of Louisiana wears corruption as a badge of honor.

Back in the '50's, when Barry was growing up, the town was booming and it was a great time to be a kid, to ride bikes to the Rex or Regina theaters for Saturday matinees starring cowboy heroes like Wild Bill Elliot or Lash Larue, and afterwards dash across the street to Edward's Orange Bowl for orange drinks and cake doughnuts, or harass the soda jerks at Dayton and Dileo's drug stores, begging them to concoct sickening mixtures of ice creams and syrups.

Though Barry will later become the most successful drug smuggler in American history, the '50s were a time when, as Jimmy Buffett says, "only jazz musicians were smoking marijuana." So the young Barry would join a group of guys and pile into somebody's daddy's car, usually a big old clunky Ford or Chevy, and head out to some dance hall to stand around holding a cold Falstaff or Jax longneck, listen to the music, and try to look cool while working up the nerve to ask the girls to dance.

There were also the football trips, which involved long bus rides. And this is where young Barry Seal first began to stand out. He didn't take the bus to out-of-town game. Instead, he *flew...* in "barnstorming" fashion, landing wherever he could find a smooth, flat surface.

"Barry flew his helicopter right down onto the field at a high school football game one time," recalled Ed Duffard, his first flight instructor. In a bit of prophetic whimsy that would still resonates four decades later, under Seal's high school yearbook is the caption, "Full of fun, full of folly."

Later, while most young men his age were still working up the courage to ask a girl to go steady, the young Seal was demonstrating *his* courage by flying daring undercover missions into Cuba, bringing Fidel Castro's insurgents weapons courtesy the CIA.

Today, at the mention of Seal's name, Eddie Duffard smiles and stretches up from the small aircraft engine he is bent over. He wipes a greasy hand across his brow before speaking, gazing out across the blazing asphalt apron in the shimmering mid-summer Louisiana heat at the general aviation terminal at the Baton Rouge Airport.

"He was just a skinny kid with a paper route," remembers Eddie. "Barry was likeable, but not very tall, and so he was always trying to prove something to you. But he could fly with the best of 'em. That boy was first cousin to a bird!"

At fifteen, Barry already knew what he wanted to do: *fly*, so bad that he found shortcuts to help him pay Eddy's fat-in-'54-dollars fee of $14 per lesson.

"He was always scheming to pay for his flight lessons," laughs Duffard. "Once he even tried to sweet-talk me into helping him siphon gasoline from cars around the airport to pay for a lesson."

"Barry was a wild one, the black sheep in his family. That's why when his mom came by to see me, begging me not to teach her son to fly, I said, 'ma'am, that boy of yours *is* gonna find a way to learn to fly...no matter what. Somebody's *got* to be the one to teach him," says Duffard.

"Barry was a daredevil, alright," states Clifford Rice, an owlish-looking man who today himself instructs young pilots in Northern Louisiana. Back then; he was just another young and hopeful pilot in the closely-knit bunch hanging out at the airport. "I remember he flew into a hurricane with some news people one time, just for fun."

The Louisiana flying fraternity is a smallish one. Rice, who later bought Barry's flying service from him in the mid-sixties before becoming the personal pilot for long-time Louisiana Governor McKeithen, recalled several hair-raising incidents with the young Barry.

"I used to go skydiving with him, drop him out of the Champ (a small private plane) from three or four thousand feet. The Champ's a tandem airplane, meaning one person sits in front of the other, and when Barry opened the door to jump, there was absolutely nothing on that side of the plane but blue sky. The first time we went up together in that plane to jump, Barry waited until he was almost out of the plane, and then turned back and hollered to me, "Hey, Cliff, this plane's got a little center-of-gravity problem!"

"'What do you mean?' I shouted back.'"

"He shot me a devilish grin," Rice recalls. "Then he shouted, 'When I get out, you've got to move from the back to the front seat!'"

Rice grimaces. "So I had to climb over the seat—I've got no parachute on, no harness, *nothing*—and the damn door's yawning wide open, and I can hear Barry laughing his head off as he floats down to earth."

"That was the Barry Seal I knew."

Out at the small Baton Rouge airport, where he kept a plane for business purposes, Joe Nettles, then a businessman in his early forties, became a mentor and something of a second father to the young Barry Seal.

Today, at age eighty-eight, Nettles' eyes still gleam with memories of the boy he came to think of as his adopted son. "Barry was always out at the airport, ever since he began high school. One day I asked him, 'what are you gonna do when you get out of high school?' And he said, 'Why, I'm gonna go to work for *you*, Joe!'"

"He was always fooling around with airplanes," Nettles remembers, "and he was just a natural born pilot. My wife and I had four girls, and Barry got to be a member of our family. I remember he had a Donald Duck imitation that always made our youngest daughter laugh, and he just adored the girls, he was like a big brother to them."

"When he got out of the service, the first place he came was our house. He would come take us for rides, and the girls would get him dates… Barry was just a likeable person, he was loveable," Nettles says firmly.

But along with the fun and frolic came hints of trouble to come… like the early incident over Pikeburden Plantation (today part of LSU) that almost ended in disaster.

"He was flying my old Piper Tri-Pacer, and they landed on a private strip to look at an old plane," recalls Dr. Philip West, an LSU medical sciences professor. "When they took off again he thought he'd put a scare into the two friends joyriding with him, so he shut off the power as soon as the plane cleared the trees."

Seal deliberately stalled his rented plane just to scare his friends. But the plane refused to restart. It forced the young aviator to summon his entire cool to 'deadstick' land in a nearby field, clipping several trees.

One boy broke an arm, and Barry broke his ankle in the crash-landing. It was an injury that would nag him all his life.

"He was a good pilot, or he wouldn't have walked away from that crash," says Dr. West. "But I never let him fly my plane again."

"I was out at the airport when the hospital called after Barry's accident," another early pilot friend, David Holmes, said. "The wives of the two guys flying with Barry that day were waiting for them to return. When I told them they'd crash-landed and were all in the emergency room, they were about beside themselves."

By 1958, hot-shot pilot and daredevil Barry Seal, well before turning twenty-one, was ferrying weapons down to Cuba and delivering them to Fidel Castro's men, according to Clifford Rice and other pilots of that era at Baton Rouge's Downtown Airport.

This is not as outlandish as it seems, we learned. The CIA was supplying *both* sides of the Cuban civil war. But when the CIA turned on all things *Fidelismo,* numerous sources report that Barry soon thereafter began flying sorties *against* Castro, in P-51 Mustangs, a surplus WWII fighter.

"We would sit out at the airport and chat, about planes and girls mostly, is how I found that out, " Rice recalls. "We'd talk about his girlfriend, Ava, a real dish. We all used to kid him when he'd take her flying around the airport.... How come your plane was rocking up and down, Seal?'"

"I remember when that Cuban business was starting up," stated Holmes. "Barry would disappear for a week or so, and then show back up, and we heard he was flying a P-51 down there. But although Barry and I were good friends, he always remained a mystery. It was like he had two sides—one side was jovial and free-spirited, but the other side—well, that was the side where you'd be standing around a hanger out at the airport and somebody from the FBI would walk over and start asking you questions about him."

"That Cuban thing—that's when Barry's fortunes changed," Holmes recalls. "That was when he would start showing up with really nice twin-engine airplanes, and then disappear with them for weeks at a time. And money was somehow by then no longer an object for him, like it was for the rest of us young pilots hanging around out at the airport. Pretty soon he owned three planes: a Comanche, an Aranca Chief, and a Champ."

Holmes smiles. "We called his little company "Beatnik Airlines" if I recall."

"Barry was just wild back then," Eddie Duffard told us. "He didn't seem to know what it was to be afraid. But he was really smart, which saved him a lot of times. But the good times didn't last for him forever, no sir. I saw Barry later in life out at the airport, and now he's flying a Beechcraft with a cargo door on it that opens outwards. 'That plane looks just perfect for smuggling weed!' I called out to him."

"Barry didn't say nothing. He just shrugged."

Joe Nettles remembers the moment when he believes Barry's life pivoted and took a turn down 'the road less traveled.' "One day out at the airport Barry was walking with a friend when he spotted me talking to somebody, and Barry said to his friend, pointing to me, 'see this man here? This man taught me everything I know!'

"I shook my head, and said, 'No way Barry. I surely didn't teach you to get arrested flying arms into Cuba. See, he was going to get $2000 to fly a load of weapons to Castro, I think it was, before we knew he was a Communist.... And the FBI caught him in the process of taking them to Florida, and he never got them there."

A cloud passes over Mr. Nettles' wizened old face. "If he hadn't gotten out of that, he wouldn't have gotten involved with any of the other mess," he says sadly. "When he got out of that he thought he could get out of anything. Barry showed me a letter that he got from the judge exonerating him. After that, he felt invincible."

His wife puts a consoling hand on Nettles arm, and suddenly events of forty-five years ago are as real as the red catsup we have just finished pouting on our eggs in this coffee shop along the I-12 Interstate north of New Orleans.

"There there, honey," she whispers soothingly, before looking across the table to us and smiling sadly. "Sometimes Joe will hear a plane fly over the house, like Barry used to do, buzzing the house just for fun, and I'll find him just looking up at the sky for the longest time afterwards," she explains. "Joe misses Barry."

"That boy was the best pilot in the US—bar none," Mr. Nettles says, recovering. "When Delta Airlines sent him an application, he tore it up. They weren't *big* enough for him. He didn't smoke or drink. He had no bad habits at all. I don't know what happened..." he says, his voice choking slightly before trailing off.

Though Joe Nettles has an obvious deep personal feeling for Barry Seal, over and over again in Louisiana we were surprised to hear people express admiration and affection for Seal, as well as outrage at his treatment by the federal government... from people one would never suspect would harbor such feelings. Men who would not hesitate to pull the switch on Angola Penitentiary's electric chair for a sleazebag drug smuggler, for example, like an elderly businessman of clearly right wing tendencies we sat beside on a shuttle flight from Houston into Baton Rouge, who expressed affection for Seal we found shocking, and indicative that there was much more to this story than had surfaced.

When Joe Nettles told us, "I don't know what happened," he might have been speaking for us as well. Until, well into the second year of our investigation into the life and times of Barry Seal, we finally began to learn what had really happened.

Barry Seal met David Ferrie.

CHAPTER THREE

LEARNING TO FLY—THE CIVIL AIR PATROL WAY

IN 1955 BARRY SEAL joined the local Baton Rouge Civil Air Patrol and learned to fly along with another kid from the neighborhood, John Odom. And Odom remembers a joint training mission their unit held with David Ferrie's New Orleans CAP unit…

"We boys from Baton Rouge weren't nearly as sophisticated as the New Orleans unit, so Barry was much enamored of David Ferrie, whose unit was a quasi-military outfit," said Odom. "They met at least three times a week—two evenings and each Saturday—and Lee Harvey Oswald was a member of Ferrie's elite 'little boys' club. Both Barry and I met Oswald, who was what I would call a 'CAP super geek.' All of Ferrie's CAP guys were 'geeks,' but Oswald epitomized the unit. He was extremely bright, though, and spoke Spanish and some Russian."

When the House Select Committee on Assassinations tried to find Oswald and David Ferrie's records in Civil Air Patrol files they discovered that "most of the records of the squadron had been stolen in late 1960." As we will see, something about people like David Ferrie (and Barry Seal) requires government records about them to be misplaced with uncanny frequency. One record which had escaped being 'stolen' reveals that Oswald joined the Civil Air Patrol on July 27, 1955 at the same time he was at summer camp with David Ferrie and Barry Seal.

By the time the Select Committee had wrapped its investigation half a dozen former cadets could be found who were in the Civil Air Patrol in 1955 and could link David Ferrie to Lee Oswald. Even the New Orleans Police Department knew it. One Vice Squad Detective—more about him later—had reported, "Ferrie assumed control at Moisant Airport at about the same time Oswald joined."

David Ferrie's methods of recruitment are no great mystery, after you've met and interviewed a number of former cadets. He looked for bright kids from troubled homes. Seal's father, for example, was alcoholic, and belonged to the Ku Klux Klan as well, a fact which several Southern law enforcement authorities stated was often indicative of abuse in the home. A childhood friends of the young Barry Seal, John Prevost, confirmed the outlines of the story.

"I grew up on the street behind Barry," said Prevost. "He was one year behind me in school. He didn't get along with his folks that well. They wanted him to stay in his yard, and I would always hear them calling him to come home, 'Barry! Barry!'"

Later, after he had become a CIA pilot himself, Barry Seal would recruit young boys to work for him in the same manner in which he himself had been recruited by Ferrie. Charlie Montgomery, today a boyish 43-year-old flight controller in Houston, was a bright youth from a troubled home, who went to work for Barry Seal at the tender age of fourteen. "Barry had a helicopter sitting in a trailer in front of his house. That was a tremendous inducement for a young kid looking for a little excitement. My father was an architect, and a bit of a drunk. Working with Barry was my haven," says Montgomery. "I was a minor who could disappear for a week at a time without my parents asking any questions. Barry had something he would say all the time: 'Are you ready for *adventure?* I was."

Was it David Ferrie who got an impressionable young pilot named Barry Seal into flying drugs for fun and profit? Seal's friend John Prevost stated that while serving jury duty in Louisiana on a drug case, he had encountered David Ferrie, acting in some manner for the defense. "David Ferrie came to Baton Rouge, he had something to do with a defendant, a black guy, on trial for distributing drugs. That's all I recall, but I knew it was him. Ferrie is someone you remember."

This was our first indication that we should look closely for evidence indicating the young Seal's recruiter might have been 'connected' to the same narco-underworld inhabited by Mob guys like Jack Ruby...

Who was David Ferrie? Into what sort of enterprise did he induct both Barry Seal and Lee Oswald? If we hoped to understand the organization to which Barry Seal devoted his entire business career we would first need to learn what is known about Ferrie…. And David Ferrie's story, we were to learn, leads to the heart of the spooky netherworld of American covert intelligence, narcotics, Cubans, and the Mob…. It is without question the darkest subbasement of the secret history of our life and times, the place where many of the biggest American tragedies of the past four decades were set in motion.

For over thirty years the uncomfortable fact that Lee Harvey Oswald had come under the influence of David Ferrie while a member of the Louisiana Civil Air Patrol has been a source of embarrassment and consternation to the peddlers of the official story featuring a crazed lone gunman in the assassination of John Fitzgerald Kennedy. Officials flatly denied it…until photographs of Ferrie standing beside Oswald were finally unearthed, taken at the July '55 Civil Air Patrol summer camp at Barksdale Air Force Base the young Barry Seal is on his way to in the poignant picture we had seen.

So Ferrie and Oswald were acquainted. What we found, to our delight, is that instead of further muddying the waters, adding Seal's name into this already heady mix brings some light and clarity to this critical place and time where so much of this country's recent history was set in motion. Stated simply, Seal's recruitment by Ferrie just adds to the growing evidence that recruitment was one of Ferrie's primary jobs in the Civil Air Patrol, which was itself, we were to learn, a by-product of the most dark and awful days of the Cold War.

Far more than other youth organizations like the Boy Scouts, America's Civil Air Patrol has always been a quasi-military entity. It was to become fertile ground for recruiting hotshot daredevil pilots into this country's then-forming paramilitary forces.

Created one week before Pearl Harbor propelled the United States into World War II, the CAP's role was to harness the nation's aviation resources to aid in the event America entered the conflict. The American military immediately supported the effort, and Civil Air Patrol members became the 'Minutemen' of World War II, volunteering time, resources, and talents to fill the gaps as men and resources were mobilized to fight abroad. The War Department placed the organization under the jurisdiction of the Army Air Forces.

Congress later established the CAP as the Auxiliary of the new U.S. Air Force, giving the Secretary of the Air Force authority to provide financial and material assistance to the organization. This explains why it was a US Air Force plane that ferried the 16-year-old Barry Seal to Civil Air Patrol summer camp at Barks-dale AFB in 1955.

Within days of President Kennedy's assassination Oswald's involvement with the CAP in New Orleans had become the subject of intense speculation and investigation, and David Ferrie, widely regarded as one of the most mysterious people to figure in the investigation of the assassination, briefly was under suspicion by the New Orleans District Attorney's Office. The FBI and Secret Service had then taken over from the local authorities, and released Ferrie with an apology.

Despite the efforts of the FBI, it is today well established that Oswald was part of David Ferrie's circle during the period when Ferrie was a private investigator and pilot in New Orleans.

During the week following the President's murder, the FBI made a perfunctory inquiry into Oswald's membership in the Civil Air Patrol in New Orleans. They discovered that Oswald had joined the Patrol as a cadet in 1955, and that David Ferrie, an airman of skill and renown, was at that time a leading light of the local Patrol unit... the same man called in because of suspicions he may have had something to do with Kennedy's assassination, less than 48 hours after it happened.

Yet they did nothing. How the *FBI* dealt with this inconvenient knowledge illustrates a seemingly-deliberate obstruction of justice by the Bureau, evidence for which we were to experience first-hand, when, while a retired FBI gumshoe did some investigative work for us, he returned excellent results on everything we'd asked him to do—except to ascertain for us, if he could, whether Barry Seal had been in the CAP as a youth. Coincidence? Perhaps, but we heard the same pattern of cover-up recounted in book after book about the Kennedy assassination, in which are rattled off example after example of how the Bureau was used, three decades ago, to thwart any real investigation into Kennedy's murder. It is just like the Kenneth Starr probe, which ended any real investigation of drug smuggling through Arkansas. *La plus ca change...*

"On the Kennedy thing, Hoover said to his agents, everything gets 'bagged and tagged,' and then sent to me directly," former New Orleans CIA operative Gordon Novel told us. "If you wanted to keep your job in the Bureau, you bagged it and tagged it, and sent it to Hoover, who promptly shit-canned everything."

Gordon Novel, today a wizened imp with still-bright blue eyes behind bottleneck glasses, has figured around the fringes of American scandals from the Bay of Pigs to JFK's murder to Watergate to the Waco tragedy. He was one of the most colorful characters in New Orleans DA Jim Garrison's ill-fated 1967 probe, was eventually suspected of being one of the "second Oswalds," and has even been accused of having been present in Dealey Plaza when JFK was 'hit,' a charge Novel vehemently denies.

But there's something *else* about David Ferrie which makes the FBI's treatment of him look especially sinister. David Ferrie was one of their own. As we will see in the next chapter, Ferrie himself was recruited into America's "clandestine services" way back in 1942, and spent World War II working undercover in South America...at that time the only place outside the US where the FBI ran all covert intelligence activities.

"I saw Dave Ferrie's name on a list of 'disowned' agents," FBI agent Delbert Hahn admitted to us grudgingly, when we told him we had discovered Ferrie's Bureau connection.

After the assassination, Ferrie had been almost immediately fingered as a suspect, we learned to our amazement, by a Jack Martin of New Orleans, who said he thought he recalled seeing a photograph of Oswald with other onetime CAP members in Ferrie's home.

Ferrie claimed to remember nothing, and denied ever having any relationship with Lee Harvey Oswald. But he has lied about so much else, too, about other important and easily verifiable things like his knowledge of Cuban Revolutionary Council operations out of Camp Street, for example.

Lying is what spooks do.

So his denials should have been viewed with some suspicion by investigators...but there *weren't* any real investigators, it turns out, looking into David Ferrie in 1963. Instead, that task fell to the FBI. They immediately muscled the locals who had developed the lead, like New Orleans DA Jim Garrison, aside. Garrison had called Ferrie in for questioning about Ferrie's now-famous trek by car through a blinding rainstorm from New Orleans to Texas the day of Kennedy's murder...to go ice-skating.

Thanks to the FBI, it's true purpose, even today, remains unknown.

In an interview with FBI agents in New Orleans on November 25, 1963, Ferrie denied any contact with Oswald in the CAP, saying he'd served as a commandant of the CAP from 1953 to 1955 and that his unit had met at New Orleans Lakefront Airport. When his CAP cadets were instructed in the use of rifles, he had not participated in that training, Ferrie maintained.

The FBI and Secret Service investigation came to a quick conclusion a few short days after the allegation was first reported. A Secret Service report concluded "information furnished by Jack S. Martin to the effect that David William Ferrie associated with Lee Harvey Oswald at New Orleans and trained Oswald in the use of a rifle was "without foundation."

It stated further "Jack S. Martin, who has the appearance of being an alcoholic, has the reputation of furnishing incorrect information to law enforcement officers, attorneys, etc." Further it stated that the FBI had informed the Secret Service that Martin had admitted to FBI agents—in a meeting whose hidden agenda virtually defines what is meant by 'secret history'—that his alleged information about Ferrie and Oswald had been just "a figment of his imagination and that he had made up the story after reading the newspaper and watching television."

Quite a turnaround, one wonders what it took.

Slandering people who possess both inconvenient knowledge and the bad manners to speak of them is SOP (standard operating procedure) in these precincts. We discovered to our horror that it nearly always works like a charm. So we went to interview Warren DuBrueys, famous as the FBI Agent who trailed Oswald in New Orleans and then followed him to Dallas. He has spent the past three decades being tight-lipped about it.

Today Dubrueys is a vigorous 78-year old man whose blue eyes are still piercing when he wants them to be. He gave us nothing but the well-rehearsed 'official story,' even after we trotted out our knowledge of the Texas Attorney General having called the Warren Commission to report Oswald had been recruited by the FBI, a piece of 'inconvenient knowledge' which prompted a special executive session of the Warren Commission that was quickly classified top secret.

Nor did Dubrueys change expression when we cited his fellow New Orleans FBI agent William Walter, who said Oswald would meet with FBI agents in New Orleans in the summer of 1963, presumably Debrueys himself, and that the FBI had two different files on Oswald, the second of which "was a security file that had to do with espionage and Cuban activities." His sworn testimony to the House Select Committee remained classified until recently.

CIA pilot and lawyer Gary Eitel, a Texas Ranger in the 1970's, told us he heard FBI agents talking about Oswald being taken to train in marksmanship by Bureau agents while he lived in Dallas...So Eitel visited the Grand Prairie Gun Range for himself, confronted the owner with the hearsay he'd overheard, and learned, he said, that it was *true*.

The Senator who launched the intelligence committee probe, Richard Schweiker, said, "Oswald had intelligence connections. Everywhere you look with him, there are fingerprints of intelligence. The Warren

Commission was set up at a time to feed pabulum to the American people for reasons not yet known and one of the biggest cover-ups in the history of our country occurred at that time."

Still, it will take an act of God to get even a morsel of useful information from Warren Debrueys, who will take to the grave what he knows. So we changed tack and attempted to get him to at least divulge to us the rationale for keeping the American people in the dark. Because of Barry's Seal's alleged involvement, we had been forced to read, we told him, a three-foot high stack of books relating to the Kennedy assassination just to get up to speed… and we had come away with just one question.

"What's that?" Debrueys asked blandly.

"Did Lee Harvey Oswald know anyone who *wasn't* involved in intelligence?" we asked.

Debrueys façade dropped for a moment. Puzzled, he considered the question. "Ruth Paine?" he offered weakly, not bothering to pretend he believed it himself. For an instant we felt some spark of truth struggling to the surface.

"Warren," we pleaded, pressing the momentary opening, "explain to us, if we're not allowed to know who killed Kennedy, why we were taught in school that we were citizens of the greatest democracy on the face of the planet? If all we really are is what we were back in the Middle Ages— serfs on some feudal Lord's fiefdom—wouldn't it have been kinder to have clued us in when we were young?"

"Human nature does not change all that quickly," he replied, meaning, we thought, serfs we were and serfs we more or less remain…

So although the Feebies (FBI) had questioned former CAP members on whether Oswald had known Ferrie in the Civil Air Patrol, and an uncomfortable number had answered 'yes,' back in 1963 when the truth might still have mattered… that was pretty much that.

Moreover, it appears as if this "inconvenient knowledge" on the part of some of the hapless former cadets was clearly dealt with severely, by *somebody*… as when one of Oswald's former schoolmates, Edward Voebel, first stated that he and Oswald had been in the Patrol "with Captain Dave Ferrie," and then—quite suddenly—"could no longer recall" the matter.

The FBI was indifferent to the fact that Voebel stated he had been scared by "crank-type telephone calls" and a visit to his home by a strange man. Nor was the Bureau stung into action when another former cadet said Ferrie had scurried around just after the assassination asking whether any old group photographs of his (Ferrie's) squadron featured Oswald.

One wonders today what ham-handed methods were used to gain Voebel's retraction. After he died in 1971 of an aneurysm at the premature age of 31, his parents had proclaimed his death "no accident," but attributed it to his 'inconvenient knowledge.'

This suspicion was reinforced when we learned that Edward Voebel had spent the entire summer of 1963 in Mexico City. Could he, too, have been a David Ferrie recruit from the Civil Air Patrol? Barry Seal, we will learn, was also in Mexico City a lot that year, along with guys like Felix Rodriguez and Frank Sturgis. Supposedly, so was Lee Oswald.

But in the frightening aftermath of the assassination, back at a time when American citizens still believed in the integrity of this nation's security services, even New Orleans DA Garrison initially accepted the conclusions of the FBI's inquiry into Oswald's membership in the Civil Air Patrol. The matter was dropped.

But fifteen years later the House Select Committee on Assassinations had no trouble at all discerning that in 1954 Oswald had joined Ferrie's unit of the Civil Air Patrol, that he not only knew Ferrie, but knew him so well apparently, that in an interview with Look magazine his brother, Robert Oswald, had speculated out loud that Ferrie might have been instrumental in recruiting Lee Oswald... into *what*, exactly, he didn't seem sure.

"According to Lee's own later statement, 1954 was the year when he first became interested in communism," stated Robert Oswald. "I can't help wondering whether it might have been *Ferrie* who introduced Lee to Communist ideas. I realize that I have nothing solid on which to base such a speculation, except the timing."

Robert Oswald was very likely suspicious with good cause. Lee, a notoriously poor speller—"Sincerly" and "Becaus"—wrote in flawless prose to the Young People's Socialist League, "Dear Sirs; I am 16 years of age and I would like some information about your Youth League, I would like to know if there is a branch in my area, how to join, ect., I am a Marxist, and have been studying socialist principles for well over 15 months and I am very interested in your Y.P.S.L. Sincerely Lee H. Oswald."

If Oswald received help from David Ferrie in composing this well-written note, it would fit, since Ferrie's boss, CIA/ONI/FBI big shot Guy Banister, for whom Barry Seal too, we will hear, worked in the early '60's, ran a New Orleans office devoted to collecting material about "communistic fronts." Jerry Milton Brooks had told the FBI that at Guy Banister's insistence, he too had written to Communist Party

Headquarters in 1961 to inquire about membership, and had subscribed to Communist publications—odd for someone also a member, with Banister, its head, of the racist right wing Minutemen.

We turned up a half-dozen former Ferrie protégés from the Civil Air Patrol, who are today just ordinary citizens, like Colin Hamer, a research librarian in the New Orleans Public Library, a pleasant soft-spoken man who told the House Select Committee (HSCA) of meetings Oswald and David Ferrie had attended in an Eastern Airlines hangar at Moisant Airport. Oswald had attended more than a dozen such gatherings, while "Ferrie was a unit leader. I can clearly recall that Ferrie headed the Civil Air Patrol Unit during the period that Oswald attended. They were both there."

Hamer told us the story of why Ferrie had moved his CAP unit from the small Lakefront Airport to New Orleans International Airport (Moisant.) "Our CAP unit was all-boy... just the way Ferrie liked it," smiled Hamer. "Then a woman named Gladys Durr brought her girl scout troop over to join our unit en masse, and we all sort of paired off, boys and girls together, understand? Ferrie didn't like *that* one little bit, and he and Durr got into a hot clash, and after that he moved to the other New Orleans unit."

"That was where he started the Falcon Squadron, right," confirmed Colonel Mary Berkowitz, a Louisiana state official who has been active in that state's CAP since 1959. The Falcon Squadron, we had heard, was an elite unit of Ferrie disciples, which included an even more elite inner circle called "the Omnipotents."

Eager—even after all this time—to distance the CAP from Ferrie in every way possible, Berkowitz added, "But he didn't have a legal (CAP) charter for that."

The momentous clash between David Ferrie and the Girl Scouts in 1955 was contemporaneously chronicled by the FBI. They looked into the mess after receiving disturbing news. "Mrs. Ruby Nichols advised the FBI on September 26, 1955, that she was not the source of the information to the effect that Ferrie had stated he could see no reason to salute the flag," reads an FBI report. "She stated Ferrie had addressed a Scout meeting under the direction of Mrs. R.J. Durr, and that Mrs. Durr reported information to the effect that Ferrie might be a communist. Mrs. Nichols said she is a member of the Seniors of the Moisant Squadron of the Civil Air Patrol, and is in charge of the Girl Scout Squadron."

That David Ferrie might be—of all things—a *communist* was an idea quickly dispelled. Joseph Lisman, an agent of Delta Airlines and

Commander of the Cadets of the Moisant Squadron of the Civil Air Patrol, described Ferrie to the FBI as being brilliant, but not a genius, as "a person who goes off on tangents just short of becoming berserk." He added, "David Ferrie is a good organizer; he made the Civil Air Patrol at New Orleans airport what it is today; he has a large following among the Civil Air Patrol Cadets, and is an excellent flying instructor. He gives six hours of his time each week to instructing Moisant Squadron Cadets and considerably more of his time associating with them."

Lisman said, according to the FBI report, "Ferrie is a woman-hater, and that he, himself, personally disliked Ferrie because of his personality traits."

For her part Mrs. Durr told the FBI she was sorry that the matter had gone as far as it had, and said she could think of no disloyal statements made by Ferrie. But then she did mention that he was greatly disliked by her Scout Troop, principally because of the fact he arrived at the meeting on his motorcycle, his clothes were not pressed, and his hair was unkempt.

Anyone who grew up in the 1950s remembers how suspiciously our culture regarded unconventional behavior... like riding a *motorcycle*. But one can also hear in this an echo of Oswald's brother's question about whether it might have been Ferrie who introduced Lee to Communist ideas. CIA agent Ferrie (more on this shortly) had, clearly, been a part of his boss Guy Banister's operation to keep tabs on American pinkos.

Colonel Berkowitz of the Louisiana CAP told us, "The only real recollections that I have of David Ferrie was of him barking orders, looking weird, with the pasted-on eyebrows that everyone comments on. He had a cap on when I met him so you didn't see his wig. When I joined, when I was fourteen, he was the commander of our squadron. I do recall we had one young man in Moisant (Walter Sharp) who transferred over to Ferrie's Falcon Squadron and became one of Ferries protégés, and Ferrie got him an appointment to the Air Force Academy in Colorado Springs. But then he had an unfortunate car wreck while driving Ferries' Corvette, and couldn't go."

That so-called eccentric "weirdo" David Ferrie had enough clout to wrangle appointments to the Air Force Academy came as news to us. It would have been news to the Warren Commission, too— had they only been interested.

Even Oswald's mother, in the days immediately following the assassination, tried to hint in the right direction. Marguerite Oswald told the FBI that she was going to "divulge information that had never before been discussed. "When Lee was 15 years old he was a Civil Air Patrol Cadet," she said. "While he was in the Civil Air Patrol, a civilian, who was associated with the Civil Air Patrol, induced him to join the United States Marines."

She was referring, almost certainly, to David Ferrie. Yet despite this, or perhaps *because* of it, Warren Commission apologists like Gerald Posner have stridently insisted that David Ferrie was expelled from the Civil Air Patrol in 1955 and therefore Oswald could not have been in his group. Here, one recalls the accusation leveled against the Clinton Administration that their favorite stonewalling tactic was to "deny, deny, deny."

Clinton, clearly, has learned at the feet of people *who wrote the book.*

When Ferrie was interviewed by FBI agents after the assassination of President John F. Kennedy, he recommended Jerry Paradis as a Civil Air Patrol member who could verify whether Oswald had been in his unit. They finally got around to interviewing him... in 1979. And no wonder, since he told the HSCA, "I specifically remember Oswald. I can remember him clearly, and Ferrie was heading the unit then. I'm not saying that they *may* have been together, I'm saying it is a *certainty.*"

But by 1979 this statement made no headlines. It would have 15 years earlier. The tactic of "deny, deny, deny," had worked once again.

When John Kennedy Jr., was asked, at the press conference announcing his media venture George magazine, about whether he would use the magazine to investigate his father's assassination, his answer was extraordinarily poignant. No, he answered, too much time has elapsed...

"Time," Kennedy replied, "is the great enemy of the truth."

So while there is absolutely no doubt at all today about David Ferrie's association with Lee Oswald in the Louisiana Civil Air Patrol, the 'boys' have managed to make it seem to be a contentious issue for over *thirty* years.

That is certainly a neat trick... and one we will see often, and examine more closely later, when CIA pilot Barry Seal is smuggling cocaine to fund Bill Casey and George Bush's war in Central America in the early 1980s.

David Ferrie also used his Civil Air Patrol mentor-ship both to further his pedophile tastes, a purpose far removed from teaching young boys to fly, and in recruitment of young pilots into American 'clandestine' services. Lee Oswald, Barry Seal, Edward Voebel.... After Voebel's CAP days with Capt. Ferrie, he attended the Marion Military Institute in Alabama and then served six months in the United States Army. Interviewed later about Oswald's supposed 'leftist' political views by the New Orleans Police Department, he couldn't be any help, he stated blandly; he had been in Mexico during the summer of 1963.

The final use Ferrie had for the CAP was in the procurement of young boys for what former cadet Collin Hamer wryly called "unauthorized physicals."

Edward Shearer, one of Ferrie's many Civil Air Patrol cadets we spoke with who had never before been interviewed, told us what young men were attracted to in Dave Ferrie. "The entire reason for the existence of the New Orleans Cadet Squadron was the national drill competitions, which we attended three years in a row," Shearer stated.

"The accent in the New Orleans unit was totally on professionalism, because almost all of Ferrie's cadets intended to go into the Air Force later. And if you had your CAP "Certificate of Proficiency" when you entered, you automatically had one leg up, and started basic training with one stripe already."

From what we were beginning to learn about the young Barry Seal, that sounds as if it would have suited him just fine.

CHAPTER FOUR

WHO IS DAVID FERRIE?

NONE OF THE VAST array of mysterious and enigmatic characters surrounding the assassination of President John Kennedy has been as consistently described as "mysterious" and "enigmatic" as David Ferrie. His life is uniformly described as being full of strange activity and puzzling behavior. Cuban exiles christened him the "master of intrigue." New Orleans DA Jim Garrison called him "one of history's most important individuals."

At the time of the Kennedy hit Ferrie was a forty-five year old New Orleans resident, well-acquainted with all of the most notorious names linked to the assassination: Lee Oswald, Clay Shaw, Guy Banister, Jack Ruby, and Carlos Marcello. According to Banister lieutenant Joe Newbrough, he had many other talents as well...

"Ferrie spoke fluent Italian and Greek," Newbrough told us. "He flew to Italy on several occasions I can recall, on arms deals I think."

Hmm. Arms dealer. Speaks Italian. Ferrie's assorted talents and eccentricities included being a hypnotist, medical researcher, amateur psychologist, victim of a strange disease (alopecia, which made his body completely hairless) and senior pilot with Eastern Airlines, until he was fired for homosexual activity... on the job. He is also described as a CIA "contract" pilot, which is only accurate if Babe Ruth was a New York Yankee "contract" ball player.

Barry Seal will also be tagged with this label. When the CIA gets caught with its hand in the multi-billion dollar cocaine cookie jar, Seal is dismissed as a CIA "contract" pilot, who did the 'bad stuff' on his own time, or on the side, or while the *real* agents were looking the other way… though the cocaine blizzard which eventually surrounded him on all sides must have made finding another way to look somewhat difficult.

In addition to both being labeled CIA "contract" pilots, Seal and Ferrie shared similarities too numerous to be coincidence. This is not really surprising; both held—at different times—the same job, Southern Regional Manager—Aircraft Procurement and Deployment. So if they are operating out of the same play book, the same 'Company' manual, maybe we can deduce a few hints on domestic disinfo.

We noted with surprise that it was not that difficult to discover new information about the much written about Ferrie, facts both important and trivial (he was called 'Dave,' and not 'David,' for example, by everyone we interviewed who had known him.) A little poking around in New Orleans revealed ample evidence that Ferrie spent his lifetime in American "clandestine services." Maybe make that "contract" clandestine services, just to be safe.

Since it was Ferrie who set a young Barry Seal on his path to "spookdom," we wondered how Ferrie *himself* had been recruited. No one had been able to find out. And while 'Dark Side' recruitment officers don't leave behind a paper trail with mundane details like date-of-employment application, we were able, with a little digging, to discover when and how Ferrie's spook career began.

Dave Ferrie was born in Cleveland in 1918, to a family that made their careers in public service. His father was a police officer who rose to the rank of captain, his uncle a battalion chief in the Cleveland Fire Department. Dave was reared a Roman Catholic, and attended parochial schools until entering Cleveland's St. Mary's Seminary at the age of twenty to prepare for a lifetime of service to the Roman Catholic Church as a priest.

However, the irrepressible Ferrie was unable to disguise his lust for altar boys long enough to don the purple vestments. He was judged unsuited temperamentally for the role of priest by *two* separate Catholic seminaries.

Ferrie then began to learn to fly, at his father's suggestion, to take his mind off of his failures at the seminary, according to the House Select Committee on Assassinations. The HSCA's investigation states— without even a raised eyebrow—that Ferrie had become a pilot in 1942 and then gone to work for an oil-drilling firm which had jobs in South America.

We found this highly curious. Ferrie, 23 in 1942, prime draft age in the middle of World War II, at a time when you needed more than a note from your local Congressman to evade military duty. And he's a *pilot* to boot! But instead of being drafted, the HSCA report blandly states, he "goes to work for an oil drilling firm with interests in South America."

The oil business has certainly produced more than its share of spooks... Oil and intelligence work seemingly hand-in-glove... witness for example the two George's, George Bush and George DeMohrenschilt, Lee Oswald's CIA baby-sitter in Dallas. Both of them, strangely enough, "worked" in the oil business in Latin America.

Yet *no one* has questioned David Ferrie's utterly transparent "cover story" before. And the biggest question this brings up has nothing to do with Dave Ferrie. It has to do with *us*...

Have we *always* been such sheep?

Our suspicions about Dave Ferrie's entry into American intelligence were confirmed by Ferrie's own godson, Morris Brownlee, in an interview about a man he still remembers fondly. Brownlee was one of America's first beatniks, a mystic when even Unitarians were frowned on, and a student of philosophy who recently, in his mid-50's, graduated from college.

"Back in World War II the development of South American oil resources was a high priority item for the Nazis," he told us. "Remember, they had no oil of their own. The U.S. had a preemptive strategy of denying them these resources. I heard Dave mention his service with the Jade Oil Corporation. His job was to scout a situation, under cover of pursuing sociological studies, and then report what he found back to the appropriate authorities in the States."

"He was a pilot, and a good one, and he had a gift of gab as well, which I always assumed he inherited from his dad, who was an Irish cop and attorney," Brownlee continued.

A former NSA agent, who lived and worked in Central America since 1964, told us unequivocally, "Ferrie worked under cover for (CIA front) Southern Air Transport, which was just Air Transport back then. That company housed a lot of weird shit."

So what have we got here? Dave Ferrie, under suspicion of involvement in the assassination less than 48 hours after it occurred, a mentor to Lee Harvey Oswald in the Louisiana Civil Air Patrol, and a CIA pilot.

In Ferrie's life, his path was greased by the same forces which will later smooth the way for Barry Seal. For example, while many have the uncomfortable feeling that their government seems only too willing to track them to hell and back over 20-year old traffic fines, those fortunate enough to be "connected," like Ferrie and Barry Seal, have the most enviable dumb luck in their dealings with the government.

Ferrie, for example, got himself involved in a series of serious misconduct incidents at the Cleveland Civil Air Patrol in 1948, charges which eventually drove him from Ohio. He appropriated a squadron airplane which had been grounded by the U.S. Air Force, and flew, after dark and without landing lights, from Columbus to Cleveland, identifying himself as a lieutenant in the U.S. Air Force.

But when the Cleveland CAP commander tried to have Ferrie dismissed, the paperwork was somehow "lost." So Ferrie was still on the books and in good standing two years later when two Ohio CAP cadets reported that their instructor Ferrie had taken them to a house of prostitution in a nearby town. While he was not charged with a crime, his dismissal from the Cleveland CAP became imminent. That's when enterprising Dave transferred himself to a post in the Louisiana CAP.

Ferrie had become *persona non grata* with the Cleveland CAP after being accused of sexually corrupting young men in his charge. But when the Louisiana Civil Air Patrol requested his records from Ohio, these papers, too, had somehow been "lost."

Predictably, the Civil Air Patrol has never been able to satisfactorily account for either of these inexplicable lapses. Nor for that matter can they explain to this day how their records of Ferrie and Oswald happened to be 'stolen' after Kennedy's assassination. So tracking Barry Seal's recruiter Dave Ferrie has already paid off; we've just learned a lesson: "Being connected means never having to say you're sorry...because your paperwork gets lost so often."

Another telltale sign of Ferrie's covert connections occurred when, while just a lowly rookie pilot at Eastern, he was nonetheless already known and admired by none other than Eastern's President General Eddie Rickenbacker. Rickenbacker, no slouch himself in the spook department, somehow found it necessary to have placed in the file of the seemingly inconsequential junior employee David Ferrie a glowing letter of recommendation.

"This man's efforts bear watching and his qualifications justify his being *used and helped* whenever possible in line of duty—*and even beyond*," Rickenbacker wrote.

Much later Barry Seal, by all accounts an outstanding young pilot, becomes first the youngest 707 Captain, and then later the youngest Captain of a 747 while at Howard Hughes' TWA... and in all fairness it must be asked whether ability alone led to these early accolades. Or was it also a Dan Quayle-like case of "its not what you know, but who?"

In a small final irony, thirty years after Ferrie and Rickenbacker's paths cross, and twenty years after Barry Seal is recruited by Dave Ferrie, Barry Seal's C-123 was specially outfitted—by the CIA, natch—for its mission into Sandinista Nicaragua, at Rickenbacker Air Force Base.

Small world.

As we began to delve into the life of Dave Ferrie, clues to his checkered career as a spook were visible all around. But some came from sources considered less sporting than others: his fellow spooks. Former Aide to the Deputy Director of the CIA Victor Marchetti was told by a CIA colleague, "Ferrie had been a contract agent to the Agency in the early Sixties and had been involved in some of the Cuban activities."

Marchetti was convinced that Ferrie was a CIA contract officer and involved in various criminal activities, telling author Anthony Summers "he observed consternation on the part of then CIA Director Richard Helms and other senior officials when Ferrie's name was first publicly linked with the assassination in 1967."

But because the boys in trench-coats exude such a smug (George W. Bush-like, actually) sense of their own superior intelligence, it is far more fun—as well as more sporting—to find 'civilian' witnesses. We found Eddie Shearer, one of Ferrie's cadet disciples in the late 1950's and early 60's, who had much to say about Dave Ferrie.

For example, Shearer spent time in the gas station which Carlos Marcello gave Ferrie right after the Kennedy assassination. Many writers, no doubt afflicted with over-active imaginations, believe the station was a pay-off for Ferrie's role in the hit.

"There's never been any doubt in my mind that Dave's gas station, a Gulf station out on Airline Highway, was a CIA cover," he told us. "Some people I knew pretty well hung out there, and it was the funniest thing, if you drove in to fill up with gasoline— which is what a gas station is supposed to be for, right?—you could sit in your car forever waiting for someone to come out and tell you they were "closed" or something. Whatever they were doing there, pumping gas wasn't it."

Much-maligned New Orleans DA Jim Garrison apparently noticed the same thing. "Although Ferrie to all intents and purposes was unemployed at the time," he said in "Heritage of Stone," "an examination of his bank account revealed that during the three week period prior to the President's assassination he deposited $7,093.02. Then a few months after the assassination, Ferrie suddenly acquired a large service station. He apparently ran it in much the same way he maintained his apartment. On one occasion he had just filled the gas tank of an acquaintance and he waved him away, turning down payment for the gas. "Forget it," he said. "The government's paying for it anyway.'"

Barry Seal, like David Ferrie, will also own a gas station, among a dozen small businesses, in the 60's and 70's. One of the most revealing insights we received about Seal came from someone from military intelligence who had known him in the 60's.

We had spent several weeks looking through boxes of business receipts from Seal's various enterprises before we asked this man for an explanation of some of the nuances of covert operations.

"Is an agent like Seal primarily a small business owner and suburban father, someone who gets a call to do something for 'the boys' one or two days a month," we asked him.

"That's not how it works," explained this intel veteran, smiling at our naiveté. "'Cover' was very important in the 60's and 70's. In the 80's things got sloppy and it became less important...but back when you're talking about, your 'cover' was very important."

"So," we asked incredulously, still distracted with thoughts of Seal's (and Ferrie's) "contract pilot" status, "do you mean Seal was a full-time CIA guy whose various businesses were—just *cover?*"

His answer was matter-of-fact. "Yes."

And so it was with David Ferrie, who in addition to his pilot duties also conducted wide-ranging and bizarre experiments, at the exact same time the CIA has admitted doing freaky CIA mind-control MKULTRA research...

"Out back of Ferrie's house, he had a workshop in his backyard," Ed Shearer told us. "And I know this sounds weird but he had a skull out there, hooked up to a skeleton, and to simulate a nervous system he had used different colored electrical wire—blue, red, green—in an effort to understand human physiology."

"Dave was a brilliant individual, interested in all kinds of things," continued Shearer, who related how Ferrie's mother, whom he knew from visiting Ferrie, had told him that Dave's brother was a nuclear physicist. When we tracked Ferrie's brother the nuclear physicist, living in California, he was unwilling to talk. Nuclear physicists are notoriously smart.

"There were almost-constant examples of Dave Ferrie's brilliance when you hung around with him," said Shearer. "He had a little lawnmower, just to give you one 'for instance,' that he couldn't get to start. So I was out back one day repeatedly pulling on the little rope to get it started, while he watched."

"'What a waste of efficiency,' Dave mused out loud. 'If we could only just get rotary motion from a motor at the start!' Remember, this was years before the rotary engine was patented, before anyone had ever even *heard* of a Wankel motor. But Dave had had the same idea, just talking out loud."

Like many in New Orleans, Shearer was accustomed to seeing Ferrie at the airport in the company of Sergio Arachna Smith, the Cuban Revolutionary Front leader for whom he (Ferrie) was training exile pilots. "There were a lot of things about Dave that just didn't fit, unless you added them up another way," he says today. "Just his appearance... good god. You have to wonder how Eastern was able to keep him as long as they did. I remember him taxiing his Eastern Convair one time, on his weekday Houston-New Orleans 'milk-run.' He would always pull in way faster than any other airline pilots did, and he'd be leaning out of one side of his cockpit window, looking like some damn railroad engineer or something."

"Then two weekends every month Dave flew a Constellation up to Washington DC and back. And if while he was up there he was meeting with his CIA contacts, it would make sense. Because I was with him on three or four occasions when he returned, and when he opened his wallet I noticed he had several one hundred dollar bills."

"That doesn't seem very extraordinary," we replied. "He was a pilot at Eastern, and they made decent money, didn't they?"

"You gotta remember, this was in the *Fifties*," Shearer stated. "Anyone who was working back then can tell you: you got paid in twenties. *Nobody* got paid in hundred-dollar bills back then. You hardly ever *saw* hundred dollar bills."

Shearer got conclusive proof of Dave Ferrie's career in clandestine services less than five years after Ferrie's death. "In 1972 I was asked to join the senior Civil Air Patrol, an outfit with no cadets," Shearer relates. "There I met Herb Wagner, a Navy flier in World War II, who had then been recruited by the OSS, the CIA's precursor, at the end of the war. When we got friendly, I'd go over to his house, and sometimes he would reminisce about things he'd done for the CIA back in the middle '50's."

"Herb told me, 'once you're in the CIA, its hard to get out.' He tried to get out when he got married and settled down. He and his wife had adopted a baby daughter, and he wasn't the daredevil he had once been. But they still pressured him to fly."

Said Shearer, "I visited him one time just after he'd gotten a 'visit' from the CIA, to go do something he no longer really *wanted* to be doing, quite obviously, because he was really down when I talked with him. And that was when he loosened up and told me, about Dave Ferrie, saying that 'if the truth was ever known about Dave Ferrie, he would be recognized as one of the true unsung heroes of the United States...' and this was coming from a man who did not hand out praise real easily. And that's when I realized that Ferrie had been a regular CIA guy, not just some asset or 'contract operative.'"

Confirmation of Ferrie's status often came in casual conversation with pilots who had worked in New Orleans... "I first met Dave Ferrie out at Lakefront Airport in 1965," pilot James Poche told us. "He was running a fixed-base operation with five DC3's and some PBY's."

That is quite a little fleet of planes Ferrie is handling out of the CIA's FBO (Fixed-Base of Operations) in New Orleans. By 1972, five years after Ferrie had been 'suicided,' his protégé Seal will be using, according to transcripts of Seal's 1972 trial for exporting munitions, the same fleet' of five DC3's and PBY's which David Ferrie had controlled.

Just how much *can* a CIA agent get away with in America? Would you believe... child molestation?

David Ferrie was arrested in New Orleans on August 8, 1961, for contributing to the delinquency of a juvenile, and re-arrested three days later for extortion, engaging in homosexual behavior with a 15-year-old boy, and indecent behavior with three others.

The extortion charge, reported the New Orleans Times Picayune on August 29, 1961, was related to a 16-year old who had made statements to police that Ferrie showed up at the grocery store where he worked, threatening the youth into signing papers stating he would not press "the crime-of-nature charge" in the case.

What has never been told is what happened *after* Dave Ferrie was arrested, to the cops who had executed the warrant. When authorities with the Jefferson Parish Sheriff's Office entered Ferrie's home with a search warrant on August 22, 1961, they found munitions, maps of the Cuban coast rifles, ammunition, and two miniature submarines later used to infiltrate CIA operatives into Cuba. An FBI report a year later stated that the Cuban Revolutionary Council, of which Ferrie was co-founder and leader, gave one "Jose Rabel" a highly sophisticated assassination weapon and sent him into Cuba via a "CIA-supplied submarine."

Anyone busted on a morals charge should be as lucky as Ferrie was: he had an OJ-like Dream Team defense, consisting of such legal luminaries as Kennedy assassination suspect and FBI/CIA/ ONI (Office of Naval Intelligence) made guy Guy Banister, and his attorney, G. Wray Gil, who spent most days toiling as Mafia Kingfish Carlos Marcello's main attorney.

Guy Banister will come up again later, in 1972, in connection with Barry Seal's munitions trial. On trial with Seal was New York Mobster Murray Kessler, who authorities assumed had met Seal when both worked for Banister in the early 1960's.

We interviewed the police officers who executed the search warrant and arrested David Ferrie on morals charges back in 1961, and discovered that no one, until now, had talked to them about what both considered the most bizarre experience of their law enforcement career.

When Ferrie was arrested, according to both their accounts, all hell broke loose. Former Sergeant Ronald Fournier of the New Orleans PD shakes his head in disbelief today at what transpired.

"It started out as just a regular arrest. We were receiving complaints from parents that Ferrie was taking good kids and corrupting them, getting them to break into the gunrooms of high schools and steal guns, because he was into gunrunning to the Cubans. We also had complaints that he would sit with the kids, sit around in a room and masturbate, in a circle-jerk, I guess you would call it," stated Fournier.

"Ferrie was the Great Imposter," he continued. "He could be just about anything he needed to be under the circumstances, like treating the kids medically, as if he were a doctor, which he did. He had a card identifying himself as a doctor, which is kind of funny, since he looked like he had moss from a tree glued to his scalp."

"So we raided his house. We knew he was carrying on sexually with the children. But, good lord, what we found…. We found maps, guns, high school official Air Force recruiting films, books on the occult and hypnotism lying around…and chalices and other instruments used in Mass."

"And then the next day, to our shock," Fournier continued, "we discovered that warrants had been issued for *our* arrest, my partner and myself, the cops who had executed the search warrant! Ferrie had gone to a judge and gotten warrants issued. Nothing like it had ever happened before. And that's when it all began to be a little bit intimidating, frankly."

Charles Jonou, Fournier's partner in the New Orleans Police Department search of Ferrie's premises in 1961, agreed with this account, and offered something else. "I handled surveillance on Ferrie for Garrison later," he told us. "Garrison was on this guy like rice on gravy. I'd watch Ferrie pacing around his apartment nude, smoking one cigarette after another. That's what he'd do: pace and smoke. It was strange to watch a guy do that. Ferrie would talk to you like he was a friend of yours, but I was never fooled. I knew he'd stab you in the back as easy as look at you."

After Ferrie's arrest, a bizarre series of negotiations began regarding the charges against him. "We were trying to get these runaway kids away from him, and return them to their parents, and we began to get phone calls setting up meetings held under mysterious circumstances with Cubans in khakis who said they would produce the kids *if and only if* Ferrie was not prosecuted," stated Fournier.

This story—of almost state-to-state negotiations—is too similar to be mere coincidence to the incredible offer which the Louisiana State Police will make to Barry Seal twenty years later in 1981, when they implore him to move his drug smuggling operation out of their state, and in return they will cease efforts to indict him for crimes he has *already* committed.

"It was the most generous offer I ever heard made to a criminal," says one cop who was there. "But instead of accepting gratefully, Barry's response was that he would have to first 'check with his people.'"

Almost forty years later, Fournier is still amazed at the hornet's nest stirred up by Ferrie's arrest. "There I was, I'm just doing my job, and some strong high-powered organization is getting a warrant issued for *my* arrest. And the thought occurred; I'm dealing with some awfully high-level Cubans here. This Captain Ferrie—someone here has a LOT of pull. This guy is a powerful man with a lot of powerful friends."

Powerful enough to get the charges dismissed? You bet.

Morris Brownlee told us how it happened. "I led a small informal delegation of influential citizens to visit the Jefferson Parish DA to persuade him to drop the charges. Included were Father Mullaby from Loyola, myself, and Herb Wagner. We went to tell him about all the good things Dave Ferrie had done. And though the process was a bloody mess, because both Orleans and Jefferson Parish's had filed charges against him, we were eventually successful and the charges were dropped."

"Could this be the same Herb Wagner who Eddie Shearer had told us about? OSS and CIA pilot Herb Wagner?" we asked.

"You knew him?" Brownlee replied, unruffled.

Perhaps it is just coincidence, but this is not the last time in our story in which the Jesuits (who ran Loyola) will figure. Seal's longtime CIA 'handler' Dave Dixon had had close ties to Loyola University New Orleans, and its president Bernard P. Knoth, S.J. So hearing about the intercession of the Church on behalf of a man charged with child molestation led us to wonder if there might some *institutional* connection brought to bear. Later a former high-ranking official from the National Security Agency would tell us that it had been "no mistake" that Manuel Noriega had sought refuge in the *Vatican's* embassy during the American invasion of Panama, since Noriega had been the Vatican's 'boy.'"

Former New Orleans Police Sergeant Fournier shakes his head in disgust at the memory of his '61 debacle. "The whole thing was out of this world. And then, the night of the President's death we began to get phone calls from the DA's office about Ferrie. When he got caught up in Garrison's probe? None of us believed Ferrie committed suicide, or died of natural causes. He was, remember, in flight condition—he had to be to pass his annual physical—how much better does it get?"

Charles Jonou, who had been watching Ferrie the night he died, concurred.

While CIA recruiter David Ferrie is usually described as rabidly anti-Castro, and anti-Communist, this is not altogether correct. Ferrie had also run guns to his idol of the fifties, Fidel Castro, when the Cuban revolutionary was raiding Batista's forces from the Sierra Maestra.

As reported by two New Orleans reporters on the scene, Jack Wardlaw and Rosemary James, in their book, *Counterplot*, according to a Captain Neville Levy, Ferrie was engaged in gun smuggling to Fidel Castro and raising money for his 26th of July Movement. Ferrie even went so far as to carry a loaded gun while fund-raising for Fidel, Levy said.

No evidence of this appears in Ferrie's FBI file. But then neither do records exist today of Barry Seal's own arrest for weapons smuggling into Cuba… We found several early friends of Seal's who confirmed and expanded on the story we had first heard from Joe Nettles. "Barry got busted with a plane-load of weapons in the tiny town of Long View, Texas, located half-way between Dallas and Shreveport," stated Reggie Griffith, a man who knew Seal his entire adult life.

Griffith, who had the Piper airplane distributorship in Baton Rouge, ruefully recalls 'the way things were' in the pilot fraternity in Louisiana in those early feverish days of the secret war with Cuba. "One time I rented a brand new Aztec twin engine airplane to a man named Matthew Edward

Duke, at right about the time Barry was busted in Texas," Griffith states. "I did it after getting a phone call from an aircraft dealer in Houston, JD Reed. Duke was an ex-commander in the Army Air Corps, and said he'd be back a little after dark."

"Two or three days later this guy (Duke) calls up long-distance, says he's down in Cuba, and can he keep the plane a few more days till Monday? Well, what am I going to say? Monday morning rolls around and the Border Patrol shows up, telling me my plane had just been shot down over Cuba, the pilot was dead and what did I know about it."

Griffith pauses. "What I knew about it was nothing. But what I was *about* to know about it was that my insurance company was only going to compensate me $10,000 on a $92,000 plane."

Reggie Griffith had made, in other words, an unintended $80,000 'contribution' to the cause.

Numerous inquiries about Seal's expunged weapons smuggling arrest in Long View, Texas yielded an interesting glimpse into the problems associated with bringing to light matters some people prefer were left in the dark. We called around to find out if there was a local newspaper in that tiny Texas town between Shreveport and Dallas which might have some record of the arrest, only to be told by the local librarian, "Don't even bother calling the local paper. A lot of things which happened in this town never really happened, if you know what I mean."

Then we got a little lucky. Long View, Texas has a law library, we discovered, and the librarian was a friend of the 80-year old judge who was the only sitting jurist at the time. She checked with this man, a Judge Atkinson, who recalled the incident, if vaguely, but was unable or unwilling to say more.

Now intrigued, the law librarian e-mailed a cousin who had worked in national security in the White House under two Presidents, she told us, asking him if he knew of Barry Seal.

"Yes, I do—but that's all I can say," came his terse reply.

The official story about David Ferrie states that when Castro announced he had become a Marxist, Ferrie furiously turned against his former idol and began to pilot bombing missions into Cuba, as well as sabotage raids on behalf of various Cuban exile groups, as if the CIA's changing attitude towards "*all things Fidelismo*" had nothing to do with head-strong Dave's sudden change-of-heart.

In 1961, well before the Bay of Pigs, Ferrie flew to Cuba dozens of times, sometimes on bombing missions, sometimes making daring landings to extract anti-Castro resistance fighters. Anthony Summers in

Conspiracy states it was "rumored that he had piloted Oswald to Cuba in 1959."

But true to the CIA's tactic of denying the obvious until things die down, Ferrie even claimed he had never even *been* to Cuba. But he regularly boasted of his exploits there, regaling his more trusted young CAP admirers, like Eddie Shearer, with tales of his activities as a commando spy at the Bay of Pigs.

Ferrie often told a story of how he had been knifed in the belly by a Castro militiaman during a midnight hit-and-run mission to the coast of Cuba in early 1961. When he died on the eve of being called to testify to Garrison's Grand Jury, Garrison related in "On the Trail of the Assassins," "One of the numerous legends about David Ferrie and his adventures as a soldier of fortune pilot involved a take-off he had made from the Escambray mountains in Cuba, after delivering munitions to the anti-Castro rebels operating there. As the legend went, a counter-attack had almost trapped him, and he was forced to take off in his plane while fighting one of Castro's soldiers with his free hand.

He had, according to this tale, received a bad stab wound in his stomach before he got the plane off the ground."

"When Lou Ivon (a Garrison investigator) returned from the morgue, he was holding a freshly taken photograph. The dead man on the slab, his bald head and aristocratic profile somewhat suggestive of Julius Caesar, bore the scar of a knife wound running up the center of his stomach."

So much for never having been in Cuba…

An airline pilot we met who had flown with Ferrie went even further. "They (Fidel's boys) were looking for Ferrie, and that's a fact. The first Communist Cuban hijacking of a plane was of an Eastern plane on Ferrie's normal run. They took an Eastern plane to Havana that Ferrie would normally have been piloting, but for some mysterious reason, he wasn't there that day."

But there is one subject concerning Dave Ferrie which seems at first glance to be so *unbelievable*—so akin to Dead Elvis sightings— that we were highly skeptical when we first heard of it. But after we received first-hand eyewitness testimony on this topic, delivered so matter-of-factly as to be utterly believable, we are convinced of its importance.

Of the many controversies swirling around Dave Ferrie's life— like the one about whether he was attempting to induce cancer in lab mice kept in cages in his apartment—none is "fringe-ier" than Ferrie's supposed talent for hypnotism. But the evidence for this is not merely persuasive… it is overwhelming. Even so, we would not believed it had we not heard unsolicited testimony about Ferrie's preoccupation with hypnotism, and his ability to hypnotize people.

Almost immediately after the assassination the stories began, starting with "alcoholic" Jack Martin, who in his first investigative interview suggested that Oswald had been put into a hypnotic trance state by Ferrie, who then imposed a posthypnotic order to go to Dallas and kill the President. Martin, strangely enough, never recanted this story, and never told federal investigators that his first story was untrue. And since he manifested tremendous apprehension when Ferrie died, expressing fear for his own life and fleeing New Orleans for some time, maybe he was telling the truth…

One could easily dismiss this claim if it stood alone. It sounds like it originated somewhere just slightly west of Area 51. But there are Freedom of Information Act documents released on the CIA's MKULTRA mind-control experiments which state that several Cuban immigrants were found upon whom hypnosis was tried, with the apparent goal of planting an agent in Cuba who, when triggered, would kill Fidel Castro. Ferrie is the likeliest candidate to have been doing the programming.

The CIA once released a statement saying this (mind control) didn't work. But independent research turned up first person witnesses who stated that classically conditioned MPD, Multiple Personality Disorder; agents were at work within Cuba from the time of Castro's rise to power in the late 1950's.

Okay, maybe *this* stuff is from Area 51 too… but what, then, does one make of the FBI interview with a Ferrie CAP cadet-turned New Orleans cop, Fred O'Sullivan, on November 26, 1963? O'Sullivan told the FBI that Ferrie might have had contact with Oswald at the Moisant Airport CAP, and that, according to the FBI report of this interview, "Ferrie had acquired a reputation for being able to hypnotize people, and that he had once hypnotized a man following one of the CAP meetings."

And there's a report prepared by FBI agents in Los Angeles on December 2, 1963, referring to remarks made by Gene Barnes, an NBC cameraman. "Barnes said Bob Mulholland, NBC News, Chicago, talked in Dallas to one 'Fairy,' a narcotics addict now out on bail on a sodomy charge in Dallas. 'Fairy' said that Oswald had been under hypnosis from a man doing a mind-reading act at Ruby's Carousel. 'Fairy' was said to be a private detective and the owner of an airline who took young boys on flights 'just for kicks.'"

Bob Mulholland will later become President of NBC News; "Fairy" (Ferrie) who *did* own an airline, United Air Taxi Service, will die a desperate man.

Eddie Shearer brought the subject up himself. "The hypnotism thing with Dave Ferrie was the one thing about him that bothered me the most. One time I remember we were marching in formation—drilling—out at Lakefront Airport, getting ready to go to the CAP national drill competition. And this kid was twirling a 'guidon'—a metal thing, a fleur-de-lis on the top of a pole with the units' colors—and it got away from him and it cut his hand up pretty good. I mean a real deep gash."

"And the kid gets up, holding his hand, and there's blood running all down his arm past his elbow, and Dave walks over to him and puts his hand out in front of the kid's face, like he's giving him a stiff-arm, and says, 'You will feel sensation but no pain,'" Shearer continued.

"And then, while we're all waiting for an ambulance to take the kid to the hospital, the kid is bleeding all over, but he's not in pain anymore.... And then Dave goes over to him again, and says to him, 'You will stop bleeding.'"

"And he did."

"Now, later, when I was in the Air Force," Shearer continued, "I learned that this is all possible, that it *can* be done. But it *can't* be done with a subject unless you've been working, hypnotically, with that subject for a long period of time. You can't just walk over to someone, in other words, and tell them to stop bleeding."

"So it became clear to me that Dave Ferrie had been working hypnosis with that kid for a long time without anyone knowing it. At least I had never heard of it before, and I spent a lot of time out there, hanging around that airport."

One of the earliest books on the Garrison probe, *Plot or Politics* by two local New Orleans reporters, said of Dave Ferrie: "He was a Civil Air Patrol leader for a number of years and numerous persons have reported that he had the high school boys under his command then, and others in a later Ferrie-formed outfit known as the 'Falcon Squadron,' *completely mesmerized.*"

When CIA agent Richard Nagell was with Oswald in New Orleans, according to Dick Russell's book *The Man Who Knew Too Much*, he discovered that Oswald was "undergoing hypnotherapy" from David Ferrie. Nagell dropped this potential bombshell in a single phrase in a letter in the Seventies, which included a set of "cartoons" one sequence of which shows Oswald, armed with a rifle, at the sixth-floor window of the Texas School Book Depository, when he suddenly awakens from a hypnotic trance.

The House Assassinations Committee said that Ferrie "frequently practiced" techniques of hypnosis on his young associates. And the New

Orleans police officers who discovered Ferrie dead in his apartment in 1967 found several voluminous abstracts on posthypnotic suggestion, as well as a whole library of books on hypnotism.

All of which makes more plausible the idea that the character assassination to which whistle-blower Jack Martin was subjected might have had a very good reason: Jack may have been telling the truth. He told the FBI, just three days after the assassination, "that he believed Ferrie was an 'amateur hypnotist 'who may have been capable of hypnotizing Oswald."

Was Oswald manipulated through applications of "mind control" techniques? The notion seems fantastic. But the CIA and American military intelligence worked diligently—*for years*—on the manipulation of human behavior, and on the creation of a "Manchurian Candidate." So the question hangs unanswered, for the simple reason that no judicial review appears to have the power to compel truthful answers from those who know.

The truth about the extent to which Dave Ferrie used hypnotism during the course of his duties as a CIA agent—and prototypical elite deviant—will likely never be known. Author John H. Davis, a member of the Board of Advisors of the Assassination Archives and Research Center in Washington, D.C., reports, for example, that a 30-page FBI report on Ferrie is—whoops again! —Missing.

Not to be outdone in withholding the truth from the American people, the CIA confessed in a 1975 presidential commission report that it had "lost" 152 files concerning drug testing and a much larger program studying means for controlling human behavior, exploring the effects of radiation, electric shock, psychology, psychiatry, sociology and harassment substances.

An enormous number of documents about Dave Ferrie remain classified until well after everyone reading this sentence is dead.

But even back in 1958, there were people interested in what he was up to. "Another thing I remember back then in '58 and '59," states pilot Shearer, "was Dave would always warn us not to say anything on the phone we didn't want to have overheard. He was convinced his phone was tapped. And when he would pick it up, before dialing he'd swear a blue streak into it, as if he were talking to whoever was tapping his phone."

During exactly this same time period there was also quite a bit of FBI interest in the young Barry Seal as well. According to Jerry Chidgey, who was Barry's roommate and friend, he became aware— in early 1960—that the FBI was following Barry.

"When I met Barry I owned 'The Amber Bottle,' a folk club in Baton Rouge. We were capitalizing on the folk craze," Chidgey recalls. "And that was where Barry used to hang, and we became good friends and ended up living together. And one day I remember two FBI guys showed up asking questions about him, while Barry was gone on a trip."

"Another time that same year (1960) I flew to Dallas, and two men in black suits followed me there and back, and the only reason I could ever figure out was because of Barry," says Chidgey. "Unless, that is, they were making a practice of surveilling folk club owners."

Barry Seal and Dave Ferrie share yet-another highly unusual trait, we discovered, a trait which is a big plus for any secret agent. Both men had photographic memories.

When we interviewed Ferrie intimate and CIA "asset" Layton Martens, he had attempted to dispel the belief that Ferrie had been plotting the Kennedy assassination during the two weeks prior, while Ferrie had been staying at Churchill Farms, Marcello's Louisiana countryside estate. Many have wondered why Marcello would have used a mere pilot on his legal team.

"Dave Ferrie had a photographic memory," Martens told us. "That's why Carlos used him. He was useful because he had sat down and memorized the Louisiana Napoleonic Code in six weeks—in its entirety!"

Barry Seal went Dave Ferrie one better.

"Barry not only had a photographic memory," his widow Debbie Seal says, "but he was also able to read upside down. He could go into an office and sit down in front of somebody's desk and, while still carrying on a normal conversation, read what they had in front of them and remember it completely later."

A photographic memory… the ability to surreptitiously read upside down… being as good a pilot as any alive….These are all clearly useful traits in the world of clandestine services. But they don't explain why the FBI was so interested in both David Ferrie and Barry Seal.

What were Seal and Ferrie doing which warranted FBI surveillance back in the early '60's?

The answer opens what's been called "*an endless can of worms.*"

CHAPTER FIVE

An Endless Can
of Worms

ON THE BALMY SPRING afternoon of March 30, 1961 in Washington D.C. the high hopes of Camelot met the nightmare that the '60's would later become. Having heard rumors of the impending Bay of Pigs invasion, the Chairman of the Senate's Foreign Relations Committee, Arkansas Senator William Fulbright, was on a determined mission to get the attention of the President of the United States, John Kennedy, just then quite a busy man.

But get it he did. And as Pierre Salinger was announcing the creation of the Peace Corps in the White House Press Room, Fulbright joined Kennedy aboard Air Force One, and handed him a memorandum which still resonates four decades later.

"As the Cuban exiles intensify their activities aimed at overthrowing Castro, it will become even more difficult to conceal the U.S. hand," Fulbright's memo warned Kennedy. "The prospect must also be faced that an invasion of Cuba by exiles would encounter formidable resistance which the exiles, by themselves, might not be able to overcome."

Kennedy and Fulbright huddled in serious conversation in-flight while en route to the lustrous green enclave of Palm Beach, Florida, where the well-known affectations of the wealthy—the Range Rovers and Rolexes, the little Chanel purses and personal chefs—get stepped up yet a further notch. Meanwhile a few hundred miles south the Cuban Invasion forces were launching themselves from half a dozen sites around the Caribbean towards their rendezvous with ignominy. Still further south, at a secret

CIA airbase in Central America where a rag-tag armada was preparing to launch air raids into Cuba, young American pilot Barry Seal sent his mom a postcard reading "Hi, Everything is very pretty. I'm fine and will see you soon. Will bring 'home movies' back to show! Berry."

Fulbright's memo continued, "The question would then arise of whether the United States would be willing to let the enterprise fail, in the probably futile hope of concealing the U.S. role, or whether the United States would respond with progressive assistance as necessary to insure success. This would include ultimately the use of armed force; and if we came to that, even under the paper cover of legitimacy, we would have undone the work of thirty years in trying to live down earlier interventions."

Maintaining 'plausible deniability' was clearly on the mind of the outspoken Senator from Arkansas. But Fulbright had another equally-pressing concern, which in retrospect makes him look as clairvoyant as one of Nancy Reagan's psychics...

Fulbright worried about the consequences not just of *failure* at the Bay of Pig's... but also of *success.* "Consideration must also be given to the nature and composition of the government which succeeds Castro," he cautioned. "The Cuban Revolutionary Front is without the kind of leadership necessary to provide a strong, vigorous liberal government.... and we would also have assumed the responsibility for public order in Cuba, and in the circumstances this would unquestionably be *an endless can of worms.*"

Later that evening, against a blue-black tropical night sky sparkling with stars, it became too late for second thoughts, and both David Ferrie and Barry Seal witnessed the premiere of Fulbright's 'endless can of worms' in all its Technicolor glory. Neither could have known how profoundly each of them would be affected by the events which they were helping set in motion.

The Bay of Pigs invasion launch was a "special op" that would raise forever the ante for CIA covert ops from mere paramilitary activities to full-blown military-style invasions... the culmination of a decade of intriguing whose true nature has never been revealed. One reason the story of Barry Seal is so interesting is because it provides a look at what 'the boys' were up to in that crucial region.

As we began to learn of Seal's flights to arm Fidel, for example, we wondered: how had Castro managed to get himself so well ensconced? For a bearded communist guerrilla in the mountains, Fidel was, according to numerous accounts, extremely well heeled. And in the last few months of

1958, as it became increasingly clear that the Cuban Dictator Fulgencio Batista was being forced to flee, his band was described in the press as "well-financed rebels."

But just *who* was supplying Castro with all that money and all those arms? And why? Where had Fidel's rag-tag band of guerrillas gotten the money to pay for arms obligingly delivered by pilots like Ferrie and Seal?

We were like most Americans: "Cuban history" brought to mind nothing more than the progression of Desi Arnaz's marriage to Lucille Ball. Clearly, a little remedial history was in order...

Start with Dr. Carlos Prio Soccarras, who was President of Cuba from 1948 to 1952. Prio headed the Authentico Party, a Party so authentically "Authentico" that shortly after he was elected he built himself a $2 million home on his Presidential salary of $25,000 a year... a nifty trick.

Alas, this sort of unabashed love of *capitalismo* left him unable to persuade the other grafters in his government to walk the straight and narrow, and a rapid deterioration in public services was accompanied by a slump in tourism... which more than offset the boom in luxury housing. Meyer Lansky's Mob, which controlled the Havana gambling industry, was not amused...

And now they wanted *Prio* overthrown. So they tapped ex-President Fulgencio Batista, who had staged enough successful Cuban coups before to get good at it, and he obligingly seized the Cuban government and canceled the 1952 presidential elections. Things once again looked rosy for the most 'Original Gangsters' of them all, the Syndicate.

But then a young lawyer in Havana with an impoverished clientele named Fidel Castro wrote Batista an extraordinary personal letter, calling down on him the wrath of God. Castro actually had the temerity to *sue* the newly installed dictator in the high courts of Cuba, demanding that the nonplussed judges sentence the dictator to *no less than one hundred years in jail* for violating the Cuban Constitution of 1940.

That's a ballsy move; especially for someone whose gonads will shortly be discovered to be slightly pinker than they should be.... "When the worst is enthroned, a pistol at his belt, it is necessary to carry pistols oneself in order to fight for the best," Castro said. He made good his threats against Batista by leading an attack on the Moncada army barracks in Santiago on July 26,1953, a date which gave his group its name, the July 26 Movement.

Outnumbered ten to one, half of Fidel's force was immediately captured, systematically tortured, and murdered by Batista's army and his secret police. Newspapers in Batista's control then printed photographs of the dead men dressed in clean clothes after being murdered, in a clumsy attempt to show that they had been killed in battle.

Few Cubans were fooled. The atrocities won for Batista a reputation as a monster in the press. Once again, tourism began to suffer…what was a long-suffering Mob Boss to do? Meanwhile the Moncada assault had become the stuff of legend. Curiously, the Cuban Communist party, which had made its own arrangements with Batista, actually *attacked* Castro for what it called his "putschist" methods. Go figure.

Three years later, on December 2, 1956, Fidel Castro and 82 followers left Mexico aboard the yacht Granma, and landed in Cuba's Oriente Province, where they used the Sierra Maestre Mountains as a base of operations to launch a guerrilla war against Fulgencio Batista. This gave the CIA boys in the Havana station something to write home about…

"Many high ranking officers [in Batista's Army] are not noteworthy for their military acumen," read one droll report on Cuba's prospects, "and it is generally known that they are more interested in the graft they are able to secure than in winning battles or skirmishes against the rebel forces."

The lure of perfumed nights in luxury villas must not be restricted just to politicians…. In a pinch, to try to suppress Castro, Batista was forced to call on Cuban warlords like Rolando Masferrer, a man fingered in a cable to Washington, as "an opportunist of the first order, a staunch friend of President Carlos Prio under whose regime he had served as a Representative, but when Prio was ousted he turned up overnight at the side of Fulgencio Batista, becoming a Senator in Batista's Government."

Clearly a heads-up guy, Masferrer was described as "a powerfully-built man of 39, who has the reputation as a gangster and a killer. He has a private band of 80-armed men who serve as a sort of personal bodyguard and act as hatchet men if violence is called for. He is known to have killed certain enemies and to have scared the wits out of others. In 1950, for instance, he was found by the police, machine gun in hand, standing over two frightened men who were actually digging their own graves."

This is not a bad clipping to walk in with if one is applying to the Mob for a job as an enforcer…. Both Rolando Masferrer and Fulgencio Batista soon were working hand-in-hand with Meyer Lansky. But the Mob had also begun hedging its bets through the recently deposed President Prio, who, a full thirty years before Sly Stallone and Madonna rolled into town, had taken to living the high life in Miami.

According to *Deadly Secrets*, the definitive book on the CIA's Secret War with Castro, "Since his exile to Miami in 1952, Prio had been putting money into anti-Batista plots the way a gambler feeds the slots, hoping one will eventually pay off. He participated in these intrigues from his penthouse—one of those revolutionaries that Castro disdained as 'heroes from afar.'"

When Prio met Castro in a McAllen, Texas motel in 1957, Castro was looking for money and weapons, and Prio was looking for a surrogate warrior. "Castro sat on the couch next to Prio, the better to convince him. As he talked, he jabbed the former president's chest with his finger. His brown eyes blazed inches from Prio's eyes. The words came in deluges, like tropical rain. He talked at full speed, all energy and enthusiasm and concentration. When he finished, it was dark, and Prio had agreed to give him $100,000," report authors Hinckle and Turner.

Texas gunrunner Robert McKeown told of *his* association with Carlos Prio before a secret executive session of the House Select Committee on Assassinations. In the mid-'50s McKeown had a successful business in Cuba until forced out by Batista. He was eventually arrested in Texas with a house full of arms and munitions he was planning to smuggle to Fidel Castro.

McKeown was fronting for Prio, with whom Frank Sturgis also worked. According to House Assassination Committee investigator Gaeton Fonzi, the FBI had—after the Kennedy assassination—discovered that Jack Ruby *himself* had contacted McKeown to ask him for a letter of introduction to Fidel...

"I was getting guns into Castro," McKeown stated bluntly, in his executive session testimony. "As a matter of fact, Prio and Castro were good friends. Prio financed Castro. He trusted Castro."

Here was part of our answer: Castro had been financed, at least partially, by Prio. To its credit, the Committee investigators then wanted to know exactly the same thing we did:

"Where did Prio get *his* loot?" they asked McKeown.

"Well, you hate to talk about the dead you know, the man is dead," McKeown said. "He was supposed to burn up $300 million and he did not burn it up. He brought it to the United States."

"Where did he get the money?" the committee's investigator persisted.

At that point, even though he was testifying in a closed Executive Session that would be sealed from the American public for twenty years, McKeown took a Forrest Gump-like "And that's all I have to say about that," stance...

"He was supposed to burn this money up in Cuba and he did not burn it up," he repeated, as if that explained everything. And it must have, at least to the investigators present, who quickly moved on to something else.

Gordon Novel acknowledged to us that it had been the *CIA's* $300 million which Carlos Prio was passing out so freely in the late 1950's. This explanation goes a long way towards explaining why so many enterprising Americans—Barry Seal, Jack Ruby, David Ferrie—were running guns to Castro like there was no tomorrow.

Twenty years before the phrase became popular, these men were already "following the money." And they weren't the only ones...The reason the House Committee on Assassinations took testimony from McKeown in the first place was because he had been involved in gunrunning to Castro with Jack Ruby *and* Lee Harvey Oswald.

"Mr. McKeown, when did you first meet Lee Harvey Oswald?" he was asked.

"Well, I was sitting in my home in St. Leon, Texas, and I would venture to say that it was around 9:00 or 10:00 in the morning and I seen this car drive up, it had a big picture window," the garrulous McKeown related. "I seen this car drive up and these two people got out and they came and knocked on the door and my wife was in her negligee and she ran upstairs, you know, and Sam was there, we were getting ready to go get some oysters or something, I don't know."

"This fellow (Oswald) knocked on the door," he continued. "As I opened the door he says, well, golly, I finally found you. You are McKeown, are you not? And I said yes. And he said well, I have looked for you quite awhile but I am sure that you are McKeown. So I invited him in. He had another gentleman with him and he was more or less in his shirtsleeves, you know, he was not dressed up or anything. But this other fellow was dressed up."

"He says, I understand that you can supply any amount of arms. I said, who told you that?' He says, 'well, I am pretty sure that you can do it.'"

"Then he (Oswald) says, 'we are thinking about having a revolution in El Salvador.' That is what he said."

"I said, 'El Salvador?' He said yes."

The incident being recounted occurred nearly two years *after* the abortive Bay of Pigs had ruined the Agency's chances for a really big—perhaps even nuclear—war in Cuba. But the 'boys' weren't giving up on having a war in Central America; illustrating the lengths those in clandestine services will go in pursuit of their ends.

Clearly, none of them could have been exactly *happy* at the prospect of having to settle for war in tiny little El Salvador.... But the "Cuban Project" was by no means the CIA's only big 'play.' Like a gambler playing three blackjack hands at once, the boys were also laying bets in Indonesia... and Vietnam.

A war in El Salvador would have been a sad little consolation prize.

Since Prio's corruption-riddled presidency, his financial interests had interlocked with those of Lansky's through the "Ansan Group," which had been buying up southern Florida with money looted from Cuba. According to congressional investigators, "Lansky, Trafficante and other racketeers supplied funding in the expectation of securing gambling, prostitution and dope monopolies in a Cuba rid of Castro."

We've come full circle. Castro got his money from Carlos Prio. And Prio, who will play a role in the Kennedy assassination just a few short years later, got his from Allen Dulles... and Meyer Lansky.

This is somewhat confusing.... First, Fidel Castro overthrows, with American help, Cuban dictator Fulgencio Batista, who had been friendly both to U.S. corporations and U.S. organized crime interests running massive gambling, prostitution, and narcotics operations out of Havana.... Then the Eisenhower administration immediately elects to use the CIA to try to resolve their *new* "problem" almost as soon as Castro took power.

But hadn't the CIA in large part just *created* this "new problem?" Now, as soon as the CIA's $300 mill helps ol' Fidel over the top, they begin to lay plans to take *him* out! Might the *real* mission of the CIA be as some kind of "make-work" organization like the WPA during the Depression?

When President Eisenhower authorized the Bay of Pigs project on March 17, 1960 he admonished CIA officials that "the main thing was not to let the U.S. hand show." Eisenhower approved a CIA plan to create a Cuban-exile force to be used for "time-to-time" opportunistic raids against Cuba, and to stir up the Cuban public.

Colonel Fletcher Prouty was responsible to the Joint Chiefs of Staff for providing the CIA with the military material it needed for its paramilitary activities. "CIA agents from Air Division came to my office and asked for suggestions for a training camp," he says, recalling the genesis of the Cuba Project...

"At that time it was made clear that President Eisenhower, the Commander of the Normandy invasions of World War II, had not the slightest idea of authorizing an "invasion" of Cuba by unskilled exiles."

The CIA plan in 1960 had been to hit Cuba from the air with air drops of supplies and U.S. Marine Corps-trained Cuban exile paratroopers; and from the sea using over-the-beach guerrilla operations conducted with U.S. Navy support, according to Prouty.

Throughout this period in 1960 Eisenhower directed that the Cuban exiles' training and arming be kept at a low level. Then, as the political campaign picked up momentum, so did the Cuban exiles' activities, with John Kennedy playing a quiet role on their behalf. His support endeared him to the CIA, because the anti-Castro project was their biggest special operation.

Most baby-boomers remember President Eisenhower even more dimly than their old baseball card collections…. Few if any recall that during the Summer of 1960 Ike was on a "Crusade for Peace," and had planned a farewell Paris Summit conference with British Prime Minister Harold Macmillan, French President Charles DeGaulle, and Russian leader Nikita Khrushchev, to de-escalate Cold War tensions.

Because of that significant meeting the White House had ordered that all "U2 over-flights" of the Soviet Union and its Communist allies to cease during April and May.

This Presidential order covered *all* U-2 flights. According to Colonel Prouty, "This caused serious problems. A special request was made by the Secretary of Defense to the White House that we be permitted to continue some flights, like in Tibet, for humanitarian reasons. The request was denied. We were grounded with no exceptions."

Thus Prouty was stunned on the morning of Friday, May 6, 1960, to see front-page headlines screaming: SOVIET DOWNS AMERICAN PLANE; KHRUSHCHEV SEES SUMMIT BLOW.

"I met an officer from the U-2 program whose Pentagon office was across the hall from mine," he relates. "He was an old friend, a high-ranking Pentagon official. And he rushed into my office waving a note that contained four names and gave it to me, saying 'They did it,' and left. I had never seen that longtime, battle-hardened employee so distraught during the decades I had known him."

America's secret history includes the uncomfortable knowledge that someone in the CIA, responsible for the U2 missions, ignored Eisenhower's orders for the purpose of sabotaging the President's parting peace initiative. This all but caused the cancellation of the Paris Summit and *did* cause the withdrawal of the invitation to President Eisenhower to visit Moscow on his "Crusade for Peace."

The question is *"why?"* The answer is, *"Money."*

When President Eisenhower made the decision to provide "cover" for Allen Dulles and the CIA and accept responsibility for the U-2 flights over the Soviet Union, he preserved the fiction that the President of the United States is in control of the United States Government. As subsequent events indicate, nothing could be further from the truth.

Kennedy will pay a steep price for his inability to accept his "conditions of employment." But as we can see, he wasn't the first President to have big trouble with "the boys."

That dubious honor goes to Eisenhower. Dwight Eisenhower spent his career in the military; yet as president he resisted pressure to send U.S. forces into Vietnam. In a recording of an Oval Office conversation—yes, he did it too—with newspaper publisher Roy Howard on Feb. 24, 1955, he says, "I tell you, the boys were putting the heat on me" over Vietnam. "But I was not willing to put the American prestige on one gol-durned thing in there."

The same might have been said of the Cuba Project.... Any undertaking employing the best efforts of Howard Hughes, Richard Nixon, and Meyer Lansky is by definition a spectacularly shady enterprise.

Later, when Barry Seal goes to 'work' for Howard Hughes' TWA in the mid-60's, its a good business move for Hughes, whose passionate corporate embrace of the CIA is akin to a beauty queen marrying not for love but money. Hughes, who nets a paltry $547 million when he sells TWA, by that time, will have racked up $6 *billion* from paramilitary contracts and clandestine warfare hardware.

Does the vehemence of Eisenhower's famous parting speech owe something to this bitter knowledge?

"The conjunction of an immense military establishment and a large arms industry is new in the American experience," he said. "The total influence—economic, political, even spiritual—is felt in every city, every statehouse, every office of the Federal Government. In the councils of government we must guard against the acquisition of unwarranted influence by the Military Industrial Complex. The potential for the disastrous rise of misplaced power exists and will persist, and we must never let the weight of this combination endanger our liberties or democratic processes."

The nation paid no heed to Eisenhower's cautions about the dangers of a military-industrial complex. Soon something even nastier began making its presence felt: the intelligence-industrial complex. This went largely unnoticed in the nation as a whole.... But to a host of CIA paramilitary cowboys like Dave Ferrie and Barry Seal it must have felt like they were newly-minted CEO's sitting atop a hot Silicon Valley Internet start-up, beginning to price next year's Ferraris.

They were riding the Big Wave.

CHAPTER SIX

WHO ARE 'THE BOYS?'

WE ASKED RUSSELL WELCH, the criminal investigator for the Arkansas State Police who kept pestering his superiors to do something about the massive criminal activity taking place under his nose at Mena: would it have made any difference to his investigation if had he known Barry Seal was working for American intelligence?

"I was concerned about the Mena airport," he told us calmly. "That was my sole focus. When journalists come up here to Mena and start poking too far into who Seal knew, they end up going off the deep end."

We can appreciate the sentiment.... Probing into Seal's connections in the world of clandestine services leads into a bewildering fog-shrouded swamp teeming with gangsters, arms dealers, corrupt politicians, 'spooks' and mil-intel types, who collectively, or so the theory goes, make up the "secret government," what Undersecretary of State Eliot Abrams called at the Iran Contra Hearings the "shadow government."

It is this group, this organization that has no name (that we know of anyway) that we prefer to call, simply, '*the boys.*'

We thought at first that the Bay of Pigs would be the ideal place to begin to wade into their activities.... every member of the Watergate break-in, for instance, was also part of the Bay of Pigs Invasion. And at least one of them—the infamous Frank Sturgis—not only knew Oswald but had also sat at a nightclub table with Barry Seal in Mexico City in January of 1963.

But there is an even earlier event that served as a blueprint for the Bay of Pigs, and which brought many of our major characters together for the first time. Just as Americans were settling down to watch the first episode of Captain Kangaroo in flickery black and white, 'the boys,' were taking an introductory bow in history at the CIA-staged Guatemala coup in 1954.... It was an out-of-town tryout for many of the stunts they will later pull stateside.

In his autobiography Howard Hunt recalls that he recommended the ouster of Guatemalan President Jacob Arbenz shortly after he was elected, but that his superiors at the CIA refused to act until Arbenz threatened the profits of United Fruit. Then, however, things very quickly shifted into high gear. Allen Dulles selected Richard Bissell as a special assistant, an apprentice, as Bissell described it, and he immediately went to work on the coup plan. Bissell will run the Bay of Pigs op... Dulles will get a seat on United Fruit's board.

The CIA chain of command in the Arbenz operation included Bissell, Deputy Director Frank Wisner, Tracy Barnes, and Colonel J.C. King... and somewhere in there is Nelson Rockefeller, whose Latin American interests seemed endangered by Arbenz. He joined the Eisenhower Administration as something called an Assistant for Cold War Strategy.

Starting the ball rolling was David Atlee Phillips, a spook born on Halloween, who set up a clandestine radio station in Mexico called the Voice of Liberation which pretended to be broadcasting from within Guatemala. He orchestrated a crescendo of false reports about legions of rebels which didn't exist, and major battles which never took place.

Phillips termed the technique "the big lie." Later he'll head the Mexico City CIA Station near the time of the Kennedy Assassination. And E. Howard Hunt, later anointed the Propaganda Chief of the CIA's anti-Castro operations, and still later spotted as one of the three tramps in Dallas on November 22, 1963, was "an officer who worked brilliantly on the Guatemala Project," according to one pipe-smoking CIA man.

The New Orleans contingent included Guy Banister, key liaison man for U.S. Government-sponsored anti-Communist activities in Latin America through the Anti-Communism League of the Caribbean, used by the CIA to help engineer the overthrow of the 'leftist' Arbenz regime in Guatemala. Banister, a key player, had his hand in lots of pies... when Seal was busted with C4 plastic explosive local officials figure two of the principals, Barry Seal and New York Mobster Murray Kessler, met each other through their common association with Banister.

From Miami came Johnny Rosselli, and Clare Booth Luce's "great friend" CIA agent William Pawley, using a CIA front called the Pacific Corporation, an offshoot of Flying Tigers airlines.

Pawley later fronts for the CIA's anti-Castro activities; Henry Luce's wife will fund anti-Castro Cubans whom the House Committee on Assassinations suspected of involvement in the JFK assassination.

Also from Miami came pilot Donald Edward Browder, associated with Jack Ruby in arms smuggling into Cuba as early as 1952, another 'soldier of fortune' type, busy in the Caribbean since he stole a cache of machine guns from an Army base in Augusta, Georgia, and was indicted for unlawfully exporting a P-38 airplane to Havana... way back in 1947.

The "home team" contingent from Alexandria, Virginia included Samuel Cummings, President of the CIA's Interarms, one of whose first deals is supplying M-l rifles, bought in Britain, for the coup in Guatemala. In the following decades of dictators, business will boom, and Cummings will sell arms to Haiti's Francois Duvalier, the Dominican Republic's Rafael Leonidas Trujillo, and Cuba's Fulgencio Batista.

When Batista fled Cuba before a shipment of Cummings' Armalites arrived, the resourceful CIA arms-dealer flew immediately to Havana to demonstrate the assault rifles for a new customer. "Fidel Castro picked up that Armalite and knew what to do with it immediately," Cummings recalled admiringly.

Overwhelmingly rural Guatemala was a place where less than three percent of the landowners owned 70 percent of the arable land, a medieval world where farm laborers were roped together by the Army for delivery to lowland farms, where they were kept in debt slavery by landowners who paid them annually the princely sum of $87.

Guatemalan President Arbenz appropriated 240,000 acres of United Fruit's uncultivated holdings, which he distributed to approximately 100,000 landless peasants. He offered United Fruit $525,000 for the land, the company's own declared valuation for tax purposes. United Fruit thought this a very bad joke. The company's influence among Washington's power elite was impressive: CIA Director Walter Bedell Smith was seeking an executive position with United Fruit at the same time he was helping to plan the coup. He will later be named to United Fruit's board of directors... joining Allen Dulles.

The CIA arranged the coup by approaching disgruntled right-wing officers in the Guatemala army with offers of arms. But the ensuing uprisings were quickly put down by troops loyal to Arbenz. The CIA resolved to do the job right the next time around. Bananas were becoming a matter of national security.

Thirty airplanes were assigned for use in the "Liberation." The CIA's air force of P-47 Thunderbolts and C-47 transports flew out of Managua International Airport. They were by far the most powerful military element in the coup.

The pilots were Americans... like daredevil Jerry Fred DeLarm, a slim, short, hawk-featured man who liked to lay a .45 down on the table in front of him when talking to a stranger. A native of San Francisco, DeLarm was a barnstorming, adventurous flier well known in Central America, according to the book *Deadly Secrets*, where he did skywriting and aerial broadcasts for Arbenz's election campaign. Promised $20,000, he was understandably disturbed when—after Arbenz won—the money did not come through. That, DeLarm reflected later, was when he began to suspect Arbenz was a Communist...

Another legendary cowboy flying for the CIA's air force was William "Rip" Robertson, a hulking Texan. Like many lifetime spooks he had transferred to the CIA after fighting in the Pacific in WWII. During the Guatemalan coup he dispatched a pilot to bomb a Soviet ship, which accidentally sent a British merchantman to the bottom instead. This forced the CIA to quietly indemnify Lloyds of London to the tune of $1.5 million, but it didn't sour them on Robertson, who flew again at the Bay of Pigs after having become a good buddy of the Somoza family in Nicaragua.

Barry Seal made an equally good impression on the Somozas; with Somoza's brother-in-law safely aboard, he piloted the last plane out of Nicaragua when the Sandinistas took over.

The offensive began with planes dropping leaflets over Guatemala demanding that Arbenz resign immediately, and Hunt's CIA radio station broadcasting the same message. Then planes returned to machine-gun houses near military barracks, drop fragmentation bombs and strafe the National Palace.

That same day a CIA-backed rebel army crossed the Honduran border into Guatemala after the CIA-sponsored air force had bombed San Jose, a large Guatemalan port city. The rebel troops dug in just inside the Guatemalan border, waiting for further air strikes.

Over the following week, the air attacks continued daily: strafing or bombing ports, fuel tanks, ammunition dumps, military barracks, the international airport, a school, and several cities. One nice touch: during one night-time raid a *tape recording* of a bomb attack was played over loudspeakers set up on the roof of the US Embassy, heightening the anxiety of the capital's residents. Arbenz went on the air to try and calm the public's fear. The CIA radio team neatly jammed the broadcast.

The disinformation made it appear that military defenses were crumbling and that resistance was futile; it provoked confusion in the Guatemalan armed forces and caused elements to turn against Arbenz.

The psychological warfare was directed by Howard Hunt and David Atlee Phillips, a newcomer to the CIA, who, when first approached about the assignment, protested to his boss Tracy Barnes, "But Arbenz became President in a free election. What right do we have to help someone topple his government and throw him out of office?"

'For a moment," wrote Phillips later, "I detected in his face a flicker of concern, a doubt, the reactions of a sensitive man." But Barnes quickly recovered, and repeated the party line about the Soviets establishing "an easily expandable beachhead" in Central America.

Arbenz finally received an ultimatum from army officers: Resign or they would come to an agreement with the invaders. His back to the wall, he tried to arm civilian supporters to fight, but officers blocked the disbursement of weapons, and the Guatemalan president knew the end was at hand.

The CIA intervention in Guatemala stirred up a great deal of ill will toward the United States in Latin America, amid complaints about a Yankee double standard that used "free world" rhetoric against communism but ignored the transgressions of right-wing tyrants. *Life* magazine blandly noted these protests, observing that "world communism was efficiently using the Guatemalan show to strike a blow at the U.S."

Following the success of the Guatemalan coup d'etat, its veterans moved on to overthrow Fidel Castro in Cuba. Another result was to install Carlos Marcello as a major criminal presence in the country by 1957, according to Professor Peter Dale Scott in *Deep Politics and the Death of JFK*. Gambling in the capital became the province of one of Meyer Lansky's associates. And John Martino and Johnny Roselli, two major Mob figures in accounts of CIA-Mafia plots to kill Kennedy, begin to pass through regularly.

This is how it came to pass that the educated, urbane men of the State Department, the CIA and United Fruit decided that illiterate peasants of Guatemala did not deserve the land which had been given to them. The pipe-smoking, comfortable men of Princeton, Harvard and Wall Street decreed that workers did not need their unions, and that hunger and torture was a small price to pay for being rid of the scourge of "communism."

Ambassador John Peurifoy went before a congressional committee and told them: "My role in Guatemala prior to the revolution was strictly that of a diplomatic observer."

But no one, according to the book *Deadly Secrets*, had told his wife, Betty Jane, who in the days after the coup penned some commemorative verse about her hubby:

> "Sing a song of quetzals
> Pockets full of peace!
> The junta's in the Palace
> They've taken out a lease.
> The commies are in hiding,
> Just across the street
> To the embassy of Mexico
> They beat a quick retreat.
> And pistol packing Peurifoy
> Looks mighty optimistic
> For the land of Guatemala
> Is no longer communistic!"

The new rulers celebrated the liberation of Guatemala by arresting thousands on suspicion of communist activity, many of who were tortured or killed, and by passing a law which disenfranchised three-quarters of Guatemala's voters, as many as 150,000 people would be killed in violence that would continue with hardly a pause for 40 years.

It is in the sidelights of the Guatemala affair that the outlines of the secret history to come can be seen in rough draft form. The Carlos Castillo government, post-coup, for example, got almost a billion in aid from the U.S., but was judged inept by the CIA, which was described as being "dismayed." So in July of 1957 new President Castillo was shot and killed just as he and his wife sat down to dinner at the Presidential Palace.

Betty Peurifoy—by then no longer around, having moved on with her "pistol-packing" hubby to bring light and grace to the people of Laos—might have written:

> "It does not pay
> The CIA
> To dismay."

One last sidelight: Castillo's killer was identified as an unlucky young man who was also very possibly clinically depressed. Because—according to the first authorities to arrive on the scene after the shooting, who were, probably as luck would have it, all military men—right after killing the President the depressive assassin committed suicide with the very same rifle he used in the assassination.

The Guatemalan Government described the hapless assassin, Romeo Vasquez Sanchez, as a "Communist fanatic" who had been expelled from the Guatemalan Army six months earlier for "Communist ideology," but who had then—slippery communistic fellow that he was—wormed his way into the Presidential Palace Guard.

And they claimed to have found a 40-page handwritten diary of the assassin's, in which he supposedly wrote, "I have had the opportunity to study Russian communism and have a diabolic plan to put an end to the existence of the man who holds power."

Since this first 'lone nut,' several subsequent generations of lone nut assassins have emulated this trailblazer, keeping diaries of their own. Propaganda specialist Howard Hunt, there when this trend began, no doubt has had himself a smirk or two behind his pipe smoke when recalling how terribly clever it all has been…

The boys' had set up shop in Guatemala.

CHAPTER SEVEN

THE 'THIRD' GEORGE

THE BAY OF PIGS adventure marked the first time in the Agency's history that its army of hired adventurers were extensively employed inside the United States. Just what, we wondered, had been the qualifications for being hired as a "hired adventurer?" We recalled Paul Newman's famous question in Butch Cassidy and the Sundance Kid. "Who are those guys?"

Were they like relief pitchers in baseball, hanging out in a 'hired adventurer' bullpen somewhere, waiting to enter the game? Were they paid by the day? Was there a Teamsters hiring hall somewhere, for "apprentice adventurers," and "journeymen soldiers of fortune?"

This speculation is, of course, silly... but not as silly as the CIA's pretense that its paid employees are somehow not CIA, but rather 'contract' labor. If the English language means anything a CIA pilot is someone who makes his living flying for the Central Intelligence Agency. Such people are not 'freebooting soldiers of fortune,' 'rogue agents,' or emissaries from the Spiders From Mars. They are 'employees.'

The doctrine of 'plausible deniability' is Orwellian double-speak, a fig leaf which 'the boys' place in front of the secret history, in which CIA pilots become a "splendidly checkered crew" who accepted as a risk of doing business with the CIA the disagreeable fact that it would disavow them if they were caught. When they *do* get caught, 'the boys' in the Ivy League ties backpedal as fast as their shifty feet can shuffle. The hapless agent caught in the spotlight suddenly becomes an 'aging former

OSS derring-doers,' an 'out-of-work Green Beret,' or an 'on-the-make mercenary.'

Anything but an 'employee.'

Dave Ferrie and Barry Seal are just two of the more recent in a long line of barnstorming brigands who left their union cards at home when they went to work.

They didn't have to ask who their employer was. They *knew* whom they worked for…

They worked for George Doole.

George Doole created the largest airline in the history of flight. Though little known outside certain circles, George Doole's name deserves to be as famous some other George's, DeMohrenschilt and Bush, as the man responsible for airborne plagues which have included the cheap and easy availability of heroin in America's inner-cities after Vietnam, and the cocaine epidemic of the 1980's.

Doole's 'Spook Air,' still headquartered in the desert at Marana, Arizona, was used in operations at the Bay of Pigs, in Laos, Vietnam, and on innumerable other black ops. During the 1980's, it will be where Barry Seal will get his planes. Today it is still there, looming out of the cactus and tumbleweed, a sprawling airplane hangar large enough to house a 747, edging up to the shimmering tarmac of a remote airfield set in shimmering Arizona desert 90 miles south of Phoenix. When CIA proprietary Evergreen Air opened a huge new hangar in 1996, they dubbed it the George A. Doole Aviation Center.

On a wall inside is a plaque reading "George Doole (1909-1985). Founder, Chief Executive Officer, Board of Directors of Air America, Air Asia company, Civil Air Transport Company." The plaque is the only memorial to the man who created and ran the largest airline in the free world.

Evergreen repairs and refits commercial airliners, in addition to keeping their hand in 'the game.' They were involved in the mid'90's in the selling of C-130's—which the Forest Service was supposed to use to help fight the scorching blazes which plague the Western US in summertime—to a Mexican drug cartel.

Under Doole, the CIA established a bewildering number of proprietary airlines. Asked by then-Deputy Director Helms to account for all the planes in Doole's regime, a staffer once spent three months on the project before confessing he could never be more than 90% certain. The problem, he explained, was that Doole was forever leasing planes between his shell corporations, and changing their markings and tail numbers.

In the heyday of the Cold War, Spook Air not only owned more planes than any other airline, but, with nearly 20,000 employees, it employed more *people* than the CIA proper.

George Doole's career began when he won a commission in the Army in 1931, and learned to fly. He became a pilot for Pan Am, flying old Ford Tri-Motors on the Guatemala-to-Panama run, and helping chart new routes through South America, where he almost certainly rubbed elbows with that other "conquistador of the air," David Ferrie.

Along the way he chartered the Pacific Corporation, a CIA front, in Delaware, long 'the boys' corporate domicile of choice. Doole's empire quickly grew to include Air America, Civil Air Transport, Southern Air Transport, and dozens of small puddle-jumper lines. Under the cover of legitimate freight and charter services, they supplied a 30,000-man secret army in the mountains of Laos for a ten-year war against the Pathet Lao, dropped scores of agents into Red China, and helped stage revolts in every corner of the globe.

Doole's pilots—invariably described as a 'raffish lot'—flew in and out of tiny jungle fields in abysmal weather and under enemy fire. They referred to the CIA as "the customer," ammunition as "hard rice." Being under heavy fire was "sporty;" brushes with death were 'fascinating.' To be "absolutely fascinated" meant scared witless, professed a writer for *Time* who covered them.

Doole was kept busy traveling the world orchestrating his vast air armada, visible at CIA bases from Vientiane to Panama City. But he stayed aloof from the pilots, many of whom regarded him as a bit a snob. "I never saw the man without a tie on," scoffed one.

All that flying about aroused *some* curiosity, even in the *New York Times*, one of whose reporters brashly asked Doole in 1970 if Air America had any connection with the CIA.

"If someone out there is behind all this," Doole airily replied, "we don't know about it."

Doole died as he had lived, in anonymity. When he passed away in Washington at the age of 75, there was no formal obituary in the *Washington Post* or the *New York Times*, no memorial service, no flowers. He was quietly buried at a private funeral in Liberty, Ill.

In an article which appeared the year after his death he was described by *Time* magazine as "a portly, tastefully dressed man." Doole was both reserved and sometimes highly sociable. To Washington society matrons, he seemed the very image of discreet old money. A lifelong bachelor like David Ferrie, he often squired wealthy widows to embassy dances in the capital.

"George Doole? Oh, he was a perfect gentleman," recalled one.

At the Chevy Chase Club, a Wasp bastion in a well-to-do Maryland suburb, Doole liked to while away afternoons playing bridge and backgammon. He usually won. "George? Well he was quite a boy," chuckled a fellow clubman, retired Rear Admiral Raymond Hunter.

But just what did he *do?* "I rather thought he was in investments," stated one society matron, Margaret Wimsatt told the *New York Times.* "He was a bit mysterious. I remember at a party at the Chinese embassy, he spent an awful lot of time talking to the Taiwanese ambassador. I asked him why, and he just said, 'We had a lot to talk about.' He would sort of peer at you through those thick black-rimmed glasses."

Once, she recalled, she mentioned the name Richard Helms, former director of the CIA. "Do you know him from the Chevy Chase Club?" she inquired.

"Oh, I know him better than that," said Doole.

Doole's airline empire was known by half a dozen different names. During Vietnam it was sometimes called the "Shy Airline." "Shy Air" flew where few tourists wanted to go. Passengers were often obliged to exit by parachute. And some of its cargo would probably be unwelcome if it were to turn up in the bridge mix at a society matron's card party.

In the public revulsion against covert operations after Watergate after the extent of the CIA's covert operations was revealed by newspapers to the American public, the Agency was forced to dismantle Doole's huge aerial empire and sell off the various planes and airfields.

But *The Empire Struck Back.*

Representative Otis Pike, who chaired some of the committee hearings, had himself been a WWII marine fighter pilot, and was a moderate-but highly independent Democrat who represented a rock-solid Republican district on Long Island where he was regularly reelected with ease… *until* he undertook the investigation of 'the boys' sordid behavior.

'The boys' proceeded to make an example of a patriotic congressman. Pike was defeated in the very next election after a smear campaign that would have made a Stalinist commissar blush. Outside money had poured into Pike's district as a warning to any future politicians who might have the temerity to exercise oversight over the apparatus of the national security state.

Today the airfield with the huge hanger bearing George Doole's name shimmering in the Arizona desert sun seems perfectly ordinary and unexceptional, rather like the George Doole who enjoyed playing bridge at the Chevy Chase club and dancing with wealthy widows. There is probably nothing remarkable about the reports of unmarked black Chinook helicopters that take off regularly from a far corner of the airfield... headed south.

And although Mr. Doole's connections with the CIA and his role in founding the Agency's air operations have been documented in books and by congressional reports, the CIA does not acknowledge the relationship.

According to a spokesman at Agency headquarters at Langley, Mr. Doole's name is not listed on any official file. Officially, the CIA says it has no record that Doole ever worked there.

If you check with them, they'll tell you the same thing about David Ferrie and Barry Seal.

CHAPTER EIGHT

DOUBLE-CHECK COWBOYS
AT THE BAY OF PIGS

WHO RECRUITED THE PILOTS, guerrilla fighters, and saboteurs needed for the Bay of Pigs and subsequent anti-Castro operations? For that job the CIA used the Double-Chek Corporation, a Miami and New Orleans-based CIA front.

Double-Chek was run by Alex Carlson, a big, blond, heavy-set man towering well over six feet who had seen three years of combat during World War II in the Pacific. While finishing law school at the University of Miami he went to South America on an "exchange" scholarship.

Funny how the continent of South America has such a seemingly-strong allure for so many in our story… George Doole, Barry Seal, Dave Ferrie. Even Nelson Rockefeller, who ran psy-ops there during WWII.

Double-Chek, just one of a number of interchangeable CIA fronts used, was first exposed in *The Invisible Government* by Washington journalist David Wise.

Barry Seal, who was already flying missions into Cuba, was 'sheep-dipped' into the Alabama Air National Guard in Birmingham, run by General Reid Doster. And even after the Bay of Pigs debacle was over, the Alabama Air National Guard would continue to be used as cover for pilot Seal, who participated in a number of Caribbean and Central American operations while based in Alabama.

One post card home from Seal came from Montgomery, Alabama at the end of June of 1961, complete with a photo of the "completely air-conditioned" Albert Pike motel on the front. "Just call me a Freedom rider!" Seal writes. "I'd better shut up before I get shot."

In another a month later bearing the same Montgomery postmark he calls himself a "watermelon eatin' son of the South."

The pilots Seal learned to fly with—Barry's young contemporaries in Baton Rouge—could now only look on in envy at their young hotshot friend. They were still flying small single-engine craft while Seal—barely out of his teens—now flew in and out of Baton Rouge in a rotating series of ever-more powerful twin-engine aircraft.

The brewing covert war was pretty much an open secret among Southern pilots. It was nothing to see paramilitary flights taking off from commercial airports under transparent 'business' covers, or from isolated airstrips and mothballed military fields in Florida and Louisiana. Less visible were the landings at the other end, at improvised runway strips hacked out of the jungles in Guatemala, Nicaragua, Costa Rica, and Cuba… landings which provided Seal excellent training for his later career.

Under General Doster was assembled a CIA air force that eventually numbered eighty Americans. The CIA gave Doster forty-five days to get ready. The general worked almost around the clock. The mission sounded foolproof to him, although he had been told next to nothing except that his part of the operation would be as "just a small cog in a large machine."

He "had confidence and had to assume that the logistics were available and the planning had been done," he said later. His briefings convinced him that the surprise invasion would throw Cuba into turmoil. The population "was supposed to be waiting for this and would gladly join the men of the Brigade as they landed."

Doster did his best to measure up to the CIA's intense feelings about secrecy. Every new recruit heard from him, "If you open your goddamned mouth, I'll have your ass."

One of the enduring secrets about the Bay of Pigs Invasion concerns the large role American pilots played, far beyond the admitted training of exile Cuban pilots and combat flights on the last day of the invasion. So great was the stress on secrecy that even today one of the last remaining living American Bay of Pigs pilots, James Harrison, is reluctant to discuss his Central American 'training' mission.

"I didn't train anyone, frankly," he finally admitted to us. "I was expected to fly combat."

What happened was that—in a foretaste of things to come in Vietnam where the South Vietnamese army was usually nowhere to be seen—invasion planners came to have doubts about the motivation of some of the exile Cuban pilots they were training, and in January of 1961 the Agency requested the use of American "contract" pilots.

Barry Seal's first postcard home from Guatemala bears a February, 1961 postmark.

None of the CIA advisers used their real names... but they used names which sounded enough like their real names so they would remember to respond when somebody shouted out their alias. Thus the CIA air force commander at the Happy Valley air base, whose real name was Garfield, became "Gar." General Reid Doster used the name "Reid' when he was at Retalhuleu as a CIA adviser.

"We all used aliases," Harrison told us. And while the eccentric-looking Dave Ferrie's alias remains a mystery, Barry Seal's became known when we discovered that one of the CIA pilots had used the alias "Billy Belt."

Billy Belt. Barry Seal. And "Billy Belt's" description in "The Invisible Government" as a "young instructor" fits the 21-year old Barry Seal, who still dutifully wrote home from Guatemala to his parents during the preparations for the invasion, letting everyone know he was all right.

One postcard he sent from Guatemala features a picture of the Lake at Amatition. Dated three weeks before the April 19th invasion, Barry writes, "Hi, I am probably going to stay at this picture a couple of days. See you soon!"

Barry also stayed at the Mayas Excelsior Hotel in Guatemala City, where the CIA pilots were put up, and that is where his anxious mother wrote him back, assuring him the postcards were appreciated. "Received your two cards and the letter as well. Thrilled to hear from you!"

Sentimentally, Barry kept his mother's cards his entire life.

Four "Alabama guard" pilots were killed during the Bay of Pigs, all on a mission to cover the beachhead on the final day of the invasion. According to the excellent *Deadly Secrets*, the exile Cuban pilots had become an intractable problem by then...

"The brigade pilots were grim. All were exhausted. Many were disgusted. Some had turned chicken. They were no longer making extra turns over the targets. "Gar" found that only about one third were "ready to go." With the others, the Americans "had to beg them to go." By now, "it took several hours to get some of their crews in the aircraft, and then they aborted the mission." They constantly "found excuses not to do the job. You could count the number of 'tigers' on one hand."

The Cubans had been asked to fly a support mission at the beachhead, where the situation was deteriorating rapidly. They demanded to know why the mission was so important. "We must hold twenty-four hours more," a CIA adviser told them, in an allusion to the seventy-two-hour period after which a government-in-arms could be declared, and "outside" (American) military assistance requested.

Castro, too, was aware of this deadline. He later told foreign newsmen "it became an urgent political problem for us to oust them as quickly as possible so that they would not establish a government there."

The reason was simple: once the "magic hour" arrived, the anti-Castro Cuban 'provisional' government would be flown in to proclaim a new government. When that happened, CIA planners had convinced themselves, President Kennedy would permit the Marines to save the day.

Led by American pilot Buck Persons, who had had combat experience in Mustangs during World War II, the mission was to land at the Bay of Pigs airfield and refuel from drums that had been dropped off there. Six B-26s took off in pairs at half hour intervals beginning at 3:00 A.M. The pilots believed that the mission would be given air cover by Navy jets starting at 6.30 that morning.

As dawn broke over the Bay of Pigs, the first B-26's arrived. One had no co-pilot; a Cuban copilot had jumped out of the cockpit and vanished into the woods as the plane was taxiing at Happy Valley. The planes picked out concentrations of Fidel's blue-clad militia and began strafing. Soon more B-26s with American crews were on the scene in bombing and strafing runs. But they soon became alarmed that the promised cover of Navy jets hadn't shown up.

"How about our little friends?" one pilot radioed another. "See anything of them?"

"I didn't see anybody," the other replied, and then heard the first pilot shout, "I'm hit and on fire!"

T-birds (Cuban jet fighters) shot them up before the Navy jets due over the beach showed up—right on time, they thought— but a full hour too late to help the beleaguered flyers.

The timing foul-up was not satisfactorily explained until the report on the CIA's performance was declassified and released 30 years later. It showed a monumental breakdown in communication between the CIA and the Navy had cost four American pilots their lives…due to the difference in time zones. The Navy was on East Coast time, and used 6:30 as the hour of dawn, while the CIA's pilots at Happy Valley in Nicaragua used Central Time, and had already scheduled the B-26s to begin arriving at the first glimmer of light nearly an hour earlier.

What happened to the dead pilot's widows, known as the Birmingham Widows, is instructive because it is repeated to the widow of Barry Seal. It is a story of misery inflicted on the widows by the CIA's insistence on keeping the American people in the dark. The CIA knew it wasn't pulling anything over on Castro; he was *well* aware of who his adversaries were.

Alex Carlson, the lawyer fronting for the Double-Chek Corporation, had the task of keeping the lid on the deaths of Americans in the invasion. He visited the widows, telling them that their husbands had vanished on a C-46 cargo flight in Central America.

He said that Double-Chek had hired the four at a monthly salary to fly cargo. "These men knew what they were getting into," he added. "It was a calculated risk. If they came back, they had a nice nest egg."

The widows were furious at Carlson's words. To cover its role the CIA was willing to imply that their husbands had been mercenaries, and they resented the implication.

"Riley wasn't a 'soldier of fortune,'" one said. "He didn't do this for the money. He was a test pilot at Hayes Aviation, and was paid a good salary there. He was an operations officer for the Air National Guard."

Another told a newspaper interviewer her husband was no "soldier of fortune" either. She said he was paid $1880 a month during the short period of time he was away. She, too, had been visited by Carlson.

"He said my husband was dead and to start life anew. He said they had spotted one of the plane's engines floating in the water. I didn't think engines floated," this widow stated bitterly.

All they could get out of authorities in Washington was a runaround. One dead pilot's mother (Riley Shamburger) took it on herself to do something about it. She carried on an energetic correspondence with the Federal Government to find out what had happened to her son, even writing the Swiss Government, which handled affairs for the United States in Cuba.

She received a reply from the acting chief of the Protection and Representation Division of the State Department. It said: "Your letters to the Department of State concerning your son have been referred to me for reply. The records in this office do not contain the circumstances surrounding your son's accident. At the time he was not on active duty in his military status. For more detailed information it is suggested you contact the Hayes Aircraft Corp., Birmingham, Alabama, since he was under their jurisdiction at the time in question."

Hayes Aircraft, a private corporation, has no one under its "jurisdiction." So the letter was deceptive. A lesser woman might have been discouraged. Instead she wrote CIA Director John McCone, and received a reply on CIA stationery: "In Mr. McCone's absence, I am replying to your letter of June, 1962, requesting information concerning your son. I am sorry to disappoint you, but this agency is unable to furnish you any such information. Also, we have made inquiries of other government departments, and these, too, have no pertinent information. We have every sympathy for you in your natural concern for the fate of your son, and I am sorry, as I can be that we cannot help. Please be assured that if at any time we are able to furnish information we will contact you promptly."

Mrs. Shamburger then went right to the very top. An aide to the President, a Brigadier General, wrote back…

"If any information is ever obtained on the circumstances surrounding the loss of your son, you will be informed immediately. Unfortunately, at present neither CIA nor any other government agency possesses the slightest pertinent information on your son's disappearance."

Riley Shamburger's mother was determined to keep trying. "I am not going to give up," she said bitterly. "They take your boy away and never let you know what happened."

After a brief flurry of publicity right after the Bay of Pigs, the story of the four missing Americans dropped out of the news, until Senator Everett Dirksen of Illinois leaked the "news" that four American fliers had been killed at the Bay of Pigs. He said he had learned this in the course of a one-man inquiry into the Cuban invasion.

Dirksen's disclosure was embarrassing for the Kennedy Administration. Just five days before the invasion, President Kennedy had said: "This government will do everything it possibly can—and I think it can meet its responsibilities—to make sure that no Americans are involved in actions inside Cuba." And Attorney General Robert Kennedy had stated no Americans died at the Bay of Pigs.

After Dirksen's statement, when newsmen sought out the elderly Mrs. Shamburger, she told them plaintively, "If no Americans were involved," she said, "Where is my son?"

Now alarmed, the White House issued a statement extending the President's "heartfelt sympathy," and explaining that the government had, unfortunately, "no information to add to that which had been conveyed before."

The charade finally ended at a press conference, when Kennedy was asked, "Mr. President, can you say whether the four Americans who died in the Bay of Pigs invasion were employees of the government or the CIA?"

Kennedy hemmed and hawed, but to his credit finally gave a truthful answer, one which helped the widows bring closure to their questions of what had happened to their loved ones.

"Let me say just about these four men: they were serving their country," Kennedy declared. "The flight that cost them their lives was a volunteer flight, and while because of the nature of their work it has not been a matter of public record, as it might be in the case of soldiers or sailors, I can say that they were serving their country."

Secret history always repeats itself... at least until it's exposed. Debbie Seal, Barry's widow, raised their three small children without knowing what to tell them about who it was their father had been. Was he just a "sleazy drug smuggler," or was he, instead, a CIA pilot whose job was flying drugs?

"When Barry was murdered, we never received one call from anyone in the government," Debbie Seal told us. "It was as if no one he worked with knew who he was."

A "sleazy drug smuggler" was what Seal was called by Arkansas politician Larry Nichols—no stranger to sleaze himself—in the *Clinton Chronicles*, intel agent and Baptist minister Pat Matriciana's million-selling video slamming Bill Clinton.

If Nichols were right, and Barry Seal was, indeed, *just* a "sleazy drug smuggler," then the far right was correct in calling Bill Clinton a "Dixie Mob President."

But Barry Seal was, as we are beginning to see, a life-long employee of American "clandestine services."

The Republicans behind the *Clinton Chronicles* presumably knew this. If they didn't, they're not the slickly efficient fat cats we all know them to be.

When Barry Seal died, his widow lived for more than a decade after his death underneath the threat of a $29 million dollar jeopardy assessment from the Internal Revenue Service which she had absolutely no hope of paying.... This did wonders to keep her from doing much talking to reporters.

One time, while defending herself from the IRS's inquisition, she stumbled on a frequently called phone number in Barry's phone records. Thinking it might be some vendor from whom she could procure receipts to show the IRS, she dialed it.

"Where did you get this number?" a hostile voice demanded, after she had explained the reason for her call. "This is a secret DIA (Defense Intelligence Agency) phone number. You are never to call it again!"

Later that day she received a friendlier phone call from someone else in Washington D.C. "Debbie, you're young, you have a whole life ahead of you, and you have your kids to think about," a kindly voice advised her, in an ironic echo of Alex Carlson's advice to the Birmingham widows twenty-five years earlier.

Then in a stern tone the voice on the phone issued a warning. "I'm going to speak to you now as I would to one of my two daughters. You've got a whole life ahead of you. Don't call anyone in Washington again."

CHAPTER NINE

A PERFECT FAILURE

BEFORE EVENTS IN DALLAS made questioning moot, President Kennedy commissioned a study of the Bay of Pigs fiasco, called the Taylor Report. It was so critical of the CIA that it was classified until recently. But the conclusions it drew became obvious when Kennedy fired the top CIA leadership of Dulles, Cabell, and Bissell.

Militarily, the 1400-man Cuban exile force was crushed by Castro's far larger military and militia in 72 hours. The exile force could neither hold nor break out of the beachhead at Playa Giro. 114 Cuban Brigade members were killed; 1189 captured.

The Bay of Pigs was, as historian Theodore Draper has observed, "one of those rare events in history—a perfect failure."

"It doesn't take Price Waterhouse to tell you that 1,500 Cubans aren't as good as 25,000 (Castro fighters)," Secretary of State Dean Acheson told President Kennedy as the operation collapsed.

As a covert operation which Washington could "plausibly deny" the invasion also failed miserably. Kennedy, in office less than twelve weeks, called it "the worst experience of my life," but nonetheless assumed responsibility. "There's a saying that victory has a hundred fathers and defeat is an orphan," he told the press. "I am the responsible officer of the government."

U.S. credibility as a world leader was also dealt a harsh blow. "Acute shock and disillusion" dominated the reaction in Western Europe.

With an unprovoked attack on Cuba's sovereignty that left over 1800 military and civilian dead and wounded, European hopes for Kennedy's intelligence, vision and "fresh" approach to the Cold War had been "wiped away" and Washington was perceived to be as "self-righteous, trigger-happy and incompetent as it had ever been."

It was the decision to invade, and not its failure, that bothered Western European political leaders, Arthur Schlesinger noted.

"Why was Cuba such a threat to you?" they asked. "Why couldn't you live with Cuba, as the USSR lives with Turkey and Finland?'"

Kennedy thought he was approving a plan that could succeed with help from Cuban underground fighters and military deserters, and an eventual uprising of a rebellious population.

"He was not informed of Castro's relative popularity," stated Taylor's report.

The cancelled second airstrike, the cause of controversy and the wedge the CIA used against Kennedy with its Cuban charges, is, like the later Gulf of Tonkin 'incident,' and the Sandinista drug smuggling 'uncovered' by Barry Seal, much ado about nothing…

It is a clear example of the CIA doing what the CIA does best—*lying*. Because even *with* full control of the skies, the ragtag 1800-man invasion force could never have defeated Castro's forces without an all-out American invasion. And this would—almost certainly—have resulted in a wider war with the Cuban's Soviet backers.

We read startling revelations about the Bay of Pigs affair in the matter-of-fact testimony of a New York City detective who later arrested Frank Sturgis for planning the murder of former girlfriend Marita Lorenz. Lorenz had decided to go public and testify about what she knew about the Kennedy assassination to the House Select Committee in 1976. The event had prompted a *New York Daily News* headline reading "Ex-Spy Says She Drove to Dallas With Oswald & Kennedy 'Assassin Squad.'

NYPD detective James Rothstein intercepted the infuriated Sturgis on his way to Lorenz's home to murder her, in what he said that Sturgis had described as a "sanctioned hit."

Rothstein told the *Daily News*, "I talked to Sturgis when I arrested him. See, I had Frank Sturgis two hours before anybody knew we had him. I told Sturgis about being in the Bay of Pigs invasion on an aircraft carrier that 'didn't exist.' And so when I grabbed Sturgis, the first thing I did was congratulate him for assassinating John F. Kennedy."

"I purposely did that. And when I told him that I had been on the Essex and that we had bombed that place (Cuba) for 3 days and 3 nights,

Sturgis said, 'The only way you knew that is if you were there.' Because it *was* unknown… and after that, he took me in as one of his confidants, we talked for 2 hours."

Rothstein had been a boson's mate on the aircraft carrier Essex, he told us. "The ship had all its markings painted out, and we took down the American flag. The pilots all wore white coveralls on their bombing missions. And the destroyers, also with markings painted over, bombed the shit out of the Cuban coast."

Rothstein told us the Essex had put people ashore for the Invasion, and that they had practiced for what would have been a first time invasion landing off a carrier off the coast of Virginia.

None of this square with the official story, yet it sounds plausible; the bungling on the part of the CIA top echelon was so extreme that it very likely was deliberate, and the only way the Bay of Pigs invasion makes any military sense is if Kennedy authorizes a full American invasion. Clearly, this was something he would not do.

What Dulles and his friends really wanted was a full-scale U.S. invasion of Cuba, numerous scholars attest; they were hoping to put Kennedy in such a compromised position that he would feel compelled to order it.

Maybe Dulles thought he could manipulate Kennedy as easily as he and his brother John Foster had run the Eisenhower administration. What he could *not* have counted on was Kennedy's refusal to fall for the logic of a full American invasion; his willingness to accept defeat rather than be pushed into an overt invasion he did not want.

"The CIA hardball artists were convinced that when faced with the realities of the invasion, Kennedy would send in American forces rather than swallow defeat," said CIA Technical Services man Robert Morrow later.

They were wrong.

On the eve of the Invasion, CIA insiders began buying the stocks of sugar companies, the earnings of which had been depressed by the loss of Cuban plantations. Stockbrokers became curious about the sudden influx of orders on what one broker called the 'tip' that cheap sugar shares might prove a sweet gamble. Prices were climbing sharply when the brigade hit the beach…

In the Bahamas, Meyer Lansky lieutenant Joe Rivers waited with a satchel stuffed with gold for word to rush in and take charge of the dark casinos…

Off the north Cuban coast two gambling pals of Frank Sturgis and Mafia boss Russell Bufalino bobbed on the seas in a Syndicate-owned boat with a CIA man aboard, ready to land and dig up the $750,000 they had buried in Havana before fleeing Castro…

Afterwards, though Kennedy was outwardly calm and hopeful, rallying the morale of his men and planning ahead, one of his closest aides, Ted Sorensen, found him "beneath it all angry and sick at heart." He seemed "a depressed and lonely man."

Kennedy had handed his critics a stick with which they would forever beat him. "How could I have been so far off base?" he inquired aloud. "All my life I've known better than to depend on the experts. How could I have been so stupid (as) to let them go ahead?"

Intended to overthrow Castro, the invasion succeeded only in helping him to strengthen his regime internally, and enhancing his image as a David defeating Goliath. "Castro's position is stronger than before the invasion attempt," the CIA reported later.

In a secret meeting in Uruguay five months later, Che Guevara even expressed Cuba's appreciation for the Bay of Pigs to White House aide Richard Goodwin. "He wanted to thank us very much for the invasion," Goodwin reported to Kennedy. "It had transformed them from an aggrieved little country into an equal."

As the invasion ground to its ignoble conclusion, in Guatemala City the CIA station chief was growing frantic, not just about the project's failure but also about the state of the Americans who had trained the Brigade…

Several of the CIA men had been on a drunk for three days, locked in a CIA safe house from which they refused to emerge. Their fury at the politicians in Washington was limitless, he would say later, reporting that he thought they were unsettled enough to kill people: "If someone had gotten close to Kennedy, he'd have killed him. Oh, they *hated* him!"

Somewhere down there in Guatemala, amidst all that self-justifying hatred towards Jack Kennedy, was an enraged David Ferrie, and a young Barry Seal.

CHAPTER TEN

GORDON'S LIST

WERE IT NOT FOR an often-remarked upon quirk of human nature one large chunk of what little is today known about the story of Barry and 'the boys' would have sunk back into the shrouded mists and murky deeps of the 'official story.'

Today, our understanding of the importance of the CIA front Double-Chek Corporation as a link between the Bay of Pigs Fiasco and the Kennedy Assassination comes only because of the oft-cited female complaint about men that most of them can be legally-classified as "cleaning-impaired."

The male in question is Gordon Novel, regarded as the CIA's man in New Orleans in the early 1960's. Gordon had beat a fast retreat out of town after Jim Garrison's probe discovered that he had been sheep-dipped into their midst as a spy for the Agency, a charge which Novel today freely admits.

After Novel fled New Orleans, his vacant apartment was rented out to two young co-eds, who, predictably, cleaned it from top to bottom before they would consent to move in. While giving the kitchen a thorough going-over they found a letter wedged under a plastic drain board on the kitchen sink, written by Novel to his CIA handler. The girls thought it might be important, and gave it to a reporter for the *New Orleans States-Item*, who recognized its significance and brought it to the attention of Garrison.

Jim Garrison called Gordon Novel, with typical hyperbole, "the most important witness in history." Others were equally impressed with Novel's historical importance; one reporter dubbed him "the most slippery and loquacious fugitive in the history of American jurisprudence."

Novel was carrying some heavy-duty secrets when he fled Garrison's investigation, related to having worked closely with David Ferrie and anti-Castro exiles in New Orleans. He headed first to the Virginia home of the Central Intelligence Agency, and then to Canada, where, true to the Agency playbook, he denied all ties to the CIA.

He later changed his story, and admitted that he *had* served as an "intermediary" between the CIA and Cuban exiles. But, his attorney stressed, his CIA activities "had absolutely nothing to do with the assassination of President Kennedy."

Written before Garrison's probe was public knowledge, the letter reads like a chapter from a Tom Clancy novel. "I took the liberty of writing you direct and apprising you of current situation, expecting you to forward this through appropriate channels," Novel writes. "Our connection and activity of that period involves individuals presently about to be indicted as conspirators in Garrison's investigation.... Garrison has subpoenaed myself and an associate to testify before his Grand Jury on matters which may be classified TOP SECRET."

"We have temporarily avoided one subpoena not to reveal Double-Chek activities or associate them with this mess," the letter continued. "We want out of this thing before Thursday. Our attorneys have been told to expect another subpoena to appear and testify on this matter. The 5th amendment and/or immunity and legal tactics will not suffice."

Novel warns that Garrison may expose "actions of individuals connected with Double-Chek Corporation in Miami in first quarter of 1961," which involves a secret important enough to lie to the FBI about...

"Mr. Garrison is in possession of sworn portions of this testimony. He is unaware of Double-Chek's involvement in this matter but has strong suspicions. I have been questioned extensively by local FBI recently as to whether or not I was involved with Double-Chek's parent-holding corporation during that time. My reply on five queries was negative. Bureau unaware of Double-Chek association in this matter."

Lest anyone rashly conclude he is expendable, the impish Novel then writes that he has a form of insurance policy. "Our attorneys and others are in possession of complete sealed files containing all information concerning this matter. In the event of our sudden departure, either accidental or otherwise, they are instructed to simultaneously release same for public scrutiny in different areas."

While the Double-Chek connection is what we're interested in here, Gordon Novel tells such colorful tales that a few points should be made before moving on...

When Novel fled to Montreal after visiting Langley, he was traveling a well-worn path. Garrison's office had evidence indicating Montreal was visited by David Ferrie before the assassination, in the company of Clay Shaw and A.J. Hidell, an alias of Lee Harvey Oswald's, and was the North American headquarters of a group of eastern European and Cuban exiles linked to the CIA through Major Louis Bloomfield.

When Barry Seal is arrested on major drug felony charges in Florida more than a decade later, it will be in the company of some of these same shadowy Montreal underworld figures with links to the Kennedy assassination, like Norman "Roughhouse" Rothman.

But the clearest illustration of the covert world in New Orleans that young Barry Seal moved in—often visiting the same Playboy Club favored by Novel—is provided by the list of things Novel told Garrison he would be willing to testify about if granted immunity.

The list includes: "International fraud; public and official bribery; intimidation; the probable murder of David Ferrie; seditious treason; mysterious intelligence activities from November, 1959to-date in the southern quadrant of the USA and certain islands off Florida; hot war games and cold munitions transfers; ten Canadian Vampire jet fighters; and Cuban-Anglo-French sabotage affairs of the early 1960's."

Even three decades later, it's still quite an impressive list. So we asked him about it. "Gordon, *ten* Vampire jets?"

"There was a whole bunch of Canadian Vampire jets sitting down here (New Orleans) then," he replied. "Some people were trying to sell them to the anti-Castro Cubans, who were going to fly them out of Miami. It (controversy) was just something I was going to create so I could come home, because being away was costing me money."

Seeing Gordon's list, Garrison had remarked, "These are all intriguing aspects of Novel's career as a U.S. Intelligence agent and I'd love to hear about them—especially his knowledge of seditious treason."

In a preview of the financial fraud later associated with spook activities in the '80s the *New Orleans States-Item* reported that one of Novel's duties prior to the Bay of Pigs "was to operate the Evergreen Advertising Agency as a front for CIA communications. With funds funneled to him by the CIA, Novel says he prepared special radio commercials used on three hundred stations in the United States and Canada. Their cryptographic messages, he claims, were to alert agents to the invasion date. The commercials advertised aluminum Christmas trees, he says, and the key alert code names were 'Star Christmas Trees' and 'Holiday Trees.' In late 1960, $72,000 of fraudulent radio time was placed.

"Evergreen Advertising—that was me and Sal DeAnGroso—we had a giant idea," Novel told us. "I was into promoting things, can you tell? And we knew that radio stations are crooked during the holidays, as regards whether your radio spots got aired or not. Radio stations are universally crooks at Christmas time, the only way to check 'em is to monitor or have access to their logs. So Sal knew if they've got it sold out, they won't even run it."

"So we created a phony advertising company—put 4A Advertising across the top—and got 30-day billing from radio stations, cause we looked so legit. So we billed out $500,000 worth of ads, saying 'buy this 6-foot Christmas tree!' Then we put a corporation behind Evergreen Advertising Agency, so you have to come through shell after shell to collect your money. And we made two dollars for every tree we sold on the radio, and never paid a penny for advertising."

Novel sued Jim Garrison, after Garrison did a *Playboy* interview. But then he received a communication from FBI Director J. Edgar Hoover, Novel says, letting him know of the Bureau's displeasure at his filing suit against former FBI agent Garrison.

Novel, unintimidated, went instead to James Angleton, the CIA's counter-intelligence chief, who gave him pictures to show Hoover, Novel insists, of "ol' Edgar with his lips pursed around somethin' they shouldn't have been pursed around…"

This was enough, he says grinning, to relieve him of any further pressure from the FBI.

The FBI got revenge with an FBI document that made news in 1998, which revealed that Novel while with the CIA had tried to doctor photographs to make it appear that Oswald had met with Fidel Castro. When that effort failed, Novel tried to doctor the picture to make it look as if *Jack Ruby* had met with Castro.

Gordon was nothing if not flexible.

The discovery of the Novel letter by two co-eds may someday perhaps be equaled in importance by the discovery in the safe of Barry Seal's widow of a photograph of a dozen well-dressed men in black suits and skinny ties, taken on January 22, 1963, in a nightclub in Mexico City.

Barry Seal left the picture to his wife, Debbie. When she turned over Barry's records to the 7-man "clean-up crew" which visited her in early 1995, the photo, which she considered a keepsake, remained in her safe.

And a good thing, too, we've seen the eagerness with which the minions of our government's "investigative services" confiscate inconvenient evidence which never again sees the light of day...

The picture is remarkable photographic evidence of what it was "the boys" were up to that fateful year of 1963 in Mexico City. We knew nothing about an individual named "William Seymour," for example, until he seemed to match, in another picture taken in 1963, the photo taken in the Mexico City nightclub.

Only then did we learn that Seymour was well known as being a long-term Guy Banister "employee" working for Double-Chek in New Orleans, as a recruiter of pilots for the CIA.

This, all by itself, is truly earth-shaking news. If the biggest drug smuggler in American history was consorting as early as 1963 with a man whose job was recruiting pilots into the CIA, the massive drug smuggling through Mena, Arkansas takes on a whole new (sinister) light.

William Seymour, we found, is in virtually all of the literature about the Kennedy assassination. He was the same size and weight as Lee Harvey Oswald, and resembled him enough to become the focus of speculation that he had been the 'second' Oswald, using Oswald's name to criminally implicate him—and hopefully Fidel Castro as well—in the assassination.

According to Garrison, Seymour and two of his running mates, Loran Hall and Lawrence Howard, were elements of a plot pieced together by anti-Castro Cuban exiles, and what Garrison called "lower echelon" CIA operatives, that cumulatively fashioned the weapon that struck down JFK.

A second famous operative appearing in that Mexico City nightclub photo with Barry Seal is Frank Sturgis, Bay of Pigs operative, Watergate burglar, and a man who researchers say made a written confession of his participation in the Kennedy assassination to a Cardinal of the Catholic Church before he died. In the picture, he is hiding his face, though his swept-back pompadour gives him away.

But by far the most intriguing person clearly visible in that Mexico City night club (And he's still alive!) is Felix Rodriguez, one of the CIA's most vicious assassins, whose long list of murders includes that of Che Guevara in Bolivia in the '60s. What was Rodriguez doing in Mexico

City in January of 1963... at a time when his official bio has him at US Army training at Fort Benning, Georgia?

Ask him. He denied being there to us. But when people lie, it is always for a *reason*.... We had listened, for example, to Layton Martens, a Dave Ferrie intimate, lie to us about even Ferrie's whereabouts at the time of the Bay of Pigs. "Dave Ferrie could not have been at the Bay of Pigs—he was with me, listening to a short wave radio," said Martens straight-faced.

Why would anyone dissemble about the activities of a dead man? Especially when there was the dead man's own testimony to refer to... From the House Committee on Assassinations: "Ferrie, as a contract agent for the CIA, claimed to have flown on several hazardous missions into Cuba, *one on the night of the Bay of Pigs*, where he landed.

Ferrie's role as a CIA agent was confirmed in 1975 when Victor Marchetti, former Deputy Assistant to Richard Helms, said that Helms had disclosed, in discussions during Garrison's investigation, "Ferrie had in fact been employed by the CIA."

CIA technical services officer Robert Morrow said he'd been on a flight with Ferrie into Cuba on the day of the invasion: "I was glad it was Dave Ferrie at the controls of the Beech. In civilian life he was an Eastern Airlines pilot and I was comforted by his confident and conscientious manner at the controls. He was very thorough, and clearly very competent."

Ferrie even addressed an audience after the Bay of Pigs and announced that JFK should be shot, after being invited to speak on the Bay Of Pigs invasion failure before the New Orleans chapter of the Military Order of World Wars. Present were witnesses who said Ferrie was introduced as a pilot in the invasion, and spoke so emotionally about Kennedy's "double cross" of the invasion force that several people walked out of the meeting.

Covering up what is already on the record always inspires suspicion. Why? What secret is so big that it requires lying about almost forty years later?

We didn't know; what we did know was that we had photographic proof of some "men in black"—and they *were* all wearing black suits—who looked to be involved in some highly profitable intrigue. So we began to look at the record of lucrative enterprises that were being traded on the central exchange of the highly active Caribbean black market.

And there, in the secret history of American covert operatives engaged in smuggling, gunrunning, and murder-for-hire, is where we finally found our answer.

CHAPTER ELEVEN

NOT JUST AN
ADVENTURE... BUT A JOB

"YOU KNOW, THERE aren't all that many players out there," former US Customs official Steve Wallner, who had tracked Barry Seal in the 80's, told us. "You can count 'em pretty much on one hand."

Professor Peter Dale Scott talks about the Kennedy assassination being the result of "deep politics," as opposed to "conspiracy theory." Secrecy and law breaking are how our 'deep political system' works, Scott says…. Its not a high cabal of Satan-worshipping Illuminati that brought the scourges of the past forty years: the assassination of a President, Vietnam, Watergate, Iran Contra, CIA Drugs. It's just 'the way things are.'

This concept of 'deep politics' sees 'what happens' as the normal result of how our system works. And it fits with what we're learning about the young Barry Seal, and the organization to which he belonged.

Did Seal wake up in the morning, rub his meaty paws together, and exclaim out loud, "Today I'm going to conspire to fly weapons to rebel insurgents? Or, "Today I'm going to go out and create a cocaine epidemic in America?"

We don't think so…. We think "Secret Agent Man" Barry Seal got up in the morning exactly the same way most Americans do, rubbed his eyes, sprinkled too much sugar on his corn flakes, and said, "Today I'm going to go to work."

After you've been doing it for a while, it's not just an adventure… it's a job.

A bunch of guys conducting business as usual...

Here's a big question: just what *is* this business that work-a-day soldiers of fortune toil at so diligently? What, exactly, *is* it that spooks do, during the odd hours when they're not busy making the world safe for democracy?

What activity do Lee Harvey Oswald, Jack Ruby, Barry Seal, Guy Banister, David Ferrie, Gordon Novel, Michael McLaney, and Meyer Lansky all share in common? Under normal circumstances, would homosexual and pedophile Dave Ferrie hang out with cigar-chomping commie-hating Guy Banister? What would they find to talk about? And what did violence-loving Jack Ruby—he enjoyed being his own bouncer in his strip clubs—Jack Ruby share in common with supposed 'Marxist intellectual' Lee Oswald?

They *worked* together. They all saw each other at the office, at the airport, or at the odd Klan cross burning that functioned as 'cover' for some of them. Its not that they're personally close... they're like people who see each other maybe once a year at some Gift Show Convention.

As it happens, the industry these men were in was enjoying a major boom at the time. Their business is weapons and narcotics, which together comprise just one industry... because who controls the one inevitably controls the other.

Jack Ruby, to cite just one example... Professor Scott shows him to be involved in narcotics trafficking as far back the late *1940's*.

Talk about being ahead of the curve!

We were amazed to learn that by 1956 Ruby was doing so well in narcotics that he was showing *training films* to potential recruits into the organization. When a pimp named James Breen met with Ruby to discuss collaborating in running three prostitutes, he found Ruby bursting with 'loftier' ambitions.... Ruby showed Breen an early narco-industry training and recruiting film, exciting enthusiasm in his new recruit in "an extremely efficient operation in connection with narcotics traffic." Typical loads were valued at over $300,000. In 1956, that was real money.

The other big action is in weapons. This perhaps explain why— to a startling degree—the lead characters in our story are almost all involved in smuggling weapons, as if they all worked for a giant superstore called *"Guns R' Us."*

This is why they all know each other; our US Customs agent friend was right about there not being all that many players. Lee Oswald knows Jack Ruby, based on too many witnesses for even the FBI to ignore.

Oswald also knows Dave Ferrie, Oswald knows Barry Seal, Seal knows Ferrie, and, based on flight plans in his pilot logs, may have also known Jack Ruby.

And *everybody* knows Guy Banister.

Jack Ruby was deeply involved in the gunrunning to Cuba. Even back in 1964, this was hardly a secret, except to the Warren Commission. Tales of Ruby running guns abounded in FBI reports taken in the first weeks after the assassination. But neither the Warren Commission nor the House Select Committee a dozen years later pursued those leads very far. Dallas agents expressed concern over this cover-up late in 1963, saying, "neither Oswald's Cuban interests in Dallas nor Ruby's Cuban activities have been adequately explored."

By the late 1950s, according to his own Warren Commission testimony, Jack Ruby had developed an affinity for all things Cuban... and his trail crossed with those of the most powerful organized crime figures in America. While the Syndicate was engaged in Cuba, Ruby was in on the action, and his Cuban activities provide a glimpse behind the heavy velvet drapes shielding the American people from the facts about their "national security" and the Mob.

According to a former Ruby associate, James Beard, Ruby stored guns and ammo in the late '50's at a house on the South Texas coast, before ferrying the equipment into Cuba. Beard said he personally saw many boxes of new guns, including automatic rifles and handguns, loaded aboard military-surplus boats, and claimed that "each time the boat left with guns and ammunition, Jack Ruby was on it."

The shipments, said Beard, were destined for the followers of Fidel Castro, then still fighting Batista.

Jack Ruby may even have been into gunrunning as far back as the late '40's. After the Kennedy assassination a pilot in Miami named Mack Blaney Johnson told the FBI that while he was flying cargo from Miami to Havana he learned of illegal flights for the Castro organization arranged by Ruby, then known as Jack Rubenstein.

And a recently declassified CIA report shows CIA agents in New Orleans making inquiries about Ruby... in 1959. Why would a CIA operative be interested in the activities of a small-time Dallas huckster... during the same time Federal investigators are also tracking the activities of both Barry Seal and Dave Ferrie? Because all three are doing the same thing... they're running guns to Cuba.

A Miami FBI report on Ruby revealed his connections to pilot Eddie Browder, who had flown cargo to Cuba and was 'affiliated' with a

Miami gambling casino in which Jack Ruby also held an interest, whose principals included Meyer Lansky—a name which will most assuredly *not* surface in the Warren Commission report. Browder had *also* been a pilot in the CIA coup in Guatemala.

Small world.

His son later told reporters, "My dad got shot down in that operation. And when the surviving members of the Arbenz Government fled they took some prisoners with them. My dad was in an unofficial prison that the Mexican Government let the Guatemalan exiles run in Mexico."

Ruby also turns up in exactly the same place in the Florida Keys which had been used earlier as a storage point in the Guatemalan coup. His pilot, Browder, was also smuggling with mobster Norman "Roughhouse" Rothman, one of Santos Trafficante's close associates, who ran a Havana casino. Rothman was known as "the slot-machine king of Cuba," through the practical expedient of having gone into partnership with the brother-in-law of Cuban Dictator Fulgencio Batista.

Almost two decades after the Kennedy assassination Rothman and Barry Seal will be arrested as part of the same major drug bust in Florida. The *Miami Herald*, in its coverage of the arrests, said of Rothman, "Norman (Rough House) Rothman, 67, asthmatic Surfside gun-runner and organized crime associate, has been convicted three times, most recently for selling a machine gun to federal agents. He once ran a Havana casino and in 1960 was convicted of trying to fly stolen weapons to anti-Castro rebels in Cuba."

Roughhouse Rothman is not a name that has surfaced with Barry Seal's before. The official story attempts to describe Seal as an historical anomaly, an once-in-a-lifetime Comet Kahoutek of drug smuggling. As we are beginning to see, nothing could be further from the truth.

Rothman first came to the attention of the CIA while residing in Dallas in 1958. That year he masterminded the nifty heist of over $13 million in bonds, cash and jewelry, stolen from the Brockville Trust in Ontario, Canada. When Montreal investigators later busted Guiseppe Controni, described as an "eastern Canadian rackets figure," they found $10,000 worth of the stolen bonds.

What had happened was the Canadian branch of the Mob, the Controni Family, had received a hurry-up order for guns from Fidel Castro. Mobsters Rothman and Controni got the call; soon there was a big weapons heist from a National Guard Armory at Canton, Ohio.

Knocking over National Guard Armories had become, for the boys, something like the hula-hoop fad then sweeping the country. During a rash of such robberies across the South, Barry Seal, we learned, had been 'given' the keys to the Baton Rouge Armory... in preparation for a heist.

It happened in 1960, according to one of Seal's life-long friends, Jerry Chidgey. "Barry came in after a trip to St. Bartholomew island, out at the furthest tip of an island chain not far from Venezuela. And somebody had given him the keys to the armory and the gun racks," recalls Chidgey.

"I was just a little punk kid with a coffee house, and Barry said he had a way we could make $5000. Two plainclothes cops were to stand guard. And they drove the guns in an unmarked police van out to the Hammond, Louisiana airport, where they were loaded into a DC 3 and then flown to Guatemala."

Chidgey found it all amazing.

"Here is a guy (Seal) who at the age of 22 has secured keys to an armory, the support of plainclothes police, and an escort to a DC-4 in Hammond. It was incredible!"

"The cops said that in exchange for their help they had been promised appointments to the FBI Academy," he continued. "So that would seem to establish an FBI connection of some kind. But later I flew to Dallas and two guys in black suits who I took to be FBI followed me, so I never could quite figure it out. But that was Barry, I guess. Always a bit of mystery there, for sure."

Less than a month after Rothman and Controni's similar Canton, Ohio Armory raid, the weapons had been loaded onto a plane bound for Cuba which was tracked on radar by the Border Patrol. The weapons stolen were recovered, and Roughhouse Rothman was, presumably, on his way to the Big Barn, charged with arms smuggling, interstate transportation of stolen property, and conspiracy.

But being connected means never having to say you're sorry.... By the end of the year he was back on the street, helping Fulgencio Batista establish an exile headquarters at the Biltmore Terrace Hotel on Miami Beach, which he 'managed.'

Wait a minute.... We've just seen that it is thanks to CIA-backed gangsters like Rothman and Ruby that Fidel Castro out-gunned Batista in the *first* place! Why is Rothman now backing the man he just helped replace? What's going in here?

During the Cuban Missile Crisis, when school-age American kids were taught to hunker under their school desks in the event of Russian nuclear attack, were we learning these skills… just so some Mobsters and CIA guys could make a buck churning weapons?

Roughhouse Rothman *was* eventually convicted of attempting to smuggle guns stolen from the National Guard Armory… but it didn't slow him down. When interviewed while out on appeal, he stated bitterly that he was being prosecuted for the *same activities* which were being regularly conducted by the CIA.

Also doing a bit of time for the stolen securities heist was pilot Eddie Browder. And while the FBI supplied several reports to the Warren Commission concerning Browder, they withheld hundreds of others featuring his involvement in gunrunning to Cuba and the stolen Canadian securities in activities controlled by Norman Rothman.

Browder stated in a deposition that he received the stolen securities from the 26th of July Movement, Fidel Castro's group, in exchange for arms during the summer of 1958… and in another bombshell admitted that he'd traded them for weapons from the International Armament Corporation (InterArms) in Alexandria, Virginia…

And since InterArms is just another way to say "CIA," it looks as if it was no coincidence that Norman Rothman first came to the attention of the CIA at the same time as the big heist. The conclusion in unmistakable: 'the boys' were demonstrably splitting the take from the sale of stolen Canadian securities.

Last, but clearly not least… CIA agent Frank Sturgis also admitted having being involved in this operation, to the Rockefeller Commission in the mid-1970s. The weapons had been hidden in the marshes of Islmorada, Florida… exactly where Jack Ruby will be identified as having been "babysitting" a large arms cache.

When Barry Seal is arrested with Roughhouse Rothman twenty years later, another man arrested is William "Obie" Obront, called the financier for Controni, the Canadian Mobster who started the stolen Canadian securities ball rolling way back in '57.

"The 60-year-old Obront, of Bal Harbour, a former Montreal meatpacker, has been described by the Royal Canadian Mounted Police as a financier for the Controni Organized Crime Family," read the *Miami Herald*. "Obront, a 59-year-old French Canadian charged last year with running a $50 million Quaalude-smuggling ring, has reportedly told undercover drug agents that "every Quaalude tablet in South Florida is controlled by me."

Controni was also described, during the Senate Narcotics Hearings in the early 1980's, as "head of the largest and most notorious narcotics syndicate on the North American continent."

During the decade-long intrigue leading up to the assassination of John Fitzgerald Kennedy, these are the people, with whom, and for whom, Barry Seal worked flying missions into Cuba.

Much later, when the 'ghost' of Barry Seal and the Mena Scandal stand briefly in the path of Bill Clinton's Presidential ambitions, drug pilot William Bottoms will rush forward to assure us that Barry Seal was "nothing but transportation for the Medellin Cartel."

As we're beginning to see, Barry Seal's roots in the deep political system 'might could' go, as they say in the South, quite a little bit deeper than that.

CHAPTER TWELVE

FULL OF FUN, FULL OF FOLLY

"THE CIA WILL HAVE to be dealt with," John Kennedy said after the Bay of Pigs fiasco. Instead, it was Kennedy who was dealt with. In the 20 months between the Bay of Pigs and Dallas there will be enough cloak and dagger intrigue to keep spy novelists busy for lifetimes...

S pies were in vogue. Spooks were hip. The whole James Bond craze took off. JFK even cornered author Ian Fleming at a cocktail party seeking tips on bumping off Castro.

"Elvis," some of his buddies called Barry Seal during this period, and it suited him…. He hung out, between bouts of derring-do, at the Playboy Club in New Orleans. Maybe Elvis had moments when he wished *he* could be Barry Seal, and avoid the cheesy Vegas fate awaiting him. He always *did* want to be a spy.

"Barry had the James Bond Syndrome, all right," life-long friend James Poche told us. "He would go off for two weeks at a time, and then be back like nothing had happened."

"We used to fly to New Orleans from Baton Rouge for the evening," Poche continued, "and drink at the Playboy Club, or visit the sheriff's brothel in Opelousas, that sort of thing. We lived together in his airplane hanger and palled around with Johnny Rivers, the musician. That was how Barry met Elvis, through Johnny."

Now this *is* a curious sidelight: Barry Seal and Elvis Presley knew each other.

Today James Poche is a living embodiment of the laid-back 'Margaritaville' lifestyle popularized by singer Jimmy Buffet, wearing sandals, his shirt outside his jeans, and a 'do-rite' rag on his head. ("It makes your hair 'do-rite," he grinned, when we asked him what it was called.)

He began working for and flying with Barry Seal in the early 1960's and later went into 'marijuana importation' with him in the mid-70's. Then he watched from the sidelines when Barry entered cocaine smuggling. While Seal built an increasingly paramilitary organization Poche had held fast to the colorful life of the lone bush pilot/marijuana smuggler.

In the small world that Louisiana was—and is—James Poche knew many of the players. "I knew Dave Ferrie, and flew around with him a couple of times. He was a friend of mine. Me and another friend, Charlie Heck, had bought a Cessna 170 and based it out at Lakefront (Airport), where Ferrie was. I've got copies of David Ferrie's signature in my log books."

We learned that what is known today as Lakefront Airport was not, back in the early Sixties, just a small public airport, but also a Naval Reserve facility where Cubans were being trained as pilots for the Bay of Pigs invasion.

"Baton Rouge is kind of a go-nowhere place," Poche told us. "And Barry had a lot of 'soldier of fortune-type' ideas, which was what made him seem so glamorous to kids like me around the airport. I was just a snot-nosed kid hanging out with the pilots, and Barry had a bunch of secrets, and was pretty mysterious. He was an enigma in Baton Rouge; no one there had ever seen anything like him. We could never figure out what he was up to."

Poche continued, "I used to make signs and banners for him, after my oldest sister had hooked me up with him. She went to school with Barry. So I took a couple of flying lessons from him in 1958, and that's how I got to know him. I was a young kid and wanted to learn to fly, partly just to have some escape from a dysfunctional family, and all that entails… the son of a Louisiana state trooper who ran security at the State House in Baton Rouge. So I had some family connections, in the Louisiana way of things, and I gravitated towards Barry. He taught me a lot. "

Poche has just described a troubled family situation remarkably similar to Seal's own, where he had moved in and out of the house during adolescence during the '50's, a time when this did not often happen.

Seal had spotted something in Poche; had Seal's own recruitment officer, David Ferrie, also been looking for boys in just these circumstances?

"We would fly down to New Orleans and bring back some girls, to where we were living at a Howard Johnson's motel in Baton Rouge," Poche remembers. "We were always flying around at night, usually ending up in the French Quarter, spending the night there and having breakfast, then flying back to Baton Rouge."

"Once I remember we went to Mexico on vacation—it was in 1960, I think—with an older married lady who had a crush on Barry, a woman named Diane, and her young daughter," Poche related.

Jerry Chidgey shared an apartment with Barry during the same 'swinging '60s.' "It was right at the beginning of luxury apartments. Barry and I shared a 'pad' overlooking the pool, and got a famous Baton Rouge interior designer, Wally Young, to decorate it. We had great times there, till one night Barry brought some people back from New Orleans and they all got naked in the pool—this is in the South now, understand—and we were asked to move out."

Up in Washington, it has been reported; John Kennedy was similarly distracted by the sexual thaw.

When his stint at the Bay of Pigs rout was over, Barry did not return immediately home to Baton Rouge. One witness claimed he was involved in continuing CIA operations in the Caribbean...

"Barry was involved with removing Trujillo from the Dominican Republic," CIA pilot Tosh Plumlee said. Plumlee, whose word, like that of most ex-spooks, should be taken with a healthy grain of salt, said that Seal had, by this time, been inducted into military intelligence.

"He and I were 4th Army Reserve, in military intelligence, based out of Dallas Love Field," stated Plumlee. "Barry Seal was involved with military intelligence in the early days, way back before he was with TWA. Military intelligence was the real game, with the CIA just acting as logistical people. Barry was a peripheral player back then, but he was a CIA 'contract' pilot all the way back to 1956 or 1957."

There is no doubting Tosh Plumlee's bona fides as a CIA pilot, and first hand witness to a lot of secret history. But doubts persist as to his veracity. Plumlee, for example, insists that he was part of a military abort team that went into Dallas to *stop* the Kennedy assassination, and that Life magazine has a picture of him on the infamous Grassy Knoll.

Does anyone today believe the American military wanted to *save* Jack Kennedy's life in November 1963?

The bigger story during this period involves how someone can be a CIA 'contract' pilot and at the same time is involved in military intelligence, as Plumlee insists Seal was. This period is, of course, the beginning of Special Forces, the Green Berets, which Seal, upon his return to Baton Rouge after a six-month stint in the Caribbean, will join.

In a characteristic move he used his connections to keep himself and James Poche from enduring the full rigors of the Airborne Ranger program…

"Barry knew a Major John Folse in the National Guard in Baton Rouge," Poche says, grinning. "I don't know from where…I was just glad that he had 'stroke.' He was able to fix it so we both entered the service and beat the draft in the late summer of 1961. Hell, we had it made… Barry would fly the Major around, and I was the cook. I only had to go to one summer camp in seven years."

Seal's life-long contempt for what he considered the 'stupidity' of government employees, "GS-pukes," and rank-and-file military was already well honed by this time.

Said Poche, "The Major had a lisp… and he also had a hard-guy military attitude. It was a combination we both found *very* amusing. Barry always laughed and talked too much for this guy's liking. 'Theal,' the Major would bark, 'Button your lip, Theal!'"

As part of the increased emphasis on Special Forces, in late 1961 the Armed Forces set up a Special Ops Air Base in the middle of the Eglin Air Force Base complex in the Florida panhandle, pulling in aircraft and crews from the world-wide Air America system to this base at Eglin. Seal's pilot's logs reflect this his flying regularly to a destination which he coyly lists as "Pensacola," the town nearest the base.

At the age of only 22, Barry Seal was learning tradecraft.

Wheeling around in a '58 Thunderbird, the swinging young spy was soon the proud owner of several thriving businesses: Seal Sky Service, Aerial Advertising Associates, Seal's Texaco, Helicopter Airways…

He also had an office in the International Trade Center run by Clay Shaw, perhaps not-coincidentally the only person ever charged with conspiracy to kill the President… the same Clay Shaw, who, according to Garrison, had such intriguing connections up in Montreal, where Seal does business as well. Could this be how Barry Seal met Norman "Roughhouse" Rothman?

A pilot's flight logs are a sort of airborne diary in progress, recording when and where they went, and in what type of aircraft. And Barry Seal, like most pilots, was meticulous in his notations—in those logs of his which escaped being 'cleaned-up' by Federal investigators.

Still, there are huge unexplained gaps.

When he was heavily involved in Cuban weapons smuggling, for example, he reported that his pilot's logs for those two whole years—most of 1959 and 1960—had been "lost."

The benefits of a strategy in which records are "lost" as easily as geometry homework—and equally as often—should by now be beginning to become apparent. We no longer viewed as sloppy bookkeeping or 'happenstance' that Seal had spent 1959 and '60 flying in and out of airports whose names he did not deem it prudent to commit to his pilot logs...

Nor are these the only gaps in Barry's early flying history. During *two* separate four-month stretches in 1962 and early 1963 he leaves no records at all in his log books of where he is flying, and with whom...at the exact same time the Agency was training Cuban exiles and "soldiers of fortune" for a second invasion in Guatemala, on No-Name Key in Florida, and on the north shore of Lake Pontchartrain in Louisiana.

His pilot's logs then begin to drop all pretense to accuracy, and every other day, month in and month out, Barry's logs state that he is "banner-towing," always for precisely five hours. For example, on a day for which we have photographic proof that he was in Mexico City, January 22, 1963, his pilot's logs read, "banner towing in Baton Rouge. Five hours."

When we showed his friend and fellow-flying instructor Cliff Rice these pilot logs his face showed dismay. "His flight logs raise a lot of red flags," Rice told us slowly. "He made a lot of flights to Dallas, and to Florida, I see. As well as to Waco, pretty irregular."

We asked former CIA pilot Gary Eitel to inspect Barry Seal's official military records for us. Eitel's recent career includes a stint as an attorney, where his court testimony helped convict two CIA miscreants in Arizona in the mid-'90s, who were selling C-130 military cargo planes to Mexican drug cartels.

"It says Barry was 1st Special Forces from Baton Rouge, La., assigned to duty that's been 'redacted.' His duty specialty codes are redacted, so that won't tell us anything..." Eitel started, reading the records aloud.

"On 31 Aug 61, he joined a reserve Special Forces group," he continued. "Then on 15 Dec 62, he's assigned to the 21st Special Forces Group—Airborne, and goes to Fort Benning Jump School.

And then, in January of 63, he's transferred to Company 'B' of the 21st Special Forces group."

That would be the same month of the picture we saw in Mexico City. We had questions. Could the people in that nightclub somehow constitute Company B? And why had Seal joined the Special Forces *reserve?*

"You get a little more freedom in the reserves, a little more cowboy style," Eitel replied. "You can take a leave of absence without losing your service number. See, in the military, once you prove yourself once, the juicy opportunities start to come your way. And once you're into *that* club… you're okay. The gravy train rolls in."

Has someone, or some organization, smoothed Seal's progress?

"Barry found a little niche in the Special Forces Reserves," Eitel stated. "One reason might be that good pilots often flunk out of flight school, because of the discipline. In 1960 he was 20. In 1962 Seal would have been 22 years old. The draft was big time then. He *could* have gone to Vietnam"

Indeed, Seal *had* flunked out of his one semester of college, at LSU. Could the CIA have smoothed his way into the Special Forces Reserve? "Its highly possible," stated Eitel. "In 1962, remember, Special Forces wasn't well-known yet at all. Army Rangers didn't have the badass reputation they developed later. There wasn't a 'Ballad of the Green Berets' yet…. What *is* clear is that Barry was in some kind of unit that had a *special ops* focus."

"Here's something… on 1 May 63 he's assigned to company D Special Ops Detachment of the 20th Special Forces Group Airborne. Now he goes up to the next grade of Special Forces—Special Detachment Special Ops. The CIA could easily have recruited him right out of the service," Eitel concluded. "If he wasn't already working for them."

Was there anything unusual about Barry Seal's 20th Special Forces Group? Yes….When it was discovered that the Birmingham-based 20th had sent a detachment of Green Berets to Memphis to carry out an unknown mission on the day Martin Luther King was assassinated, the local paper, the *Memphis Commercial Appeal*, had investigated. They discovered that the 20th was chock-full of veterans of CIA assassination ops in Southeast Asia. The paper quoted former army counterintelligence major as stating that the 20th had even had a domestic intelligence network, operated for them by the Ku Klux Klan and dubbed 'Klan Special Forces.' The major said, "The rural South was 'in-country' to these guys, and at times things got out of hand."

Barry's reserve service continues until his release in November of 1966. For the last two years of his 6-year hitch he was assigned to headquarters of 245th Engineer battalion based in Saint Louis.

"That fits," Eitel told us. "Engineers and Special Forces just go hand-in-hand. Engineers are the first guys in, they're road maintainers. They build airstrips where covert ops can go in the dark. Barry was an owner/operator. The CIA contracted him for work. They said, hey Seal... we're gonna pay you."

Gary Eitel was also a CIA pilot, a lifelong member of the same fraternity of flyers to which Seal belonged. He knew him only slightly, but, living in neighboring Texas, he *heard* quite a bit about him.

"I was working out of Tyler, Texas in 1981," Eitel recalled, "flying for oil companies. And I knew this one guy pretty well who was an 'airline transport' pilot, working for Barry Seal. One day I'm talking to him—we were friendly—and he tells me that Barry's just given him $25,000 for a flight. But he doesn't look at all happy."

Eitel continues, "He says to me, 'man, I'm just worried to death. Sheriff Smith (of Tyler) has me fly him down to Hot Springs Arkansas to chase whores, and he never pays me for the trip. And it just pisses Barry off. But there ain't nothing I can do about it. I gotta take these cops and prosecutors to this in-country R&R center."

In Seal's flight logs we had seen that the young Barry Seal had made a number of trips to Hot Springs, Arkansas, at a time when *Partners in Power* reports it was a swinging Dixie Mafia gambling Mecca...

Had the young Barry Seal back then been performing the same 'duties' for which he would later be berating his employees?

Numerous reports, such as trooper L.D. Brown's, attest to Barry speaking familiarly of Bill Clinton in the early 80's. "How's the Guv?" Barry asks a slightly awed Brown. A young Seal could have met a young Clinton back in the 60's in Hot Springs.

"I never will understand why we spent so much time in Little Rock," stated Charlie Montgomery, who worked for Seal during the late 60's and into the 70's. "Barry took me up there numerous times, supposedly on sign business. We'd stay at the downtown Holiday Inn in Little Rock. But we didn't do much sign business there, is all I know."

Montgomery also remembers often waiting outside while Barry went into an antique store in the French Quarter "a few blocks down from Maspero's," which jibes with the location of Dave Dixon's antique store at the time.

We asked Gary Eitel, "Have *you* heard anything about Seal flying a getaway plane out of Dallas?"

"It would have had to be an awful damn big plane," he replied slowly. "There were so many people involved in that thing, they'd have needed a 747 to get 'em all out. Its downright embarrassing."

But life isn't *all* covert ops. Along with the intrigue and the swagger, a more human side of Barry Seal was emerging… like the time he flew on a 'snake run' to Chatahoochie to pick up a bag-full of live snakes that a radio station needed to hold a snake-sitting contest on the air.

Recalls Charley Montgomery, "The snakes got loose in a hotel room, and there was hell to pay."

There were also romantic interludes. "Barry used to fly his girlfriend, Ava, who was a real looker, every chance he got," Cliff Rice told us. "Afterwards everyone at the airport would kid him about seeing his plane bouncing up and down as it flew over town."

In his pilot logs there is this notation, in Barry's own handwriting, from January 4, 1959: "Took Ava for first ride in Comanche N5230P. Me, her, Kenneth and Ginger went for a ride.

Had to fly with a bad leg." (A reference to his accident at Pike-burden Plantation.)

Later, things must be progressing nicely, because Ava's parents come along: "Took Ava and Mr. and Mrs. Durham for a visit to Feniday in Dr. West's plane."

Stories of Barry Seal's generous spirit came from a number of people, including DEA agents and state police who tracked him…too many to not give them credence. One example we heard involved a young Barry Seal, driving in downtown Baton Rouge one day with a friend when they came across a traffic accident.

"It was on Government Street, we just happened to be there before the paramedics," Jack Temple told us. "It was bad. Barry ran over to a lady lying in the street, her eyeball was hanging out on her cheek, and he held her hand until the ambulance got there, speaking to her soothingly. And then he rode with her in the ambulance to the hospital, even though he'd never seen that woman before in his life."

"Full of fun, full of folly," read the inscription under Barry Seal's picture in the Baton Rouge high school yearbook.

"Full of life" would be right in there, too.

CHAPTER THIRTEEN

CUBA, THE GUNS, NEW ORLEANS, EVERYTHING

NAPOLEON CALLED IT Isle d'Orleans, the only independent island state in America. From the start, there's always been something a little different about New Orleans, the city that care forgot…

The Big Easy anchors a state whose longtime Governor, John McKeithen, was the 'great good friend' of the father of the New Orleans Superdome, New Orleans 'antiques dealer' and Barry Seal's CIA handler, Dave Dixon. Presumably to cover all his bases, McKeithen also had a phone on his desk which was a 'hot line' wired directly to the Mafia Kingfish himself, Carlos Marcello.

After his arrest for murdering Lee Oswald, Jack Ruby had moaned out loud that now *everybody* was going to find out, about what Ruby called "Cuba, the guns, New Orleans, everything."

Mr. Ruby, we think, had an instinctive notion that "everything" does not include New Orleans and the state of Louisiana, which comes under some other heading altogether.

"Louisiana is the kind of place, where as soon as you cross the Sabine River coming in from Texas, the road begins to go galump, galump, galump…" said Nancy Poche, a childhood friend of Barry Seal's. "And this is on the *Interstate*, for god sakes, and you wonder, where does the money go?"

It didn't start with Carlos Marcello or Barry Seal or the 60's Cuban intrigue… There's always a former state official on trial for something or other, the latest being former Governor Edwin Edwards, for bribery involving everything from casino licenses to insurance.

For all that, Edwards is a relatively beloved figure here, having survived eleven grand jury investigations, $2 million worth of influence peddling, a penchant for gambling and women other than the first lady, and the most amazingly bald public declaration any public figure has ever made, saying that his only undoing would be if he were "caught in bed with a dead girl or a live boy."

Is the populace outraged? Ask a New Orleans cabbie. "I like him," said Clement Johnson. "They haven't nailed Edwin yet. Don't think they will. Least he's honest about his dishonesty."

According to an eyewitness, Governor Edwards' friendship with Barry Seal was warm enough to have once loaned Seal $10,000 at the gaming tables in Las Vegas, on an occasion when Lady Luck had not been kind to "Biggie."

Seal later repaid the money by casually sending his secretary over to the State Capital bearing that favorite of politicians everywhere, a paper bag-full of money.

Another eyewitness said Seal's operation passed so much money in bribes to Edwards that it took *three* separate flights in a private plane to get it all safely offshore. This seemingly confirmed in a notation we found in Seal's own handwriting. "$200,000 to Marion," it read.

"Marion" is the name of Edward's brother and erstwhile bagman.

Because of his experience around the South, DEA agent Dick Gustafson had an interesting vantage point from which to compare the 'up-and-comer' governors of Louisiana and neighboring Arkansas.

"You could get a bushel basket full of peas in their pods and not find two more alike than Edwin Edwards and Bill Clinton," he stated. Hauling up the ghost of the Kingfish, Huey Long, or his brother Earl or "Sunshine" Jimmie Davis or Edward "Grady" Partin may help in explaining to Louisiana's peculiar tolerance for corruption and its affinity for scoundrels.

Or maybe it's just something in the air…

Barry's smuggling buddy James Poche's father was a local legend, Pappy Poche, Gov. Earl Long's personal bodyguard.

"Pappy would go partying on Bourbon Street with the Guv at the Famous Door," James recalls, "and the girls would come around passing the cap, and Pappy would just take his gun out and set it in the hat, and they'd just go nuts. One time we heard he pulled out a .38 and commandeered a horse carriage in Jackson Square, just threw the tourists out. You could get away with that kind of thing back then."

Louisiana was the kind of place where, James told us, "If you had money you could buy liquor as a kid."

It was also small enough so that everyone knew everyone else... Clinton's famous reptoid campaign manager James Carville grew up just around the corner.

"James Carville's mother was a World Book salesman in our neighborhood in Gonzales," Poche told us.

His sister, Nancy Poche, was present when young Barry Seal met his first wife after returning from his six months Special Forces training...

"James and Barry came into the house, and we hadn't seen Barry for a long time. He'd lost a *lot* of weight. Barbara (Bottoms) was my brother David's girlfriend, and she was over visiting at the house when Barry walked in. That was all it took, I guess. They got married just a couple of months later."

Barbara's brother, Bill Bottoms, later became one of Barry's chief pilots, though years after he and Barbara had divorced. Since surfacing during the presidential campaign in 1996 he has attempted to 'debunk' what he calls the "Mena Myth" on the Internet, where he is well loathed. "Back in high school though," according to Nancy Poche, "Billy was just really really cute, with real real blond hair and blue blue eyes."

In addition to his careers in gunrunning, narcotics trafficking and thwarting the investigation into the assassination of the President of the United States, Jack Ruby was a longtime FBI and law enforcement informant.

"I first met Jack Ruby at the Heavyweight Championship bout between Floyd Patterson and Pete Rademacher in Dallas in the mid-'50's," Southern lawman Rex Armistead told us.

"I was there with a District Attorney I've known for 30 years, and we were invited over to a table at the 3525 Club at which were seated Murray "the Camel" Humphrey, jockey Willie Shoemaker, Buddy Fogelson, and his wife, the movie star Greer Garson. Their host was Jack Ruby."

"The next time I saw Ruby he had his hand in a cast. He told me somebody had accused Patterson of throwing the fight and, incensed, Jack had broken his hand punching on the guy's face."

"Thereafter," Armistead continued, "every time I went to Dallas either Jack Ruby or his sister picked me up at the airport in that long blue automobile of his, with his two tiny dogs in the back seat. I can remember walking into his nightclub office. When he shut the door, on the back of it was a large picture of Jack Kennedy."

Ruby was well known for his public relations with Dallas lawmen; now we heard that this solicitousness extended to lawmen from across the Gulf Coast. "When he heard my Daddy was in the hospital, he sent a dozen roses to his room," another law enforcement veteran recalled about Ruby. "When we had a vexing murder case with a Dallas connection, Ruby always knew the killer. Titanic Thompson and RD Matthew's are just a couple I recall ol' Jack dropping a dime on."

One law enforcement source told us he had wanted to visit Ruby in jail after his conviction for killing Lee Oswald. So he phoned an old friend, Captain Will Fritz of the Dallas Police, Ruby's jailer. Fritz dissuaded him from stopping by. "He said the jail Ruby was kept in was a CIA facility now, and entirely under their control."

"Colorful" doesn't begin to describe the wide-open corruption that exists in New Orleans.... During the 1970's, for example, Rex Armistead told us he had headed an Organized Crime Task Force in New Orleans, where he noted that the local New Orleans FBI had a cozy relationship with Carlos Marcello...

"I drove back behind Carlos' Town and Country motel on several occasions late at night, where I found FBI agents in government cars conferring with Marcello, sitting in the front seat. When I finally had to go to (then-FBI Director) Clarence Kelly and have him sweep 'em all out of there... was when I discovered they were tampering with my criminal investigations."

Is it any surprise, then, that FBI analysis of Jack Ruby characterizes him as a small-time operator "unable to cultivate friendships with important figures in organized crime?"

The Feebs can always be counted on to protect one of their own.

Cozy relationships abounded in the steamy New Orleans climate. In the late 1970's our lawman friend had also learned something else we heard from numerous sources: Barry Seal was known to be working for the DEA.

"An informant?" we asked incredulously.

"The DEA preferred the term 'source,'" smirked this nationally recognized expert on Organized Crime.

"I always assumed Seal was CIA, which was why he was let alone."

New Orleans was as important in the Cuban intrigue of the early '60's as the more-publicized Miami.... Just below New Orleans, a peeling banana boat named the Santa Ana slipped her moorings at Algiers naval base on the Mississippi River a week before the Bay of Pigs invasion, and began steaming towards the Gulf of Mexico, with a CIA adviser and exile troops wearing the uniform of Fidel Castro's Cuban Army onboard…

Trained at a CIA wilderness camp north of New Orleans on Lake Pontchartrain that will later 'go black,' the men onboard were about to attack—not the Cuban communist "enemy"— but the *American* base at Guantánamo. The plan was to make Castro look like the aggressor and justify direct American intervention. These men will later provide, attest numerous sources, one of the so-called 'shooter teams' in Dallas at the Kennedy assassination.

According to Colonel Fletcher Prouty, intimately involved in the Cuba Project, "Ike directed that all military-age Cubans be put into the service as a means of controlling them. The CIA began to create the Brigade, but in the process, there were a lot of Cubans who were not politically acceptable to the others. The CIA took these men and put them in the camp near Lake Pontchartrain. This was the misfit camp and it had the misfit instructors."

"When the Brigade put to sea for the landing at the Bay of Pigs," continued Prouty, "all of the Louisiana Cubans were on a boat that just sailed around in the Gulf. They were never in on the landing. Hundreds of these men, irate about the turn of events, later wrote to Kennedy and the CIA saying what they thought."

"For some reason those letters, bales of them, were sent to my office. Not only were the Cubans mad at Kennedy; the instructors were too. This created the nucleus of that gang down there."

"That gang down there," Prouty maintains, meaning Barry Seal, Guy Banister, David Ferrie, et al, was responsible for plotting and carrying out the Kennedy assassination.

Layton Martens lived with Ferrie and worked for Carlos Marcello's lawyer Wray Gil. He described to us conditions in the Crescent City in the Spring of '61. "New Orleans received 60,000 Cuban refugees. The town was inundated with people, and the infrastructure was sorely taxed.

I was just eighteen and went to work fundraising from local businesses to provide Refugee Relief for the Provisional Government of Cuba."

Though Layton doesn't say it, this "Provisional Government of Cuba" was a largely fictitious entity housed in the 544 Camp offices of Guy Banister. Banister served as munitions supplier; according to former members of his staff, the offices of his 'detective agency' were littered with guns of every distinction, housed in a building located within shouting distance of the local offices of the CIA and FBI.

Banister, who also organized the right-wing paramilitary Minutemen, purveyed a racist periodical, and supported the 'renegade' off the-books anti-Castro exile training camp north of New Orleans on the shores of Lake Pontchartrain, was clearly quite the busy fellow.

Kennedy's death knell may have sounded when he reached an agreement to stop the "secret war" against Cuba with Nikita Khrushchev at the end of the Cuban Missile Crisis in late 1962. The Joint Chiefs could not have been pleased, after having pressed for an immediate attack on Cuban missiles during the crisis. Knowledge of this fact is still secret history, discussion of its ramifications—so far as we could tell—virtually non-existent.

Nor could those true 'original gangsters,' the Mob, who, to get Castro out of Cuba and the casinos reopened must have been willing to entertain alliances with the strangest of bedfellows…

"General, this is Guido. Guido, meet the General."

Shakespeare said it best, when he told us why treason never prospers… because, of course, then "none dare call it treason."

Clues to what happened come from all over…Attorney General Robert Kennedy, fore example, was sent to meet with Soviet Ambassador Anatoly Dobrynin. In his memoirs, Premier Nikita Khrushchev quotes Bobby Kennedy as saying: "The President is in a grave situation…We are under pressure from our military to use force against Cuba…If the situation continues much longer, the President is not sure that the military will not overthrow him and seize power."

Layton Martens told us, "We (the CIA) discovered the missiles in late May of '61, and at that point the second invasion became moot. I was there, seeing US Govt. estimates of what would have happened if Kennedy had moved on Cuba. 'You can expect 150,000 troop losses,' it said, and the Southeast United States will be irradiated.'"

"The Soviets would have engaged us in a shooting war," continues Martens. "Subsequent to that realization, everything else—especially including the phony plans for a second invasion—became nothing but a political "chit."

A bitter internal struggle was underway.... Angered over the Bay of Pigs fiasco, the CIA refused to bend to Kennedy's will, and continued their destabilization campaign against Castro of sabotage raids and plots against Castro's life undertaken by Mob figures Johnny Roselli, Sam Giancana, and Santos Trafficante.

In the wake of the Cuban Missile Crisis, which had brought the world to the brink of nuclear war, Kennedy sent FBI and other agents to Florida and Louisiana to clamp down on the cowboys in the training camps. His orders to disband CIA paramilitary bases in Florida and Louisiana went unheeded.

Soon renegade exile commandos were attacking Cuban ports without approval from Washington. On March 26, 1963 an offshoot of Alpha 66 severely damaged a Soviet ship, prompting Moscow to protest vehemently. President Kennedy moved firmly to disassociate himself and the United States from the raids.

Strict federal action against exile extremists dated from this episode. Antonio Veciana and other activists were severely restricted... thirteen years later he made a startling revelation under questioning by the Senate Intelligence Committee, identifying an out-of-control element of the CIA as being behind the unauthorized provocation.

Veciana testified his group attacked Soviet ships in Cuban ports on orders from "Maurice Bishop," the code name for his American intelligence handler David Atlee Philips, chief of the Mexico City CIA station, and veteran of the glorious victory over landless peasants in Guatemala.

Said Veciana, "It was my case officer, 'Maurice Bishop, who had the idea to attack the Soviet ships. The intention was to cause trouble between Kennedy and Russia. 'Bishop' believed that Kennedy and Khrushchev had made a secret agreement that the U.S.A. would do nothing more to help in the fight against Castro, and felt—he told me many times—that President Kennedy was a man without experience surrounded by a group of young men who were also inexperienced, with mistaken ideas on how to manage this country. He said you had to put Kennedy against the wall in order to force him to make decisions that would remove Castro's regime."

Here's the real secret history: A shadowy extra-constitutional presence deliberately sabotaged Kennedy's search for an understanding with the Soviet Union just as they had deliberately sabotaged the search for peace of Eisenhower before him.

This is not conspiracy theory; it is, instead, conspiracy fact.

There *was* a secret war going on in 1963, but *not* between the Kennedy Administration and Fidel Castro. The *real* secret war was a no-holds-barred fight to the death between the President of the United States of America and his Central Intelligence Agency. Though Kennedy clearly distrusted the CIA, he still made longtime CIA operative General Edward Lansdale (the Ugly American of the famous novel of the same name) head of the CIA's assassination program against Castro, Operation Mongoose.

Kennedy had made too many powerful enemies. And now he had committed a fatal mistake, giving his foes the 'keys' to a souped-up 'assassination machine' which had, in short order, turned on its creator.

The battlefield had now been, in the CIA's phrase, "prepared."

New Orleans sits alongside the Mississippi, and also on the south shore of a large fresh water lake, Lake Pontchartrain. On the lake's north shore lay Carlos Marcello's hunting lodge in Lacombe, where researchers suspect one of the 'shooter teams' bivouacked.

According to an FBI informant, Marcello associate Sam Benton had almost 2,500 pounds of dynamite hidden there, and was negotiating to obtain a B-24 aircraft to bomb Castro's oil refineries in a joint operation between two extremist anti-Castro groups, the Christian Democratic Movement and the DRE (Student Revolutionary Directorate).

The raid was set for August '63, with two aircraft to take off from an airstrip near the Lacombe camp on a flight to bomb Havana's oil refineries.

Prodded by Bobby Kennedy, the FBI raided the house in Lacombe storing the dynamite, and the training camp nearby. Royal Dutch Shell Oil Corporation retained a fondness for their seized refineries in Havana, it seemed, a reluctance to return in the future to find bomb craters where the refinery had been, and a willingness to make their feelings known at the highest levels of official Washington...

Fervent anti-communism is all well and good. But business is business.

Press reports in the New Orleans papers reveal that in the early morning hours of July 31 FBI agents swooped down, seizing a cache of arms, forty-eight cases of dynamite, twenty 100-pound bomb casings, napalm, blasting caps, primer cord, and over a ton of explosives.

But they declined to reveal to reporters if any arrests had been made, or even to name the owner of the property raided. As it turned out, it belonged to Mike McLaney's brother, William Julius McLaney of New Orleans.

McLaney's wife told reporters that the cottage had been loaned to a Cuban exile friend. She said she and her husband had operated a 'tourist business' in Havana, but left "because Castro made things impossible down there."

The Lacombe raid assumed a prominent role in Jim Garrison's investigation of the Kennedy assassination. He believed that the exiles training there—for an assassination attempt on Castro—had been 'spun off' into the successful attempt on Kennedy.

He accused the McLaney brothers running the camp of serving the CIA with a "renegade off the books" training site and arms cache. And he asserted there had been *two* anti-Castro groups training north of Lake Pontchartrain, one "overt," the other "covert."

The *covert* group, he said, was led by the ubiquitous David Ferrie, who drilled five-man commando teams in guerrilla warfare practice and infiltration techniques on a site adjacent to the McLaney cottage. According to the New Orleans States-Item, "Immediately after the Lacombe raid, the so-called 'overt' Cuban group disappeared."

"The thread that winds through the story involves one of the central problems of John F. Kennedy's two years, ten months and two days in the White House—the problem of Cuba," stated Pulitzer Prize-winning reporter Haynes Johnson in contemporaneous coverage of Garrison's investigation. "It is Garrison's obvious contention that Cubans were somehow involved in the President's death."

"His case appears to rest" writes Johnson, "on one theory about the assassination: that Oswald was working with an anti-Castro right-wing organization and actually intended to kill Fidel; that Oswald's publicly pro-Communist activities in New Orleans and his attempt to enter Mexico and secure a Cuban visa were a ruse."

This was heady stuff in the 60's, before Americans had learned to become suspicious of people who kept diaries, traveled constantly, and looked slightly dazed after committing their 'senseless' act.

Garrison charged that David Ferrie, Jack Ruby, and Lee Oswald were all involved in training paramilitary groups of Cuban exiles and American "neo-Nazis" north of Lake Pontchartrain near the McLaney home. After Kennedy ordered a crackdown on these CIA-supported activities, he believed, the Cubans had turned their sights on him. The raid on the McLaney cottage in Lacombe signed Kennedy's death warrant.

His investigators easily discovered that Bill McLaney's brother, Mike McLaney, had operated a gambling casino in Havana for Meyer Lansky.

Three months before the FBI raid McLaney's Havana casino had been nationalized by Castro at a loss of many millions to its owners.

Mike McLaney sent the CIA a detailed plan for knocking out three Havana refineries, but instead of getting his plan approved, he got an urgent phone call warning him "not to attempt such a thing under any circumstances."

Years later McLaney was organizing a multimillion-dollar effort to take over casinos in the Bahamas for Las Vegas Mobsters. When his bribery of public officials in Nassau was exposed, the Bahamian government fell, amid accusations that McLaney had tried to engineer the assassination of the Prime Minister...

It has to be admitted that these acts are consistent with someone who could credibly have been associated with the Kennedy assassination.

The exiles arrested at Lacombe worked with a group of CIA contract agents led by Gerry Hemming known as the No-Name Key group for their training base in the Florida Keys. A decade later, when witnesses and evidence began to point to CIA/anti-Castro involvement in the assassination in the 70s, former CIA agent Victor Marchetti claimed the CIA was considering a limited hangout, in which it would admit that some of its members were involved in the assassination.

These are those guys.

Howard Hunt wrote, "Nino Diaz had been dusted off, and together with a hundred untrained followers, sent to the CIA's amphibious base on Lake Pontchartrain, Louisiana."

But back in 1967 the hapless FBI could find no traces of this base. "During the years 1960, 1961, 1962, no information was obtained from sources regarding a camp where guerrilla training was given to Cuban exiles in the Lake Pontchartrain area."

In 1967, the mere *existence* of the Pontchartrain base was still secret history. It was the camp that wasn't there... until Haynes Johnson wrote of Garrison's notions about the "existence of a training camp for Cubans in St. Tammany Parish across Lake Pontchartrain in the summer of 1963 where, supposedly, Oswald went for the purpose of participating in the plot to kill Castro."

The CIA denied in 1967 even having knowledge of the camp at Lacombe...

"Old hands at station confirm JMWAVE (Miami) was the only Agency-sponsored training camp. To the best of Station knowledge there was no station or agency support or funding of the [Christian Democratic Movement] training camp."

By the time the truth finally *did* start to dribble out, the coup plotters had such a firm grip on the media that it made barely a ripple...

New Orleans resident George Wilcox told historian Michael Kurtz he had observed "Ferrie, Oswald, and numerous Cubans, all dressed in military fatigues and carrying automatic rifles, conducting what appeared to be a 'military training maneuver' near Bedico Creek, a swampy inland body of water (a bayou) near Lacombe, on the north shore of Lake Pontchartrain, in early September 1963, two months after the government raid on anti-Castro guerilla camps in the United States."

Then, something major happened...

In 1979 investigators for the House Select Committee on Assassinations discovered a training film from the archives of Georgetown University. Ferrie, Oswald, Banister, and David Atlee Philips were all on an 8 mm 'home movie' shot in the summer of 1963.

Grab yourself some popcorn. We're going to see a *movie...*

It's a shadowy landscape, almost a moonscape, at dusk, and the film is grainy—an old 8 mm film, taken during September of 1963. Trees and bushes are dark looming shapes in some semi-tropical clime with palmettos and Spanish moss and hanging vines.

Coming down an open road we see a line of two-ton military trucks. When they stop, a group of soldiers leap out and fan across the road, wearing fatigues and carrying rifles, machine guns, and mortar components.

The scene changes.... We see flashes from rifle muzzles as soldiers practice laying down fire, while their comrades rush across the field. A mortar team lobs rounds off into the distance, covering their ears with their hands.

An open jeep roars past; its headlights pick up a road sign with the shape of the state of Louisiana and a number.

Cut to five men in huddled conversation in the dusk around the jeep. They include Antonio Veciana of CIA-backed Alpha 66, and Guy Banister, whose 544 Camp Street office address is stamped on Lee Harvey Oswald's Fair Play for Cuba Committee literature even though Banister is CIA, and Oswald is supposed to be a commie symp...

Then we see a tall figure wearing civilian clothes, dark hair, a prominent nose, and deeply impressed wrinkles under his eyes, turning away from the camera to avoid being photographed. Its the infamous "Maurice Bishop," CIA officer David Atlee Phillips from the Mexico City station, who Veciana will later finger to congressional investigators as being with Oswald in Dallas just a month before the Kennedy assassination.

The camera goes slo-mo to move to another group loitering at a nearby truck. One of the men in this group turns to the camera and starts to smile, or smirk, really, the famous smirk of Lee Harvey Oswald, caught on 8mm film training with the CIA's renegade anti-Castro Cubans.

Cut to a daylight scene. Men shooting guns, posing with weapons. And there are several more long shots of Oswald wearing a black T-shirt and a ball cap, and close-ups of a round-faced man with a "fright wig" and "impossibly thick phony eyebrows."

"It's Dave Ferrie," breathed House investigator Robert Tanenbaum, today the mayor of Beverly Hills, California, when he first saw the film. "Nobody else looks like Ferrie."

Someone took a *film* of the infamous paramilitary camp in Lacombe, the camp which housed the killers of John Fitzgerald Kennedy.

"The men at the Lacombe training camp were the top terrorists in the Cuban community," American adventurer and CIA agent Gerry Patrick Hemming admitted twenty years later.

"The movie was shocking to me because it demonstrated the notion that the CIA was training, in America, a separate army," Tanenbaum said later. "It was shocking because I'm a true believer in the system and yet there are notorious characters in the system, who are being funded by the system, who are absolutely un-American. And who knows what they would do eventually.

What if we send people to Washington who they can't deal with? Out comes their secret army?"

Then something *else* happened... can you guess? No, the film didn't get *lost*... it was *stolen*. After the discovery of a film as important as the Zapruder film, this 8 mm "home movie" taken in the summer of 1963 *vanished*.

While in the custody of the House Select Committee on Assassinations, of the House of Representatives of the United States of America, it was stolen, and never recovered.

Who has the power to pull a black bag job in our nation's Capital on one of the three co-equal branches of the United States Government?

Probably not the *Ghostbusters*...

CHAPTER FOURTEEN

WHO ARE THE
BROTHERS MCLANEY?

"MIKE MCLANEY WAS a wonderful athlete, a national tennis champion, and a splendid golf hustler," New Orleans antiques dealer Dave Dixon, Barry Seal's CIA handler, had told us...

B ut none of these attributes which Dixon ascribed to his friend made McLaney important enough to burglarize the US House of Representatives.... But his training camp in Lacombe, for terrorists, mercenaries, and assassins, is a whole other story...

"One of the most significant eyewitness observations was of Ferrie, Oswald, and numerous Cubans, all dressed in military fatigues and carrying automatic rifles, conducting what appeared to be a 'military training maneuver," wrote historian Michael Kurtz.

Longtime CIA hit-man Colonel William Bishop, shortly before his death in 1990, told author Dick Russell, "I did look into Oswald's background. I'd never met him, but I'd seen him in a training film in New Orleans the past summer. He just happened to be in the group out there at the Pontchartrain camp."

In July of 1963 a group of Cuban exiles had arrived in New Orleans from Miami, according to numerous accounts. They bivouacked at the anti-Castro guerrilla training camp at Lacombe, where Marcello maintained a hunting lodge, on property belonging to Havana casino operator Mike McLaney, who worked for Meyer Lansky. After the

Miami exiles arrive Lee Oswald shows up. Now whether Oswald is patsy or conspirator or Emissary from the Spiders From Mars, what is significant here is he *was* in the company, once again, of Guy Banister, David Ferrie, and David Atlee Philips.

Had the film ever been shown, it would have demolished the "lone nut" explanation of the assassination.

When we asked engaging-but-slippery "CIA's man in '60's New Orleans" Gordon Novel if he had known the McLaney brothers, his answer was interesting.

"I knew Mike McLaney by name, a CIA guy, supposedly. Dead now. But," he continued, "here's the problem in dealing with intelligence: its a beehive. Everybody operates in separate cubicles; our operations never overlapped. Just because we were both in New Orleans doesn't mean we ever came in contact."

The CIA, which at first denied having knowledge of the training camp at Lacombe, eventually reversed field a bit, saying, "The New Orleans CIA station ignored the Christian Democratic Movement camp, since it had Agency backing."

Reversing themselves a final time in June 1975, the CIA's Jerrold Brown said "an unknown group" had backed the camp.

For its part, the stolid FBI has always had trouble lying with the panache of their better-educated brethren at the Agency. They ignored the existence of the camp; Warren Debrueys stated grimly to the House Committee on Assassinations, "because they felt one Federal Government agency should not investigate the alleged official activities of another unless specifically instructed to do so for suitable reasons by higher authority."

The Bureau does have *one* slick trick, however, which they use repeatedly in their reports. They misspell the name of whoever they're 'protecting,' so it won't turn up in computer searches later. So in a memorandum Special Agent Debrueys recalled Senator Richard Schweiker "seemed to be interested in an anti-Castro training camp which was alleged to have been located in a rural area across a lake in New Orleans. I did state that there was a case in which a search warrant was effected by me and other Special Agents of a residence located on the other side of the Lake from New Orleans some time in the Summer of 1963.... The owner of the property was a man named McLany (ph.) who I recall may have had some prior gambling connections in Cuba..."

Saying McLaney *may have had* some prior gambling connections in Cuba is akin to saying that Hitler might have had something to do with killing Jews. Southern lawman Rex Armistead told us, "The three most over-rated things in this world are home cooking, home loving and the FBI."

So who *were* Mike and Bill McLaney? Mike was, as already stated, a casino owner in Havana. One of his lieutenants, Lewis McWillie, was Jack Ruby's best friend. When Fidel Castro took power, Mike McLaney was arrested, then freed, and continued to operate under Castro in hopes of becoming gambling czar of Cuba, hopes nurtured by having paid a $102,000 bribe to Fidel Castro's Ministry of Gambling, future Watergate burglar Frank Sturgis.

When his Casino Nacional was nationalized McLaney lost at least $7 million. His brother Bill owned the Carousel Club in Las Vegas. It is presumably 'coincidence' that Ruby's club in Dallas was also called the Carousel Club...

But when *Life* magazine printed a story linking McLaney with Meyer Lansky, he filed a multimillion-dollar lawsuit. The magazine produced newspaper clippings confirming that no casino operated in Havana without Lansky's consent; the suit was thrown out.

Because of the *Life* story the Miami Police began a brief investigation of McLaney. "Mr. McLaney named some of his close friends," their report said. "Those named included J. Edgar Hoover, John S. Knight, publisher of the *Miami Herald*, and Rocky Pomerantz, Chief of the Miami Beach Police Department. He (McLaney) stated that he could use these people as references, along with the Chief of Police and Mayor of New Orleans."

McLaney could probably have quit after mentioning Hoover. But Mob guys like to boast.

But fame is the kiss of death to mobsters and spooks like John Gotti or Barry Seal. McLaney is no exception. His notoriety finally prompted the Internal Revenue Service to file income tax evasion charges him. He was convicted of evading $118,000 in taxes, but was sentenced, typically, to just three months in Federal prison.

Being connected means never having to say you're sorry.

Of his erstwhile employer, Gerry Hemming stated, "Mike McLaney was in with some of William K. Harvey's people and JMWAVE type assholes."

CIA agent Harvey had been, literally, licensed to kill, and ran the CIA assassination operation ZRIRIFLE. Its targets were heads of state, and it recruited a pool of assassins, including Thomas Eli Davis, involved with Jack Ruby in gunrunning operations since 1959.

Even the apartment house on Magazine Street where Lee Oswald lived during his stay in New Orleans was probably not just an ordinary apartment building...

Ed Haslam, author of a book about Dave Ferrie, told us of visiting Oswald's apartment house while scouting locations for a Frontline documentary, and meeting the current owner, who stated he had purchased the property from "a guy with a business out at the racetrack named McLaney."

Mike McLaney's brother, William Julius McLaney, had operated a racehorse feed business at the New Orleans Fairgrounds. If true, Oswald's apartment was a CIA safe house.... No wonder J Edgar Hoover was concerned with wrapping up the Warren Commission in such short order.

The raid on McLaney's camp netted a large cache of armaments and eleven men, arrested and then released. Their number included:

—Richard Lauchli, an arms dealer who supplied Fidel in the late 1950's, and co-founder of the Minutemen. In 1976 he told the *St. Louis Post-Dispatch* that federal law enforcement agencies "know more than they are telling about the assassination of President Kennedy, but I don't want to say which ones because I'm friendly with them. Some day it will all come out but now just isn't the time."

Lauchli's fellow Minuteman, John Thomas Masen, was middleman for military weapons smuggling from Fort Hood through Dallas, an operation with Jack Ruby as paymaster.

—Mobster Sam Benton. "Sam would never get near anything that might explode," Mike McLaney had said about Benton. Benton was a con artist, setting up the Cuban Refugee Relief, for which Layton Martens and David Ferrie collected money, before police began looking into the fact that over 90 percent of the money contributed was being eaten up by "administrative overhead."

—Cuban exile fighter Victor Panque. Carlos Quiroga told the New Orleans District Attorney's Office that Panque was in charge of training at this camp. "His file contains no information to indicate connection in the Lacombe, Louisiana, area," the CIA said.

—'Ricardo' Davis, who told a fellow worker later, who in turn reported it to the FBI, that while living in New Orleans his living expenses were paid for by an anti-Castro organization known as the Minutemen. Davis stated Lee Harvey Oswald was also connected in some manner with the Minutemen organization. With assistance of John Birch Society members, Davis said he had set up a training site in Lacombe.

Fidel's Commies later straightened out our feeble FBI gumshoes. In a documentary never shown publicly in the U.S., they fingered the Lake Pontchartrain bust as the "turning point" in the war for control of America.

When the FBI let everybody go with no charges being filed, the documentary said, it was a clear signal to extremist CIA Mafia and Cuban exile elements that Kennedy's policies were no longer being carried out, and that Kennedy himself was no longer being protected from executive sanction.

A permanent solution could now be devised.

CHAPTER FIFTEEN

DID BARRY SEAL
FLY A GETAWAY PLANE
OUT OF DALLAS?

IN THE AFTERNOON of November 22, 1963 John Fitzgerald Kennedy was murdered. Several hours later Dave Ferrie's friend Lee Harvey Oswald was captured by the Dallas police. At about 1:00 P.M. that same afternoon, half an hour after the president was shot, neighbors who lived along the road that runs by Redbird Airport near Dallas began calling the police to report a private plane behaving peculiarly. For an hour it had been revving its engines, they reported, not on the runway but parked at the end of the airstrip on a grassy area next to the fence. The noise prevented nearby residents from hearing their TVs, as news came over about the terrible events in downtown Dallas. Shortly thereafter the plane took off.

An FBI file of March 10, 1967, describes statements made by an air traffic controller Louis Gaudin, on duty at Redbird at the time. We tracked Gaudin down in retirement in the tiny town of Long Branch, Texas, and coaxed him into speaking for the first time about the shocking events he had witnessed. "I filed that report in '67 for only one reason," Gaudin said. "I had received a visit from an assistant district attorney in Jim Garrison's office, who showed me four pictures of possible pilots involved in the incident that day. One of them was a weird-looking character with a funny-looking wig. A week later I saw him on the news. They said his name was David Ferrie, and that he had committed suicide. That's when I smelled a rat."

"I was an air traffic controller working in the tower at Redbird that day. When I came on shift I was told we'd received a bulletin to report any suspicious activity immediately to an FAA Security number. And we did, we kept calling that number all afternoon, but all we got was a busy signal. Then, when we heard they had caught the 'lone gunman,' I guess they called it, we stopped calling, and let the matter drop."

And that's where the matter rested until Gaudin became alarmed at the death of a man whose picture he had just been shown. He called the FBI, and filed the report which, he said, became something of a burden to him for the rest of his life. "There was no Freedom of Information Act back then," he says today. "That is what's created some problems for me."

From his perch atop the control tower, Gaudin had noticed something suspicious about the three well-dressed men in business suits standing alongside several suitcases beside a Comanche painted green-and-white. He grew so suspicious, he related, that when the plane took off, on runway 17, he asked the pilot if he needed any assistance, just to establish contact. The pilot said no. Gaudin then asked which way the plane was heading. The pilot stated south.

Gaudin the watched as the plane flew south for two miles, made a hard left, and flew *north*… towards Love Field. The pilot had lied. Suspicions now fully aroused, he went to the control tower's receiver and listened as the plane made an approach and landed at Love Field, eight miles north of Redbird.

What happened later clearly indicates that Gaudin witnessed something he had no business seeing. From the control tower, he says, he was too far away to be able to identify the people aboard the plane. But there was one person who *could*: Merrit Goble, who ran the fixed-wing operation, TexAir, at Redbird Field.

"Merrit and I were friends," Gaudin relates. "So one day after filing the FBI report, I went down to see if the FBI had been to visit him too. They hadn't, he told me. I asked him if he had anything, gas receipts or any record of the fueling of the plane in question. And he acted very strangely, and told me it was none of my business. He said 'I will only answer questions from bona fide law enforcement authority.' And that I've always thought was real strange, because, like I said, we were friends."

Merrit Goble died last year, taking any secrets he possessed to his grave. But Redbird Field was not just a small general aviation airport, according to a native Texan, former CIA pilot Gary Eitel, who owned a facility there in the 1970's. "The FAA had its general aviation headquarters there. Howard Hughes had a huge old WWII hanger there, with heavy security, people from Wackenhut all over the place. And there were the Porter planes from General Harry Byrd's outfit."

Was Barry Seal at the controls of that suspicious Comanche? He did own a Comanche, like the one drawing suspicion at Redbird. And even without a picture of Seal with the CIA assassination squad Operation 40 taken in Mexico City on January 22, 1963, based on the evidence and given a government at all *interested* in solving the crime, it is clear that Seal—at the very least— should have been considered a prime suspect in an investigation into that suspicious-looking 'getaway' plane.

A spectacular pilot… a 'known associate' of all of the 'usual suspects'… David Ferrie, Carlos Marcello, Guy Banister, and Grady Partin (more on him later)…

Seal, a gunrunner to Cuba, a veteran of the Bay of Pigs, and a CIA pilot, was never questioned. In the protracted and indifferently motivated investigations to follow—and this *is* highly significant—Barry Seal was "protected."

Lacking an eyewitness, both willing to come forward, and enough of a survivalist to live to testify—the truth of that day in Dallas will never be completely known. We believe Seal did indeed fly that 'getaway' plane out of Dallas, and that this fact remained his 'ace in the hole' for the rest of his life during his often-acrimonious dealings with his superiors.

For the purposes of history, it appears indisputable to us at this time that Garrison got it (mostly) right. Back in Coup Central, New Orleans, Oswald's arrest must have been received as horrifying news to Ferrie and Carlos Marcello, who would otherwise have been celebrating their triumph over Bobby Kennedy's Justice Department that very day in the Federal Courthouse…

Now a live Oswald was screaming "patsy!"

So that evening Ferrie rushed off into a blinding thunderstorm in his car with two young male companions to Texas, to go ice-skating, he says. This is a clumsy and implausible lie; Ferrie probably was coordinating the finishing of the job.

We can all certainly imagine what a cop would say if *any of us* used that line. "Tell it to the judge." Do people drive all night through blinding rainstorms—right after the murder of their blood enemies—to ice-skate?

What other reasons might there be to explain why the FBI and Secret Service showed such disinterest in David Ferrie as an assassination suspect? If their investigations were controlled by the coup plotters themselves, they would have acted exactly, we think, as they did, in fact, act.

And we are left with the chilling certainty that the rulers of the present Republic shot their way into power, just as Hitler's Nazis did.

Some have said that Ferrie's mission to Houston and Galveston was to himself fly a getaway plane, hooking up with the plane from Redbird and then continuing overseas…

Raymond Broshears, a roommate and friend of David Ferrie, told writer Dick Russell, "David was to meet a plane. He was going to fly these people on to Mexico, and eventually to South Africa, which did not have an extradition treaty with the United States. They left from some little airfield between Dallas and Fort Worth, and David had a twin engine plane ready for them and that was the purpose of his mad dash through a driving rainstorm from New Orleans."

Redbird Airport is a little airfield between Dallas and Fort Worth. Broshears sounds as if he got the story just a little garbled in translation.

Sam Giancana later confessed to participation in the assassination, stating a planeload of killers were flown to the Texas border, according to his brother Chuckie Giancana, in *Double Cross*.

From there they were, supposedly, driven to a Mob hideout in Monterrey, Mexico, where Giancana himself hid out after the slaying.

In addition to the well-known suspects, Chuckie says 'Momo' 'said that two of the hitters had been Santos Trafficante's "friends," one a crooked former Batista cop (Felix Rodriguez?) and the other a US Customs officer.

The noose began to tighten around David Ferrie less than 48 hours after the assassination. On the morning of November 25 an FBI teletype said Ferrie's library card had been found on Oswald when he was arrested.

Savvy Dave knew he was hot, and stayed away from New Orleans until the following Monday, when he was interviewed by the FBI, the Secret Service, and the New Orleans police…

Transcripts of these interviews were (*natch!*) immediately classified. They were never mentioned in the FBI summary report and were not turned over to the Warren Commission.

Following the theory that the most likely suspects are the people who *should* have been considered the most likely suspects—if this weren't Casablanca—deserving special scrutiny today should be Felix Rodriguez, unquestioningly one of the CIA's most successful assassins.

In 1959 Rodriguez was a top cop in Cuba under Batista. When Batista fled to Miami Rodriguez went with him, along with Frank Sturgis and Chi Chi Quintero. Officially Rodriguez didn't join the CIA until 1967, well after both the CIA invasion of Cuba in which he participated, and the assassination of JFK. But records recently uncovered show he actually joined the CIA in 1961, when he was recruited by a certain fella' named Bush, which is, Rodriguez says, how he became such a "close personal friend of Bush."

Rodriguez and Bush share another bond. Neither remembers where he was when Kennedy was shot. Rodriguez, asked by a Rolling Stone reporter where he was the day JFK was shot, claimed he couldn't remember. And on the day of the assassination George Bush was in Texas, too, but he denies knowing exactly where… and Texas is an awfully big state…

The *Nation* magazine discovered a memo written by J. Edgar Hoover on November 29, 1963, summarizing oral "briefings" given on the day after the JFK murder to, among others, "Mr. George Bush of the Central Intelligence Agency."

This puts Rodriguez and Bush in company with a few select others who can't recall where they were when Kennedy was shot…. Richard Nixon, and Howard Hunt, both of whose stories changed so often as to be embarrassing to anyone with a decent regard for tradecraft.

Nixon, Hunt, Rodriguez, and Bush. Not the Disappeared Ones… The Forgetful Ones.

Was Bush CIA as far back as '63? When the question came up in his Presidential campaign, Bush had the White House stonewall the matter. But Bush has been, it has been reliably reported, with the CIA since before 1961, using Zapata Oil, as 'cover' for Agency activities with anti-Castro groups before and after the Bay of Pigs.

CIA agent David Atlee Philips should also be called in for questioning. Now that he's dead it's probably even—almost—politically feasible. Author Anthony Summers found a deposition of Howard Hunt in which he answered a question concerning the radical anti-Castro Cuban organization DRE, with which Oswald was associated in New Orleans. Hunt said, "The DRE. Dave Phillips ran that for us. But that is classified, I think. He was the head of it…"

This admission clearly links Oswald's activities in New Orleans to Phillips and the CIA; also, to Dallas, the DRE safe-house in Dallas, the gun running involving Jack Ruby, and the renegade training camp which the CIA denies existed on the shores of Lake Pontchartrain…

a place so top secret that film taken there of Lee Oswald, David Atlee Philips, Guy Banister and Dave Ferrie had to be stolen from the House Select Committee.

The question always arises of how a conspiracy so vast and intricately-planned and involving so many people, could possibly have been kept secret all this time. It is usually phrased like this: "Why hasn't anybody talked?"

The answer is simple. They *have*. The talking started before the assassination and has continued to this day.

Carlos Marcello bragged in front of Ed Becker that Kennedy would be killed and described how it would be done...

Santo Trafficante, Jr. stated Kennedy would be killed...

Joseph Milteer, a 'right-wing nut,' said Kennedy would be killed and even described how it would be done...

Johnny Rosselli, Sam Giancana's right-hand man, told Jack Anderson that Ruby was "their man, and was ordered to silence Oswald."

Lyndon Johnson's mistress, Madeleine Brown, said Johnson implied before Kennedy was killed that it was going to happen...

Marita Lorenz, CIA agent, relative of Ambassador Henry Cabot Lodge, and mistress of Fidel Castro, said under oath that she was with Frank Sturgis, Felix Rodriguez, and a group of anti-Castro Cubans present at the Kennedy assassination...

Even David Atlee Phillips, alias 'Maurice Bishop,' perpetrator of the multiple Oswalds, said before he died that 'fringe' elements of U.S. intelligence *may* have been involved in the conspiracy...

Sam Giancana. Homer Echevarria. And many more not mentioned here, because this book's focus is not on any one single atrocity, but on the "team" to which Barry Seal belonged, 'the boys,' and on their amazing 40-year long crime spree...

The American embassy in Mexico City housed the largest CIA station in the Western Hemisphere in the 1960s, home to the CIA assassination squad, dubbed Operation Forty.

Mexico City was where a photographer immortalized Barry Seal and his CIA/Mafia cohorts in a picture taken in a nightclub on January 22, 1963, in the company of Frank Sturgis, CIA operative William Seymour, and Felix Rodriguez.

David Atlee Phillips *aka* Maurice Bishop was the CIA's covert action chief in Mexico during 1962-63, when this picture was taken. Reliable testimony has him meeting with Oswald in Dallas before the assassination.

In *Deadly Secrets*, authors Warren Hinkle and William Turner name Raul Villaverde, Rafael 'Chi Chi' Quintero, Lois Posada Carriles, Felix Rodriguez, Frank Sturgis, and Ricardo Chavez as members of Operation Forty.

Joaquin Sanjenis directed Operation Forty until his death, under the overall control of Howard Hunt. Thomas Clines, the notorious Edwin Wilson and "Blond Ghost" Ted Shackley, Mr. Spook himself, were all involved with Operation Forty.

Frank Sturgis, member of the team that broke into the Watergate complex in 1972, admitted to having been part of Operation Forty.

So was Barry Seal. "Yeah, Barry was Op 40," Gerald Hemming confirmed to us. "He flew in killer teams inside the island (Cuba) before the invasion to take out Fidel."

Richard Nixon is generally given credit for planning Operation 40, during his 1959 campaign for President. After Batista was kicked out and Castro came to power, American corporations which Castro nationalized—Pepsi, Ford, Big Oil, the Syndicate— asked Nixon to put the hex on Fidel.

Nixon started planning Operation Forty. It's "him" all over.

CIA Colonel William Bishop told author Dick Russell about Operation Forty, showing him a series of photographs of "Latin-looking individuals. On the backs of the pictures were the words "Special talent 1960-65, Ice pick man... Butcher... Sniper and demo [demolition] expert... Propaganda... Knife man... Pilot and navigator... Mutilator."

Bishop said, "We weren't playing a nice game."

Russell wrote that on some of the pictures were inscribed "Destino-Mexico," and asked whether this meant that these particular people had operated out of Mexico. "Yep," said Bishop, "A lot of times they would cover their tracks by declaring themselves as nationals of Mexico or Nicaragua, Panama. It didn't make any difference."

In *The Man Who Wasn't There* Russell wrote that Bishop conceded that he had been in Mexico City "two or three times in 1963." When Russell asked about his purpose there, Bishop replied that he would rather make no comment on that, saying it was a matter of national security.

"It had something to do with Cuba," Bishop said, "but not as such."

When Chuck Giancana discussed Mob Boss Sam Giancana's strategic move to Mexico in early 1963, he touched on Op Forty...

"It was to be an all-out, no-holds-barred Latin American push. Mooney settled into a lavish Mexico City apartment and went right to work, drawing on the expertise and mammoth resources of the recently formed CIA team of assassins and operatives specifically trained for

Latin American clandestine operations. CIA insiders jokingly dubbed the team the "White Hand," an allusion to the Mafia killer progenitors the "Black Hand'"

In March-April 1962, Seal associate Gerald Patrick Hemming was approached by Guy Banister, he says, to assassinate John Kennedy. Hemming said he turned him down, saying, "Are you fucking crazy? "Banister is also implicated by Cuban General Fabian Escalante, CIA Colonel William Bishop, FBI and CIA documents.

Hemming said, "Colonel Bishop worked for General Magruder (of military intelligence) too, just like (the CIA's William) Harvey. Harvey worked both sides. He worked in direct contact with Sullivan and Hoover while he was on the CIA Payroll."

"A lot of these people had different loyalties, because back in World War II they'd excluded OSS from the Western Hemisphere. So it was the FBI guys that had all the Intel when CIA and INR and the State Department picked 'em up."

This description fits Barry Seal's recruiter, David Ferrie, who 'played' in South America during World War II.

The central thesis of most researchers on the assassination is that it was the work of the Mafia, elements of the CIA, and right-wing Cuban exiles aligned with Guy Banister, Clay Shaw, and David Ferrie, all of whom were CIA-connected.

Jack Ruby was Sam Giancana's "man in Dallas" for years, running guns for the CIA as well. He had demonstrated loyalty and the ability to work with both groups during the planning for the Bay of Pigs invasion. Ruby had friendships with undercover agents, with men like Oswald, and even offered David Ferrie a job in his Carousel Club. So it is logical that it was Ruby who was ordered to silence Oswald.

And Barry Seal knew them all.

But the most persuasive evidence that Barry Seal was "in" on the hit came nine years after the assassination, when he and six others were on trial for attempting in 1972 to send seven tons of plastic C4 explosive to anti-Castro Cubans in Mexico. In the middle of the trial the judge received an anonymous letter, threatening to blow the cover off matters pertaining to "national security" unless the charges are dismissed.

Its contents, reprinted here in full, reveal a bald attempt to blackmail a Federal judge into dismissing felony charges, by convincingly demonstrating first-hand knowledge of the Kennedy assassination... exactly the same threat Nixon tried to use to get the FBI to call off the

Watergate investigation. Though the letter is anonymous, the envelope bearing it is in Barry Seal's handwriting:

Dear Mr. Lestage:

Due to personal initiative and desire to see justice done this letter is mailed to you and your associates.

The United States two-count indictment against seven men on charges of conspiracy to ship "implements of war" out of the United States, without having approval of the government, has no chance to succeed.

In the years 1956, 1957, and 1958 I worked for the CJ Simpson de Cuba Drilling Company, which had three rotary drilling rigs operating in Cuba.

Whether you or any of your associates are aware of the number of "implements of war" shipped by that company out of the United States as components of drilling equipment, I have no idea. But I advise you to find out!

These shipments of "implements of war" by the CIA had no known open approval of the United States Government. Yet I am sure that your attitude towards it would be that as long as it is done by a federal agency, it is correct.

If this is your assumption, then you are dead wrong. I can name names of agents involved in these shipments.

This whole sorry mess of the CIA putting Fidel Castro into a position to overthrow the government of Juan Batista has never been told to the public.

An open court of law would be a fine place to bring the truth of this entire matter out.

My testimony to this affair of 1956,1957, and 1958 as being relevant to the government's case against these seven men cannot be repudiated.

As you can see, this letter is unsigned, and for good reason. Copies of this letter are filed with a number of people, and you are herein advised that mention of this letter will be made in the effort to squash the two-count indictment against the seven.

If you have any reply, hand-carry your reply, open and not sealed, to Lee Young of the Alexandria Bureau of the *Shreveport Times*, who will, in turn, deliver it to me.

145

Signed,
Former liaison officer for CJ Simpson de Cuba A 45177

What was *this* all about? "Lee Young" cannot, 27 years later, be found. But CJ Simpson de Cuba *can...*

In a Secret Service report from Chicago about former CJ Simpson de Cuba employee Homer Echevarria, it stated Echevarria had had *foreknowledge* of the assassination. The incident was found particularly disturbing by the House Select Committee on Assassinations, especially given that it had come to the attention of the Secret Service within days after John Kennedy's death.

The memorandum reported a tip from an informant that a Cuban activist, Homer S. Echevarria, in a discussion about an illegal arms sale, said that "his group had 'plenty of money' and that his backers would proceed [with the arms deal] 'as soon as we take care of Kennedy."

When the Secret Service investigated Echevarria they discovered that his father had been a pioneer of the oil industry in Cuba, and that he had left Cuba in 1960 for Miami and then Dallas, where he worked for the CJ Simpson Oil Drilling Company.

In a Secret Service report after the assassination, an informant "reported that he had knowledge of a group of Chicago Cubans, allegedly anti-Castro, who were bitterly opposed to President Kennedy, including Cuban exile Homer Echevarria, who was connected with the DRE and the 30th of November Movement, who learned from Paulino Sierra that President Kennedy was going to be assassinated prior to November 22, 1963."

"For the information of all offices concerned," the Secret Service reported, "(Moseley) advised on November 26, 1963, that he had been attempting to negotiate a sale of machine guns to one Homer S. Echevarria, and that Echevarria allegedly made a comment the day before the assassination of President John F. Kennedy that 'we now have plenty of money as soon as 'we' (or 'they') take care of Kennedy.'"

In the estimation of Maurice G. Martineau, acting special agent in charge of the Secret Service office in Chicago, it had been a hot lead. A reliable informant, Thomas Moseley, had told one of his agents the day *before* the assassination that a Cuban exile with whom he had been negotiating the sale of machine guns had boasted his group now had "plenty of money" and would make the buy "as soon as we take care of Kennedy."

In an urgent communication to headquarters Martineau advised he was undertaking a top-priority investigation. From what Echevarria disclosed, he learned that the arms deal was being financed by Paulino

Sierra's provisional government with money obtained from "hoodlum elements," who were "not restricted to Chicago."

The House Select Committee discovered that the organization run by Paulino Sierra was backed financially by organized crime.

It would have blown the case wide open. Martineau prepared to place an undercover agent inside the Echevarria group. An expanding investigation would have uncovered the Sierra cabal's link to the Lake Pontchartrain camp, the Mafia, and the Castro assassination plots, which, in turn, would have opened a Pandora's box of leads to Ruby and Oswald.

But after LBJ ordered it to assume primary jurisdiction in the JFK case the FBI effectively choked off the investigation. The Bureau "made clear that it wanted the Secret Service to terminate its investigation," said the House Select Committee. When the Secret Service complied, turning over its files, the FBI chose not to pursue the matter.

Less than a week later newspapers across the nation were reporting, "an exhaustive FBI report now nearly ready for the White House will indicate that Lee Harvey Oswald was the lone and unaided assassin of President Kennedy."

One of the three so-called Dallas "tramps," Chauncey Holt, testified that Homer Echevarria was supposed to have been his contact in Dallas when Kennedy was killed.

And the two exile Cuban groups with Echevarria worked, the DRE and the 30th of November Movement, were the same groups using the CIA's renegade training camp on the north shore of Lake Pontchartrain...

Evidence was surfacing, within just a few days of JFK's assassination, of networks of militant Cubans and Mafiosi with connections to Lee Harvey Oswald and involvement in gun running to Cuba... with one of the Cubans even bragging about "taking care of Kennedy" before the assassination took place.

Homer Echevarria, with foreknowledge of the Kennedy assassination, worked for the CJ Simpson Oil Drilling Company...

And nine years after the JFK assassination Barry Seal is pointedly referencing this same obscure company, CJ Simpson, in an attempt to blackmail a Federal judge into dismissing his indictment.

Seal was using the same threat Richard Nixon tried to used to wiggle out of Watergate...

Knowledge of 'that Bay of Pigs Thing.'

Finally we turned back to writers Sally Denton and Roger Morris, from whom we had first heard a rumor of Barry Seal's involvement in the Kennedy assassination. When we inquired where *they* had first heard it, we learned from author Sally Denton that her father had been Mike McLaney's lawyer.

Small world.

CHAPTER SIXTEEN

THINGS AIN'T ALWAYS BEEN JES' *RIGHT* DOWN HERE

LATE JUNE IS THE TIME of year in Louisiana when the Spanish moss hangs limply in the heavy air, and it was no surprise when Saturday the 26th of June, 1969 dawned hot and humid in the muggy swamps north of New Orleans... so hot that even the live oaks dotting the antebellum Oaklawn plantation home outside of Clinton were letting their branches droop to the ground. On the airstrip adjoining the property a small private plane made a poor takeoff, narrowly missed a tree while struggling to gain altitude and went into a nosedive, plummeting to earth from 100 feet in the air.

Two men were killed instantly. One, the pilot Jerry Sylvester, was Louisiana Teamster Boss Edward "Grady" Partin's 'strong-arm' man in Clinton...

Just *before* turning into charred flesh in burning wreckage Jerry had been talking to investigators for Jim Garrison's probe, about CIA agent and International Trade Mart exec Clay Shaw, who had been seen in Clinton with Dave Ferrie and Lee Oswald in the feverish months before the Kennedy assassination.

"He could tell you who Shaw knew in Clinton, and why he was there," a local informant had muttered darkly to a Garrison staffer.

Garrison had been successful in tracking down numerous witnesses who had seen Oswald and Ferrie together during the summer before the assassination. In addition to the eyewitness sightings of the two men in military fatigues carrying automatic rifles in military training maneuvers in Lacombe, witnesses saw them together at a private party, where they discussed a coup d'etat against the Kennedy administration, at a local New Orleans amusement park, in the Napoleon House Bar in the French Quarter, and at a political meeting in Barry Seal's hometown Baton Rouge.

Oswald and Ferrie traveled extensively together that summer. Six separate witnesses testified they saw them both in the company of Clay Shaw in Clinton, a subject about which Jerry Sylvester was talking just before he died.

According to the brother of Sylvester's passenger, who perished even though *he* hadn't blabbed about anything... even the fact that Jerry Sylvester had cleared his meeting with Garrison's investigators with Grady Partin beforehand wasn't enough to keep his plane airborne...

Sylvester had told investigators that he'd checked with Ed Partin before talking to them, and that he would "tell Partin what we discussed, because he doesn't want to do anything to hurt Partin."

Garrison's investigators assured him all they were concerned with was Clay Shaw...

Gerry Patrick Hemming had this to say about people who 'talk.' "You're 'card' that keeps you alive may be that you're keeping quiet, or if you aren't keeping quiet, that you're giving out wrong answers that satisfy the people who are going to let you live."

Sylvester's death, which illustrates the fact that there is a large cast of characters in the Louisiana contingent of the Kennedy assassination drama, became more interesting after we had learned that Barry Seal was a 'close associate,' as they say, of Grady Partin's, the undisputed lord of Local No. 5 of the Teamster Union in Baton Rouge, and whose hiring hall was a hangout rivaling any Mob 'social club' in Queens.

Barry's childhood friend and smuggling buddy James Poche told us, "Barry was hanging out at Grady Partin's all during this time (62-63). We used to live together in (Barry's mother) Mary Lou's spare bedroom, and he was involved as usual in all sorts of strange things. I remember, for example, helping him figure out how to drop 50,000 political leaflets over Baton Rouge, with pictures of apples with a worm in them. It got a guy named "Apple" Sanders un-elected from the State Senate that year, as I recall."

What football is to Nebraska, state politics is to Louisiana: a contact sport, one in which Barry Seal was engaged at Grady Partin's behest. An old Louisiana Teamster official confirmed Barry's friendship with Grady, telling of Seal's frequent appearances at the Teamster local.

"Hell, back then we was kings in this state," Butch McKeown told us. "We ruled this state back then."

Who is the 'we' Butch is referring to? Clearly, we needed to learn more about Grady Partin...

In 1967, at the height of the media smear campaign against Garrison led by Henry Luce's spear-carriers at *Time* and *Life*, Edward Partin was featured prominently in a *Life* cover story about David Ferrie and the goings-on in New Orleans.

"I'm a Teamster, and some people think, a hard one," Partin told the magazine. "I've been in fights and jails and packed a gun, and I've been shot twice and knifed once. I joined the Marines but hit an officer and went to the brig on bread and water. And once I helped roll a sailor. They put me in front of a summary court and gave me a bad conduct discharge."

Exactly the right credentials needed for a quick rise to the top of the Teamsters... Partin, who in between knife fights did three years in the Washington State Reformatory, joined the union in the early 1950's and moved to Baton Rouge. After Kennedy's assassination, Irving Davidson, a Washington lobbyist, Lansky associate, and Washington 'public relations man' doing business with government officials in Israel and Latin America, told the FBI that he had heard there was a photograph of Partin in the presence of Jack Ruby.

So, had there been a place card reading "Edward Grady Partin" at the table of those sharpening their knives for Kennedy? Partin knew Ruby and perhaps even Oswald, according to Professor Peter Dale Scott, through their common activity: smuggling guns to Castro.

"Are you aware that Partin was under investigation for smuggling weapons to Cuba?" asked an attorney of a character witness for Partin during one of the Hoffa trials which were the battlefield upon which Bobby Kennedy fought his losing war with Organized Crime.

"I was right up there on several occasions when they were loading the guns," Partin admitted, about his Cuban gunrunning. "Hoffa was directing the whole thing."

The solicitousness of so many patriotic Americans in making sure that Castro had enough weapons to defend himself is, even 40 years later, truly astonishing. Without a doubt Fidel Castro, thanks to the CIA/Mafia alliance, was the best-armed Communist dictator ever to run afoul of the United States.

Partin's account of the Teamster assist to Organized Crime's weapons smuggling to Castro implicated union officials William Presser and Irving Davidson, who we have just seen has been trying to implicate *him*.

Grady Partin had taken very seriously the possibility, after Garrison began his investigation of David Ferrie, that he too would be ensnared in the probe, through a story being told that Ferrie had once been *his* pilot, too.

What were Barry Seal's ties with Grady Partin?

We visited a savvy native for a quick tour of the Louisiana political 'swamp,' and Bill Maux, veteran TWA purser and friend and associate of Barry Seal's, took us into his confidence during a long lunch at a riverside French restaurant located in the darkest depths of Acadiana. Over crawfish étouffée he gave us a short course in the arcane relationships between political power centers in the state of Louisiana...

"I remember one of Mr. Hoover's assistants by the name of John Sullivan came to New Orleans and spoke at the American Legion," Maux began, speaking about former FBI agent John Sullivan, a Banister intimate who died soon after the assassination. "Sullivan used to talk to Judge Leander Perez, who was very concerned about the activities in New Orleans," explained Maux patiently.

"Now Leander *controlled* Plaquemines Parish, y'understand, and even though there was a state law on the books against gambling in Louisiana, there is only one road in-and-out of Plaquemines Parish, and Leander controlled it. And Leander dearly *loved* his slot machines..."

"But when McKeithen was elected Governor, he appointed a certain Colonel Grevenberg to head the State Police, and with orders to show the flag in Leander's parish, and 'take care' of the slot machines."

Maux smiled. "Grevenberg proceeded to go down there to 'take care' of the slot machines, but very soon found himself more-or-less literally on his butt—with Leander looking down at him— saying, 'stay the hell out of my Parish.' And Grevenberg did *not* go back."

Well into the modern era, we had just learned, the head of the Louisiana State Police was unwelcome in parts of the state.

Maux said, "Barry Seal's first helicopter came from Leander Perez... that didn't mean Barry really *knew* Leander. He *didn't* know Leander. If you weren't family you didn't know Leander."

Another Leander Perez associate was George Singleton, according to the House Select Committee...

"Mr. George Singleton was close to Judge Leander Perez in the fight against integration," Banister's partner Joseph Oster testified. "And he and Mr. Guy Banister were also close friends. Singleton wrote for the Citizens Council and Colonel Buford Balter, Mr. Singleton, Mr. Stewart and others around Mr. Banister were interested in ultra-conservative politics. Alvin Cobb was also a friend of Banister. Mr. Cobb was a supporter of the KKK..."

The informant whose whisperings put Jerry Sylvester into a dive at the opening of this chapter lived next door to Alvin Cobb's brother, Lloyd, Clay Shaw's superior at the International Trade Mart.... We have seen rent receipts from Barry Seal's Helicopter Airways in the 60's, which at that time housed itself in Clay Shaw's International Trade Mart...

In 1973 James Earl Ray swore that he had provided his attorneys with two telephone numbers given to him by his mysterious CIA "handler, "the anti-Castro Cuban who Ray was only ever able to identify as 'Raoul.'

Predictably, Ray had first met 'Raoul' in New Orleans' sister city of Intrigue in the North, Montreal.

Ray told the *Atlanta Journal:* "Look, I know the telephone numbers of two men in Louisiana. The authorities could have got their names."

One of those two numbers Ray "knew" rang into a line controlled by Edward Grady Partin.

This all came into sharp focus one day in conversation with Southern lawman Rex Armistead...

"Grady Partin had been a part of the infamous Murder Incorporated, along with another Louisiana mobster named Onofio Pecora," he told us. Armistead, who deserves his own book, had spent the late Seventies as head of a multi-agency Organized Crime Task Force in Now Orleans...

"You know," he once informed us casually, "things ain't always been jes' *right* down here."

During a two-year long investigation, this was, hands-down, the most true thing we heard.

CHAPTER SEVENTEEN

SINNERS IN HEAVEN

WITH JACK KENNEDY reduced to a flickering flame over a gravesite in Arlington National Cemetery; 'the boys' were firmly in the saddle, and ready to pursue their dreams in that section of the planet known as Southeast Asia. They moved to Laos, because that was where the money was, a man who spent over 20 years in Special Forces, who we'll call Colonel Nick, told us. He'd been stationed in Laos in the mid-'60's, he said, in charge of an 'A' base in the hills. His job had been to pay hill tribesmen $6 per kilo for their opium.

"The Chinese only paid $4, and that was how we "bought" their allegiance," this Special ops vet told us. "And once a month we would pile all of the acquired opium down on the end of the dirt runway and burn it in a bonfire. Then, as I recall, some of the guys would run around quick to get downwind. There's not that much to do in Laos."

Everything changed in early '65, Col. Nick said. Then an order came down to burn no more opium, but to "store it" instead, for removal to a more "secure" location." That order coincided with Ted Shackley, Oliver North and Richie Secord coming into the theater of operations," he stated crisply.

Soon the planes from Air America started landing in Laos much more frequently, then lumbering out towards Saigon filled with opium, where their cargo created thousands of GI addicts who brought their habits home with them. This is such an open secret that they even made a movie about it, *Air America,* starring Mel Gibson. What they don't tell you in the movie, said Nick, is about the number of Air America planes that were subsequently brought down by friendly fire, by grunts on the ground who knew how dirty the war had become.

"Do you want to know why the Vietnam War lasted so long?" he asked. "Because too many people were making too much money."

During a time when the 'official story' of Barry Seal's career has him flying for TWA, numerous sources stated they were spotting him in Southeast Asia. "Barry Seal did a lot of damn good stuff in the late 60's," CIA pilot Tosh Plumlee told us. "In 67 and 68 he was with Air America in South Vietnam and Laos doing Search and Destroy and Special Ops with Ted Shackley's boys. He'd been recruited for Special Ops because of the 'Cuban thing.'"

Was Seal's job at TWA just his 'cover?' Several military intelligence veterans said 'yes,' including one who told us he had first encountered Seal while flying into and out of Burma's Golden Triangle, tracing international flows of money for military intelligence.

"Barry and I were both in Southeast Asia during the same time frame," one stated. "I began seeing his name on cables in early 1964. In retrospect, after spending years trying to piece everything together, what I think was going on was half of us was chasing the other half... but we were *all* reporting to the same people."

"In '68 I was in San Francisco, and by then he had become a 747 captain, flying internationally," said one of Barry's closest lifelong friends, Joe Hurston. "I know that Barry was in Special Forces at the same time, and that he made some extraordinary flights while working for TWA, over in the Orient."

"I worked for Barry all during those years," Joe continued. "I ran several businesses for him: Seal Sky Service, Aerial Advertising, Seal's Texaco. And I would be the one to pick him up at New Orleans International Airport when he'd return from overseas."

"What did he tell you he was doing?" we asked.

"Very often he would just shake his head, and say, 'Man, if you only knew where I've just been!'"

"Was that it?"

"Once or twice, he said a little more. One time he told about having flown a 707 into Southeast Asia, landing on an isolated runway somewhere, and taxiing underground."

"What do you mean? He taxied *underground?*"

Hurston shrugged. "That's what he said. I'm just telling you what he told me."

Later, we checked with a former Special Forces operative who had done three tours in the area. "There *was* an underground facility—a huge one," he told us. "It was in Thailand, at a place called Nakhon Phanom, near Udorn."

We discovered a document in Barry's own handwriting which shed a little light on what he had been doing. In a note to his attorney coaching him on what to say during a pleading for dismissal in his 1972 explosives bust (covered in the next chapter) he wrote, "Don't forget that while in the employ of TWA I volunteered for hazardous duty without extra compensation to fly TWA's contract US Military flights into hot war zones in Vietnam, which I did with tons of explosives and war material. Youngest captain for TWA on Boeing 707's, too."

CIA electronics expert Homer "Red" Hall gave another inkling of what Seal had been doing. "I first met Barry probably in the middle '50's. I was a pilot too, working with Hair Flying Service, which is where Barry worked. They sold airplanes and had a maintenance hangar, and that's where everybody was hanging out, there and at the downtown airport."

"Then I went into the Navy. When I came out of the service I'd see him around. We didn't actually chum together, but you're around in the hanger, you get friendly. We were both pilots, slapping each other on the back and all that. We were all very young."

What is the significance of Barry Seal having been involved in the secret war in Laos? The secret war in Laos, we discovered, had had an 'Alice in Wonderland' quality. Certainly the pilots didn't understand it. Could it have been a war fought over drugs?

"It was all not quite real," one Air America vet recalled, in the book *Air America*, from which the movie was made. "Our wives would run across Communist Pathet Lao soldiers in the marketplace in Vientiane doing their shopping. Crazy."

In the early sixties American pilots were even housed in the same hotel in the Laotian capital that the 'enemy' Soviet pilots used. Every morning the Americans would fly out in their C-46's and C-47's to drop supplies to rightist troops, while the Russians would take off in Ilyushin transport planes to drop supplies to the Pathet Lao. "I watched T-28's loading up with bombs while two Russian 144's taxied across the runway," Air America pilot Wayne Lannin said. "The T-28's took off on bombing runs, the Russians took off for Hanoi, and we took off to do *our* thing. It was all very strange."

At night, all the pilots drank Pernod together in the hotel bar, swapping war stories.

Former *Newsweek* reporter John Robaton concurred. "The whole thing was ridiculous. There were these three half-brothers, and one was in charge of the government, one was in charge of the Pathet Lao and the third was the King, politically neutral. Crazy."

But according to experts like Professor Alfred McCoy, it had a *very* rational purpose. Opium. The enterprise in which Barry Seal took part in Southeast Asia is replete with names we are becoming familiar with, from Shackley's Miami team that was moved en masse to Laos, bringing at least three of his Operation 40 assassins to Laos with him: Felix Rodriguez, Jose Pasada and Chi Chi Quintero.

But the Sixties weren't the start of the CIA dealing drugs. Before there was a CIA there had been the OSS. The heroin that the OSS dealt was grown in Burma, and refined in Shanghai. They stumbled upon this import when they were in Asia with the Flying Tigers trying to stop Mao from assuming power. The poppy-to-ghetto connection actually began in World War II, with Colonel Paul Helliwell of the OSS, who brought heroin from Burma to the U.S. as far back as the mid-1940s.

"You have to understand the mentality that these guys developed during and after the Second World War," CIA pilot Gary Eitel told us. "It was, 'let's root out communism and while we're at it steal all the gold and art.'"

We will later hear evidence that Paul Helliwell is linked to the ownership of Barry's fleet of drug smuggling aircraft during Barry's '80's heyday.

Drugs produce untraceable cash for the things covert ops love best: mercenaries, fixing elections, and buying politicians. Strapped for cash in the early 1950's, the French secret services used Corsican opium dealers throughout Indochina to finance their operations against the Vietminh. They set up a system for the collection and distribution of opium and morphine base from all over the Golden Triangle of Laos, Burma and Thailand.

Morphine base is easily manufactured in makeshift jungle labs. Opium's major alkaloid is precipitated out of the raw sap by boiling it in water with lime. The white morphine floats to the top, is drawn off and boiled with ammonia, filtered, boiled again, and then sun-dried. The resultant clay-like brown paste is morphine base. That's where the Corsicans came in, refining the morphine into heroin, preferred by addicts because it is quicker acting and more potent than unrefined morphine. When the French decamped, the CIA was only too willing and eager to inherit this network. Could this have been behind Eisenhower's proscription against 'the boys' running amok in Vietnam in 1954?

History shows that the CIA disregarded President Eisenhower's order. CIA Colonel Ed Lansdale was the lead 'unconventional warfare officer' attached to the Saigon Military Mission. His 12-man team was in place less than 2 months after the French defeat at Dienbienphu. They found that the well-organized Bin Xuyen street gang directly controlled Saigon's police force.

Lansdale used American money to buy the defeated French Vietnamese army, the ARVN, and he used it to in a savage 6-day battle to take Saigon back from the Bin Xuyen that left 500 dead. He worked in tandem with Lucien Conein, about whom we will hear more, later in our story. During WW2 Conein had led OSS paramilitary operations in North Vietnam, fighting in the Tonkin jungle with French guerrillas. His intimate knowledge of French forces and his skillful use of troops helped Lansdale take Saigon.

Later, when opium warlord Vang Pao went to war with two rival drug-lords for control of the Southeast Asian opium trade, he met first with CIA station chief Ted Shackley. Vang Pao wanted total control of the opium trade, while Shackley was looking for a military intelligence foothold in the trade. The two struck a bargain… and US Air Force jets then bombed the compounds of both of his rivals out of existence.

The young major who coordinated the bombing attacks on Vang Pao's rivals was Richard Secord. When Vang Pao became undisputed lord of the Southeast Asian opium trade, he donated a share of his profits to the training and equipping of Laotian tribesman for incursions against North Vietnamese supply lines, and to carry out assassinations against suspected communist sympathizers. Drugs were—once again—paying for assassinations.

While Secord coordinated the flights that ferried arms, personnel, and heroin to various points in Europe and Asia, John Singlaub ran the assassinations arm of the enterprise. One of the pilots who made these flights was a Special Forces lieutenant named Adler Berriman, *aka* Barry Seal, who will in the 1980's fly a fleet of drug smuggling aircraft, many of them procured for him by Singlaub.

Mafia Don Santos Trafficante visited Vang Pao in a Saigon hotel, and walked away the leading importer of China White heroin in the world. Vang Pao's profits soared; so did his contributions to the training and equipping of the Laotian tribesman. What had been a relatively small scale operation blossomed into the Phoenix Project, an epic intelligence debacle that resulted in a bloodbath: the assassination of nearly 40,000 noncombatants in Vietnam, Laos, Cambodia and Thailand.

"The boys" had established an important precedent, using an existing criminal infrastructure to finance intelligence community operations that never would have received funding through standard appropriations channels. Subverting the will of Congress and the American people would now be easy.

Long after Shackley returned to the US to run the western hemisphere operations of the CIA, his agents were raking in millions of dollars from Vang Pao, and transferring it to a bank in Australia called the Nugun Hand Bank. They also began to pilfer tons of military equipment from depots around Asia and transfer it to a secret base in Thailand.

The operation became public knowledge in the late 70's, when Bo Gritz and Ross Perot drummed up support for bringing home the remaining American POW's. Gritz, the most decorated Green Beret commander of the Vietnam Era, was asked to surreptitiously enter Laos looking for Americans. Gritz ended up meeting the recognized overlord of heroin in the world, Khun Sa. On a Gritz-produced videotape, Khun Sa said that US government officials have been and are now his biggest customers, and had been for the twenty years.

"We fought a war in Laos and Cambodia, even as we fought whatever it was in Vietnam," Gritz says. "The point is that there are as many bomb holes in those two other countries as there are in Vietnam. Five hundred and fifty plus Americans were lost in Laos. Not one of them ever came home. Yet we heard a president say, "The war is over, we are out with honor—all of the prisoners are home.""

"We ran the war in Laos and Cambodia through drugs," Gritz continued. "From '65 to '75 there is one CIA guy in Laos, named Shackley, involved in the narcotics business. And you know whom he used for distribution? Santos Trafficante, old friend of the CIA and mob boss. Later, Richard Armitage, who stayed in Asia after the Vietnam war ended, was reportedly a prominent trafficker in Bangkok during 1975 to 1979. He was one of the embassy employees. Armitage was (also) responsible for recovery of US prisoners of war."

Richard Armitage later joined Bob Dole's staff, then Reagan's campaign staff and ended up the Assistant Secretary of Defense. Gritz says, "Ross Perot had reports on Armitage. And he ended up pinning Richard Armitage—a giant of a man—up against a wall, demanding that Armitage resign. Perot accused him of being a drug smuggler and an arms dealer. That takes pretty big cajones."

"Perot then went to his friend, George Bush, and gave him evidence of wrong doing by Armitage. And Bush told Perot to go to the 'proper authorities.' So he called on William Webster, later head of the CIA, and made at least one visit to the White House carrying a pile of documents. He received no support from the Reagan administration. In fact Frank Carlucci, the secretary of defense—before that he was Deputy Director of the CIA—called him in to ask him to *stop* pursuing Armitage!"

Clearly, then, spooks dealing drugs isn't an aberration of the 1980's. They flew heroin in Asia on the CIA proprietary airline Air America during the Viet Nam War, where it was refined in Asian soft drink bottling factories owned by PepsiCo. Later we will support a Contra army led by Adolpho Calero, whose involvement in narcotics trafficking is notorious, and who also owned the Nicaraguan soft drink concession for Coke.

Jack Ruby, it has even been suggested, might have been recruited into the Burmese heroin business while still a soldier during World War II, when the main smuggling trail for opium to the West was from Burma overland to Turkey, then by various routes to Marseilles.

But during World War II this route was disrupted, and other routes took up the slack, the main one being from China and Burma on US military ships around South Africa and ending in Florida, which had the main supply ports for the China-Burma-India Theater.

Ruby had been sent to the Republic Aircraft Factory in Farmingdale on Long Island, where Army Air Corps Intelligence was developing the first two prototypes of a photoreconnaissance aircraft being tested at that time for use in the Pacific Theater. He received specialized reconnaissance aircraft mechanics training, before moving to Chatham Air Base near Savannah, Georgia.

Irving Zakarin, one of Ruby's fellow soldiers, remembers that Chatham was a secret logistics base to reconnaissance units in Asia. Could this have been where Ruby became involved in OSS officer Paul Helliwell's smuggling?

While this is still secret history, its outlines *are* dimly visible. We already know that by 1947 Ruby was involved with the major international heroin operation in North America. And Farmingdale on Long Island is a place Barry Seal, like Jack Ruby a generation before, will spend a lot of time during the 1960's, even teaching brother-in-law and future smuggling pilot Bill Bottoms to fly there.

But whom is the wizard pulling the strings behind the velvet curtain? One likely candidate might be CIA agent Colonel Paul Helliwell, who somehow managed to toil in anonymity in the cocaine-filled 1980's, when he was the true owner of 'drug smuggler' Barry Seal's Lear jet.

A new generation had taken control. We were all about to experience the consequences.

CHAPTER EIGHTEEN

DEEP WATERGATE

"When you've got them by the balls, their hearts and minds will follow."
—Charles Colson, Nixon White House Advisor

IN JULY 1, 1972, ten days after the arrest of burglars in Washington's Watergate Complex, the TV series Bewitched aired it's final episode, and Attorney General John N. Mitchell resigned as chairman of President Nixon's re-election committee because of the brewing Watergate scandal; and as Sammy Davis Jr's., single "Candy Man" made a move up the charts pilot Barry Seal was arrested in New Orleans, for conspiracy to export enough C4 plastic explosive to blow the island of Cuba half-way up the Florida Keys.

We discovered that the arrest of Seal and six co-conspirators is part of the secret history of the Watergate Scandal. And it points towards what might have been behind it all...

Because the most amazing thing about this most amazing scandal is that, even after all these years, we still don't know.

What connection could Barry Seal have had to Watergate? When authorities swooped down on a DC-4 being loaded with C4 plastic explosive and arrested everyone involved in the operation, it temporarily shut down what became known, after the release of Nixon's tapes, as the "Mexican Connection."

Remember Watergate? If you're like most Americans, like we were, you remember it wrong.... We remember cheering Nixon's removal as his just desserts for various unconstitutional abuses of power. And we didn't mourn his passing; after being elected in 1968 with a "secret plan to end the war," he had instead *prolonged* Vietnam for almost as long as World War II had *lasted...*

The Watergate Scandal, we discovered, had an unexplored narcotics trafficking, arms smuggling component. On the tapes Nixon referred to this as 'the Mexican connection.'

Barry Seal's big 1972 arrest was as the result of working for this ongoing operation during the Watergate summer of 1972, when it was disrupted as part of a larger war between the CIA and Nixon over the newly-created apparatus he had devised to bring control of drug intelligence into the White House.

The pilot arrested with Barry has told us that this was by no means the first CIA-sponsored weapons-for-heroin flight Seal and his associates had flown.

Like something right out of a "Gangland" column in the *New York Post* two Mob families went to war for control of the drug trade.

Except that these were *federal* families.

Barry Seal's 1972 bust, while it was big news for a day or two, was never connected to Watergate in the press, even though it occurred less than two weeks later. On July 3, 1972, The *New York Times* reported that Federal officials had arrested seven men in Texas and Louisiana on charges of conspiring to smuggle munitions to Mexico. A DC-4 was seized at the Shreveport Regional Airport loaded with almost seven tons of plastic C-4 explosive, 7,000 feet of explosive primer cord, and 2,600 electric blasting caps.

The explosives, said the U.S. Attorney's Office in Louisiana, were headed to Cuban exiles in Mexico, who were going to use them in an effort to overthrow the government of Fidel Castro.

This much at least turns out to be right on the money...

"Barry and I were involved in an operation which I know Barry believed was fully backed by the CIA, a plot to get rid of Castro in 1972," states James Miller, the pilot arrested with Barry in the bust. "When we were arrested, it took Barry completely by surprise."

What had they been up to?

"We were planning the overthrow of Cuba with the assistance of the Mexican Air Force," Miller told us. "We had flown several times into Mexican Air Force bases, and met for that purpose."

Had Miller, an ex-military pilot, known he was involved in what was to have been a weapons for heroin transaction?

Turns out, he did...

"This was not the first time this pipeline had been used," says Miller. "That was why it was such a shock when we were arrested."

The principal players in the scheme were Richmond Harper, millionaire rancher and Director of the Frontier State Bank of Eagle Pass, Texas; Marion Hagler, a former Inspector with the INS; Mob associate Murray Kessler, and Barry Seal.

"Murray and Barry had known each other since the Cuban business in New Orleans," explains Miller, a lifelong member of the clannish Louisiana pilot's fraternity. "Kessler was a Gambino family associate."

Miller stated that Barry Seal had known—and taken numerous meetings with—the head of what was then the most powerful of the five New York Mob families, Carlo Gambino.

"Barry and I flew to New York to meet Mr. Carlo Gambino. Barry had an idea for importing shrimp from Panama to restaurants in New York. Mr. Gambino said he liked the idea, but said that all of his restaurant business had to be cleared through his nephew Mannie," Miller said.

Mannie Gambino told us that he was too busy to talk just then," he continued, "to call him back in three days to set a meeting. Well, three days later, Mannie was missing, never to turn up again. His bloodstained car was found out at Newark International airport, and no one has ever seen poor Mannie again."

Mannie Gambino's partner was New York Mobster and Guy Banister partner-in-the-Cuban-business Murray Kessler.

Small world.

Seal was supposedly working for TWA full-time as a pilot during this period. That turned out to have merely been his cover, as Barry Seal had been busy with a lot more than flying tourists to Italy and Greece. He was planning wars in Central America.

TWA realized the exposure it had with its spy on the payroll, and the airline nervously pleaded with Seal not to get caught doing anything while he was wearing his Captain's uniform...

We discovered a letter in which the airplane's v-p of personnel is pleading with Seal to 'be good,' to "not bring the company into disrepute with his extra-curricular activities." The letter reflects not an employer/employee relationship, but something more akin to state-to-state negotiations.

Though Howard Hughes' 'marriage' with the CIA was a happy one—Hughes' companies served the CIA worldwide as its largest private contractor—TWA could be embarrassed if one of its pilots made headlines for launching a Central American coup.

Charles Colson had told Watergate investigators that Hughes had "close organizational ties with the CIA," and thus by implication with Watergate. But few among the Washington press corps at the time professed a clue as to what he was talking about...

Barry's co-conspirators were a rich assortment of people connected with everything from organized crime to the White House's new drug enforcement czar.

Murray Kessler, for example, an associate of the Gambino organized-crime family, was a frequent houseguest at Richmond Harper's ranch; and Harper, according to Barry Seal, had "deep deep ties right in to the White House."

Kessler's rap sheet included six convictions on charges of interstate theft, transporting stolen property, bookmaking and conspiracy to possess heroin.

A Customs agent tailing him through an airport described Kessler in his report as "50-ish and Jewish-looking, wearing a open-collar gray shirt with a gray sports suit, accompanied by a "bleached blond in white slacks and a red polka-dotted jacket."

Lucky guy. "Bleached blondes in white slacks and red polka-dotted jackets" were power accessories back then. Murray was 'connected:' he had been "an anti-Castro guy, since his days with Guy Banister," according to retired DEA agent Dick Gustafson, who knew him. "It was like a mantra he carried around with him."

The men arrested were all intricately "connected."

Kessler had been, as they say in crime-land, a "known associate" of Guy Banister and David Ferrie in the 1960's, and Barry Seal. Richmond Harper was connected too: the middle-man in the weapons-for-heroin deal was a "tall lean guy wearing a cowboy shirt with the monogrammed initials "RCH," a string tie and cowboy boots," according to author Pete Brewton.

It's a description with which Debbie Seal agrees. She once saw him on the airport tarmac in Eagle Pass, after flying in with Barry to confer while awaiting trial. This is also where Oswald's "buddy" George DeMohrenschilt entered Mexico on his way to Guatemala for the Bay of Pigs.

Small world.

Harper was also an associate of Carlos Marcello's front man, Herman Beebe, funny credentials, one should think, for a man with deep deep ties into Nixon's White House.

Those ties included access to the head of Customs and Special Consultant to the President on Narcotics, Myles Ambrose…as well as to John Erlichmann's aide Jack Caulfield, who, in addition to his duties as a bagman, had helped to set up the White House Plumbers unit.

Ambrose visited Harper and went hunting with him on his ranch in Mexico, according to former Customs officials who worked under him, and was Harper's guest at the wedding of the century in tiny Eagle Pass, the 'hitching' of Harper's own daughter, an event commemorated by the slaughtering of 600 steers.

No bull.

Myles Ambrose's chatfests with the colorfully-connected rancher were first discovered by the House banking subcommittee investigating the Texas rent-a-bank scandal.

"We tried to warn him [Ambrose]," stated one Customs official to the committee. "Tell him that this guy [Harper] is bad. He wouldn't listen."

Since he had shepherded the establishment of the DEA through Congress, when we reached him (in Virginia), we asked him about his curious associations…

On Harper, Mr. Ambrose was emphatic, stating he had only ever visited the Harper ranch… *once*. But about the creation of the DEA, he had more interesting things to say.

"I got to Tip O'Neill," he told us, about the deal to set up the Agency. "And that kept the partisan stuff out." (Oh, to have been a fly on the wall during *that* negotiation.)

A former Customs Agent who worked for Ambrose described him as a fearsome autocrat…

"I was the top graduate in my class at the Treasury Department," the agent told us. "I wasn't afraid of anyone or anybody. But my first day in Washington I learned just how much fear Ambrose instilled in people. He was an Orangeman—you know what that is? A follower of William of Orange? And he took it so seriously that no one in Customs was allowed to wear green. And my first day on the job—not knowing this—I had on a green suit, and he came over and read me the riot act."

This agent's anecdote came to mind when we found ourselves feeling Mr. Ambrose's displeasure at the thrust of our questions. Finding himself out of sympathy with our speculations about the *true* nature of the pie being carved up at the DEA's inauguration, Ambrose became eager to share with us his thoughts on the involvement in the drug trade by the folks on the *other* side of the aisle.

"I was with Treasury back in the late Fifties, when Bobby Kennedy was running the Kefauver Committee Hearings on Organized Crime," he said angrily. "And I know for a fact that there was a yellow sheet (investigative report) on a meeting in Havana where Meyer Lansky gave two kilos of heroin to Frank Sinatra to bring back to the States so he (Sinatra) would have a little 'walking-around' money…. But because Sinatra was helping Kennedy get elected, his brother removed all reference from the Committee's report."

Sinatra's dead, and can't defend himself. Ambrose still can, so we wanted to know why, when warned by Customs agents to steer clear of Richmond Harper, he hadn't listened? He had no recollection of the warning, he told us.

Later we will discover that Richmond Harper, a strange friend one might have thought, for a man who had created American Drug Enforcement Administration, had once been on trial for mislabeling dog food—food not intended for humans—as fit for human consumption, and shipping it over the border from Mexico to the United States.

After his friendship with Harper was revealed, Ambrose was forced to leave office. Later Nixon aide Charles Colson told Senator Lowell Weicker "Ambrose had set up the CIA in the Drug Enforcement Administration."

"Certain Mafia figures had cordial relations with Ambrose," Colson also stated with—as we've seen—some justification.

One of the benefits of studying Seal's 1972 arrest is the number of previously hidden, 'underground' associations it reveals… For example, the plane used, a DC-4, was owned by James Boy, owner of Fort Lauderdale Leasing in Miami, who we have been able to identify as a "known associate" of the Central Intelligence Agency…

James Boy's planes will a decade or so later fly Ollie North's mercenaries in and out of Honduras; he will also be arrested with Seal in 1981, in the big DEA drug bust called Operation Screamer.

The Customs Service undercover agent who carried out the '72 sting, Cesario Diosdado is also part of the secret history… In one of the strangest episodes to occur on the day of the Kennedy assassination Alpha 66 head Antonio Veciana said Diosdado had mysteriously shown up unannounced at his Miami home.

"You don't know anything about Kennedy, do you?" Diosdado asked.

When Veciana replied "no," Diosdado seemed satisfied. Veciana felt he was being tested, and so didn't tell Diosdado that he had seen Oswald in Dallas a month earlier, he testified, because "he didn't want to get involved."

House investigator Gaeton Fonzi later reported: "Veciana said as soon as Diosdado walked in the door he told him, 'hey, don't worry about a thing, I don't even know why I'm doing this, they just told me to do it, interview some Cubans.'"

Syndicate boss Sam Giancana had said one of the shooters in the Kennedy hit had been a US Customs officer, according to Chuckie Giancana's *Double Cross*. When the House Select Committee interviewed Diosdado in 1976 he was working for that home away from home for wayward souls, America's Drug Enforcement Administration.

Diosdado insisted that he worked for United States Customs from 1957 to 1968, not for the CIA, and said he never questioned anyone about the JFK assassination.

But a variety of CIA documents confirm that he *was* a CIA agent... "Presently resident Customs Agent-in-Charge, Key West, Florida. At this time Subjects (Diosdado's) salary was being paid by WAVE Station." When an informant claimed that Diosdado had sent arms to Castro prior to Castro's taking over Cuba, as well as getting individuals in and out of Cuba for a price, the FBI shrugged, stating they "do not interfere with his activities since the FBI believes he is acting for the CIA."

So, Diosdado was running weapons to Fidel Castro too. This is not a huge surprise. Why is Diosdado lying? Out of principle? Just to keep in practice?

Barry Seal was on to Diosdado. According to Seal, "through records I have obtained from a private investigative agency in Denver, Colorado, the Customs Service undercover agent who carried out the sting, Cesario Diosdado, has been proven to have been an ex-CIA agent who worked in the Bay of Pigs invasion and had been working both sides of the fence in the Miami/Cuban area."

In his landmark book *The Mafia, CIA, and George Bush: The Untold Story of America's Greatest Financial Debacle,* Peter Brewton was the first to connect Seals' explosives bust to the same crew of 'elite deviants' who later created the savings and loan scandal.

Brewton called Seal's bust with Mafia associates and CIA operatives "one of the most bizarre and inexplicable criminal cases on record."

Seal had been taking some sick leave from his job as a captain flying 707s and 747s out of New York to Europe for Trans World Airlines, according to Brewton. "When he walked out of his motel room near the New Orleans International Airport, he was arrested by federal agents and charged with violating the Mutual Security Act of 1954, which prohibited the exportation of weapons without the permission of the State Department."

The saga began, CIA/Customs Agent Diosdado later testified, when he was sent to Mexico City to meet with U.S. and Mexican agents to map out a strategy for breaking up an arms smuggling ring. He said he had been summoned by the Federal Bureau of Narcotics and Dangerous Drugs and told by a special agent of the Bureau to investigate a group that had "approximately 10,000 assorted weapons and then trying to trade the weapons for 25 kilos of heroin."

Leland Briggs *was* that special agent Diosdado referred to in his testimony. When we tracked him down in retirement, he told us, "I knew Diosdado had been working with the CIA in Florida back in the 60's, but he was with Customs when I called him in. He was a pain in the ass. Back then the CIA was working against us most of the time."

While in Mexico City, Briggs had witnessed something extraordinary: Myles Ambrose flew in, he told us, along with then-Asst. Attorney General Dick Kleindienst and Jack Caulfield, who was, of all things, a member of Nixon's George Bush-led Cabinet-level Committee on International Narcotics Control...

"Caulfield was a good guy, a former New York cop, who was laundering money at that time for the Republican National Committee," Riggs remembers. "I set up meetings with the Mexican Treasury Department for them."

Drug smuggling through Mexico had been Meyer Lansky's main narcotics operation, according to the inestimable Professor Peter Dale Scott. Scott said the Federal Bureau of Narcotics consistently diverted attention away from this key trafficking pipeline, reportedly the biggest drug smuggling channel into the United States.

It was so well established, Scott had been the first to report, that Jack Ruby had been involved in it as far back as *1947.*

What was Nixon bagman Jack Caulfield doing in Mexico City at precisely the time $50 million of untraceable cash was flowing -much of it from there—into Nixon's re-election war-chest?

If you answered, "discussing stopping the flow of narcotics into the US from Mexico," your faith in America's political class exceeds our own...

During Barry Seal's trial it was revealed that even the Mexican whose report initiated the undercover operation, named Fregoso, had unsavory associations. He was a DFS officer (Mexican CIA) of singular stature, so corrupt that he will be drummed out of that agency—in what has to rank as a Mexican first—for accepting bribes from a narcotics dealer.

The initial deal had been 10,000 automatic weapons for 25 kilos of heroin. Diosdado met retired INS agent Sandy Hagler in Eagle Pass, and was told that the operation had a fleet of five DC3's as well as 3-5 amphibious PBY aircraft...the same fleet of aircraft which Dave Ferrie controlled five years earlier.

But when Diosdado produced the first few kilos of heroin it was judged defective by the Harper/Kessler/Seal group, which now wanted *cash*. To cover the cost of the transaction Diosdado deposited a million in cash in a safe-deposit box at Chase Manhattan in New York City, and another million in cash in a safe deposit box in San Antonio.

Harper then put Diosdado in touch with Murray Kessler, who invited him to visit a steel plant in Newark which, Kessler stated, was used to manufacture weapons and make spare parts.

So Diosdado went to New York to meet "Mr. Big," placing an initial order of 4,500 M-1 rifles with 500 rounds of ammunition for each weapon, after Kessler boasted of being in business in Virginia, with the "biggest arms supplier on the face of the planet."

This turns out to be absolutely true. Customs Agents found in Kessler's address book the name and phone number of Sam Cummings of Interarms, the CIA's proprietary armaments supplier in Virginia.

Samuel Cummings, we recalled, had been recruited, while still young, to arm the 1954 Guatemala secret invasion.

Small world.

For over half a century the genteel Philadelphian peddled arms, rising quickly to the top of the global small-arms trade. He helped foment the history of post-World War II America: a long run of wars, coups and revolutions, from the '50s to the '90s.

His company, Interarms, sometimes equipped both sides.

Cummings and his Swiss wife lived in jet-set comfort in a 14room apartment in tax haven Monaco, and a sprawling chalet, 4,000 feet up, in Switzerland's Bernese Alps. Though born an American, he became a British subject. The guiding principle of his business strategy was the idea that "the military market is based on human folly, and not normal market precepts. Human folly goes up and down, but it always exists—and its depths have never been plumbed."

Philosophical niceties aside, in the trade Cummings had a nickname: "the merchant of death."

For Murray Kessler this was not, all in all, the best of times. His partner, Manny Gambino, had just been kidnapped. When Mannie's car was found at Newark Airport, with blood all over the trunk, in certain New York circles this was not considered a good sign.... "Manny left to meet some people in Jersey," Kessler said to Diosdado.

Manny Gambino, nephew to the all-powerful Carlo Gambino, ultimate Mafia don, had been kidnapped and held for ransom. Kessler was designated as the bagman to deliver the loot. But even after the kidnappers received part of the $350,000 ransom they demanded, Manny Gambino was murdered. His corpse was later found in a New Jersey garbage dump.

The enraged Carlo Gambino sent out his top enforcers to avenge his nephew's death. One of the kidnappers was found and killed in a Staten Island bar by a Gambino soldier named John Gotti, who was sent to prison for seven years.

Gotti will, of course, later emerge to do major cocaine business with Barry Seal—distributing to "retail" massive amounts of cocaine, according to pilot Richard Brenneke, in a deposition to Congressman Bill Alexander—brought into this country through the remote airport in Mena Arkansas.

Brenneke, predictably ridiculed and 'discredited' when he first came forward, now appears to be telling the truth.

James Miller, the former military pilot arrested on the tarmac with the plane and the weapons in the '72 bust, had told us of flying to New York with Barry to meet with Carlo Gambino several times that year. Once they went to see Gambino to ask the don's blessing on a shrimp-importing scheme Barry had hatched.

This confirms the connection between life-long CIA agent and pilot Barry Seal and the highest levels of the Gambino Family, at the time New York's most powerful.

If Barry's planes were, in the mid-'80's, being met in Mena by Sal Reale of the Gambinos, as Richard Brenneke claimed, we can now see that it fits an already-existing pattern...

When Diosdado flew in to the big Apple to talk 'turkey' with Kessler, Murray the Mobster rose to the occasion, putting thoughts of his dead partner aside. He regaled undercover agent Diosdado with his views on life while squiring him around New York.

And since Diosdado was wearing a wire, today we can let the entertaining Mr. Kessler speak for himself for a few moments, from official court transcripts that read like dialogue out of a David Mamet gangster movie...

Diosdado tries to give tailing agents listening in to the conversation in Kessler's limo clues to the car's location, through the ruse of asking about passing Manhattan landmarks...

> DIAZ: How many lanes in this tunnel?
> KESSLER: In the tunnel? Two.
> DIAZ: Is this the only tunnel in town?
> KESSLER: No, we got the Holland Tunnel, that's farther down, the Lincoln tunnel. This takes you right into the heart of Manhattan.
> DIAZ: UNINTELLIGIBLE.
> KESSLER: You see a lot of nigger hustlers in this part of town.

Then, maybe because his partner Manny had just been "iced," Kessler begins to wax philosophical on his methods of doing business...

> KESSLER: See, one of the biggest problems in this kind of situation is an untrusting situation. And I know a man has to have some way where he's dealing with somebody with *family*. This man is not going to do anything bad because he *knows* the people he's dealing with have *got* to be bad people—people with blood—you understand?

The easiest way, the way we dealt with previously *(Would I tell you a lie?)*, we had a man from Manhattan, and a girl and five guys would come over every month with two suitcases—$600,000 or $700,000. We built a hand grenade factory in Kansas, our own, with a general named Smith. Our own! We started out the same way (as we are with you), you know...

> DIAZ: Yeah?
> KESSLER: Then later they said, 'listen, these people are real people; they're not interested in stealing nothing! They're in this deal, they want to make what they're supposed to make. What we agreed and that's the game.
> I'm not interested in dying for money, understand? You must deal with *real* people—not in a hotel room—but with

people who *live* someplace! People who know, you know, my mother, your mother, and my kids. I *know* these people, you understand?

You're entitled to make one mistake here. That's the problem, we pay you, whatever you make I pay you, but honor, honor! *That's* the way I do business. This is where my children and my family live, and maybe I'll get killed, but they'll say, listen, he got killed doing his job. *That's* the way I like to do business, the only way you can know honor with people of this caliber. There's no other way, no other way. People who trust you— when people who trust you with things like this here— God forbid you make a mistake! That you *lose* something. There's no going back and saying you're sorry. This game has no "*I'm sorrys.*"

Kessler discusses the importance of transportation, and boasts of his association with Barry Seal...

KESSLER: I'm in a position where I've got a man that's flying around the world all the time. This is no nickel aviator! A real captain, like you came on the airlines with! Captain! Need him—he's gold! He's experienced. I was in the cigarette business here. I bring cigarettes from Panama with this guy. He comes into the country, the United States, and never lands! Throws out everything on Long Island, its a three hundred yard field, everything, never lands!

Barry Seal's own deposition stated that he had flown to Panama with a Carlos Marcello associate, Joe Mazzukka, to discuss "importing" cigarettes with an RJ Reynolds official there.

Curiously, this same RJ Reynolds official also agreed to go into business with Seal and his Mob buddies, fronting for them in setting up an oil exploration company on the island of Aruba to facilitate exporting explosives.

Kessler also discusses doing business on an international level, stating his preferences right into Diosdado's microphone.

KESSLER: If we had met four or five months ago I might have said, come on, let's go to Israel. They've got more guns there than you've got hair on your head. Millions of them! What's going on in the United States I don't understand, why only a few people in this country do what has to be done. Because of what happened here the past 2-3 years—since the niggers started with the revolution shit here—they have a gun control law here now. If you go to buy a rifle you got to show where it's going, who bought it, everything!

Diosdado and Kessler agreed that Barry Seal will fly with Kessler to Vera Cruz Mexico in advance of the deal, to check out the airports suitability for landing a fully loaded DC-4

Kessler now turns mysterious—strange, since he's just given away CIA Mob secrets to everyone with access to transcripts of the wire—and begins speaking in code…

"My driver has to look at the racetrack so he knows how to drive the car on it."

From Seal's later trial testimony, we can piece together what happened next…

Barry Seal must have been wilting in the suffocating heat of Vera Cruz, Mexico—never a place particularly known as a vacation getaway. The humid Gulf air was oppressive, and there was no shade on the isolated airstrip on which stood Seal and two sweltering companions, just a swarm of mosquitoes and a lone burro nibbling garbage along the edges of the runway…

Rings of sweat expanded underneath the armpits of the bear-like Seal's flight suit as he and the two smaller figures flanking him peered intensely at a map of Cuba, spread out on a picnic table near the dilapidated shed which served as the strip's air terminal.

One of them was CIA agent Cesario Diosdado, the other Mafia lieutenant Murray Kessler. Their eyes followed Seal's forefinger to a spot on the map, as a droplet of sweat dripped from Barry's forehead directly—we like to imagine—onto the word 'Havana.'

Could these three huddled figures be—two weeks before the Watergate burglars are arrested—involved in the complex of scandals that will come to be known as Watergate?

If you're not sweating in the bright sun of Vera Cruz, as Barry Seal was in June of 1972, it's easy to forget how important the Mexican connection was to the Watergate scandal.

When hush money was paid to the Cubans busted at the Watergate it came in the form of Mexican checks, turned over first to Maurice

Stans of CREEP (Committee to RE-Elect the President) and then to Watergate burglar Gordon Liddy, who passed them to Bernard Barker of the Miami Cubans arrested the night of the final Watergate break-in.

Barker, a CIA operative since the Bay of Pigs invasion, was walking around carrying this "Mexican" cash when he was apprehended.

The money came from one of George Bush's intimates, and at the request of Bush, a member of the Nixon Cabinet since February 1971. Just two days before a new law made anonymous donations illegal, $700,000 in cash, checks, and securities was loaded into a briefcase at Pennzoil headquarters by a company vice president who boarded a Washington-bound Pennzoil jet and delivered the loot to the Committee to Re-Elect the President.

Later, the Banking and Currency Committee of Texas Democrat Wright Patman began a vigorous investigation of the money financing the break-in. The largest amount, he discovered, had been sent in by William Liedtke, longtime business partner of George Bush.

On the day Nixon resigned Patman wrote to Peter Rodino pleading with the chairman of the House Judiciary Committee to *not stop* investigating Watergate...

And though Patman died in 1976, his advice still holds good, though nobody, any longer, is holding their breath waiting.

Was George Bush implicated in the activities of the Plumbers? Bush was knee-deep in deep doo-doo, as illustrated by the notorious White House meeting of June 23, 1972, whose exchange between Nixon and Haldeman provided the *coup de grace* to the agony of the Nixon regime.

Haldeman says (on the tapes): "Now, on the investigation, you know the Democratic break-in thing, we're back in the problem area because the FBI is not under control, because [FBI chief] Gray doesn't exactly know how to control it and they have… their investigation is leading into some productive areas because they've been able to trace the money…. Not through the money itself, but through the bank sources, the banker. And, *and it goes in some directions we don't want it to go.*"

Nixon's famous answer is, "When you get in—when you get in say look, the problem is that this tracks back to the Bay of Pigs, the whole problem is that this will open the whole, the whole Bay of Pigs thing and the President just feels that ah, without going into the details…. Don't, don't lie to them to the extent to say there is no involvement, but just say this is a comedy of errors, without getting into it, the President believes that it is going to open the whole Bay of Pigs thing up again and, ah, they should call the FBI in and (unintelligible) don't go any further into this case period!"

Nixon's references to Howard Hunt and the Bay of Pigs are an oblique allusion to the Kennedy assassination, according to chief-of-staff Haldeman. So clearly Nixon knew more about the killing of Jack Kennedy than he was ever held accountable for—placing him, no doubt, in the company of scores of others.

Now comes the moment which defines the shady character of George Bush. White House officials, including Bush, spent the morning of Monday, August 5, 1974 absorbing the impact of the just-quoted "smoking gun" tape... in which Nixon ordered the CIA to stop the FBI from investigating how various sums of money found their way from Texas and Minnesota via Mexico City to the coffers of the Committee to Re-Elect, and then into the pockets of the Plumbers' arrested in the Democratic Party headquarters in the Watergate.

The revelations established a case of obstruction of justice against Nixon, fine with Bush; he wanted his patron and benefactor to resign.

But Bush's main concern was that the tape called attention to the money-laundering mechanism which he—together with Bill Liedtke of Pennzoil and Robert Mosbacher—had set up... the mechanism which had been shut down by Barry Seal's explosives-for-narcotics bust... When Nixon had talked about "the Texans," and "some Texas people," he was referring to Bush, Liedtke, and Mosbacher.

The threat to Bush's political ambitions was great. And the White House that morning was gripped by panic. Nixon would be gone before the end of the week...

And in the midst of the furor White House Congressional liaison William Timmons wanted to know if everyone who needed to be informed had been briefed about the smoking gun transcript.

In a roomful of officials, some of whom were already sipping Scotch to steady their nerves, Timmons asked Dean Burch, "Dean, does Bush know about the transcript yet?"

"Yes," responded Burch.

"Well, what did he do?" inquired Timmons.

Replied Burch, "He broke out into assholes and shit himself to death,"

There was a lot more going on in Watergate than ever surfaced... otherwise the nation might have had to endure the ordeal of witnessing

'Texan' George Bush breaking out into assholes and shitting himself to death.

Haldeman said "the CIA was an agency hostile to Nixon, who returned the hostility with fervor," and adds that throughout the Watergate investigation "the multiple levels of deception by the CIA are astounding."

He supported the thesis that Watergate was a highly sophisticated CIA plot to destroy Nixon, and that Jim McCord, a former CIA security chief who was intensely loyal to the agency, deliberately sabotaged the Watergate break-in in order to cripple the Nixon White House and frustrate its attempts to centralize control of the intelligence community.

This is, of course, still only a "modified limited hangout." Unstated by Haldeman is the fact that Nixon wasn't taking control of *all* intelligence—just *drug* intelligence.

Today scholars agree with the conclusions of the book *Silent Coup*. Nixon was done in—deliberately—by the CIA. What we *thought* happened during Watergate is just a gossamer fairy tale for the chumps sitting in the cheap seats...

It was not the righteous indignation of the American people, coupled with the vigilance of a free press, that brought Richard Nixon down.

It was the CIA.

The first thing the White House was frantically looking for, after the burglars were discovered and "driven downtown," was *money*. Hush money. Lots of it...

John Dean quickly summoned CIA war-horse General Vernon Walters to the White House to try squeezing money from the burglars' old employer.

When the general arrived in Dean's White House office they fenced a bit: Dean said the "bugging" case was becoming "awkward," and that one of the FBI's theories was that it was done by the CIA, which Walters denied vehemently.

Walters later wrote, "Dean then said that some of the accused were getting scared and 'wobbling.' I said that even so they could not implicate the Agency."

This barely-veiled threat was because the CIA had long relationships with everyone involved, including Hunt, then 'working' for the Mullen Company, a known CIA front.

Dean seemed taken aback, Walters noted later with some satisfaction, at the CIA's refusal to come up with cash, but asked again if there was anything the CIA could do. Walters agreed to carry the request to Helms. But he told Dean he knew what Helms would say.

The next day Walters was again summoned to Dean's office, and reported that he had spoken with Helms, who did not want to pay the burglars. Walters recalled raising the metaphorical ante of his warning to Dean: "Involving the Agency would transform what was now a medium-sized conventional explosive into a multi-megaton explosion and was not worth the risk."

Walters reported, "Dean looked glum but said he agreed with my judgment."

On Wednesday June 28, the two men met for a third time. Dean asked, said Walters, "whether there was not some way that the Agency could pay bail for the burglars. He added that it was not just bail, that if these men went to prison, could we (CIA) find some way to pay their salaries while they were in jail out of covert action funds."

Walters became grim after this request, and turned it off decisively.

A scant five days later Barry Seal was arrested in New Orleans, in a deal that was supposed to be weapons-for-heroin until the arms-sellers abruptly decided they would rather have *cash,* thank you very much. Coincidence? Or a White House attempt to tide the Cubans over with untraceable cash?

Dean's desperate search for money was eventually the plot's unraveling: the $200,000 in hush money paid to Hunt finally exposed the scandal. Interestingly, all of the "support" money raised for the burglars' legal and personal expenses eventually became hush money… given to Howard Hunt *alone.*

Meant to take care of the *Cubans,* and thus ensure their silence, the money never made it to them. Was this just a case of greed? Or had somebody *wanted* the burglars to talk?

What happened, clearly, was that the fix was in, the knives were out, and Nixon was going down.

It is, of course, no coincidence that the Watergate burglars were anti-Castro Cubans. They were the mechanics, or 'wetboys,' of the CIA, and had been for already over a decade. But placing the uniform of this 'secret team' on Barry Seal puts the drug scandals of the 1980's in an entirely new light, as well as illuminating some unexplored dark corners of the Watergate scandal.

The 'secret team' conspiracy theory was, of course, 'discredited' in the 1980's. But by following the career of Barry Seal we're beginning to see that thirty years of covert operations—and the political scandals that follow—have drawn upon exactly the same (cess)pool of talent. Like TV actors with familiar faces moving from one god-awful series to the next, the *dramatis personae* remain so consistent that it must be that these scandals are all the handiwork of the same group of bosses.

Author Georgie Anne Geyer said it well. "An entire new Cuban cadre now emerged from the Bay of Pigs. The names Howard Hunt, Bernard Barker, Rolando Martinez, Felix Rodriguez and Eugenio Martinez would, in the next quarter century, pop up, often decisively, over and over again in the most dangerous American foreign policy crises. There were Cubans flying missions for the CIA in the Congo and even for the Portuguese in Africa; Cubans were the burglars of Watergate; Cubans played key roles in Nicaragua, in Irangate, in the American move into the Persian Gulf."

Felix Rodriguez tells us that he was infiltrated into Cuba with the other members of the "Grey Team" in conjunction with the Bay of Pigs landings; this is the same man we will find directing the contra supply effort in Central America during the 1980's, working under the direct supervision of Don Gregg and George Bush. Theodore Shackley, the JM/WAVE station chief, will later show up in George Bush's presidential campaign.

Howard Hunt, part of the overthrow of the Guatemalan government of Jacob Arbenz in 1954, an important cog in the chain of command in the Bay of Pigs, a person accused of having been in Dallas on the day Kennedy was shot, one of the central figures of Watergate. According to an internal CIA memorandum, Hunt *was* in Dallas on the day President Kennedy was murdered; the memo discusses a concern among CIA bosses that the presence of Hunt at Dealey Plaza might be uncovered.

Victor Marchetti, the author of "The CIA and the Cult of Intelligence," suggests that the CIA thought about taking a "limited hang-out," and was willing to concede that CIA agents may have been involved in the assassination plot against JFK, that a "renegade" band of agents acting on their own may have made the hit.

Hunt vehemently disputed this, and sued the authors of "Coup D'Etat in America," A. J. Weberman and Michael Canfield, for stating that he had been one of the tramps photographed in Dealey Plaza just after the murder.

Hunt lost.

Nixon's anti-drug campaign was in reality a bid to establish his own intelligence network. According to "The Great Heroin Coup," Egil Krogh wanted the White House, instead of the CIA, handling the drug intelligence work, allowing Nixon's staff to decide which drug traffickers to pursue.

Howard Hunt told Krogh he could enlist experienced CIA figures, starting with CIA veteran Lucien Conein, a brazen move, since the CIA had just been acutely embarrassed by the discovery that a huge proportion of the narcotics smugglers arrested in the big Justice Department Operation Eagle drug bust in 1970 were CIA-paid Cubans, Bay of Pigs veterans. When Nixon instead chose William Sullivan—who had been second to J. Edgar Hoover in the FBI—"the boys down at the Masonic Lodge," (as we've heard them referred to) could not have been overjoyed.

The White House *was* out to gain control of narcotics intelligence. But even that wasn't enough. Nixon's staff also sought to control enforcement. In January of 1972 the White House set up the Office For Drug Abuse Law Enforcement (ODALE), according to a plan conceived by Gordon Liddy. Nixon named the soon-to-resign-in-disgrace Myles Ambrose to head of the newly created Drug Enforcement Office, which later became the Drug Enforcement Administration. It became the domestic strike force which soon became notorious for its record of illegal raids, no-knock entries into private homes, and beatings of innocent people. Some called it the American Gestapo.

So, if we heed Deep Throat's advice, and "follow the money," where *does* the real money lead? Down back alleys into the drugs and weapons bazaars of Central America? Who could have been expected to be a little put out, institutionally speaking, by all this maneuvering? What organization might have not been overjoyed to learn that there was a *new* drug enforcement outfit on the block... muscling onto their turf?

Remember whom Cesar Diosdado—the man who set up Barry Seal— really worked for?

On June 12, 1972 the CIA reorganized its Office of Narcotics Coordinator into the more unified Narcotics Coordination Group, or NARCOG. The following month the White House issued Executive Order 11676, providing for the establishment of the Office of National Narcotics Intelligence (ONNI), whose goal was "the development and maintenance of a National Narcotics Intelligence System."

Overlapping functions? Turf conflicts? Its *only* narcotics, right? Whose gonna get all bent out of shape over *that?*

We know what Groucho Marx would say: "Go ahead. Say the secret (three-letter) word. You may win a hundred dollars!"

CHAPTER NINETEEN

THE TRIAL OF
THE C4 SEVEN

"WITH 'THE BOYS' it's never all fun and games. With them there's—almost always—blood on the tracks.... "Whatever we come up with has got to be watertight," Erlichman told Nixon in a taped White House conversation in July of 1972. To which Nixon responds, "John, if they had the confessions of some, that's really what...." Erlichman agrees. "And they'll not only have the five burglars, but the two mystery men, (Gordon) Liddy and (Howard) Hunt.

"That'll give the public a lot of blood..."

"This is *blood* money," Diosdado had told Kessler in New York, attempting to persuade him that he was not a man to be trifled with.... Armed with C-4 explosives, endlessly conspiring, cherishing their spycraft like it was the chivalric code, riding back streets in Jeeps, defiant, dreamily-detached from the mess they make and the *blood* they spill...

These are the people we are talking about here.

'The boys.'

On a private plane cruising blissfully above the clouds, one of the best friends Barry Seal ever had told him that he was glad that Barry had been busted—*glad!*—because think of how many bodies would have been maimed by seven tons of C4. Barry Seal had broken down and cried so hard that his friend had to take over the plane's controls.

But the moments when covert operatives—risk junkies—stare the results of their handiwork in the face pass quickly. And life gets back to what passes for normal.

The day after Barry Seal's arrest the New Orleans Times-Picayune published a picture showing Seal being led in handcuffs into the Federal Courthouse to face the multiple felony charges that he *must have known* would ruin his airline career as a pilot with TWA...

Yet, flanked by grim-faced federal marshals, Barry Seal was *laughing* as the flash bulbs popped, sporting the widest grin imaginable. We've always wondered: *why is this man smiling?* Was it that he had ice water in his veins?

Or did he know something we didn't?

When Richmond Harper was arrested he said, "It's the most ridiculous thing I ever heard of."

When they slapped the cuffs on Barry Seal, he said, "All I need is a bunch of Cubans after me."

No one, as it turned out, was in any hurry to prosecute Barry Seal. The case took two years to come to trial, and as the trial delays dragged on it today becomes apparent that putting the Mexican pipeline out of commission temporarily—just for the duration of Nixon's agony—had been the real goal of the operation. The arrests of assets like Seal, Kessler, and Harper had been unintended collateral damage.

When the case finally came to trial it was notable more for moments of humor than anything else...

Outside the courtroom one morning the irrepressible Seal approached one of the undercover agents he had been with on that hot day in Vera Cruz two years previous, DEA Group Supervisor Frank Maldanado.

Maldanado remembers what happened next...

"Barry brought over his young wife, Debbie, and said, 'Frank, was it hot when we were in Vera Cruz?'"

"Very hot," I told him.

"And I was wearing a suit, and sweating a lot, wasn't I?" Barry asked.

"Yes, you were," Maldanado replied slowly, not sure where this was going.

"And the bus broke down on our way back into Vera Cruz, right?"

"I saw you standing beside it, yes, as we drove by on our way back into town," Maldanado confirmed.

"Well," Seal grinned, "tell my wife that. She thought I was out having a good time."

"It was a clear case of entrapment," stated retired DEA agent Dick Gustafson, about the government's evidence at the trial. Seal's longtime associate Bill Maux told us there had been earlier entrapment attempts which failed.

"A guy said that he needed to buy some arms—for Palestinians, I think it was. 'Where's your money?' I said. He showed me a letter of credit. I took it to the bank. I told him I would put him in touch with Dr. Ian Smalley. Come to find out the guy worked for the government and he was trying to get me for selling them arms but I never did anything illegal."

Ian Smalley was a British arms merchant working out of Houston, where he had merited the nickname 'Dr. Doom.' He will later figure into both the October Surprise and Oliver North's arms dealings with Iran which became known as Iran Contra.

"Ian Smalley was an associate of ours," Maux said. "He came to see us in Louisiana. We took him to some place on I-49, a seafood place. He was married then, but he called me from his motel and asked where all the women (prostitutes) were. So I called the Sheriff, who said he didn't fool with them no more, because they were nothing but trouble."

When the trial of the C4 Seven finally got underway government prosecutors promptly introduced into evidence an automatic weapon that had nothing at all to do with the charges against the defendants.

"Intentional misconduct," is what the Appeals Court later called this move, in denying the government's half-hearted motion to re-try the men.

The *Baton Rouge Advocate* published editorials about the case:

Why False Evidence in Government Trial?
"Some serious questions may be raised about the intentions of prosecutors serving the US Government following the failure to obtain a conviction in New Orleans of five men arrested for conspiracy to smuggle explosives to Mexico," stated one editorial, which flayed around for a reason behind the intentional misconduct on the part of the federal prosecutor. US Attorneys are not normally suspected of throwing trials like judicial Black Sox.

The editorials waxed indignant, but they could never figure out quite *what* was going on—and said so. Who, back in those more innocent times, would have guessed that the arrest of the 'C4 Seven' was meant only to *temporarily* interrupt the Mexican Connection weapons and narcotics pipeline—just until Richard Nixon's mouth could be gently but firmly removed from the money end of its feeding tube...

A mistrial in the case of the 'C4 Seven' was declared on June 29, 1974. No harm, no foul. Everybody but Nixon went back to 'business as usual.'

Less than six weeks later, Nixon resigned.

CHAPTER TWENTY

AFTER THE FALL

BEFORE BARRY SEAL could become the biggest drug smuggler in American history; he had to serve an apprenticeship. Where was Barry sent to learn his chops? The DEA. America's Drug Enforcement Agency. At this late date, this is not exactly the irony of ironies it might have been back in more innocent times.

How could this have happened? After the explosives case was dismissed in late June of 1974, according to Pete Brewton, "Barry Seal began working full-time for the CIA, traveling back and forth from the United States to Latin America."

This jibed with what he heard from Gerry Patrick Hemming...

"Barry got a Lockheed Lodestar late in 1974. It was a plane that Howard Hughes once flew, and it would do 300 mph and had a 2000 mile range."

After the explosives case terminated his airline career at TWA, Seal went to work for the CIA, 'sheep-dipped' into the DEA as an operative for the Special Operations Group of the newly created Drug Enforcement Administration. His new boss was someone we strongly suspect he already knew: Lucien Conein, called by the *New York Times* "one of the last great Cold War spies."

Seal was one of several hundred CIA assets "sheep-dipped" into the DEA while the nation's attention was riveted, during the long hot

Watergate summer of 1974, on the progress towards the political gallows of condemned man Richard Nixon...

"The boys" used this opportunity to slip covert operatives into the new DEA whose chief and only loyalty was to people for whom the term "narcotics interdiction" meant keeping out the other guy's drugs.

In the form of his devil child, the DEA, Nixon's legacy, the Drug War, would live on long after his departure from the political scene. It was time to take a look at this controversial organization that Barry Seal "worked" for...

When Nixon made his play to remove drug intelligence from the jealous clutches of the CIA, 'the boys' had retaliated on many fronts. CIA agent-in-place (in the White House) Howard Hunt strove manfully to place as many key CIA officers as he could into the forming DEA. According to Retired Brigadier General Russell

S. Bowen in *Immaculate Deception,* soon there were "more than 100 CIA-trained Cuban exiles, under cover of narcotics enforcement [functioning] as a White House goon squad..."

Unable to publicly block Nixon's "reorganization" plan purporting to heighten the efficiency of the war against heroin—everyone's against heroin, right?—the CIA had infiltrated it instead, placing its own men in positions of responsibility.

Even the Rockefeller Report later stated, "Beginning in late 1970, the CIA used one of its proprietary companies to recruit Bureau of Narcotics and Dangerous Drugs agents.

Egil Krogh explained that Hunt had taken pains to "counsel me as to how we should build, into CIA operations, 'narcotics control' as an important priority."

The ever-helpful Hunt had also suggested Colonel Lucien Conein, CIA since 1954, be brought onboard as director of the proposed White House intelligence office. Hunt also recruited Conein for the Watergate burglars; the man called "Black Luigi" turned him down.

Conein later boasted, "If I'd been involved, we would have done it right." Conein was also involved with Hunt in the perennially popular Agency sport of libeling dead Kennedys, forging cables to indicate that President Kennedy had ordered Diem's assassination.

After Watergate, Conein was put into the Bureau of Narcotics and Dangerous Drugs, in charge of a new strategic-intelligence office in the Office of National Narcotics Intelligence (ONNI) which the next year became the Special Operations Group of the newly formed DEA. He hired large numbers of former CIA officers amid published reports that he was organizing—not a plan to interdict the heroin flooding into America in the waning days of the Vietnam War—but an *assassination* program. Conein and CIA hit squads, we were to learn, go way back...

Conein's "swashbuckling tales of war and death and sex, almost all of them true," according to his *New York Times* obituary, "formed an enduring legend at the CIA." He ran agents behind the Iron Curtain in the early 1950s, and then was the CIA's contact with friendly generals in Vietnam through whom the United States gave approval for a coup as they planned the assassination of South Vietnamese President Ngo Dinh Diem in November 1963.

Others of Conein's credentials proved even seamier.... Appointed chief of covert operations for the Drug Enforcement Administration, a brief flap ensued when he indiscreetly boasted of his membership—since World War II, when he had been its liaison with the OSS—in the biggest heroin smuggling ring in the world, the Corsican Brotherhood.

Conein became a public figure in 1975 by candidly testifying about his role in the Diem killing to a Senate committee investigating the U.S. role in assassinations of foreign leaders. His own role, he testified, "was to convey the orders from my ambassador to the people who were planning the coup, to monitor those people, and get as much information as possible so that our government would not be caught with its pants down."

Neil Sheehan wrote in *A Bright Shining Lie*, "Few secret agents are ever given the opportunity to scale the professional summit by arranging the overthrow of a government. Conein was transmitting the power of the United States to influence these generals to do its bidding."

"He was a man out of his time," said historian Stanley Karnow, author of *Vietnam: A History*. "He was the swashbuckling soldier of fortune—the guy who has ceased to exist except in fiction."

From 1973 until 1984, Conein ran secret operations for the DEA. These missions remain secret even today. Why? Because they set the stage for the massive influx of cocaine during the 1980's.

"I helped place Conein in the Office of Narcotics in the White House," Egil Krogh admitted to us when we reached him at his law practice in Seattle.

"He had extensive experience, we were told, in Vietnam. And I do recall hearing things about how in Laos he was reputed to have recruited some of the tribes over there using narcotics as currency.... But I had no idea that he had been a member of the Corsican Brotherhood. He was a rough-looking customer, though, and I could see how he had gotten his nickname, which, as I recall, was 'Black Luigi."

In addition to spooks from the CIA, five hundred agents of Customs transferred into the new DEA, not all of whom were pleased with what they saw…. The DEA soon employed more than four thousand agents and analysts, and resembled the FBI as a domestic law-enforcement agency.

If the Watergate burglars had not been arrested and then connected to White House strategists, the DEA might well have become the strong investigative arm for domestic surveillance (read secret police) Nixon lusted after. They had the authority to request wiretaps and no-knock warrants, to submit targets to the Internal Revenue Service; and with a contingent of former CIA and counterintelligence agents had the talent to enter residences surreptitiously, gather intelligence on other agencies, and interrogate suspects.

The CIA agents and counterintelligence experts from the military were, under Nixon's original game plan, all supposed to work on "special projects" designated by White House strategists. Soon word spread in Washington that interdiction of narcotics was not high on the agenda… These new 'high-level' intelligence agents had a *different* approach to narcotics intelligence from that of traditional narcotics agents, who operated by spreading "buy money" around until someone attempted to sell significant quantities of narcotics.

Colonel Thomas Fox, the former chief of counterintelligence for the Defense Intelligence Agency, recalled, "they did not seem to possess any systematic intelligence about narcotics traffic. The revelation of this dearth of information raised embarrassing questions as to what the narcotics agents were actually doing."

"All they seemed to be interested in was statistics," said one still-disgruntled Customs agent we spoke to, who had finally transferred back to his old Agency in disgust.

"The whole thing was getting crazier and crazier, and finally I asked to be transferred back to the Customs Bureau."

Charges of corruption and "papering the record" led to reports, widely circulated in the press, that the new DEA was seizing far less narcotics than its predecessors, the Bureau of Customs, the Immigration and Naturalization Service, and the Bureau of Narcotics and Dangerous Drugs.

Nobody thought to ask if maybe that had been the *point…*

In fact, the DEA had such a negative effect on the narcotics traffic into the US that Senator Henry Jackson of Washington began investigating. Rebellious officials in the Drug Enforcement Agency started feeding him morsels of the scandal brewing there. Drug interdiction was a low priority of Conein's DEA Special Operations Group, the whispers said; *assassinations* were what interested the soldiers of fortune who walked its corridors.

It was soon an open secret... Howard Hunt, after all, had recruited Cuban exiles in 1972 to "waste" Omar Torrijos in Panama.

And Conein is shopping for assassination equipment with his old friend Mitchell Werbell at the B.R. Fox Company, a firm with CIA 'connections' specializing in the manufacture of sophisticated assassination devices.

Werbell, known as the CIA's master gunsmith for his innovative silencers, made machine guns quieter than IBM Selectric typewriters. A magazine profile dubbed him "The Wizard of Whispering Death." He headed a half-dozen public companies, owned a bomb-testing range, a private boot camp, and flew around the world in a private Lockheed Jetstar with a pet wolfhound and a series of stunning blondes "who were the raw stuff of Calvin Klein jeans ads," according to the book *Deadly Secrets*.

And Lucien Conein shared a Washington DEA/Special Operations Group safehouse with Werbell's "Central Investigative Agency," which included John Patrick Muldoon.

Jackson's investigators learned that Muldoon had been part of the CIA's massive assassination program in Vietnam, Operation Phoenix. Agency documents found in his safe at the DEA also disclosed, in an interesting gossipy tidbit, that he was sleeping with the wife of a *Washington Post* reporter. Unclear is whether this was on his own or on the Company's time... where he was planning a coup on the small Caribbean island of Abaco which would allow its use "as a haven for gambling and other nefarious purposes."

What was a CIA agent doing setting up "gambling havens?" How does that affect our national security?

Robert Vesco hung out with these people, too, manufacturing in Latin America Werbell's soon-to-become famous machine pistol, the Mac-10, the weapon used in the assassination of Barry Seal in Baton Rouge in 1986.

Barry Seal kept a file current on Vesco, his widow told us. Its whereabouts are, not surprisingly, unknown.

Richard Nixon had first befriended financier and soon-to-be international fugitive Robert Vesco in his '68 campaign, even helping Vesco get released from a Swiss jail through the intercession of United States Attorney General John Mitchell. When Vesco returned to the U.S. he hired Nixon's brother Donald Nixon to return the favor.

When a reliable DEA informant, Frank Peroff, reported that Robert Vesco was involved in heroin smuggling, everyone quickly made for the exits…

Peroff testified that after he dropped a dime on Vesco he was set up to be murdered. When that failed, he was arrested. The DEA was protecting Vesco at Nixon's request, said Peroff.

Bit of a sticky wicket, that.

Presidents of the United States of America don't protect heroin smugglers—do they? Thankfully, before that question could be answered before the Senate Investigations Subcommittee probing into Peroff's heroin charges, the DEA announced the disappearance of its Vesco case file.

Another file missing. Imagine that.

Setting the example for DEA leaders to come, Conein appeared totally unconcerned about consorting with a suspected heroin smuggler, and he and Werbell collaborated with fugitive Vesco in an attempt to put a DEA/Special Ops Group Operations Center in Costa Rica.

Werbell, called before the Senate Permanent Investigating Subcommittee and questioned about Vesco, repeatedly took the Fifth, resulting in his nickname, "Mitch the Fifth." Committee chairman Senator Henry Jackson felt moved to ask: "Did the US Government wish to keep Vesco away for some reason? Does he have some special information which could explain, in part, the national nightmare we've just lived through?

Smart man, that Henry Jackson. Might Vesco's "special information" be the same knowledge which later gets Barry Seal killed? "

"Vesco has information which, if he talked, would make Watergate look like a picnic," one of Jackson's Senate investigators said.

In retrospect, it seems clear that everyone knew what was going on. Chuck Colson had even stated that the Drug Enforcement Administration/Special Operations Group was responsible for kidnapping and assassination.

"I know that Gordon Liddy went down to Miami to recruit talent for the Drug Enforcement Administration's Special Operations Group," a former DEA agent, Wallace Shanley, said. "Sturgis was one of these potential assassins. I don't have any written documentation on this. I was working with these guys: Conein was one of them."

As was the case with the CIA assassination program of the 1960's, Operation Forty, the DEA Special Operations Group assassination program was headquartered in Mexico...

Charles Colson told Senator Lowell Weicker that he "should look into the surroundings of the death an Italian named [Lucien] Sarti, who was a major narcotics trafficker shot in Mexico about two years ago. Sarti bought his way out of jail and got to Mexico where he was shot. Colson said this case will show the *other* half of Conein's operation."

What Colson was referring to as the "other half" of Conein's job, is what is called "the great heroin coup."

It involved the replacement of the French Connection—a creation of the wartime OSS designed to ward off "Communist" influence on the docks in Marseilles—with CIA-linked Cuban exiles acceptable to Santos Trafficante.

French intelligence officials, assisted by expatriate Corsican criminals, had been in the opium traffic during the Indochina War. A still-classified CIA report prepared in conjunction with the DEA accused "the highest levels of French government, industry and society, including the cabinet, police, and military" of having "financial and social connections" with leaders of the worldwide Corsican underworld. The report added that "these criminal leaders can and do use their influence on the families and relatives of individuals in power to accomplish their objectives."

Conein's Operation Deacon was supposedly designed to create "an international net of deep cover assets to immobilize or eliminate international sources of illicit drugs and significant drug traffickers."

Yet Deacon produced not a single drug bust. What it *was* doing became clear, just had Chuck Colson said, when top French Connection boss Lucien Sarti was shot to death by a DEA agent in Mexico City after having been tracked there by Conein's Special Ops Group.

Sarti and his wife went out to a movie, returned to their car and found themselves surrounded by police. The unarmed Sarti was shot dead. And he was not the only French heroin smuggler to die; a score of murders followed within a week.

The subsequent American press blackout of this noteworthy event is the clearest signal of American involvement. But, like Brit Ambrose Evans-Pritchard reporting on the Clinton Drug Scandals, the European press had no qualms reporting what 'the boys' had done to the French

Connection. *Le Monde*, France's most respected newspaper, charged that the break-up of the French drug network was the result of a "close Mafia-police-Narcotics Bureau collaboration" in the U.S. to shatter Corsican influence in the worldwide narcotics traffic, and create a virtual monopoly for the U.S.-Italian Mafia connection, whose key figure was Santo Trafficante."

"This studied disinterest in the politics of narcotics (other than the propaganda, including flagrant lies, from official press releases) is a recurring, predictable phenomenon of our press; and it has visibly had a deleterious impact on U.S. politics," Peter Dale Scott wrote in the foreword to *The Politics of Heroin*.

"If the *Washington Post* and the *New York Times*, the supposed exposers of Watergate, had picked up on stories like the one in *Le Monde*, then the history of Watergate might have been altered... for the history of Nixon's involvement in Watergate is intertwined with that of his personal involvement in drug enforcement. Nixon's public declaration in June 1971 of his war on heroin promptly led to his assemblage of White House Plumbers, Cubans, and even "hit squads," Scott reported.

The "remarkable shift" from Marseilles (Corsican) to Southeast Asian and Mexican (Mafia) heroin in the United States, agreed Henrik Kruger in *The Great Heroin Coup*, was a deliberate move to reconstruct and redirect the heroin trade... not to eliminate it.

The story is evident in the life of CIA Agent Alberto Sicilia-Falcon. Within a month of Sarti's slaying, Alberto Sicilia-Falcon, an exile Cuban pederast based in Mexico and trained at the same Army facility which turned out Felix Rodriguez, had taken over the heroin trade. His business soon had revenues in what the DEA estimated was the "hundreds of millions of dollars."

It was a growth spurt any Silicon Valley start up would envy.

Falcon's career is another example of the way US clandestine services set up and then throw away—like so many Dixie cups— drug smuggling assets...He and his teenaged catamite lived in many palatial homes, including one which was a circular fortress.

"Just the way the house looked was James Bond-y," one associate recalled. His private army fought battles, pirated boats, murdered, and robbed, all with the knowledge and protection of both the Mexican government and the CIA. His money was secreted around the world in the banks of a half-dozen nations.

How did Alberto Sicilia-Falcon achieve such power? Where did he begin? Who, or what, helped him? The agents who tracked him, according to James Mill's epic exposé *The Underground Empire,* explain it all—and with good reason—in three little letters: CIA.

"By the end of their investigation, DEA agent William Coonce remained convinced that both Sicilia-Falcon and his onetime assassin Michael Decker had worked, or still worked, for the CIA," Mills wrote. "We tried to have this checked out, but the CIA won't tell you anything one way or another."

"The CIA originally recruited Falcon in Miami and then it went to his head, he went too far, got too big for his britches, had too much money, too much power," agent Coonce told Mills. "He was definitely planning to overthrow the government of Mexico. There's no question about that."

Though his arrest led to 104 indictments, 73 of them in the United States, scant attention was paid in the U.S. press to the mysterious Falcon. But our tax dollars were clearly paying for some piece of work...

"He'd (Falcon) stay in bed all day with little boys and take pictures of them," reported Mills in *The Underground Empire.* "Someone gave him a beautiful little fifteen-year-old Mexican girl, and he gave her to Carlos's brother Jaime. Jaime used to screw the shit out of her. She'd hang around the house, hardly say nothing, and I remember Jaime said, 'Hey, Alberto, can I do it to her?' 'Go ahead.' You know. 'If I walk in don't even stop.'"

The intrigue swirling around the overthrow of the French Connection illustrate that the later "goings-on at Mena" do not occur in a historical vacuum. Thus the Mena Scandal cannot entirely be laid at the feet of a wastrel hillbilly Arkansas Governor. The organization which surfaced at Mena during the 1980's has had a long and continuous history...

The beneficiaries of the "heroin coup," for whom Barry Seal worked in the '70's, are the same people for whom he will coordinate transportation through Mena Arkansas during the '80's. They include drug world "all-stars" like Santiago Ocampo, who will one day head the Cali Cartel, and Juan Matta Ballesteros, possibly the most "protected" major criminal in world history, going purely on a dollar basis.

Nixon's War on Drugs was designed not to eradicate narcotics trafficking but merely to replace the players. And the new "home team" will one day come to be called the "Cali Cartel," so "protected" that the DEA will create a "visiting" team, the Medellin Cartel, to serve as a straw man. When Medellin (and Barry Seal) were brought down, the protected "home team" continued to hum along as efficiently as the old New York Yankees.

With periodic upheavals, this same "Outfit" appears to have flourished from the late 1940's, when Jack Ruby became associated with it, through the 1980's, when its lieutenants go by names like "Barry Seal" and "Oliver North," and beyond... an organization that has furnished drugs, sponsored politicians, and likely taken over the United States of America.

"Lucien Conein was organizing an assassination program," CIA agent Gerald Patrick Hemming confirmed to us. "Once we got it underway in 74, with a bunch of anti-Castro Cuban assets, I went down to Colombia. The big thing then was sailboats and small planes, and Conein jumped in and the Quantum Corp. assholes and Stewart Mott was around."

"See, the people who control intel nets and have palace access are gun dealers and drug dealers. When I met Barry in 1974, his 'cover' was as an ex-coast guard pilot. But Barry was primarily just a plane-mover back then," Hemming said. "He's moving planes around, gunrunning, hauling cars and cigarettes and stuff."

Charlie Montgomery, recruited by Barry Seal while he was a boy in Baton Rouge, confirms the 'spook' nature of Seal's assignments during the '70's. One of Montgomery's jobs was picking Seal up at the airport when he returned from overseas trips...

"Barry would just show up at New Orleans airport at three a.m. in the morning," he recalls. "Its not like there were any airlines flying at that time of night."

Later—in the mid-'80's—Montgomery became a flight controller at Houston Hobby Airport. "I used to hear Barry's voice coming into the tower," he continues. "Are you cleared for Customs?" the flight controllers would ask him. Barry always replied, "That's already been taken care of."

He was curious enough about this special arrangement, Montgomery told us, to visit Barry while seeing his mother in Baton Rouge one holiday. "Barry just smiled when I asked him, and told me the same thing he had told the flight controller... that it was 'taken care of.'"

DEA agent Dick Gustafson was asked by Seal to visit him in his (Seal's) office in a trailer out at the old Baton Rouge Downtown Airport in 1974...

"Barry said he wanted to help me out," Gustafson remembers. "He was with his attorney, Jack Gremillion Jr., the son of the Attorney General of Louisiana at the time."

"I was shocked at the change in him. He looked like a much older man than the young pilot I had met for the first time just a few years earlier, in '68 or '69. He was already bloated and worn with care."

During that same period in '74, Gustafson relates, he had asked Seal, whom he genuinely liked and felt empathy for, how it was that he had ended up involved with people with organized crime connections...

"Barry got teary-eyed right away," Gustafson recalls, "and couldn't answer the question. But I got the feeling at the time that this was not who he had started out to be, and that he felt bad about it."

Retired DEA agent Kenneth Miley, by numerous accounts, was Barry Seal's DEA 'handler' during the later 70s. We wanted to ask him about the reports we had heard from several sources that an agent named R.A. Thompson had been fired for allowing Seal to bring back an 'unauthorized' load from Colombia in November of '77...

Miley—even 20 years later—won't talk. "Barry's dead. I'm alive," he told us. "I want it to stay that way. I don't talk. Barry was a soldier of fortune, and that led to something else. End of story."

'Soldier of fortune' Barry Seal was still working as a 'plane mover' in 1980, according to Hemming, who explained the size of the operation. "We're guaranteed money. In operations hauling weed from Jamaica, Colombians were starting to stash packages of coke inside the grass, as well as Quaaludes. Barry was a guy who wouldn't bitch if the Quaaludes were getting a 'free ride.'"

What a 'free ride' meant, said Hemming, was that "the pilots were being paid a couple hundred thou for hay (grass.) The suitcase of coke is gettin' a free ride, meaning the pilot's not getting any extra for carrying it. Of course we had to make sure it was a controlled delivery. Or a delivery whose terminus was not inside the United States. We had buyers from the States, and so we'd deliver it to the Bahamas. On the way to Nassau you'd land on Andros Island, offload, continue on, land, close out your flight plan, and go to the hotel."

Seal, according to Hemming, was "an asset in a task force, with a group that had a license to steal. Our assets were guys who volunteered to do the work, and in exchange got certain help from the government."

Hemming has been quoted in dozens of books dealing with American covert operations, and he is thought to be of occasionally dubious reliability. But something he told us that seemed inconsequential checked out completely, when we had the opportunity to verify his information firsthand...

Seal had worked with him, stated Hemming, in "running a smuggling school for a bunch of guys out of Texas in the tiny town of Eloy, Arizona. We had a little rescue school on the side, search and rescue operation for smuggling pilots whose planes had vanished, and been presumed to have gone down."

"Do you know how many pilots have gone down while on smuggling runs?" he asked. "It's not a statistic the DEA generally gives out, but there have been 6000 pilots who have met their deaths in smuggling since 1972."

He recounted a typical search and rescue mission in which he and Barry Seal had participated. "Two pilots left Jamaica, going out around Cuba. They didn't carry life jackets because they thought it was bad luck. We were hired to search the remote keys at so many thousands an hour. A dozen times we (Barry and I) did that. In between we were training people to fly heavier twin-engine planes."

We looked up "Eloy Arizona" on a map, where it is "freeway close" to the CIA's Evergreen Air terminal at Marana, and not far from Oliver North's first National Reconnaissance Operation office, located at the Laguna airfield, where, on the day the Iran Contra Scandal broke, 1400 pounds of cocaine was found abandoned on the runway.

We visited the tiny municipal airport in Eloy to see for ourselves, and discovered several pilots who remembered the DEA training school in 1975 and '76. The school had coincided with the arrival in early '76 of a C-123 military cargo plane, one pilot told us, which the local pilot fraternity all suspected was traveling to South America, and coming back with drugs.

The drug operation, to hear Hemming tell it, was all President Jimmy Carter's fault. "After Carter takes over in 1976, and Admiral Stansfield Turner cleans house at the CIA, finding jobs for longtime CIA assets like Seal became a priority that was often fulfilled by smuggling under color of narcotics interdiction," stated Hemming. "All these guys had to be placed somewhere after that choir boy Admiral started getting rid of 'em. The majority of the operators that were contract employees had to be placed somewhere. There had to be money to take care of these guys."

Hemming is referring to what *Deadly Secrets* calls "Turner's Great Terror," when the new CIA Director purged over 800 covert operatives after the Congressional revelations of the CIA's dirty laundry by the Church and Pike Committee's investigations.

These investigations, which then-CIA Director Bush fought every step of the way, led directly to the election of the peanut farmer or nuclear physicist or whatever he was, from Plains, Georgia.

Even Pineapple Face, General Manuel Noriega, was let go in the purge; it was a sign of the desperation of the times. And it prompted droves of angry CIA cowboys to enlist in the George Bush for President Campaign, where their unofficial campaign slogan must have been "Never again."

Conein had worked out a "crossover' arrangement whereby DEA would claim that any CIA asset busted for narcotics smuggling was on a deep-cover DEA assignment, Gerry Hemming, who also worked for the DEA Special Ops Group, confirmed for us…

"The deal was, anybody involved can be busted, but not convicted, because we weren't law enforcement, we were intelligence."

Documents released under the Freedom of Information Act, make clear that a so-called "gentlemen's agreement" existed between the CIA and the Justice Department, requiring Justice to ask for dismissals rather than expose sources or techniques, should any of Conein's men get in trouble.

An example of this policy can be seen in the story of convicted drug smuggler and Bay of Pigs veteran Carlos Hernandez Rumbaut. Hernandez was arrested and convicted in Mobile Alabama in 1969 with almost 500 pounds of marijuana. After bonding out of jail through Conein's DEA group, he fled the country after his felony drug conviction and landed on his feet in a job (Secured for him by the DEA!) as the top national narcotics official in the Central American country of Costa Rica. Instead of showing any displeasure at this turn of events, the US Government gave Hernandez a diplomatic passport, and he continued to smuggle drugs.

At least twenty-seven U.S. prosecutions of Latin American drug cases and two major domestic cases were dropped because of this CIA involvement with the Department of Justice. On August 23, 1976, when he appeared at the marijuana smuggling trial of Mitch Werbell, Gerald Hemming was arrested, and charged with the illegal transfer of a silencer, and drug smuggling.

In preparation for his trial, Hemming tried to subpoena documents from the Government about the Kennedy assassination, then went on an epic rant worth quoting…

"Why do I want the Warren Commission stuff?" he replied angrily to a reporter's question. "All of a sudden they're accusing me of conspiracy to import marijuana and cocaine. Hey, what about all the other things I've been into for the last 15 years, let's talk about *them*. Let's talk about the Martin Luther King thing, let's talk about Don Freed, Le Coubre, nigger-killers in bed with the Mafia, the Mafia in bed with the FBI, and the goddamn CIA in bed with all of them. Let's talk about all the people I dirtied up for 'em over the years."

"These are federal agents who are paid to advise Secret Service, they are paid to do their job in the country and instead they got into bed with nigger-killers, they got into bed with Jew killers, they got into bed with the Heinrich Himmler cocksuckers, and that ain't done in this country," Hemming continued.

"They've been doing it for too goddamn long and a faggot like J. Edgar Hoover let them get away with that shit. I can get on the goddamn phone and have six contracts out in 15 minutes on Jesus Christ himself. Right now. Cause its out there. This country is run like a goddamned Banana Republic. Have we been targeted because we're nasty motherfuckers and probably had something to do with killing him? They were purging the cowboys."

"Purging the cowboys" had its drawbacks.... After Jimmy Carter's election, his White House Strategy Council on Drug Abuse was stonewalled by the CIA and denied access to classified information on drug traffic, while this group was worrying about the influx of drugs from Afghanistan and Pakistan... apparently with good reason, since 'mechanics' like Barry Seal had begun turning up there.

"Barry would call me from the road every so often," fellow smuggler James Poche told us. "One time I got a call from him, and he was all excited. 'I'm in Karachi, Pakistan,' he told me. 'You should come right over.'"

Another of Seal's oldest friends, Bill Maux, told us Barry was connected to Mena Arkansas as far back as 1969. Maux, a Seal confidante while both were at TWA, remembers, "In the late '60's I went in the travel agency business, late '68 or early '69. Barry was working on starting a helicopter shuttle between New Orleans airport and downtown."

"But the financing fell through, so he had to put the helicopters to work. He sent two of them over to Mena around 1969, early '70 at the latest. He complained to me once about his pilots up there, said he was getting beat on the clock. Looking back, I know there was a lot of horseplay going on in Mena," Maux recalls.

"Even back then—that's about the time it started. We're talking about pedaling those left-handed cigarettes and the stuff to make them."

Left-handed cigarettes, Maux explained, when we asked, meant marijuana.

"Barry just didn't like crop-dusting," said Gerry Hemming. "Under 'cover' of being a Coast Guard pilot in '69, he took part in Operation Eagle. That, and the other things he'd done, made him qualified to be recruited for the DEA's Special Ops Group in 1974. He had been *used* for something."

The way Hemming said, "he had been used for something" sounded as if he were saying 'he had already been compromised, and could be counted on.'

"In Operation Eagle they were after Alfredo Duran," Hemming continued. "His step-father was the guy who took power for two days between Batista and Castro in Cuba. He was a rich kid, trust fund baby, goes to the brigade (2506) as a private, goes to law school, he's met with Fidel and been on CSPAN.... In Operation Eagle they were after Freddie, and ended up with something like 76 people indicted for doing smuggling that hadn't been signed off on, and Barry was involved in there doing some flying."

Hemming then gave the most understandable rationale we've heard for why American intelligence became involved in a massive way in the drug business in Central and South America during the 1970's. He offered a rationale for the nationalization of the illegal narcotics industry that makes a certain skewed sense.

"First of all, we figure, who's using this dope?" Hemming snorted. "Leftists! This is not a fact that messes up my chess game."

"You cannot allow that kind of capability to remain freelance. There is too much money. Some tinhorn asshole can come in, take over, and end up ruling a subcontinent. We were always looking for signs of foreign intelligence and military penetration of the South American drug trade, signs of Soviet or Cuban presence."

"The presence we ended up finding, and which made us have to jump in and get involved in a big way," Hemming stated slowly, "was Israeli."

CHAPTER TWENTY-ONE

BUSTED IN HONDURAS

WHILE PABLO ESCOBAR was still a petty thief in Columbia a man named Juan Matta Ballesteros was already an important player in the international drug cartel. He was arrested with 26 kilos of cocaine (in 1970!) at Dulles Airport outside Washington, D.C. Did this major bust earn Ballesteros a life sentence? Um, nope... He only got deported. Ballesteros was already being called a "friend of the CIA," as well as "one of the largest drug dealers in Latin America."

He was a partner, with Mexican drug kingpin Felix Gallardo, in the drug ring run by CIA agent Alberto Sicilia-Falcon... the man, as we've seen, who was the grateful beneficiary of all of the helpful "rubbing out" of his competition that had been carried out for him by Lucien Conein's friendly boys in the DEA.

A company controlled by Ballesteros, SETCO, will later be the grateful beneficiary of a multi-million dollar contract from our always-helpful State Department, to carry out "humanitarian" assistance to the Contras.

But despite being thought of by the State Department as an eminent "humanitarian," Ballesteros still found it in himself to participate in the torture-murder of DEA agent Kiki Camerana in 1985.

US Customs, bless their backwater agency hearts, had Barry Seal 'made' as a part of this super-organization as early as 1982.

Exuberant, infectiously confidant, and a total adrenaline junkie, Barry Seal seemed to enjoy adventure as much as making money—probably more. He was an effective organizer, and immensely resourceful under pressure. But just as these skills were really beginning to pay off big for him—he and wife Debbie purchased their first luxury home together in an exclusive Baton Rouge suburb in 1978—something went very very wrong.

While flying back from Ecuador with a load of cocaine, Seal was arrested, in Honduras, on December 10, 1979. And when we began to take a look at Honduras, we discovered that if you're interested in American political life at the dawn of the 21st Century, a good place to start is Honduras...

Honduras is where a lot of the bodies are buried—in still-shallow graves.

Just before Barry's arrest Honduras had had a coup, leading to the overthrow of Honduran president Juan Alberto Melgar. Ushered into power was General Paz Garcia. The key financier behind the coup was Matta Ballesteros, which could be viewed as comic opera, except for its serio-tragic consequences.

What happened was that a drug scandal had broken, while Melgar was in the U.S. for medical treatment. A hapless Lieutenant, chief of the Honduran branch of Interpol, had declared that he had given Paz documented proof of the involvement of high Honduran military officers in the international cocaine traffic...

Big mistake-o. General Paz had him arrested for slander, but said that *(but of course)* he was ordering an investigation of the allegations.

Meanwhile the newspaper *Tiempo* ran a series linking top Honduran officers to a rash of kidnappings and killings connected with the cocaine trade. One article, an interview with a fugitive suspect in the kidnap-murder of a couple involved in drug trafficking, fingered Ballesteros, that wonderful "friend of the CIA." For this bit of impudence, the newspaper's cartoonist was arrested.

Adding insult to injury, another newspaper, *La Prensa*, reported that Gen. Paz co-owned land outside Tegucigalpa with Ballesteros, "chief of the local Mafia organization."

The accumulation of these scandals and embarrassments brought down the government of Melgar, who, preparing to run for the presidency in the 1980 elections, had begun distributing copies of a campaign ditty called "The Ballad of President Melgar," praising himself in song:

Let me tell you about a friend
Who knows how to govern this land
He's a help to the poor peasants
Though a general so fine and grand.

Lovers of music in Honduras must have heaved a sigh of relief when Melgar was overthrown.

Under the new regime, Honduran army intelligence began to get a bigger cut of the grateful Ballesteros's drug trafficking, in exchange for protecting his operations. Honduras soon became the major point of transit for cocaine and marijuana coming north from Colombia. At the seat of power sat Leonides Torres Arias, the head of Honduran military intelligence, who, according to a US Senate investigation, begun getting cocaine money kickbacks from the generous Ballesteros right after the 1978 coup.

"What we heard later was Barry had just paid off the wrong people," his widow told us. Deborah Seal, nee Dubois, is from the tiny town of Gonzales, Louisiana forty miles outside of New Orleans, whose main claim to fame—aside from the doe-eyed homecoming princess described in *The Secret Life of Bill Clinton* as 'a ravishing country girl'—is as the "Jambalaya capital of the world." She was 20, working the cash register at a Plantation Chicken outlet just outside town when she met the dashing airline captain Seal, then going through his explosives trial. Seal was smitten, held her hand for a second too long when she gave him his change, and returned to woo her for an entire year before she consented to go out with the much-older (he was 33) man.

Seal was not yet cutting the larger-than-life figure in the narcoculture of the Deep South that he would later, when he wooed Debbie. But he *was* a 747 pilot who knew the world, which offers its own dashing romanticism, even if he in trouble with the law.

"What finally made me go out with him was when he called on Thanksgiving Day a year after I met him," she recalls. "He asked if he could take my family for an airplane ride that afternoon. That seemed safe; besides, I had never been in an airplane before."

Their first years together were lean. "He had lost his job with TWA, and the explosives smuggling charges against him (eventually thrown out by the judge on technical grounds) were on his mind constantly," she says.

Their primary income was from the sign company Seal owned. Debbie remembers traveling to different jobs around the South, occasionally sleeping overnight in their car when money was tight. Then came the smuggling career, to which the young mother—they had three children in three years—was unsuited. She dates the milestones in Barry's developing smuggling career to the births of her three children.

"Our first child was born in July of 1975," she recalls. "All that year Barry was spending a lot of time out of the country, preparing, I later learned, for his first smuggling trip, which occurred on New Years' Eve of that year. We had a second child just over a year later, and I remember Barry picking me up at my mother's—where we stayed while he was gone—that Christmas. I had my newborn on my chest, and Barry dumped a briefcase full of hundred dollar bills on the bed."

"I really didn't know what was happening at first," said Debbie Seal. "He'd be traveling, you know, and I was at home with the babies. We had a nice house, but nothing special."

Later, as it started becoming obvious, there were pitched battles over the source of his income. Barry was a traditional Southern man; his wife was not going to tell him what to do. Debbie was a traditional Southern woman, for whom 'standing by her man' came naturally. And she would need all the loyalty she could muster when he was arrested and charged with cocaine trafficking in Honduras...

"I got a phone call," she says, explaining how she learned that her husband had been arrested, "from a man who owned a hotel in La Ceiba that Barry used to stay at, saying that Barry was in trouble. Then Barry called and said he was caught with an automatic weapon onboard while refueling in Honduras. He said he would be detained a few days. For the next four or five months he'd call and say, tomorrow he'd be home."

He wouldn't. He would spend nine long agonizing months in a Honduran prison.

"I had three kids—six months old, two and three. I was terrified," says Debbie. Though the IRS would hold her hostage after her husband's murder, under threat of a $29 million property assessment, about most aspects of her husband's business she was just exactly what the IRS eventually declared her to be: an "innocent spouse." In other words, the perfect CIA wife...

"At times Barry made cryptic comments about his work for "the Company" without telling me outright whether he worked for the CIA," she says. "He would spin yarns about the Bay of Pigs, and talk of his time in Special Forces, but I never knew whether to believe him or not. I always had the sense that he was working for the government. But I don't have anything on paper to prove it. And I don't suppose I ever will."

When Seal was busted in Honduras, Tegucigalpa newspapers were full of stories about the big-time gringos arrested. A Honduran citizen who worked for Seal during the 80's, Dan McDaniel, provided us with a (rough) translation:

"The North American (Barry) was captured last Friday on the Bay Islands by national investigators. A briefcase containing forty kilos of cocaine was delivered to an American residing in the Bay Island by two foreigners captured Wednesday by Narcotic agents at the La Ceiba airport. Sources say Elder Barryman Seal was carrying a cargo of cocaine. They accused him of being the true responsible trafficker of drugs."

"Colombian nationalized Honduran Stephen Barnun was also captured at the airport in the Piper that came from Ecuador," the newspaper continued.

"An airplane was confiscated, a 45 caliber rifle, and a 56 mm AR180. The following day he (Seal) was transferred to La Ceiba along with the American who was a nationalized Colombian, Stephen Barnum."

Both men ("Barnum" was the alias of Steve Planta, a Seal associate) were sent to the capital along with forty kilos of cocaine. But by the time they had been booked in the capital, the "forty kilo cocaine bust" had miraculously shrunk to just *seventeen*...

"Twenty-five million dollars worth of cocaine was confiscated on the island," the papers reported. "The witness against the trafficker captured yesterday in La Ceiba was presented yesterday in Tegucigalpa before the public relations office of the security forces. Lebers, a Moroccan, having in his possession 17 kilos of cocaine valued at $25 million. The drugs were confiscated from Lebers two days before by the narcotics police of the island. It was established that it contained 17 packets."

Some happy Honduran General must have smiled when he read the reference to the "17 packets." Maybe he patted a suitcase into which he'd packed the other "23."

"Barry tried to keep most things away from me," McDaniels told us, when we asked him about the particulars of the arrest. "And although I didn't meet him until after his release, he later told me that he had simply paid off the wrong people. At that time Barry did not know Generals Alverez or Montoya, the generals that got into politics in the late '70's."

While stopping to refuel in Honduras on his way back from Ecuador, where he had picked up the forty kilos of cocaine, Barry Seal got caught up in a changing of the Honduran guard. While in Ecuador, he supposedly had met a Moroccan Jew, 'Lebers,' offering him a ride back to the States in his private plane after Lebers reported that he had spent 10 days in Ecuador, waiting to meet someone who never showed up.

Sounds unlikely. Remember Gerry Hemming's rationale for US "clandestine services" getting involved in the Colombian drug trade, the presence of Israeli intelligence? Could this have been a subsequent joint operation?

Upon reaching Honduran airspace, Seal had touched down on a deserted runway on one of the Bay Islands, dropping off Lebers, a briefcase filled with coke handcuffed to his wrist, as well as two military duffel bags. Then Seal hopped over to the National Airport to refuel, his plane now clean, and ready to pass inspection.

But something was afoot. The authorities searched his plane thoroughly and discovered an automatic weapon, arrested him, and confiscated his plane (one of the generals reportedly had his eye on it.)

Meanwhile our 'Moroccan Jew,' as conspicuous as a bishop in a brothel, wanders around lost for three days on a tiny island, with a briefcase filled with cocaine handcuffed to his wrist, waiting for Seal's plane to return.

A second group of smugglers was arrested the same day, including a local furniture dealer, Ali Yacub, and Louisiana pilot Emile Camp, who will befriend Seal in prison and become his chief pilot.

"After being informed that the aircraft being piloted by Emile Camp had another passenger who was unknown and who had escaped upon arriving at the airport," the Honduran papers reported, "we can say the third man responds to the name of Lester Marson Clay, alias 'Morsteo,' who in company with Ali in 1977 was arrested for one kilo of coke. The source who provided the information stated that the subject in reference is now out of the country. His location is in the hands of military police."

And a good thing, too... Honduran law enforcement has a famous zero tolerance policy for non-bribe-paying smugglers.

The man Seal had left literally holding the bag, 'Lebers,' was paraded in front of the Honduran press the next day. "I arrived from Ecuador on business as an assistant producer for American television," he said.

"A man I didn't know invited me to a drink at the bar and we conversed about many things. I confided that in two days I would be leaving to go to Miami where my wife would be waiting. He said he would introduce me to two friends who could take me as far as Honduras, thus saving on my fare. In the following days Mr. Stefan was introduced to me, a Colombian. A few minutes later an American, Adler Barryman Seal, arrived, and we left for Honduras."

They told him, Lebers stated, that they would drop him off in Honduras and let him take a plane from there into Miami…

"The American (Seal) said that there was problems entering Honduran territory, so they would drop him off," Lebers said. The following day they would stop by and pick him up.

And that was how he came to be sitting in a hotel room in La Ceiba when he was captured by three soldiers.

"At the island of (Roaton) they forced me to leave the plane. To show that they would be coming back for me they left their baggage. I accepted. I had no other alternative."

Lebers swore he didn't know that the two green military-style duffel bags left by his traveling companions contained such a large cocaine haul, and assured the press that during his questioning there had always been an American policeman present.

Through Emile Camp, with whom Seal will become close in prison, Barry will meet Ali Yacub, and his fellow Lebanese businessman, international arms merchant Gerard Letchinian. All are 'friends' of an American Barry already knows, CIA agent William Earle, whose son, Bill Jr., will four years later be arrested with a planeload of cocaine in Louisiana, involved in a Honduran coup attempt by a General Bueno Rosa funded by $10 million in cocaine, and supported by Oliver North.

Small world. And getting smaller.

William Earle was a CIA agent detailed to Honduras, running a company called International Aviation Consultants.

"Bill Earle started out with an airline operation in Honduras," explained McDaniel. "He had a business down there, an American face that Barry met at the airport. He was a little older than Barry, four or five years, a nice guy, intelligent, pink skin, reddish blonde hair, short, and fat."

"When the military built up the airport, the navy put extensive new radar arrays into a volcano, and Bill, his son, Bill Jr., Gerard Latchinian, and Mickey Soriano were helping General Gustavo Alverez Martinez in this endeavor in Tegucigalpa," Dan McDaniel explained.

"I was in partnership with General Alverez, in charge of armed forces in Honduras, and General Montoya, in charge of the Navy. I had met them back in '74 or '73 when they were just Majors."

Gerald Latchinian is in Oliver North's diary. When he writes that $14 million of the funding for the Contras came from drugs, he is referring to money that came from Latchinian.

McDaniel told us, "Barry went to jail after having paid off a Captain Lopez, who forgot he had to split with someone upstairs. It may have been Ballesteros that was angry. He was a drunk and completely corrupt."

Captain Lopez will one day soon be General Lopez, head of Honduran Armed Forces.

"Ali had a furniture factory in La Ceiba," said McDaniel, "and there is an even better one there now. After he went to jail, Ballesteros pulled him out and financed his factory. The expression 'crime doesn't pay' is not one used often in Honduras."

It took Seal nine months and a half-million dollars to figure out whom to bribe to get out of prison.

"Barry had bribed the government once to get out, but then there was an election in the middle of the negotiations, and he had to pay off a whole new set of officials," one insider said, about the protracted negotiations.

There was even a jailbreak in the planning stages.

"Joe Mazzuka, a Carlos Marcello lieutenant, was going to help spring him," one source told us. "Wendell and Benji (Seal's brothers) started formulating a plan to break him out of prison. Wendell went down to scope out the terrain to see if a helicopter could land."

Amid this intrigue, Barry Seal made himself comfortable…. He had himself built an air-conditioned house inside the prison with a movie screen and a projector. The jailer sent couriers out to fetch his meals from the best restaurants.

Debbie Seal flew down every weekend from New Orleans to the prison at LaCeiba. The staff treated her like visiting royalty, throwing her a birthday party, making little gifts. "They liked Barry," she says. "He raised the standard of living of everybody in that prison."

"I don't know when Barry graduated from pot to coke but this would have been about the time," Debbie says today. "Bill Earle was right there in La Ceiba. And Ellis McKenzie was in jail in when Barry was in jail. He had already gotten busted for smuggling on a ship. He was a ship captain, arrested with a man named Ali Yacub. Yacub was Ellis' boss, a short Spanish businessman, despite his name."

Ellis Mackenzie, a notorious hulking 6 foot 280 pound black Honduran with a violent streak, will later go to work with Barry Seal as his ship captain in a successful seaborne smuggling operation.

In one of the true ironies of history, when Barry Seal flew his CIA-sponsored drug sting operation on the Nicaraguan Sandinistas, the true registered owner of the C-123 military cargo plane which he piloted on that mission was a black Honduran drug smuggler from Honduras' Bay Islands, Ellis McKenzie.

We've got the FAA title records to prove it. The question arises: when did the CIA begin registering American military warplanes under the names of scummy Pirates of the Caribbean?

Despite the creature comforts Barry Seal constructed in the little prison, there was a very frightening aspect to being incarcerated in a foreign land, as well as a residual distance and sadness that appears to have never subsequently left their life together. "I'll never forget the first time I visited him," Debbie says. "As I'm coming to the guard desk there was a woman guard getting ready to start patting me down. And beyond her a stairway, and I could see a guard coming down the steps."

"Then I spotted Barry's face, red and frantic, behind the guard gate," she continued. "He was yelling to the guard, speaking Spanish, telling the lady not to search me, that he had arranged that I would not have to be frisked. They led me to Barry; he's standing at the gate, and they unlock the gate and we just fell into each other's arms. He was all fresh, still moist from the shower."

"He took me to a little room they had where wives could spend the night, a room where they used to hang bananas to dry," she continues. "And I'll never forget, there in that little room with the bananas hanging in it, Barry looked at me, and said, 'I'm still a man,' meaning that he was still the man I'd married."

"The room had a cot in it with little candles, and out the window you could see a bar across the street. And we laid there all night listening to American country and western music, Charley Pride, I think, drifting in from the bar. And I kept wondering if the kids were all right the whole time, our three children that I had left with my mother for the weekend, all under the age of three," says Debbie Seal, a sad note creeping in...

"They were just babies."

CHAPTER TWENTY-TWO

WELCOME TO THE
'GO-GO' '80s

IN THE SUMMER OF 1980 Barry Seal was released from prison into the chilly morning air (it sits on a 3000 foot plateau) of the capital city of Tegucigalpa, Honduras. With the sun dappling the cobblestones of the main square, and the shoeshine men and lottery-ticket vendors unhurriedly moving through their daily routine of setting up underneath the huge shade trees, the newly-freed pilot casually walked down the cool quiet streets, past vending carts offering fresh chunks of pineapple, juicy slices of coconut, and the ever-present bananas.

As Barry strolled through the peaceful Spanish Colonial center of Tegucigalpa, there was as yet no hint of the whirlwind about to descend, transforming this tiny little-visited country into the Lebanon of Central America, and earning it a dubious place in history as the biggest drug marketplace the world has ever known.

During the next few months the calm will be shattered with the roar of hundreds of millions of dollars' worth of bulldozers and huge military transport planes, as the American military presence began to build to support the contra camps tucked discreetly away in the countryside.

While in prison in Honduras, a country which gave the world the phrase 'banana republic,' Barry Seal compiled a rolodex of the current players in narcotics smuggling. When he got out he was ideally positioned to hit the ground running at the dawn of the go-go 80's in Honduras, which was just then becoming the hub of all the intrigue that money can buy...

"We turned the whole damn country into an American battleship," lamented the chairman of the House's Western Affairs Subcommittee later.

"We created the 'USS Honduras.'"

Like a little-noticed tropical depression that grows into a Force 5 hurricane, events in Honduras, that tiny and most backwards of countries—only Haiti in the Western World is poorer, and not by much—roared like a 100 mile-per-hour gale through the lives of millions of Americans.

Through Honduras, and the good offices of the Honduran Army, came the cocaine blizzard that transformed millions of American lives. During the final days of the Contras, the Honduran Army got busted with more than 6 *tons* of cocaine headed for the United States; a bust that came only *after* the end of the contra war had diminished the usefulness of these particular tinhorn generals in mirrored shades.

While in jail in Honduras Barry met William Roger Reeves, a smuggler who told him that he worked for the Ochoa family of Medellin. At this exact same time the man who will become Seal's chief pilot, William Bottoms, is 'released' from the US Navy, raising the prospect that Seal's new enterprise might have been "sanctioned" from the very beginning at the very highest levels of government.

Thus we have Seal's release from prison in Honduras, Bottom's release from the Navy—where according to his own account he flew sensitive intelligence missions—and the beginnings of the collaboration with Roger Reeves, all occurring simultaneously, as if an unseen force, or a hidden hand, were at work...

But who was William Roger Reeves? Talented amateur? Or 'connected' individual?

"Roger Reeves was an illustrious and famous smuggler who owned a house in Metairie (near New Orleans) where he kept a beautiful grand piano, which he played all the time when he was home," former DEA pilot Dave Gorman told us.

"We worked for the Jorge Ochoa cartel," Seal later told a U. S. Court in Miami, as if the Ochoa cartel were a stand-alone entity. "Reeves was a business manager, so to speak."

This arrangement collapsed in August of 1982 when Roger Reeves was arrested by U. S. Customs. But by that time Barry Seal was already becoming a legend among members of the Confederate Air Force, the loose-knit pilot fraternity in the South of former military and CIA pilots whose connections were formed in Southeast Asia.

Was the Reeves/Seal meeting mere happenstance? Just the matter of chance that Seal's later testimony indicated? We found this doubtful. Seal was a master of casually concealing just such sensitive matters of 'national security.' He had, for example, told the DEA men debriefing him in 1972 that the plane he was using to fly the seven tons of C4 plastic explosive had come from "some company registered in Delaware."

So who *was* William Roger Reeves? When we located him through the Federal prison system, in the minimum-security facility at Lompoc, California, we thought we would find an answer. Instead, what we discovered only added to the mystery.

We had contacted officials at the prison over a year earlier to request an interview with their inmate Reeves. They explained the procedures for contacting a prisoner, and a month later, we got word back that Reeves was uninterested in talking.

Then Debbie Seal offered to help. She and he had been on friendly terms, and she thought he might talk to us if we used *her* name with him. But incredibly—when we re-contacted the Lompoc prison administration—they denied ever having had him in their facility.

What's more, a second call to the Washington DC federal locator which had originally given us information as to where in the penal system he was located, this time produced word that no such prisoner had ever *been* incarcerated in the Federal system.

And as if that were not bizarre enough, we received word that he was serving out his American prison term—in Germany. Had he been moved on our account? We called a law enforcement source to inquire. "I'm not sure you want to be asking about that," came his dark response.

Then we met Rene Martin, a Cajun Carlos Marcello lieutenant and smuggling pilot, who had smuggled with and for Barry Seal many times. We had, in Seal's own handwriting, a record of their having done business together. "10/82 rene martin 148 k & jim eakes—several days later 60 more. paid 2.2 & 2.5 million," read the note we found in Seal's files.

Rene told us that he had first met Roger Reeves when Reeves walked into his Mob-run firm, Gulf Caribbean Enterprises, located at the corporate heart of New Orleans, One Shell Square.

Reeves, according to Martin, was a former Orange County, California firefighter who had taken to piloting single engine planes for fun and profit. By the time Reeves hit New Orleans, he was ready for the big time, and had soon leased a 90-foot shrimper which made an epic round the world drug run, sailing through the Suez Canal and then stopping for a load of Thai stick and heroin before proceeding across the Pacific to the West Coast.

But Martin didn't see Roger Reeves as CIA—merely entrepreneurial. Martin is also involved in the smuggling run that Seal eventually pled guilty to in Louisiana, a long and at times hilarious smuggling story involving a load of cocaine that had been flown to White Castle, Louisiana, and was ultimately purchased by Seal. Two kilos from this load were sold to an FBI undercover agent by Seal's associate, CIA man William Earle, Sr.

Barry Seal began to fly cocaine for the Ochoas in an operation staged out of the Carver Ranch, in Belize, which was run by Chester Cotter. And although these two individuals have made appearances in books about Seal and the cocaine cartels, we had read nothing giving the slightest clue to who either Cotter or Carver were…

Which was strange, because the Carver ranch is where Arkansas Governor Bill Clinton's best friend Dan Lasater flew in 1984, seeking to *buy* it. Lasater, a big player in the cocaine trafficking network as early as the mid-1970s, has the distinction of being the only man in anyone's living memory so well-connected that not one but *two* separate Organized Crime Drug Task Forces into his organization—in Arkansas, and again in New Mexico—were shut down before completing their work.

The Carver Ranch was a refueling stop for smugglers coming up from Columbia. Located near the border with the Yucatan, it has cropped up in number of investigations—one of them the "Mena" probe of Arkansas State Trooper Russell Welch, which focused on Barry Seal's smuggling empire.

No simple horse farm, Carver Ranch was part of a trafficking empire. Cotter, the manager, it was said, was a man with legendary sway over the local peons; he would personally greet arriving planes with fuel supplies at the ready on the landing strip.

Accompanied by Patsy Thomasson, later a top Clinton White House official, Lasater flew to Belize in his private Lear jet to negotiate the purchase of the 24,000-acre Cotter ranch.

But the deal fell through, reported *Partners in Power*, because of a dispute with the governor of Belize…

"He proved hard to deal with," according to one observer. One member of the Lasater party then proposed, "that the governor should be wasted."

This caused some consternation for the U.S. Ambassador who was present during the negotiations. Also present was a lawyer from

Washington, D.C. named Ed Cummings, who had flown down with Lasater, ostensibly looking for a horse farm.

This story always seemed heavily redacted to us. And we found out our instincts had been right, when we learned who the two men had been that were associated with what we learned had been the *CIA's* Belize refueling depot.

Mob pilot Rene Martin, we discovered, knew intimate details of the operations staged out of the Carver Ranch. He had helped to build the first crude 3000-ft. runway there, hacked out of the jungle by hundreds of native workers in the remote northwest corner of Belize…

Mr. Carver, for whom the ranch was named, had been a naval inventor helping perfect Allied submarine warfare back in WWII.

And Chester Cotter, who had such legendary 'sway' with the peasants in the countryside, had acquired this clout through the simple expedient of killing any of them who got in his way.

Rene Martin described Cotter as a character like the CIA agent 'upriver and out of control,' played by Marlon Brando in Apocalypse Now.

"Cotter had a silo on the ranch that was filled with corpses," Martin told us. "He killed so many that the Belize government finally stepped in and killed *him* (Cotter)."

If true, this would explain the truculence shown by the Governor of Belize to Lasater's party in 1984. Might Lasater's secret mission have been to smooth out a potentially explosive situation, with a murdered CIA agent and a sullen populace?

That neatly explains the rancor in the reported comment of the Lasater lieutenant; that the governor "should be wasted." What seemed like (rhetorical?) overkill in the context of a failed real estate deal now made perfect sense.

Was Lasater conducting state-to-state negotiations? If so, he had clout of a caliber any Mafioso of the 'dese dem and dose, y'all' variety would envy…

Labeling Dan Lasater as 'Dixie Mafia,' as some have tried, conceals his affiliation with the real organization with the power to shut down criminal investigations. Intelligence reports show that when the DEA opened a file on Lasater in 1983 and assigned him a tracking number. Lasater was tipped off at once, according to Ambrose Evans Pritchard in *The Secret Life of Bill Clinton.*

Roger Reeves introduced Seal in early 1981 to Felix Bates and the Ochoa's, and Barry soon found himself dealing with the Colombians directly. It was the birth of what later became known as the Medellin cartel.

One of Seal's top Colombian contacts was a woman who always wore a costume. According to Barry's widow, who met her several times at Miami's Omni Hotel, she would turn up in a nun's habit or dressed as a nurse. Her role is later taken by Carlos Bustamonte, who became the Ochoa's distributor in Miami, who called himself "Lito."

Seal called himself "Ellis McKenzie," using the name of the criminal black Honduran boat captain he had met in prison. Lito's real name, too, was a closely guarded secret, and Seal would contact him by calling one of three numbers on Lito's pocket telephone pager.

Barry Seal was rapidly becoming, in certain circles, something of a smuggling legend…

"Barry Seal was the Henry Ford of the drug smuggling industry," says Miami private eye Gary McDaniel, who made a specialty of drug cases.

"He brought military logistics to bear on the problem of transportation, which had been the bottleneck in the 70's."

"Seal developed a system that utilized military equipment, electronics, aircraft, communications gear, etc. He was able to succeed because local people thought it was a military endeavor," McDaniels told us.

But smuggling was not *all* Barry was doing during this time…. Some might even say that was just his *cover*…. During this same time period, Ambrose Evans Pritchard told us, he had learned that "Barry was doing recon work very early after the Sandinista revolution."

While home, Barry played the devoted family man, according to numerous accounts. One lifelong friend, John Prevost, remembers Seal's 'suburban dad' days well…

"The way I always remember Barry was how I saw him one day when he passed me on the freeway. It was the mid-70's, and he had an old station wagon and as he passed me he gave me a big wave, and I heard his good-natured laugh…"

"And he's wearing a big t-shirt, he's got a baby on his lap and another on the seat beside him, his car windows' open, and he's singing along at the top of his lungs to some song on the radio."

Not exactly a portrait of an American Drug Lord; Prevost's description of Seal described not so much a drug kingpin as a mid-level government functionary home for the weekend.

Could the two, in fact, be the same?

Seal approached his task with the zealousness of a CEO in a start-up company in Silicon Valley. He studied mistakes previous traffickers had made by reading the testimony in big federal drug conspiracy cases, and even attended trials when he could, soaking up information like a student attending seminars.

Ultimately he created a system that was nearly fail-safe. His planes departed from and returned to his Louisiana bases at night, without lights. They didn't need any; his pilots wore third generation military issue night-vision goggles at $5,000 a pair, which electronically magnified the available light from the stars and moon fifty thousand times.

Seal had such a good source for state-of-the-art night vision goggles that the Baton Rouge DEA asked *him* for some. He obliged.

Once over Colombia, Seal's fleet of planes flew through "windows" in Colombian airspace: precise periods, paid for with bribes when the military would "look the other way."

For the military, this often meant looking straight down into the red jungle dirt, which they would have needed to be doing to avoid seeing the *dozens* of flights which took off every night at dusk.

"You would be sitting in your plane overlooking the sea, on a runway hacked out of a mountainside," smuggler pilot James Poche told us.

"Then as if on cue, when the sun went down you would see dozens of tiny specks taking off from tiny mountain runways in the hills around Santa Marta, flying out over the water into the twilight, heading north. It was a beautiful sight."

Called Operation Seaspray, it was a joint CIA-military operation. In "Secret Warriors: Inside the Covert Military Operations of the Reagan Era," Steven Emerson described Seaspray as a joint Army-CIA project to move counterterrorism forces secretly into and out of foreign countries.

"We provided instant clandestine aviation to anyone and anywhere worldwide," a former Seaspray member told Emerson.

Barry Seal, we soon learned, had been an integral part of Operation Seaspray.

In March 1982, Seaspray began flying electronic spying mission with a Beechcraft King Air. Flying 4 miles above the border of El Salvador, Honduras and Nicaragua, the plane intercepted communications from left-wing opponents and right-wing death squads trying to disrupt Salvadoran elections, Emerson wrote.

In Seal's files were FAA title records we discovered detailing the hidden ownership of Seal's fleet of smuggling craft. In these documents we found the FAA title records for two identical King Air's purchased new for this program, and delivered to Seal at exactly this time.

Seaspray got its names from its pilots, who had often flown just 60 feet above the waves of the Gulf of Mexico in total darkness except for dim light from an instrument panel. They flew so low that waves would occasionally splash the aircraft's windshield.

One pilot spoke of a new co-pilot completely losing it and breaking down into tears from fear.

Re-entering U.S. airspace, Seal's smugglers slowed to 120 knots, so that on radar screens they looked like helicopters coming ashore from oil rigs in the Gulf of Mexico. The planes would pass over a radio checkpoint on the beach— usually at Grand Isle just off the marshy Louisiana coast— and if the radioman on the ground determined that the plane was not being followed, the mission was completed, with the plane following radar beacons to drop sites in remote parts of the Louisiana bayou.

Duffel bags filled with cocaine parachuted to earth to be picked up by circling helicopters, which would, in turn, drop their cargo to vehicles waiting to transport the dope to distribution centers in Miami, New York, and Los Angeles.

The operation more truly resembled an 'underground' cargo airline like Federal Express than any romantic notion of bush pilots flying loads of marijuana with a margarita in one hand.

"The dope business is all about protection," former Louisiana state police official Stan Hughes said. "Remember when Diane Sawyer went down to Colombia to interview Ochoa and Escobar? How did she could find them, when the US government couldn't? And how come all these guys have got zoos in their backyards? Come on! They *own* the government."

The surge of cocaine exports Barry managed and facilitated was for the consortium of Colombian cocaine brokers known as the Medellin Cartel... which by 1980 had acquired the dubious reputation of supplying some 75 percent of all U.S. cocaine.

This was a lie, and not a little white one either; it served to protect, until their services were no longer needed, the people whose coke *was* really ravaging America: Cali.

We began to learn a little about what we came to think of as the Myth of the Medellin Cartel...

The propaganda, first, concealed the names of the true authors of the cocaine blizzard... Juan Matta Ballesteros and the Cali Cartel didn't need machine-gun-wielding toughs; they controlled the *governments* of the countries in which they operated, including Honduras.

According to a study by the U.S. Senate, the Medellin cartel began in 1980 when the Marxist revolutionary group M-19 kidnapped a member of the Ochoa family, already a prominent cocaine manufacturing clan.

At a meeting in his Medellin restaurant Jorge Ochoa convinced the major cocaine families to contribute $7 million each for the formation of a 2,000-man army equipped with the latest in automatic weapons. Over the coming months the cartel's army fought and won a war with M-19, forcing survivors into an unwilling alliance that strengthened the cartel's hand.

More importantly, the process of fighting a common enemy tightened ties among the city's drug families, and they developed a close cooperation in the years following their victory.

Several years ago we began to hear disquieting rumors that the true story of the creation of the Medellin Cartel had not yet been told... that it might well have taken place somewhere in the *Northern* Hemisphere.

"What do you think, a bunch of peasants in the Andes got together and said, let's create our own little OPEC?" scoffed one Special Forces veteran of our acquaintance, who had spent time detailed to Peru in the 1980s.

"*We* created the cartels! It made it easier to deal with than a hundred squabbling warlords, so we put them all under one management."

Startling as it was, we had little trouble crediting his statement; it fit with the knowledge that has accumulated about the Medellin Cartel. Investigative journalists Alexander and Lesley Cockburn were the first to report that the Medellin Cartel made a $10 million "contribution" to the contras, for example, at the behest of Felix Rodriguez, CIA agent, shooter team alumnus and close friend of George Bush...

Ramon Milian testified to this fact to Senator Kerry's Senate subcommittee, to the same reaction from the major media as Gary Webb's Dark Alliance series received...

And General Miguel Maza, chief of Colombia's intelligence agency DAS, reports Cockburn's *Dangerous Alliances*, that he believed the CIA had ties to the Medellin Cartel, which the Agency has gone to some lengths to conceal.

Then in Miami we met Paul Etzel, a soft-spoken Colombian accountant who had worked in Barry Seal's organization in the mid-80s, also serving as Seal's interpreter, including in Panama in meetings with cartel honcho Pablo Escobar.

Etzel later went to jail for six years. He still displays the refined European manners of the South American elite which were doubtless among the qualities that led Barry Seal to recruit him.

"You know, of course, don't you," Etzel asked us, halfway through lunch in a Cuban restaurant in Hallandale, a Miami suburb, "that Barry Seal *created* the Medellin cartel?

Actually, we were forced to tell him, we *hadn't*...

According to insider Etzel's account, Barry Seal took warring groups, competing factions, and brought them together—melded them—showed them the benefits of acting as one.

"He brought together the Ochoas and Ledher and Escobar, all of whom were at each others' throats, and got them to work together."

"On whose orders had he done this?" we demanded.

Paul Etzel didn't know.

"Barry got big... real fast," says retired DEA agent Dick Gustafson. "When I was transferred back to the Baton Rouge DEA office in 1980, Barry Seal was all anybody in the office wanted to talk about. But we never could catch him. He would have his helicopters do drops up in Ascension Parish, and I've interviewed people out there on both sides of the Amite River numerous times, and nothing."

"I went to work undercover in 1979," former narcotics investigator Stan Hughes told us, "buying weed behind McDonald's from 16-year old kids. I hated it—it was pointless and stupid. "

"But 'working' Barry Seal wasn't a whole lot different. I still have an 8x10 glossy picture of Barry while we had him under surveillance, coming out of the Baton Rouge airport in a pickup truck after supervising flying in a load..."

"He actually stopped at the stop sign, looked both ways, waved at me and my partner, and drove away," says Hughes.

"When Barry got busted on the Quaalude thing, and I heard about there being government intervention to save his ass, I didn't believe it at first. But talk to any smuggler, and they'll tell you: they can always buy their way out of a dope deal.... It was all just a game, mostly; their (Seal's) intelligence was always much better than ours."

Hughes smiles. "One time we were watching Barry's house from the air, and he comes out waving a white sheet in surrender. And then a kid came out carrying three suitcases, and gets in a car and takes off..."

"And we think, aha! So we tracked that car all the way to Arkansas... where we found out from the kid that Barry had given him three empty

WELCOME TO THE 'GO-GO' '80s

suitcases and a thousand dollars and said, 'drive to Arkansas and get that helicopter off my back.'"

By 1982, in the words of a congressional investigation headed by Massachusetts Senator John Kerry, the Medellin cartel had perfected the cocaine smuggling business into a high-tech trade based on specialization, cooperation and mass production.

By 1988 the cartel's annual income was estimated at $8 billion and Forbes magazine put two of its leaders, Jorge Ochoa and Pablo Escobar, on its list of the world's richest men.

As the cartel's exports expanded in the early 1980s, the Kerry committee reported, there were 'signs' its smugglers were using CIA covert operations to protect their cocaine shipments into the United States.

This is like saying, after an elephant has rampaged through your living room and defecated on your Oriental carpets, that the turd left behind is a 'sign' of pachyderm presence in the neighborhood.

All major U.S. investigative agencies have been forced to admit, with varying degrees of frankness, that the Medellin cartel used the Contra resistance forces to smuggle cocaine into the United States. The State Department said that "available evidence point's to involvement with drug traffickers by a limited number of persons having various kinds of affiliations with, or political sympathies for, resistance groups."

The war in Central America contributed to weakening an already inadequate law enforcement capability, exploited easily by the organization of mercenaries, pilots and cartel members involved in drug smuggling. But the real Barry Seal was also far more impressive and well-connected than the character played by Dennis Hopper in HBO's made-for-TV movie some years ago, loosely based on the smuggler's life. The film portrayed the pudgy pilot as a hapless victim, caught in a cross fire between bungling but benign government agencies and Latin drug lords.

The truth is a richer—and altogether more sinister—matter of national corruption. Many of Seal's planes had been previously owned by the CIA front Air America, and their ownership showed evidence of almost casual passing back and forth between similarly "connected" front companies like Seal's. Three Piper Navajos involved in Barry's cargo airline were suspected by U.S. Customs as having been owned by Air America.

Louisiana State Police Lt. Bob Thomasson said intelligence reports on Seal date back to 1972. "Mr. Seal was suspected of being the head of a large drug-smuggling organization consisting of some 60 people operating in six or seven states and several foreign countries," Thomasson said.

In 1988, as cocaine was busily destroying the fabric of America's inner cities, the *New York Times* reported that the Reagan Administration was told that the Honduran military, which had been providing critical assistance to the guerrillas fighting the Sandinistas, may have been involved in drug dealing, perhaps as early as 1981. In a February 12, 1988 story the *Times* reported that a former official in the Drug Enforcement Administration said that a United States drug agent stationed in Honduras relayed the allegations to his supervisors from 1981 to 1983 but was ordered not to investigate them.

"According to a former Drug Enforcement Administration official, an American drug agent stationed in Honduras from October 1981 to 1983 sent intelligence reports to Washington charging Honduran military officers, particularly in the navy, with facilitating the transshipment of drugs to the United States," reported the *Times*. The agent, Tom Zepeda, was also said to have charged that Honduran military officers, including Col. Leonides Torres Arias, the chief of army intelligence, were protecting drug traffickers. "The most prominent of those was Juan Ramon Matta Ballesteros, a Honduran believed to have close links to the Medellin drug cartel of Colombia and who was returned to the United States this week to face drug-trafficking charges."

John C. Lawn, head of the DEA, said Zepeda's charges about corruption in the Honduran military were backed by too little evidence to merit an investigation, and were similar to the reports sent regularly from dozens of other countries. He said the agency had never been ordered to ignore the Honduran military's involvement in drug crimes. "That would be a violation of my oath of office," Mr. Lawn said.

But Lawn is lying. In 1983, the DEA closed its office in Honduras, a country that had become the biggest open drug bazaar the world has even known, for what it said were "budgetary reasons." A Federal drug official said it had not been "productive."

Finally, in 1988, the *New York Times* takes a stab at reporting what was common knowledge in Central America at least five years earlier. When they got around to 'leaking the truth' it was for a reason...it was just six days after they had run *this* headline: "HONDURAS PLANS TO BLOCK CONTRAS FROM ITS TERRITORY."

The Honduran Army had made a bid for more money. And the CIA sent a message back through the *New York Times*. It's impossible to miss the connection between the two headlines—unless, we suppose, you're a reporter for the *Times*. Not a case of investigative journalism, alas, but just the normal grinding of two tectonic plates against each other, signifying nothing more (or less) than business as usual.

Someone had merely been sending someone *else* a message about straying from the reservation.

CHAPTER TWENTY-THREE

THE COVERT OP
THAT ATE THE WORLD

HOW BARRY SEAL WENT from being, at the dawn of the 1980's, a talented amateur in the drug smuggling business to just a year later heading a paramilitary organization with almost a hundred employees on two continents, has never before been told. Like with the earlier meteoric rise of Alberto Sicilia Falcon, these are secrets the CIA is loath to have escape.... And while the effects of Seal's historic smuggling operation have been chronicled, and the relationships involved hinted at, there remain today huge questions about just who really benefited from the massive drug smuggling which took place using the Mena airport.

Seal by the end of 1982 commanded an organization with a reach spanning the Western Hemisphere. Did he do this alone? Get there all by himself?

Of course not. We recalled the four essentials that Seal had needed to make it all work...

"Every successful drug smuggling organization needs four things," Miami private eye Gary McDaniel had said, ticking them off on his fingers...

"Production, distribution, transportation, and protection."

What organization had provided the *protection*? And what was the relationship between the hundreds of millions of dollars generated by

Seal's smuggling, and the simultaneous documented infusions of vast sums into the Arkansas bond market?

Had Barry Seal been making cash and then turning it over to Dan Lasater to be laundered?

We recalled the famous exchange between then-Governor Clinton and horrified state trooper L.D. Brown, who confronted his boss after flying with Seal at Mena and discovering the cocaine importation. Clinton waved Brown's concerns off...

"That's Lasater's deal," Brown quotes him as saying. "And your buddy Bush knows all about it."

But where *did* Bill Clinton fit in? He had to have been informed of the operation at a bare minimum. Arkansas is just too small a state to conceal major infusions of men and material. But was he a part of the operation?

Had Arkansas Governor Bill Clinton helped to provide the protection? Of course he had. But no one has been willing to give direct testimony to their relationship...

Until, that is, we met James Miller, the pilot and Seal associate arrested with Barry in the '72 explosives bust. Unsurprisingly, he later went to work flying for the DEA, out of the Baton Rouge office. There, Miller heard all the latest news about the hottest topic of conversation there, Barry Seal.

"One time one of the local DEA agents had told me that Barry had been arrested in Mena, Arkansas. And I ran into Barry a week or two later—at a pay telephone—and we were talking, and Barry said, let me show you something..."

"And he showed me a piece of paper," Miller continued, "a personal release bond, you know, the piece of paper that somebody has to sign before you can get out of jail, signed by Bill Clinton, who at that time was the Attorney General for the State of Arkansas..."

Miller smiles wryly. "And that's when I began to realize that Barry was pretty heavily politically-connected."

Had Bill Clinton and Barry Seal *both* worked for the same shadowy organization?

Would the hidden connections—long the subject of speculation—between Barry's smuggling in Arkansas and the other well-known Arkansas players *ever* become visible? With, for example, shadowy Arkansas powerbroker Jackson Stephens, the biggest contributor to first George Bush in 1988, and then Bill Clinton in 1992?

Or Chicken King Tyson? His attorney Jim Blair? Had all these figures stood idly by and *watched* as Seal used their smallish state to build an empire?

Here was the Holy Grail in our Mena quest:

"Who was Barry Seal working *for?*

The Mena Scandal has been, much like the Kennedy assassination, a frustrating preoccupation of 'conspiracy theorists.' But no Grail quest is easy. The Mafia has the code of *omerta*, their blood-curdling code of silence. And the good ol' boy (and girl) Arkansas elite can also rely on its members to keep their mouths shut, through use of everything from swampy graves to concrete coffins underneath highway pylons to the spray of automatic weapons fire like that which felled Clinton bodyguard Jerry Parks... who, reportedly, had been on many cash runs to Mena with the also now-very-dead Vince Foster.

Less dramatically, group disloyalty in Arkansas is also punished by social ostracism—being denied access to the back-scratching, deal-making network that controls the scams...

But late in our investigation we met a man no longer worried about falling from favor. The reason? He already had...

His nickname in the Seal organization was "Blackie," and he had been "Barry's money man in Miami."

Numerous sources confirmed his close connection with Seal's organization, including Seal's widow, with whom Blackie maintained a friendship even after Seal died. We saw, for example, a condolence card he wrote her after Seal's assassination...

Blackie, who hails from rural Arkansas, is today a talented 50ish legitimate businessman who paid a price for his illegal activities in the 1980's, spending almost a year in solitary confinement in a tiny county jail in rural Florida, and then six years in a federal penitentiary, after being caught up in the DEA undercover effort called "Operation Screamer" which also rolled up Barry Seal.

He was, he told us, a man who had helped put Seal in touch with the other Arkansas "players."

Blackie first met Barry through two college chums of his in law school at LSU in Baton Rouge... Joseph "Beaver" Brantley IV, and ███ ████ ███ are two exceptionally interesting individuals, we were to learn.

Lawyer ████ had been deeply involved in Barry's sign companies, as well as his various smuggling enterprises...

And Blackie's other chum, lawyer 'Beaver' Brantley, has been a part of some spectacularly shady enterprises, with Edwin Edwards son, Stephen Edwards, to give just one example, where he participated in a $100 million 'bust-out' of an energy company…

Money in a publicly-traded energy (natch) company was made to just 'disappear'—to stockholder dismay—like Barry Seal's arrests disappeared, or the government's files on David Ferrie had disappeared…

"Spooks" are called "spooks" because things—and sometimes people—disappear with almost magical frequency around them.

"I became acquainted with Barry in the '74-'75 time period," Blackie related, "through Beaver and ███ and my brother-in-law at the time, a banker from the little western Arkansas town of Helena named Baker Bush….We all got along well, partied and so on, just young men on the make, I guess you'd say."

"My brother-in-law Baker Bush, had taken an interest in Barry's sign company, loaning him money to expand the business. Baker was in a wheelchair; I was married to his sister, who had just developed multiple sclerosis, so there was a lot going on."

"Then I lost track of Barry for a while," Blackie continues, "and reestablished contact by calling him up in 1980, to seek his advice about an airplane I was considering purchasing, a twin Bonanza. I was 'working up a load,' in drug smuggling parlance, putting together the various elements that must mesh perfectly for a successful run to take place. Barry was a top pilot, and an expert on planes. I had also by then heard that he enjoyed a certain level of 'protection.'"

Blackie smiled. "So I called him up, and we got to talking, and one thing led to another…"

At this point in late 1980 and early 1981, Barry, as we have seen, was a talented amateur smuggler, bringing back dope under cover of his real employment as a spook…

"Barry was working as a 'plane mover' in 1980," Gerry Hemming had said.

What Blackie did next seems truly momentous today, if only in hindsight. He had heard through the Arkansas grapevine, he told us, that Fayetteville attorney Jim Blair might be willing to entertain the idea of making a strictly off-the-books cash investment— a high risk investment that would also have the advantage of being *very* high reward…

"I went to see him at his law office in Fayetteville," Blackie said. "Jim's a tall guy, very smart, with a reputation for being highly-analytical, which I remember thinking was a little strange, because his desk was a complete mess, a jumble of papers really. When we were done cutting a deal we had a plane, and a pilot (Barry) and we did our first successful load together. And that was how Barry Seal met Jim Blair."

All we knew at that point about Jim Blair was that he was the guy who had turned Hillary Clinton's $3000 commodities investment into $100,000, a matter of financial probity on which the press had been strangely willing to accord Hillary Clinton—with her smug air of self-righteousness—the high ground.

Most impartial observers who analyzed the transactions concluded it was a straight bribe laundered through futures trading, passed through Blair to Hillary by one of Arkansas's leading industrial conglomerates.

"You and Barry went into business with *the* Jim Blair?" we asked incredulously. "Don Tyson's lawyer? The guy who turned $3,000 into $100,000 for Hillary Clinton and no one could figure out how he had done it?"

Blackie grinned. "Knowing Barry might have helped."

Ken Starr's Whitewater probe had—for one brief flickering moment—turned to the subject of "Drug Money and Clinton," looking into possible links between Clinton campaign finances and drug profits in Arkansas, before slinking back into the safer precincts of Oval Office blow jobs.

Despite substantial evidence of wrongdoing, Starr's investigation was shut down—as all the other law enforcement probes had been—according to disgusted law enforcement authorities who had been there.

Starr's 4-year Arkansas probe wasn't even the *first* 4-year long federal investigation shut down, an honor belonging to the FBI Organized Crime Drug Task Force looking into the Dan Lasater drug trafficking organization between 1982 and 1986.

Lasater had been the focus of a major 4-year FBI probe—investigations usually reserved for outfits the size of the Teamsters.

Gary Webb had made a big discovery about Lasater, he told us, while doing research for his book *Dark Alliance.*

"In December 1986," he told us, "the FBI's own report of the investigation began, 'the Little Rock, Arkansas office of the FBI concluded a 4-year Organized Crime Drug Task Force investigation involving the cocaine trafficking activities of a prominent Little Rock businessman who operated several banking investment firms in Arkansas and Florida.'"

"'The investigation revealed that the businessman was the main supplier of cocaine to the investment, banking, and bond community, the largest bond community in the United States outside of New York City. This task force resulted in the conviction of this businessman and 24 co-defendants to jail sentences ranging from 4 months to 10 years, as well as the seizure of cocaine, marijuana, an automobile, an airplane and $77,000.'"

Webb paused. "Now according to the FBI's own annual report, to warrant an FBI Organized Crime Drug Task Force you must be a major regional drug trafficking organizations with the following characteristics: 1. Highly organized. 2. Multi-jurisdictional in operational scope; and 3. Possess national significance and influence."

"Does that sound like a guy who spent like six months at a halfway house?"

The sentencing of Dan Lasater is yet another vivid illustration that being connected means never having to say you're sorry...Lasater got a slap on the wrist sentence, even though he was acknowledged to have been the Drug Kingpin.

There were also even-earlier examples of thwarted Arkansas investigations, including Federal and state undercover narcotics operations dating back to the mid-1970s targeting powerful Arkansas poultry processor Don Tyson, the major target over a span of ten years.

But the bantam-sized magnate running Tyson Foods, the state's largest private employer, had fended them off with ease...

Operating from an egg-shaped office in the company headquarters in Springdale, Tyson was, like Lasater, a major contributor to Bill Clinton's campaigns, and like Lasater was also alleged to be in the drug business.

Memoranda circulated in the Criminal Intelligence Section of the Arkansas State Police showed Tyson under suspicion of drug dealing as long ago as the early 1970s...

And the DEA had a file, "Tyson, Donald J. et al" including documents referring to the "Donald Tyson's drug trafficking organization."

A report commented that Tyson "is an extremely wealthy man with much political influence and seems to be involved in almost every kind of shady operation, especially narcotics; however, [he] has to date gone without implication in any specific crime."

Another file told of allegations by an informant that "Tyson smuggles cocaine from Colombia, South America, inside race horses to Hot Springs, Arkansas."

Smuggling cocaine inside of racehorses? This, we think, is too arcane a concept to have sprung from *two* separate sources unless it were true… Because in addition to the Arkansas reports, we also have the report of lawyer and author Richmond Odom (latest book "Sold Out") who interviewed a woman named Frances living next door to Barry Seal's "hideout" in Livingston Parish between New Orleans and Baton Rouge.

Frances, also a pilot, had bought the place from Seal because it was adjacent to a landing strip (Seal's). After Barry landed the 'Fat Lady' C-123 military cargo plane on the strip early one morning, she said, a few minutes later she heard the neighing of horses.

She went out on her sun deck, looked across the gravel road to the airstrip, and saw 5 or 6 horses grazing beside the plane. A few minutes later the horses were herded back into the plane, and it took off.

This would seem to indicate one of two things. Either Chicken King Don Tyson and Barry Seal were in the smuggling business together, or each had independently come up with the novel idea of smuggling cocaine inside of racehorses.

Then we remembered: Jim Blair was Don Tyson's attorney.

And suddenly, things cleared up, just a little.

We were able to immediately verify at least one thing we had heard from Blackie about Blair. He was, in fact, a slob: "Jim Blair, the corporate counsel of Tyson Foods, keeps an admittedly messy desk at his office at Tyson Foods in Springdale…" read a news article regaling an anecdote about a sheriff 's deputy moonlighting as a security guard at Blair's law firm. The guard had once reported a break-in at the firm based on nothing but the state of Blair's apparently ransacked office.

Cleanliness may be next to godliness, but it's nowhere near the real seat of power in American life these days… because Blair was a force to be reckoned with behind the Arkansas scene, turning up at crucial flash points in the Clinton history:

It was a call from Blair that persuaded Webb Hubbell to resign as associate attorney general…

A call from Blair that persuaded the late Jim McDougal to buy the Clintons out of the Whitewater land development project in December 1992, a month after the Presidential election…

Even Vincent Foster, friend of Blair's and law partner of Hillary Clinton's, who brought the papers over to sign, was asked to wait outside so he wouldn't hear the details of that particular Blair "power phone call."

But from that day forward, McDougal sharply curtailed his public grousing about the president.

As corporate counsel for Tyson Foods, Blair executed the deals through which Don Tyson built the world's largest poultry company, and later negotiated the plea bargain that got Tyson and his company out of the Mike Espy quagmire…

As a political operative, he raised buckets of money for Democrats, then later got the Clintons out of the Whitewater project…

And it was Jim Blair who steered Hillary Rodham Clinton to her famous $100,000 killing in the commodities market, and then later advised Bill Clinton on how to save his presidency…

Jim Blair, it seemed obvious, was what's known in certain circles as a fixer…

"Those who know Blair hate that he's labeled as a fixer," said one newspaper report. "But they respect the power he's cultivated and are careful not to cross him. His regal congeniality has a sharp edge."

"It would be easy to mistake Jim Blair for a footnote in history," read another article. "He has played his part mostly behind the backdrop. Tyson Foods' company history doesn't even mention his name. But people don't need to see Blair's name in the credits to know that a call from him means that the big gun has been pulled out."

Blair, it was said, pursued two passionate interests: the stock market and politics. His stock transactions were so profitable they were said to have made him more money than his work with Tyson.

He is also, of course, reported to have given away a few secrets to his closest pals, some of whom made a small fortune following his advice…

Could this *very* public man be the Jim Blair, who, according to Blackie, had financed the first load in what would become the biggest drug smuggling operation in American history?

Was Blair really a boy genius? Or was he, instead, just the latest Mafia and CIA-connected wonder like wheeler-dealer Allen Glick, the ambulance-chasing Kansas City attorney who transmogrified overnight into the mega-bucks owner of several of Las Vegas's biggest casinos, courtesy the Teamster Central States Pension Fund for whom he fronted?

(Speaking of the Teamsters, Barry Seal apparently made *them* a tidy profit, too. "I made a trip up to DesPlaines, Illinois once myself," Blackie coyly told us. "That *is* where the Central States Teamsters Pension Fund is located, isn't it?)

Having friends in high places can be an enormous help if you're attempting to establish a reputation as a wheeler-dealer; being a stock market whiz would be a snap if you were getting insider tips from, say, former SEC chairman Bill Casey, whose largesse extended to providing such information to New York Mobsters of his acquaintance. But if Blair and Seal had 'hooked up,' who had Blair's "*patrone*" been?

Of course, a case could always be made that he did it on his own. But if you've been to Arkansas, you likely would sooner believe that Lum and Abner were the true owners of the Federal Reserve than that any of the characters from that benighted state made their 'pile' without a (big) push from offstage. Also, the notion of Jim Blair as *the* secret Arkansas drug kingpin was absurd. It made far more sense that he would have reported to someone higher up. But who?

Hadn't Starr's probe already gone over Arkansas with a fine toothcomb? Wouldn't the national media—even if their coverage was blatantly censored—have snuck in a few clues to Mr. Big?

But then, if the national press had been on top of things back when it counted, Clinton would today still be in Little Rock hosting Governor's Quality Conferences, taking 'lunch meetings' with big-haired state clerks in Excelsior suites.

So we set about finding out for ourselves.

CHAPTER TWENTY-FOUR

THE OLD MAN
AND THE MONEY

THE PAST IS LIKE a foreign country," said F. Scott Fitzgerald in The Great Gatsby. *"They do things differently there."*

Arkansas *is* the American past, in many ways: a place where the feudal power relationships more common in America's earlier years are still nakedly visible to anyone with the stomach to look.

Arkansans don't like to hear such comments; Ross Perot's characterization of the place as "the chicken-shit state" infuriated them. Privately though, the more thoughtful indicated to us that they recognize that all is not well in the Razorback state, and has not been for as long as any of them could remember.

What was deviant in the morals, or lack thereof, of some of the state's leading elite?

"Was it something in the air?" we asked Blackie. "What *was* there, in the Arkansas ethos at the beginning of the 1980's that led you to think that a prominent lawyer like Jim Blair would consider a drug smuggling proposition?"

"I'm not really sure how to answer that," he replied slowly. "I know I never would have gotten in to see him, except for his connection to my brother-in-law Baker Bush, who vouched for me."

Blackie was reluctant to say more about Baker Bush, who he still regards as "family," other than to say that the partners in Barry Seal's sign business had bought Bush out to help him with some "legal difficulties" he got into in 1980...

Baker Hoskins Bush, the former vice chairman of First National Bank of Helena, Ark, had been sentenced to 30 months in prison following conviction for embezzlement and using forged stock certificates to obtain loans, a short article in American Banker magazine explained, totaling $1.2 million during 1979.

Where had Barry and his partners found the cash to buy Baker Bush out? Not a problem. According to Blackie during the year following the approach to Jim Blair, Barry Seal and his partners had experienced what business writers' term "gratifying profitability."

"The biggest problem we had with money was what to do with it," Blackie said. "How to physically dispose of it, I mean. It got so we just weighed it."

According to Blackie, Jim Blair served several functions for Seal's smuggling organization, including providing "protection." When one if its members got into trouble with the law, Blair was there to help...

"In 1981-82 I spent ten months in solitary confinement in Opalousa County Jail in Fort Walton Beach, Florida," Blackie told us. "And we had Blair interceding for us with the Sheriff's office there. Ask Sheriff Jerry Alford, he'll remember."

Jerry Alford, today happily retired and looking forward to many more future years as a "golden ager," declined to comment.

So Blackie explained...

"Foolishly, Barry and I had been talked into supplying some people with cocaine that we had done a little business with before," he told us.

"He was a charter boat captain in Destin with a customs contact at EPIC in El Paso that later got us busted in the federal Operation Screamer thing. Anyway, I went to meet with this guy, who I'd already given a pound of coke, at a Holiday Inn in Destin, Florida, while Barry waited at a pay phone down at the local 7-11. And I got busted for conspiracy to supply cocaine and did eleven months and 29 days in solitary confinement in a little local jail."

Blackie said, "I got out by running a bit of a sting on the state of Florida, aided by Barry and Bush's Task Force guys down in Miami. They sent somebody up to Eglin AFB to talk to me, and I pretended to roll for them, and threw a few facts in with the back-and-forth, and we got the Sheriff's Office to go to the judge privately and tell him I was cooperating, which sprung me out of jail..."

"The worst thing about that stretch was that some DEA guys went and stole $6 million of mine while I was in there, knowing I couldn't do a thing about it," he said ruefully.

Blackie had described in a single stroke the corruption endemic in the concept of the 'confidential informant.'

The little fish are supposed to roll on the bigger fish, in theory anyway; it never happens that way. The reality is that big smugglers like Barry Seal, who brought in planeloads, get probation.

Why? The answer is horrifying: they're too profitable to the those in power to take off the street.

There was a gradual increase in the number of the organization's smuggling runs, Blackie told us, each a little larger than the one before. But there was still a looseness to the operation—and its participants—that indicated that Barry Seal and his confederates had not yet lost their amateur status.

But a big change came late in 1981, said Blackie. They got a new boss, a shadowy figure Barry Seal studiously avoided even mentioning by name...

"Everything changed sometime in late 1981," Blackie told us. "After that the operation tightened up a *whole* lot. Things began to be run completely on a 'need-to-know' basis, with 'cut-outs' everywhere, and strict compartmentalization. Paulie (Paul Etzel) handled the cars; I collected the money, turned it over to Barry, and also took care of the boats.... A guy named Dick Rosen, connected with Customs at the EPIC center in El Paso, helped Barry coordinate the flights."

Nice of US Customs to help keep the Seal smuggling airline running smoothly. We asked Blackie our biggest question...

"Where did the money go?"

"Arkansas," he said bluntly. "Barry began to refer to someone 'high up' in Arkansas as being the real boss of the operation. Barry called him 'the Old Man.'"

"Now everything was, 'the Old Man wants this or the Old Man said that, always in a reverential tone which Barry almost never used. He was clearly not kidding around when it came to this man."

"Who *was* the Old Man?"

Blackie hesitated a beat before answering. "Jackson Stephens," he said. "But you didn't hear it from me."

More has been written about Clinton campaign financier Jackson Stephens than is easily digested by anyone remotely squeamish about plunging into the depths of conspiracy theory...

This much is known: Jackson Stephens grew up with five brothers and sisters on a small farm in the woods of Grant County, Arkansas, working hard to get through the Depression and learning the values of self-reliance, diligence and industry. Young Jack picked cotton and helped neighbors harvest their crops.

He graduated from Columbia Military Academy in 1941, went on to the University of Arkansas and later was appointed to the U.S. Naval Academy. In 1946 he joined Stephens Inc., a municipal-bond house founded by his brother Witt. They went on to build a financial empire.

So far, just another story of an industrious American boy making good, we thought. But regarding Stephens, things get real baroque real fast...

His name appears in almost every whispered scandal of the past several decades: the criminal bank BCCI, Mena, the death of Vince Foster, the Justice Department scandals of the stolen PROMIS software, the Indonesian money in the campaign finance scandal...

The list, as they say, it 'do' go on...

What had first piqued our interest in Stephens was the 'James Norman' angle. Norman was the senior editor for highly respected *Forbes* magazine, when he wrote an article about the death of Vince Foster which implicated Bush's Secretary of Defense Caspar Weinberger in Barry Seal's drug smuggling operation.

Called "Fostergate," it was set to run until being pulled at the last minute, despite *Forbes* own lawyers having cleared it, exactly like the *Washington Post's* spiking of Roger Morris' and Sally Denton's "The Crimes of Mena."

Editor Norman, it turned out, had sent a letter to the White House asking for comment on allegations that the recently-deceased Foster had been involved on behalf of the National Security Agency in a Jackson Stephens company, Systematics, a bank data processing company.

According to Norman's article, Systemics was involved in a highly-secretive intelligence effort to monitor world bank transactions and launder funds from covert operations, including drug and arms sales related to activities in and around Mena, Arkansas.

Norman's sources said Foster was linked to the National Security Agency (NSA) for decades via Systematics of Little Rock, Arkansas, which helped the NSA distribute software enabling them to tap into the computers of banks running it.

"It was sort of a well-known thing within the intelligence community that Systematics was, in effect, a cyber-bank for the intelligence community, a money Laundromat for covert funds that the intelligence community was moving around," stated one of Norman's spook sources.

Norman's story also implicated Ronald Reagan's Defense Secretary Caspar Weinberger in Seal's smuggling. When he was murdered Barry Seal had with him three boxes filled with documents that he carried with him wherever he went, Norman reported.

This much we had no trouble verifying from numerous sources.

Norman reported that among the documents was the encrypted code number (KPFBMMBODB) for a secret Swiss bank account containing over ten million dollars 'belonging' to then-Secretary of Defense Casper Weinberger.

A co-signatory on the account was a relative of then-Senator Howard Metzenbaum, D-Ohio, according to Norman's account, "which is why Congress is so squeamish about investigating this stuff. We are talking about bi-partisan payola," he said, in a letter to the managing editor of *Forbes*, protesting their decision to kill his scoop...

"The clear implication is that Casper Weinberger, while Secretary of Defense, was taking kickbacks on drug and arms sales by arms/drug smuggler Barry Seal," Norman stated.

"I mean, here was Weinberger, Secretary of Defense throughout the Reagan era, during which we had one of the biggest defense build-ups in history, an environment fertile for kickbacks. Payola. Corruption. And, in fact, Weinberger *was* eventually indicted by Iran-Contra prosecutor Lawrence Walsh."

Alas for poor Jim Norman... Cap Weinberger just happened to be on the board at Forbes, which spiked the piece, and then 'spiked' Norman.

Weinberger's name also came up in connection with drug smuggling in a Costa Rican legislative investigation that identified him, along with Oliver North, John Hull, and former Ambassador to Costa Rica Lewis Tambs as personas *non grata*, for helping facilitate a massive drug and arms operation which corrupted that country's society. Were Weinberger to set foot in Costa Rica, today, he would be arrested.

So if this were the tale of a good reporter (Norman) who fell off the cliff into X-Files paranoia, the country of Costa Rica is similarly delusional...

Jim Norman had worked at *Forbes* for five years, after having been recruited from *Business Week*. A *Forbes* colleague described Norman as "one of the best reporters we've got" and "not one of our ideologues at all."

Norman's Fostergate articles portrayed a Jackson Stephens immersed in an unlisted covert world of black ops…Stephens first came into his own in 1976, with the presidential campaign of Jimmy Carter, his classmate in the U.S. Naval Academy in 1946.

Then, just as he was becoming known as a national Democratic fundraiser, in 1980 he threw in his lot with the Republican party, shrewdly writing off Carter in favor of the Reagan-Bush ticket…

Smart move. Arkansas banker Stephens, we learned, has had intimate access to each of the last three Presidents, and both candidates in the 1996 Presidential election "owed him big," as one journalist put it.

A *New York Times* series on candidates' campaign finances reported Clinton received $100,000 in contributions from associates of financier Stephens as well as a $3 million line of credit from Worthen Bank of Little Rock, which Stephens controlled.

When then-Governor Clinton needed a $50,000 loan for last-minute television ads, he called on Stephens Inc. "[Clinton] was somewhat in a panic," the company's President recalled.

Though he was still a big donor to the national Republican party, Stephen's network had begun to 'fall in' with Clinton's campaign, raising crucial early money. On the eve of the triumphant Democratic national convention, Clinton's campaign owed $4 million, much of it to Stephens-controlled Worthen Bank.

Stephens was also deeply involved in BCCI. His name rang a loud gong with those who investigated the career of that "criminal bank," as law enforcement officials called it.

Yet Stephens somehow was always considered an innocent bystander or a victim. In all his dealings, his personal prestige remained unchallenged.

And it was this trait of Stephens which put us back on familiar territory. He belongs, it turns out, to the handful of notables always just off-stage in national politics, like Clark Clifford or Robert Strauss. Stephens is a big player in the Big Leagues, someone who proves, day in and day out that being connected means never having to say you're sorry…

His investment-banking house was the most important outside Wall Street; his family dominated the politics and economy of Bill Clinton's Arkansas for nearly fifty years.

Although Stephens escaped the BCCI snare, he had continued his foreign entanglements with mega-rich Indonesian banker Mochtar Riady, connected with the highest reaches of the Chinese Communist Party.

He helped Riady's Lippo Group establish connections in America, through his lieutenant, John Huang, whose business associates were instrumental in helping to start the Worthen Bank, in which, along with Stephens, the Riady family had an interest. Huang worked on Worthen matters while also helping set up Lippo bank in California and becoming friendly with Gov. Bill Clinton.

Huang also worked with the unit in the Democratic National Committee responsible for raising $7 million in campaign contributions in the Asian communities during 1996—much of which was returned when exposed as 'tainted.'

His actions precipitated the campaign finance scandal after the 1996 election, with allegations that China had bought itself a President, effectively squelched by Janet Reno's Justice Department.

John Huang's whereabouts became a mystery when the scandal broke. Granted top-secret clearance early in 1994, Senate investigators later characterized Huang as a "human vacuum cleaner" who sifted through enormous amounts of classified information dealing with China. During his 18 months at the Commerce Department, Huang was privy to at least 109 intelligence briefings...

The full dimensions of the espionage and influence-peddling scandal may never be known. But the NSA chose Stephens' Arkansas-based Systematics to construct a "Mission: Impossible" room called the Secured Compartmentalized Information Facility at Fort Gillem, Georgia, at the same time that Stephens was involved with Riady's Lippo Group, itself linked to China Resources, a front for Chinese military-intelligence operations.

This is Jackson Stephens, whom we have heard called "the Old Man" of the Mena operation. Clearly, the career of Jackson Stephens shows that the game, whatever it ultimately is, isn't about ideology, or party politics. It's about access... to the same vast network with which Barry Seal was connected, a network that clearly flourishes across party lines.

It's like that scene from the Preston Sturges movie *The Great McGinty*, where a homeless bum who distinguishes himself by voting thirty-five times in one election; his reward is to find himself being groomed by the city's political boss as the mayoral candidate of the *Reform* party.

Puzzled, he asks the boss, who controls the disgraced incumbent and his *establishment* party, how he can deliver the *reform* party nomination as well.

"I *am* the reform party," says the boss. "Hell, I'm *all* the parties."

Considering that Jackson Stephens' Systematics apparently even provided the software for the White House's "Big Brother" data base system, and his myriad other 'spooky' entanglements.... If Stephens *were* shown to be the Drug Kingpin at the top of the pyramid in Barry Seal's world, would it come as any great surprise?

We met a particularly shadowy associate of Seal's from the even-shadowier NSA, who had known Barry since 1972, whom we will call "Gus." And since Stephens name is often mentioned in conjunction with the NSA, we inquired directly about him.

"No comment," came his terse reply.

Even so, he told us later, he received a visit the next day from "a well-known man he had not seen for a half-dozen years. He warned me about talking with you because it might threaten 'current operations.' They asked me if I had everything I need," he smiled. "Got enough money, Gus? Need anything?"

If "Gus" today is perhaps understandably reluctant to have his real name bandied about, it is with good reason, according to former US Customs agent Steve Wallner. "Gus" had been so *big* in his field that Wallner told us there had been a 17-man squad of Customs Agents assigned full-time to tracking his movements in and out of the country.

And "Gus" had been with Barry Seal the night before he died.

"There's no doubt that something quite extraordinary was going on in Arkansas during the 1980's, and that Barry was very much involved with it," he told us.

"But you're missing a big piece of the Barry Seal story. Seal became famous because he had, first, been part of something called Operation Condor..."

"Look *that* up—and *then* come see me."

CHAPTER TWENTY-FIVE

THREE DECADES OF
THE CONDOR

A CONDOR, ACCORDING TO Webster's Dictionary, is "a type of vulture—found in the most elevated parts of the Andes, a large bird which feeds on dead animals."

The name of the CIA's international assassination project called Operation Condor must have been some witty Agency guy's idea of providing food—in the form of human corpses—for the indigenous birds of South America.

Condor was so big that even movie star Robert Redford had heard *something* about it…. His late 70's thriller *Three Days of the Condor* was about the assassination of undercover agents with 'inconvenient knowledge' of a super-secret covert op.

Many moviegoers can vividly recall the challenge hurled at Redford at the end of the movie by his nemesis Cliff Robertson outside the *New York Times* offices…

"Yeah, sure," sneered Robertson. "You can give it to them. But do you think they'll *print* it?"

Today Redford's movie seems more than a little prescient.

Our NSA source "Gus" was a steely-eyed man dressed, when we first met him, in a tight-fitting olive drab t-shirt. He entered the restaurant where we were to rendezvous, Dan B's in Bay St. Louis on the Mississippi Gulf Coast, unnoticed…

"I was asked if I was interested in taking a trip to Honduras in the summer of 1964," he began, sliding into a chair and anticipating our first question.

"I was so eager that I learned Spanish in just two weeks… I ended up spending the next two decades of my life living in Central and South America, eventually working for two different competing factions of the US Government: Customs and the NSA."

Gus was from the tiny town of Bunkie, Louisiana, he told us, where his thirst for adventure had been nurtured by an accomplished mother who was a writer and Ph.D.

"What did you do in South America?" we asked.

"My job was to corrupt the governments of Central and South America," he replied crisply. "I was so good at it that I didn't come back to the States for 17 years."

"I first met Barry Seal in the lobby of the Hotel Maya in Tegucigalpa, Honduras, back in the mid-70's," he continued.

"Barry was good friends with the owners of the hotel, the center of intrigue in Central America back then. And just by looking at each other, we both knew what the other was doing, although neither of us stated it openly to the other when we met, or for a long time afterwards. It was just… *understood*."

"Besides, *what* we were doing wasn't as important as the fun we were having doing it. We were—both of us—making more money than we knew what to do with, and having a great old time doing it."

"Barry Seal was one of the smartest people I ever met," Gus told us. "He was a remarkable entrepreneur. We became good friends. He was one of the few people I ever felt I could trust. And, while I was in Bolivia in the mid-'80's, he was one of my closest associates."

We showed him the picture of Seal from Mexico City in 1963.

"That picture was taken in the night club in the Aristos Hotel, on Heidelberg street off Avenida Reforma in the Zona Rosa," he responded immediately. "I know it well. It's called the Angus restaurant."

"When did you and Barry…?"

He stopped our question with a wave of his hand. "What you learned about Operation Condor?" he demanded.

We began with what is, nakedly and undoubtedly, Operation Condor's most spectacular event…

Just after dawn on July 17, 1980, paramilitary squads in combat fatigues and black ski masks—featureless except for swastika armbands—roared through the downtown streets of the capital city of La Paz, Bolivia, firing on anything that moved. They were soon joined in mutiny by marauding bands of Bolivian soldiers.

The "Cocaine Coup" had begun…

While long-suffering Bolivia had suffered a hundred fifty coups before, this one became the worst torture and killing spree in Bolivian history. When it became public in the mid-'90's, President Clinton came close to apologizing.

And it had all been engineered through Operation Condor.

A month before, six of Bolivia's biggest drug traffickers met with military conspirators to hammer out a financial deal for future protection of the cocaine trade…

According to Peter Dale Scott in *Cocaine Politics*, a La Paz businessman said the coming putsch should be called the "Cocaine Coup." He was right. And today it is…

An Argentine secret policeman told DEA agent Michael Levine the CIA knew all about the coup. "You North Americans amaze me. Don't you speak to your own people?" the officer wondered.

"Do you think Bolivia's government—or any government in South America—can be changed without your government and mine being aware of it?"

When Levine asked why that affected the planned DEA investigation, the Argentine answered, "Because the same people being named as drug dealers are the people who we are helping to rid Bolivia of leftists."

Three weeks later, Levine met with a Bolivian drug trafficker who outlined plans for the new government in which his niece, Sonia Atala, a major cocaine supplier, would "be in a very strong position."

Barry Seal, we will soon learn, worked with Sonia Atala.

The masked paramilitary thugs in the coup turned out not to even be Bolivians, but spoke French, Italian and German, and Spanish with Argentine accents. Their presence in Bolivia would later be ascribed to the CIA—and Operation Condor.

General Luis Garcia Meza was in control. His first act was to release drug traffickers from jail and destroy police records of trafficking. He had brought in the neo-fascist paramilitary squads wearing swastika armbands, calling themselves the "Fiancés of death."

Garza immediately put the Interior Ministry under the control of the nephew of Roberto Suarez, the Bolivian kingpin who went on to become exactly what he styled himself as… the King of Cocaine.

"I knew Roberto Suarez very well," Gus said quietly, interrupting our narrative. "I was married to one of the Suarez's."

Guess who financed the cocaine coup, with $50 million? It's the same man who the year before had financed the successful coup in Honduras...

The CIA's "great good friend" Juan Matta Ballesteros. He is a man who gives the term 'asset' a whole new meaning.

The Bolivian General and his Interior Minister Arce, "a potbellied gangster in a metal-laden uniform—"were in business with Roberto Suarez, Bolivia's biggest cocaine trafficker. DEA agent Mike Levine in *The Big White Lie* recounts how local counterparts informed him that a coup was imminent in Bolivia, and that Argentina and the United States, both worried about Bolivia's "leftist" government, were encouraging the plotters.

"Levine was in way over his head..."Gus told us. "He himself was part of Operation Condor, though he doesn't admit it."

And who would? Nazi war criminal Klaus Barbie had organized the Condor paramilitary groups. Barbie, known in France as the "Butcher of Lyon," lived in Bolivia for years under the alias of Klaus Altmann.

"I knew Klaus Barbie," Gus stated calmly. "We—American intelligence—worked with him. We had to: he virtually owned the damn country. Klaus Barbie controlled the Bolivian military, so we had to do business with him.

"I remember asking him at lunch one day...did he ever have any regrets about WWII? He said, 'just that I never finished killing the bastards.'"

When an outspoken Bolivian socialist, Marcelo Quiroga, called for a national strike to protest the Bolivian coup, military agents dressed in civilian clothes arrived at his La Paz union headquarters in ambulances and stormed the meeting, reportedly killing him.

He was shot, but did not die instantly; kept alive for hours by Argentinean 'torture experts' adept at keeping a person living for the longest time possible while inflicting maximum pain. Day later, his castrated and tortured body was found outside La Paz.

His wife, Christina Quiroga, was at home when a friend called; saying everyone at the meeting had been taken prisoner. All that was left in her husband's office was blood.

"They shot Marcelo, but he didn't die," Quiroga Santa Cruz said 13 years later on a visit to Chicago, in which she showed reporters a copy of a newspaper article featuring a picture of her husband's beaten face. Only years after the murder, when she saw this picture in a German magazine that bought them from a former Bolivian minister of the interior did she learn what really happened.

Enraged, she enlisted the families of others killed in the "cocaine coup" of 1980 and went to court. The man they went after was Army Commander Luis Garcia Meza, leader of the junta that seized power that day, and notorious for his involvement in drug trafficking.

The significance of the coup went beyond the borders of Bolivia. The impoverished nation had just become the latest battleground in a war.

Bolivia's neighbors to the south were ruled by authoritarian right-wing regimes. But to the north, the rest of Spanish-speaking South America was governed by democratic civilian regimes. "The Argentines and the Chileans saw the dangerous ideology of democracy arriving at their borders, and they didn't like it," said one Andean Pact diplomat.

Nor, apparently, did US proconsuls. "Forget politics," said one Bolivian businessman. "For people here, the question was: who is going to control the cocaine trade?"

For the United States the cocaine coup was a diplomatic triumph, the result of the coordinated intelligence efforts of Operation Condor.... and that it ushered in Bolivia's most repressive regime in the 20th century, well, that may well have been *precisely* the point...

"Operation Condor was the result of years of careful planning designed to take over an entire hemisphere," Gus explained. "It was the conquest and then plundering of an entire, nearly virgin, continent, for the benefit of the American intelligence operatives involved in the operation."

Two years after Fidel Castro had marched into Havana and overthrown Batista, Eisenhower and Treasury Secretary Robert Anderson had briefed the incoming President Kennedy...

"Large amounts of U.S. capital," Anderson said, "[were] planned for investment in Latin America." But the investors were holding back, "waiting to see whether or not we can cope with the Cuban situation."

Thus was planted the seed for the School of the Americas, which cultivated intimate relations between American armed forces and those of Latin America and the Caribbean... relations whose practical results were kept from the public until a lawsuit in Paraguay produced five tons of reports bearing the imprint of Operation Condor detailing the arrests, interrogations and disappearances of thousands of political prisoners during Gen. Alfredo Stroessner's 35-year dictatorship of Paraguay.

When Paraguayan dictator Stroessner, considered a neo-nazi even by his admirers, was finally toppled, word of Condor finally began to emerge...

Participating in Op Condor were the security forces of Argentina, Brazil, Chile, Paraguay and Uruguay, all of which were more or less military regimes. Until the discovery of the five tons of documents and files in Asuncion, the existence of Operation Condor was just another wacky "conspiracy theory."

But it had been a nightmare reality they had been forced to live through. Paraguayans quickly nicknamed the files the "archives of terror."

The Operation Condor documents describe a secret U.S. plan for the security forces in Brazil, Argentina, Chile, Paraguay, Uruguay and Bolivia to crush left-wing political dissent.

The plan formalized cooperation among police and military forces in all six countries, tying them to the generals to Washington, who provided the funding for the operation. These South American intelligence services, it was revealed, all used as their blueprint American military manuals that trace back to a 1965 army program to train military, police, and paramilitary forces throughout Southeast Asia and Latin America, the direct precursor to the infamous assassination program Operation Phoenix in Vietnam.

Condor allowed security officers to take part in interrogations, pursue people across borders and order surveillance on citizens who sought asylum in other countries.

In 1986, Senate investigators began to get wind of what had been going on inside the country in the CIA's name since the '70's, where the nerve center for much of this was Miami.

Jack Blum, special counsel to the Senate Subcommittee on Terrorism, Narcotics and International Operations, said, "Holy shit, what's going on? Do we franchise out pieces of Florida to foreign intelligence organizations to conduct illegal activities?"

He had just listened to Leandro Sanchez Reisse's story, just a small piece of Condor. Sanchez Reisse told Blum that in the late 1970s, while serving with the Argentine military intelligence, he had set up a secret money laundering operation in Florida with the blessing of the CIA, to help Gen. Garcia's bloody 1980 coup. Sanchez later became a DEA informant.

Blum notified the Senate Intelligence Committee about Sanchez Reisse, but they didn't delve into his story. A CIA-sanctioned operation in Florida, run by the Argentine military, had subverted official U.S. policy, supposed to be anti-drug.

The CIA had just brought to power a highly organized gang of drug thugs.

What was Barry Seal's role in all this? Louisiana State Police files indicate they were aware Seal was setting up large numbers of dummy companies in Honduras, as early as 1977, almost two years before the cocaine coup.

These dummy companies were *not* used by Seal; for his own smuggling efforts, he had dummy Cayman and Panamanian entities.

"When 'the boys' lost the election (to Carter in '76)," Gerry Hemming said, "they realized they'd been caught napping. They were going to do what it took to ensure that it never happened again. They were going to be goddam sure there wouldn't be any more nasty October Surprises."

The result of their efforts was personified in the person who became known as the Queen of Cocaine, Sonia Atala.

Sonia, a big-time dope smuggler in Bolivia and Columbia who was the most singularly evil character in DEA agent Levine's book *The Big White Lie*, may also be one of the most important figures of the Iran Contra scandal to avoid exposure... Gus, our NSA source, had known her well, in his quasi-official capacity...

"I was what was called an 'in-country private operative' in Bolivia during those years," he told us. "I saw that the deal was, they didn't ask how much money you made. But if something happened to you, you were on your own."

Sonia Atala, a slight figure often dressed in business suits, had almond-shaped eyes and high cheekbones that hinted of Indian blood. But her skin was fair, her jewelry expensive and she might have been mistaken for some Senator's petite little aide-de-camp were it not for her piercing and predatory dark eyes...

With American help, she consolidated her position as the Bolivian "Snow Queen" after the coup, becoming the main link between Bolivian cocaine producers and the Colombian cartels.

According to former DEA agent Levine she was "responsible for shipping more cocaine into the United States than any person I had ever known of."

The CIA, he charged, helped Atala by "destroying her competitors, protecting her from prosecution as she sold drugs to Americans, and paying her a small fortune in tax dollars for her 'services.'"

Sonia Atala and Roberto Suarez avoided prosecution while trillions were made; their arrests would have revealed the ties between the U.S.

intelligence community and Latin American drug traffickers, Levine writes.

When she *was* finally caught, this biggest drug baroness of them cut a deal with the federal government that essentially let her go free, in return for her help in prosecuting a few underlings, former allies, and customers like former "Minister of Cocaine" Luis Arce.

Being 'really' connected means never having to do time.

She testified, "Arce told me that the gringos had cut off financial aid to Bolivia, and the government needed money. They (the gringos) ought to take care of their borders because we're going to cover them with cocaine…to inundate the gringos with cocaine."

"Inundating the gringos with coke?"

It sounds a lot like a diabolical communist plot. (We wondered: had Arce's speechwriter ever been in Guatemala?) Levine wrote, "This all came amid disquieting rumors that at least one of the biggest cocaine labs on the continent—the one at Huanchaca—was run by the CIA to finance covert South American operations like the Contras."

Atala later slipped back to Bolivia, where she was able to recover most of her assets and jump right back into the drug business.

American drug pilot Bo Abbott was part of the same organization, he says, though just a bit player. He was caught hauling a load of cocaine out of Bolivia.

Abbott, a native Virginian, was born and raised in Richmond, where his mother was a secretary for the U.S. Department of Justice. As an 'informant' (read 'dope-hauler') for the DEA Abbott hop-scotched across Central and South America, flying planes laden with drugs, money, and guns to destinations ordained by his government handlers…

He points to Cochabamba, Bolivia, in the central mountains, and Santa Cruz to the east. That is where he used to land, he says, to make contact with Bolivia's biggest drug dealers.

"They keep their planes in Asuncion Paraguay until they need to fly a load," Abbott says, describing a web of dirt strips and supply centers that comprised the Central and South American drug trade.

Abbott said he had frequent contact in Bolivia with the people he called the two biggest drug kingpins: Roberto Suarez and Sonia Atala.

Why have neither of these names been as widely publicized in the United States as Colombia's Pablo Escobar?

Mike Levine, former DEA bureau chief in Buenos Aires, also identified Suarez and Atala as the pivotal Bolivian drug merchants.

Abbott says Atala had a warehouse in the free-trade zone in Colon, Panama, and that he witnessed drug flights in and out of that facility.

Even today reports sometimes surface that the Colon free trade zone is a major hub in the hemisphere's drug and money trade.

Our NSA source confirmed, "I saw Barry a lot at Noriega's private airport in the free trade zone."

What he had begun to learn, Abbott claimed, was that the U.S. government did not really *want* to catch the *major* drug kingpins. Instead, the goal was to control the traffic and protect certain dealers. He claims it was the CIA's way of maintaining political control over Central and South American countries—the objective of Operation Condor.

Abbot stated he had seen how the U.S. Central Intelligence Agency and the Israeli Mossad control the world's cocaine trade, skimming off "black" slush funds to finance covert political operations and the occasional assassination...

"I was not a decision maker," he says. "I was a grunt at the bottom. If I hadn't been making money, I doubt I would have done it."

Court records show that he was a federal drug informant. The DEA taught him how to fly, with special training for takeoffs and landings on short, hazardous runways.

And he drifted, federal court files show, into and out of places like Bolivia, Belize, Panama, and Nicaragua with frequency. Abbott said he and a former DEA agent, since sent to prison, flew multiple planeloads of drugs into the Addison, Texas airport where the DEA maintains its major US base.

And Abbot had worked for the same organization, as did Sonia Atala...

"Sonia was the most dangerous person I ever met," NSA agent Gus, avers. "She was absolutely fearless and also crazy, a lethal combination. One time in Puerto Rico I was at a party at her condo in a high-rise directly overlooking the international airport. She was expecting a plane-load of 'product,' and excused herself, saying she'd return in an hour, and for the party to continue without her."

"When her twin-engine plane landed, Federal agents began to drive out to surround it. And then we saw Sonia screeching right onto the runway shooting a machine gun out the window of a red Corvette at the oncoming federal agents. It was surreal—watching a regular Wild West shootout from a high-rise."

"Sonia stood there and took incoming fire from Customs agents," he continued, "and held them off long enough for most of the cocaine—at least 60 keys—to be offloaded into the trunk of her car, and for the plane to escape."

"Then she took off and led the agents on a high-speed chase through the narrow streets of San Juan, off-loaded in a safe house, and was back at her party an hour later."

"Another time she and I were at a strip club in Puerto Rico together," he continued. "We were sitting in the front row watching the show. Sonia liked girls—she later lived with (Mafia don) Joe Bonnano's grand-daughter—and she saw a girl she wanted dancing in the show, and said to me, 'See that girl? I'm going to have her!'"

"She *was* going to have her, too. I could see how determined she was… And she called the dancer over, and had her join us at our table, and poured her a glass of champagne, and then started laying her line on her. Sonia said, 'I want to take care of you. I want you to live with me.'"

"'Hey, I'm not like that!' the dancer said. 'And I already have a home.' "So Sonia pulled out a paper bag full of money and dumped a mound of hundred dollar bills right out on the table. 'Take however much you want,' she said to the girl."

"And damned if the girl didn't pick up a wad of hundreds— what must have been about 5 grand—and then smile at Sonia and say, 'Where did you say we lived?'"

"Sonia *ran* the cocaine biz in Bolivia," Gus told us. "And that *was* where the business was run from. The guys you heard about— the Ochoas and the Escobars and the Lehders—they were just Vice Presidents fronting for the Company."

"Barry Seal worked directly for Sonia Atala."

CHAPTER TWENTY-SIX

EVERBODY COMES
TO RICK'S

WHILE THE CIA'S Operation Condor was remaking the Southern Hemisphere politically; the DEA had also, strangely, had their own Operation Condor. It was, supposedly, a concerted drug eradication and trafficking interdiction program.

That two separate federal agencies—the CIA and the DEA, always reputed to be at each other's throats—had been running operations at the same time with the same code name has long puzzled writers and journalists. Why the same name? Was it coincidence? Had they just been running low on imagination?

There was only one Operation Condor—we were to learn. And narcotics interdiction was not on the agenda.

Newspapers have for years carried stories about the massive DEA operation called "Operation Condor," bylined everywhere from Mexico to Peru, their contents virtually interchangeable...

"When the Army came in the late '70s to crack down on the drug trade, it only escalated the level of violence," explained one.

"In the clandestine "Operation Condor" CIA-trained secret police from the Southern Cone nations were brought in to oversee Army anti-narco operations. Troops tortured and raped Indians, but never caught up with the country's most infamous drug bosses, Miguel Angel Felix Gallardo and Rafael Caro Quintero among them."

The DEA never caught up with drug kingpins like Gallardo and Caro-Quintero—while they still proved useful—for exactly the same reason that—while he still proved useful—America's biggest drug smuggler, Barry Seal, never went to prison for his crimes.

A few other samples of DEA Condo news clips:

"Condor 6, which got off the ground last July, uses three U.S. contracted Bell helicopters and one State Department-supplied C-123 transport plane, which are flown by U.S. pilots, according to the State Department..."

"Operation Condor, a government drive in the mid-1970s, forced traffickers to flee, most to the state of Jalisco. But many slipped back during the friendly administration of..."

"In its effort to escalate the war on drugs, the Reagan Administration has become entangled in South America's most intense and brutal counterinsurgency campaign. In Peru's Upper Huallaga Valley, Condor 6, a U.S.-sponsored narcotics control operation, works side by side with a campaign by militarized Peruvian police to wrest control of the jungle region from drug traffickers and the Maoist insurgents of Sendero Luminoso ("Shining Path")."

'Rogue' agents have been hinting at the real truth for some time. For example, in the trial in Phoenix of a 'rogue' DEA agent...

"A former U.S. Drug Enforcement Administration informant who was convicted of killing a state Department of Public Safety narcotics agent plans an entrapment defense.... Celaya claimed he was entrapped because he turned down a U.S. intelligence assignment, and refused to take command of Operation Condor, reportedly a conduit for the United States to channel money and weapons to friendly groups in Central America," the Arizona Republic reported.

DEA pilot Abbott had been right. The government doesn't really *want* to catch the major drug kingpins. Instead, the goal is to control the traffic, protecting certain dealers, ostensibly as the CIA's way of maintaining political control of South American governments.

In effect, this means that there are two different kinds of drugs: good drugs and bad drugs. Good drugs are 'our' drugs, goes this reasoning. Bad drugs are everyone else's. It's a neat scheme, and it has worked to near perfection.

And if manipulating the drug trade is the CIA's way of maintaining political control of *South* American governments, another question must be asked. Could this also be the CIA's way of maintaining control of *North* American governments?

Governments like, maybe, *ours?*

"I had pictures of DEA agents and Customs agents loading drugs onto planes in Colombia at one time," one source told us. "And I was stupid enough to think that that would protect me. But it didn't protect Barry Seal, did it?"

Then we heard from an eyewitness testimony about a meeting held in Baranquilla, Colombia in 1981 at which Oliver North had given the order for the arming of the Colombian Marxist guerrillas, the M19.

"Reagan had no idea what kind of power he was turning over to Oliver North," NSA agent Gus told us.

"I saw an idiot sitting around in Barranquilla drinking rum and coke give the order to fly weapons in to the guerrillas, thinking they'd go to war with the cartel guys. The result of North's rum-soaked brainstorm was that Barry Seal was tasked with flying in and arming the rebels, with the expectation that they would go to war with the drug dealers. But the rebels and the drug dealers got together instead."

The CIA armed Marxist Fidel Castro in the late '50's. Was it so preposterous that they would again be arming Marxist insurgents in the mountains—this time in Colombia—twenty years later?

By the end of 1981, Miami was a Smith and Wesson 45, a briefcase full of money, and a new Cadillac with a trunk filled with cocaine and a map showing the route to L.A.

Miami, when the narcotics boom took off in the mid-1970s, became the drug capital of the world. More than 70 percent of the U.S. supply flowed through it. The traffic brought that city both fantastic quantities of money and murder.

The huge influx of hot dollars made Miami a place where shady bankers gave lavish parties at which characters like the one portrayed by Michael Douglas in *Wall Street* exchanged business cards with Al Pacino's sniveling Cuban character from "Scarface," promising to 'do brunch' at Joe's Stone Crabs on the waterfront.

In Miami things got so bad that even after burning tons of confiscated marijuana in Florida Power furnaces, police were reluctant to accept new drug cases because they had no more room to store the evidence.

In Key West the sheriff's office found itself, on most days, with a stash of confiscated drugs worth at least $ 4 million on its hands; the sheriff's men spent an inordinate amount of time just protecting it from thieves—and from each other.

It was all the overburdened authorities could do just to keep a body count. As it turned out, even *that* was a challenge... so many corpses piled up at the Miami morgue that the Dade County medical examiner rented a refrigerated hamburger van to house the overflow....

Bad as things were, we were told by numerous observers, when George Bush's highly publicized Regional Drug Task Force (Division 7) showed up on the scene, they quickly got much worse.

One example: an investigation by an interagency task force led to the arrest of Isaac Kattan, the biggest drug-money launderer ever caught in Florida. An impressive catch, Kattan was a major distributor (the largest in Los Angeles) for the 'protected' coke coming through the "USS Honduras" from Juan Matta Ballesteros...

But when Internal Revenue Service agents on the task force wanted to delay his arrest, hoping he would lead them to the *real* bosses, Bush's DEA Group 7 boys demurred.

"They got twenty kilos of coke but not much else,' said one disgruntled member of the task force. "Chopping off Kattan's head didn't kill off the organization; another head popped up to do the same things. But if the DEA hadn't been in such a hurry to make an arrest, maybe we would have got the organization."

Was this outcome mere coincidence? Or might protecting the organization's lieutenants, like Isaac Kattan and Barry Seal, have been Group 7's mission?

Kattan's sophisticated operation included a network of offshore banks in Panama, the Bahamas and the Cayman Islands, as well as dummy companies incorporated in Panama and the Netherlands Antilles... the same financial centers to which law enforcement had tracked Barry Seal's money flows.

The idea is to create so many zigs and zags of intermediary stops that it becomes impossible, even given a motivated Justice Department, to follow the money trail.

And 'over-motivated' was not a charge ever hurled at Ed Meese's Justice Department.

Kattan was caught because of his own arrogance; he made only perfunctory attempts to hide his trail, and blatantly carried boxes stuffed with cash into banks like the Continental National Bank, the first Miami bank owned and managed entirely by Cuban exiles.

The first indication that Continental was accepting large dope-money deposits had come in 1978, when the Customs Service and the Treasury Department uncovered a laundering operation run by one of Kattan's associates. This is also when Louisiana law enforcement investigators were watching as Barry Seal set up large numbers of dummy companies in Honduras and all over Central America…as part, we now know, of Operation Condor.

"Casablanca on the Caribbean," one crime expert called Miami, the city where Seal came to spend more and more of his time. The intrigue and corruption reminded many observers of nothing so much as Bogie's "Rick's American Bar."

But the movie Casablanca depicted a tri-cornered game, played out by Nazis, Vichy French and the Resistance…

In Miami there were *four* groups of players to be contended with: Italian and Jewish crime syndicates; Cuban exile terrorist groups and the Central Intelligence Agency; Latin American drug dealers; and bankers.

Like every other successful 'player' there, Barry Seal did business with all of them.

It may surprise some to learn that the flamboyant Seal's operation was considerably more discreet than those of the other 'cocaine cowboys.'

His years of tradecraft provided a measure of discipline to his colorful personality… *His* couriers didn't ride around in flashy Mercedes. Instead, they used a small fleet of maroon mid-sized Mercury Marquis, as non-descript as government cars, purchased in wholesale quantity in Georgia by Seal associate Gary Seville.

"We called them (the cars) 'throw-aways,'" Blackie told us.

"We would just leave the keys in the ignition and the product in the trunk, and never see the car again. It minimized our exposure. Where we really felt vulnerable was when the money changed hands."

"Why was that?" we asked.

"Because, by agreement, we didn't come with—with a *contingent*… So the Colombians didn't either. This was good, from my point of view, because I never felt real comfortable around Colombian 'muscle.' But their bosses were a breeze to do business with."

"You mean, you *trusted* the people you did business with in the Medellin cartel?"

Blackie nodded. "Sure. They were always there when they said they would be, and the deal was always just as we had agreed to."

Morgan Hetrick, the Korea-era Marine and private pilot to aviation pioneer Bill Lear before becoming a CIA drug pilot, agreed…

"The Medellin group were 100% straight," he avers. "They were true to their word, they showed up on time, and they were a pleasure to deal with. The USG doesn't do business like that."

Hetrick lost everything when he was caught up in the 'sting' operation whose ultimate target was hapless and floundering sports car entrepreneur John DeLorean. He is scornful in his assessment of the people he worked for and with for many years.

"Compared to the Medellin Cartel, the US Government guys were a pack of lying thieves. You're in a lot better hands dealing with criminals."

The 'US Government guys' had also discovered a tasty target in Seal's organization. He was beginning to feel the pressure of what would become nearly constant surveillance…

"By 1981 or '82 everybody knew who everybody else was," said Blackie. "And from then on, we were always being harassed by 'rogue agents and agencies.'"

"What's a 'rogue' agent?" we asked.

"The honest law enforcement authorities, be it on the local, state, or federal level," Blackie replied. "Guys who weren't clued in on the protected nature of the enterprise being carried out."

No description we heard was more telling. 'Rogue' agents were guys that weren't in on the joke.

"Barry built his organization like an intelligence network," Blackie stated. "Everyone was on a complete need-to-know basis. He was the only one who knew everything. Even though I handled the money, I didn't know a lot of what Barry was doing. We had safe houses and drops all over. For example, we had two condos over on Key Biscayne Boulevard, one right on top of the other…"

"And we had drilled a big hole through the floor of the top one, so that we could come in and lift a load of money from Lito (Carlos Bustamonte) up through the floor, and then ease a load of cocaine back down. That way, we never had to be in the same place at the same time."

Using double-decker condominiums for nearly undetectable drug and money drops between the Colombians and Seal's operation is really a nifty bit of tradecraft, it seemed to us. Credit where credit is due: 'the boys' are nothing if not *smooth*…

"When something *was* interdicted by a rogue agency—and rogue DEA guys were watching us all the time," Blackie continued, "we would immediately go to a little cottage we kept in Fort Lauderdale for precisely that purpose. There we always had between $2 million and $4 million in cash, to buy us out of whatever trouble we'd gotten into."

"Sometimes things got ridiculous," Blackie said. "It was nothing for us to rent out a whole floor of the Omni hotel, just to keep our communications secure. That was a big thing with Barry. We had really high-tech data prompters with digital scramblers attached. You would type in your message and then the scramblers would scramble it so we could communicate without any eavesdropping agents understanding anything being discussed."

From Blackie's accounts, he and Seal had acted just like spies.

"Barry went to extraordinary lengths to ensure secure communications… I remember once flying in from Miami in the Lear for a meeting with Barry, and taxiing into a hangar at Lakefront Airport in New Orleans…

"Barry picked me up and we drove around Lake Pontchartrain to the New Orleans Yacht Club. There a helicopter picked us up; we choppered out to a Texaco barge sitting in the middle of the Mississippi. We got off and climbed down into the engine room of the barge, where, with deafening machinery noise all around us, we had our meeting."

"Just before the Operation Screamer indictments came out in March of 1983 was the worst time, as I recall. Agents were everywhere we went."

When we learned how *much* money there was, we began to get a feel for the immensity of it all…

"Hell, it cost us a thousand bucks a day just to have one of our boats (they eventually had three) sitting at the dock," stated Blackie.

"Barry was having all the boats retrofitted with CIA electronics from that place in Miami… the "'Spy Shop,' I think it was called. Our payroll easily ran into several million a year. But we brought in 2000 kilos a month for the two years I was most intimately associated with the finances of the organization. At four grand a kilo, the organization made about $200 million… And that's in just the two years, '82 and '83, that I handled the money. But by then, too, remember, the money wasn't really 'ours.' I was by no means a full partner, and Barry wasn't either. But there was always enough money so it didn't seem ever to matter how much we took."

Blackie smiled. "We were so flush we even imported a couple of Rolls Royce's from England. Barry sent his English mechanic at Mena, Pete Everson, over to get them. But then Barry decided that they were too flashy, and they just sat around and gathered dust…. The only thing we used them for? Christmas parades in Fort Lauderdale. We donated them every year and they rode in the damn parades."

"Barry was by then talking all the time about what "the Old Man" wanted done, and it was clear that we were part of something much larger. By the way, there may even have been two 'Old Men,' and not just one, the one up in Arkansas, and another with a place in Bal Harbor just north of Miami Beach. It was always one for us, one for the Old Man."

What had happened after 1983? Blackie shrugged. "I'm not the one to answer that question. I 'went away' after that. But the business doesn't change. Barry used to say, you can be sure of just *one* thing with anyone you meet in the smuggling business."

"What's that?" we asked.

"That they aren't who they say they are. Forty-five percent are DEA, forty-five percent are Agency, and ten percent are mercenaries… and they're the only guys who ever go down."

CHAPTER TWENTY-SEVEN

THE WAR OF '82

THE MOST TALKED-ABOUT event in Barry Seal's much-talked about life concerns the persistent rumor, around since shortly after his assassination, that he had been murdered when he threatened to make use of videotape of a DEA cocaine sting which had netted George Bush's two sons, Jeb and George W.

Rumors are just that: rumors; still, when something has been whispered about for as long as this has, its very persistence becomes a story in itself. And this one has all the makings of a major box office thriller...

Governor and Presidential contender George W. Bush and his brother Florida's Governor Jeb Bush, allegedly caught on videotape in 1985 picking up kilos of cocaine at a Florida airport in a DEA sting set up by a vengeful Barry Seal.

Seal was said to have been angry over what he considered Vice President George Bush's shabby treatment of him. In the deal the two had cut, Seal felt, Bush was to take care of his (Seal's) legal difficulties; in exchange, Seal had gone to work for Bush and North at Mena.

Now he felt double-crossed by Bush, so the story goes; his reaction had been to use his DEA cover to set up a sting that ended up netting two very red-faced Bush boys.

Seal then stepped in and 'took care' of things. The Bushies were now supposedly in his debt. Plus he hung on to the videotape shot of the sting for insurance.

In retaliation, Seal was very publicly executed for his impudence less than a year later. When caught, members of the hit team all tell their lawyers that once they got to the US their actions had been directed by a military officer who they all very quickly figured out to be National Security Council (NSC) staffer Lt. Colonel Oliver North.

Where are the tapes? What evidence was there for this story?

The evidence, if it existed, would have been in the three boxes of documents, audio and videotape that Seal had his employees move with him where-ever he went, and that were confiscated by the FBI Special Agent in Charge of the Baton Rouge office who showed up on the scene less than ten minutes after Seal's slaying.

Whatever Seal *was* carrying around with him when he died was so hot that, to get it, the FBI broke the law and violated both the rules of evidence and the US Constitution in their haste to recover Seal's files.

Was this why Barry Seal died?

Our investigation into persistent reports that there exists an incriminating videotape of Republican George W. Bush caught in an aborted (by Seal) DEA cocaine sting was unable to turn up anything to prove the allegation.

But what the search *did* uncover was almost equally shocking.

We discovered, first, that the plane from Seal's smuggling fleet suspected of being flown in the alleged incident had somehow, after Seal's death, ended up in the possession of the person who had supposedly been caught flying it in 1985, George W. Bush.

It was his favorite plane.

Small world? Or just coincidence?

We know what Bogie would have said...

"Of all the planes in all the world, he had to fly in mine."

An even-bigger shock waited. The FAA ownership records of the turboprop King Air 200, which was part of Barry Seal's smuggling fleet of aircraft, and which was supposedly caught on tape in the sting, led directly to some of the major perpetrators of the financial frauds of the 1980's, Iran Contra, and the Savings and Loan Scandal.

Intrigue swirled around the successive owners of this particular Beech King Air 200... intrigue of a characteristically *spooky* kind.

The plane, in just the five years between Seal and the State of Texas Motor Pool, where it was Bush's favorite, had been involved with owners who found it necessary to make the papers on a regular and unflattering basis...

The intrigue includes Greek shippers paying bribes to obtain loans from American companies, which would never be repaid...

An American executive snatching the charred remains of a payoff check from an ashtray in an Athens restaurant...

Swiss police finding bank accounts used for kickbacks and bribes...

In trying to explain to ourselves how this plane went from being part of Barry Seal's smuggling fleet to becoming, according to Texas officials, a favorite airplane of Governor George W. Bush, we had stumbled onto hard documentary evidence of Barry Seal's CIA involvement.

It was a major find. The FAA records confirm that Seal, with whom the CIA has *(natch)* consistently denied any relationship, piloted and controlled airplanes owned by the same Phoenix, Arizona company, Greycas, which owned the majority interest in CIA proprietary airline, Southern Air Transport.

"Barry had a lot more to do with Southern Air Transport than has ever come out," we had been told by numerous sources.

Thanks to trying to track down an unsubstantiated rumor about those wastrel Bush boys, we had clear evidentiary *proof* that the biggest drug smuggler in American history flew CIA planes.

It had started with a lead into the history of the aircraft (a 1982 Beechcraft King Air 200 with FAA registration number N6308F Serial Number BB-1014) found in records kept by Barry Seal's widow Debbie.

Through these files, and other "hard paper" records left by Seal after his assassination including leasing agreements, insurance policies and maintenance records we discovered a deliberately-confusing paper trail of convoluted ownership exactly like those unmasked in the Iran Contra hearings, and leading to the most interesting places.

Unraveling the King Air's tangled and colorful history first requires a look at the year the plane came into service... 1982 was a momentous year. The plane was spanking new. And President Reagan had just introduced "Project Democracy," which he called a "crusade for freedom."

It became, instead, a license to steal.

Here's how it started...

The detonations rumbled along the rocky course of the Rio Negro in Nicaragua throughout the night of March 14, 1982.

Concrete bridges groaned under their own weight, and came crashing in avalanches of dust in a dark landscape seen through night-vision goggles. In certain quarters of Washington D.C, it was time to uncork the champagne.

War was breaking out in Central America.

Two days later, Barry Seal took possession of the first of many planes supplied to him through CIA Director Bill Casey's "off the-books" Enterprise, a King Air 200.

By March of 1982, more than 100 U.S. advisers were in Honduras. The chief of the Honduran Army, Barry's pal General Alvarez, said that his country would agree to U.S. intervention in Central America, if it were (*but of course!*) the only way to "preserve peace."

Some Generals will say anything to make a buck.

"Up to March 1982 you could still change your policy," recalled a member of the NSC later. "The issue was still the question of support for El Salvador's rebels. If that ended, so could pressure on Managua. But once the first forces of Nicaraguan exiles were trained and set in motion, any real negotiating became much harder. The blowing of the bridges was an announcement."

Democrats, fearing that Reagan was pushing the US into another Vietnam-style quagmire, throughout early 1982 tried to cut off aid to the contras, and at precisely this time—at the height of CIA Director Bill Casey's frenetic efforts to ward off these Congressional efforts—Barry Seal acquired two brand new multi-million dollar Beech Craft King Air 200's.

The ownership of the planes was deliberately obscured through convoluted transactions involving Phoenix-based corporations, which we were "fronts" for Phoenix-based General John Singlaub's "Enterprise."

In early 1982 Singlaub had organized an American chapter of the World Anti-Communist League (WACL), with a loan from Taiwan. Seal's King Air 200's come from sources close to these efforts.

Jack Singlaub has a long history of involvement in covert operations, beginning with the World War II Office of Strategic Services (OSS). He served as CIA desk officer for China in 1949—yet another China hand—and deputy station chief in South Korea during the Korean War. During Vietnam he commanded the Special Operations Group Military Assistance Command, Vietnam—Studies and Observation Group, deeply involved in the CIA's Operation Phoenix assassination program.

Seal and Singlaub's covert efforts in 1982 were made necessary by the CIA's recent history. It had been forced, after the shocking scandals of the 1970's, to make drastic reductions in "official" CIA capabilities in the Carter years.

Until then, the CIA had controlled a huge network of planes, pilots and companies for use in paramilitary situations. But after the public revulsion at disclosures of out-of-control CIA covert operations, many of these assets, like the infamous Air America, were dissolved or sold off.

The Contra war put everything back into high gear; the Reagan Administration sought to expand covert paramilitary operations in Central America and elsewhere.

So the CIA and the Army jointly agreed to set up a special aviation operation called *"Seaspray,"* *New York Times* reporter Seymour Hersh revealed in 1987. And the Agency rebuilt its capabilities illegally, relying on assets like Barry Seal.

This is old news to local and state police in areas, like Mena, affected by these extra-constitutional government operations. They—more than most—had seen the cynical manipulation of this operation to flood America with a river of drugs.

When law enforcement authorities debriefed convicted "drug smuggler" Seal in late 1985, one of the cops present brusquely began by stating, "We already know about *Seaspray.*"

The spring of 1982 was an extraordinarily busy time. The boys were getting ready to go to war…

—CIA agent Dewey Clarridge put a proposition to Contra leader Eden Pastora. "He would become the star of the second revolution as he had been the star of the first."

—John Hull, whom Congressional sources said worked for the CIA since at least the early 1970s, rented a contra safe house in San Jose, Coast Rica at CIA request.

—Retired Air Force General Richard Secord began managing an operation in which Israel shipped weapons captured in Lebanon to a CIA arms depot in San Antonio, Texas, for re-shipment to the contras.

—Felix Rodriguez drew on his Vietnam experience and wrote a proposal for the creation of an elite mobile strike force that would be "ideal for the pacification efforts in El Salvador and Guatemala."

—Medellin Cartel moneyman Ramon Milian Rodriguez began to launder, at Felix Rodriguez' request, $10 million from the cartel for the Contras. In secret testimony to a Senate committee he claimed he was solicited by 'old friend' Felix.

—Attorney General William French Smith signs a memorandum of understanding that gives the CIA carte blanche to ignore drug operatives working in the contra movement. French's memo is widely considered the 'smoking gun' proving intent on the part of the CIA in the cocaine epidemic that coincided with the Contra war.

—And Barry Seal moves his base of operations from Louisiana to an obscure airport in the secluded mountains of western Arkansas to hook up with the CIA, which is anxious to use Seal's fleet of planes to ferry supplies to Contra camps in Honduras and Costa Rica.

Between March and December 1982, according to law enforcement records and Seal's own archives, Barry fitted nine of his aircraft with the latest electronic equipment, paying the $750,000 bill in cash… reminding us of an old *Saturday Night Live* gag about Chico Esquela, a clueless Latin ballplayer, changed only slightly…

"National security been berry berry good to me."

Early in 1982 a new cover unit of the Armed Forces was also set up. Known as the Intelligence Support Activity (ISA), it became a separate entity in the Army's secret world of special operations, with its own commander, Col. Jerry King. The secret operation ferried undercover Army operatives to Honduras where they trained Honduran troops for bloody hit-and-run operations into Nicaragua.

The Army went to outside businessmen and arms dealers to make off-the-books airplane purchases, with funds that had been "laundered" through secret Army finance offices at Fort Meade.

$325 million was appropriated for this Special Operations Division of the Army between 1981 and the autumn of 1983.

Through private front companies like the ones, which supplied Barry Seal with his fleet of smuggling aircraft, Operations Seaspray and Yellow Fruit ferried weapons like rapid-fire cannons to CIA operatives busily mining Nicaragua's harbors.

All of this was in violation of Congressional legislation barring the Defense Department and the Agency from any action aimed at overthrowing the Sandinistas.

More importantly, they ignored the manifest wishes of the American people, who strongly rejected war with puny Nicaragua. According to a 1987 *New York Times* report by Seymour Hersh, had these operations become public, they would almost certainly have caused enormous damage to the Reagan Administration.

But that's why God made Special Forces… or so, at least, goes the rationale. Whatever the reason for the Central American war, Seal's drug enterprise grew to become a truly formidable 'funding engine.'

Vast fortunes were made, covertly, during the 1980's… and these are some of the people who made them, giving them a 'leg up' in achieving the coveted distinction of being a 'global oligarch.'

Seal's planes flew from Mena to airstrips in the mountains of Colombia and Venezuela. After making a refueling stop in Panama or Honduras, they would return to Mena. En route, the planes would drop parachute-equipped duffel bags loaded with cocaine over Seal-controlled farms in Louisiana…

"His well-connected and officially-protected smuggling operation based at Mena accounted for billions in drugs and arms from 1982 until his murder four years later," said Dr. Roger Morris and Sally Denton's in *Partners in Power.*

They reported that coded records of the Pentagon's Defense Intelligence Agency (DIA) showed Barry Seal on the payroll beginning in 1982.

The effects of the Barry Seal-directed efforts to take weapons one way and bring drugs the other soon began to become visible, in ruined lives in the U.S. and maimed bodies in Central America.

"My investigation established a conspiratorial period, chronologically, with a first overt act and a last overt act. The first overt act was April 12, 1982," stated Arkansas state criminal investigator Russell Welch.

Of course, Seal's operation was not alone. When private planes began to bomb the Nicaraguan capital, resulting in the crash of a Cessna 404 at the Managua airport, an account of how three Cessna's were secretly transferred from the New York Air National Guard to Central America for the raid on Managua leaked out.

Custody of a number of planes moved from the U.S. Air Force to a top-secret Joint Chiefs operation code-named *"Elephant Herd,"* and then on to the CIA, through a Delaware company where they were first armed and then transferred to the Contras.

This company, Summit Aviation, was doing business with Barry Seal, proved by records in his widow's possession. According to congressional sources, Summit did "contract" work for the CIA, had former CIA personnel on the payroll, and had been linked through ownership records to the Cessna that crashed while bombing Managua.

And the downed Cessna's ownership records were equally as convoluted as were Barry Seal's King Air's. The 'fake paper' desk was doing a crackerjack job…

The Cessna was purchased by Summit in October 1982 from Trager Aviation Center in Lima, Ohio. They covered their tracks on the same day, selling it to Investair Leasing Corp. of Mclean, Va. Investair, which had an unlisted telephone number, and also did contract work for the CIA, according to congressional sources.

The deal was "put together" by Patrick J. Foley, Summit's "military director," a Seal associate whose name and number are in Barry's files.

In addition to work for Investair, Summit maintained and modified planes for Armairco, another company involved in covert Government projects. Armairco, organized in 1982, also bought several multimillion-dollar Beechcraft King Airs like Seal's, purchased directly from Beech in a procedure used only for military projects, according to Beech officials and aviation experts.

They were all, in other words, mil-spec planes.

When asked whether Armairco's Government work included activities in Central America, an Armairco official said, "That may well be."

The convoluted paper history of the airplane which once belonged to Barry Seal, and which was until recently the favorite plane of George W. Bush begins when the title to the new aircraft was first recorded by Portland, Oregon dealer Flightcraft, Inc, in early 1982.

Flightcraft's President, David Hinson, a former military and commercial airline pilot active in the Republican Party in Oregon, at the time was, according to *The Oregonian,* under consideration to head the FAA. The paper stated Hinson met with Transportation Secretary Elizabeth Dole to express interest in the job, even traveling to Washington to promote himself for the post.

Helping Bill Casey subvert the will of Congress and the American people presumably did nothing to hurt his chances…

The King Air, N6308F, was spoken for even *before* it arrived at Flightcraft's facilities… FAA records show a defunct Lake Arrowhead, California firm entered into leasing agreements with developer Eugene Glick in February of 1982, two months *before* the manufacturer's title was transferred to Flightcraft.

On paper the plane was 'owned' by a Greyhound Bus Lines subsidiary, Greycas, which in turn leased it to a mysterious Phoenix firm close to John Singlaub's Enterprise operations named Systems Marketing, Inc.

AP reporter Bryson Hull reported to us recently that some digging had revealed that Systems Marketing was a wholly owned subsidiary of yet-another company, called… Military Electronics.

Can you say "Iran Contra?" (We knew that you could.)

Military Electronics, through its cutout, Systems Marketing, then leased the plane to Continental Desert Properties, a firm owned by Gene Glick…

In the final step, Glick turned the plane over to Barry Seal. Insurance policies found in Seal's private papers confirm that he signed for an insurance policy on the aircraft.

What was the *purpose* of this convoluted ownership? What was it designed to conceal?

The answer lies in the very definition of "tradecraft," a term for what it is that spies and covert operators *do*: operate in the dark. The 'front' companies were in place to act as "cut-outs," layers of insulation, between the spy agency, in this case Bill Casey's CIA, and the covert operative, in this case, Barry Seal.

Gene Glick lived in the exclusive Hope Ranch, very near Ronald Reagan's Rancho Del Cielo Ranch in Santa Barbara, California. He leased not just this but several other of Barry Seal's planes and helicopters as well, during the time Seal was most active in drug and weapons smuggling.

Other documents we uncovered revealed that Glick was also actively helping Seal purchase ocean-going vessels, for use in drug smuggling activities, and as stationary platforms for the CIA to use off the coast of Nicaragua.

FBI agent Del Hahn, who had dismissed Glick's importance to us, had instead fueled our suspicions.

"He's just a money launderer," said Hahn, Special Agent in Charge of an Inter-Agency Organized Crime Drug Task Force looking into Barry Seal's organization in the mid-'80's.

Not *quite,* Delbert.... He was a *cutout.*

The circle was completed when we discovered that the Beech King Air, as well as several others used by Barry Seal, had been in reality owned all the time...by the CIA, through the company revealed in 1998 bankruptcy proceedings to have owned Southern Air Transport (SAT). Southern Air was owned by an entity called Finova, which was disclosed when no one was looking when SAT went into bankruptcy in 1998.

Southern Air is a legendary CIA proprietary—second only to Air America—connected to Secord, Singlaub, Rodriguez, Casey and Vice President George Bush.

The company that supposedly 'owned' Barry Seal's King Air's is an Agency front, set up in Arizona and headquartered in Canada to escape American financial disclosure requirements.

Among its dubious achievements Southern Air owned the C123 used by Seal in the Nicaragua sting operation; the same aircraft that was

later shot down over Nicaragua in 1986. When lone survivor Eugene
Hasenfus was captured by Sandinistas, it had precipitated what became
known as the Iran-Contra scandal.

Back then, no one knew—or admitted knowing—just who owned
Southern Air Transport, although Government officials swore up and
down that it *wasn't* the CIA.

On June 14, 1984, after passage of the second Boland Amendment
and the consolidation of Contra operations under Oliver North, the
plane was sold twice in one day, first to a Morgan B.

Mitchell of Vale, Oregon, and then to Chevrolet Dealer Merrill Bean
of Ogden Utah, who curiously gave the Dover, Delaware address of the
"Prentis Hall Corporation" on his FAA registration.

Students of the CIA have long been aware of the agency's affinity for
hiding its assets in Delaware corporations. But many other companies
do so for reasons of convenience. In an interview Bean stated that he had
incorporated in Delaware as a legal necessity because of the needs of his
investors.

"Delaware is a very convenient place for many kinds of corporations
to incorporate and many large corporations and multi-nationals do so,"
Bean said. "Because other companies I was in partnership with were
incorporated there I chose to do so also. It was much easier that way and
it was a requirement of the partners who were investing."

A good answer.... Unfortunately Delaware officials state that
Bean's company, Prentis Hall, does not exist. And in the FAA records
connected to Bean's ownership of the plane there are other gaps in the
FAA records.

When major mechanical repairs are made on an aircraft, the mechanic
is required to complete an FAA form; in December 1989, an FAA
certified mechanic installed routine de-icing equipment on the plane,
and, reviewing exact ownership documents, listed the owner as United
Insurance of Ogden, Utah.

Nowhere in FAA title paperwork does United Insurance appear as an
owner. And a spokesman for the Utah State Department of Insurance
said there had never been a 'United Insurance' licensed to do business
in the State.

So we took a closer look at Merrill Bean, and discovered that he, too,
had been involved in (*what else?*) major financial fraud, in what The Salt
Lake City Tribune called "the worst financial disaster in Utah since the
Great Depression."

The disaster was the en masse failure of Utah thrifts—hybrid financial institutions that offered high interest rates and consumer loans—and the collapse of the insurance fund that was supposed to protect their deposits. And because Utah's thrifts were essentially uninsured, the failure of Bean's thrift left a trail of broken hearts and people.

One example will suffice:

"We had just moved to Utah from California two years ago," 58-year old Irene Culver told *The Salt Lake City Tribune* in 1986. "My husband Kent was an aircraft mechanic but he has Parkinson's disease. We put half our savings in there (Western Heritage) and bought a little fixer-upper with the other half. When the state closed everything, we were ruined."

"We were going to put a new roof on and install a gas furnace, because the electricity's expensive. Now we can't do it, so we've got half the house closed off."

Bean told us, "I was Director of that failed Thrift. I came aboard when it was almost going under. And I poured some money into it to try to save it and it didn't happen. I was hoping that my $75,000 that I put into it would help revive it."

How does a savvy businessman with aircraft and car dealerships believe that $75,000 will turn around a failing Savings & Loan?

The answer may be in *The Mafia, The CIA and George Bush*, where Texas journalist Pete Brewton documented how much of the S&L scandal was connected to illegal covert operations of the CIA...

In many of those schemes a $75,000 or similar "buy-in" might have purchased a seat at a highly lucrative but completely criminal feeding frenzy.

The 'paper trail' of Barry Seal's King Air 200 revealed other connections to the unsavory perpetrators of the major financial frauds, which—like the S&L scandal—marred the 1980's.

The plane's ostensible 'owner,' Greyhound Leasing, or Greycas, for short, was also at the center of a huge and seemingly inexplicable financial fraud that, like the half-trillion dollar S&L scandal, no one ever seemed too concerned about unraveling.

The corporation was openly and eventually very publicly looted. Afterwards, company management pretended to be "baffled."

It went down like this: Greycas Inc. and another Greyhound unit, Greyhound Leasing, were bilked out of over $75 million by Sheldon Player, a Utah resident assumed to be in the machine and oilfield equipment sales business. He gained the money through fraudulently obtained loans from Greyhound.

Obligingly, Greycas then devised an elaborate cover-up scheme to prevent disclosure of details about the losses, which eventually topped one hundred million dollars.

It began with a $600,000 loan. Player would sell Greycas heavy machine tools, lease them back, and then pretend to sublease the expensive devices to end-users. In most cases the machines, collateral for the loans, were non-existent.

By 1984 Player had borrowed $8 million from Greyhound in the scheme. So he asked for $40 million in new loans to continue his transactions, and $23.5 million had been disbursed before the company got suspicious and confronted Player, telling him they wanted to inspect the machinery which they supposedly owned.

Player resisted, leading some company executives—not in on the joke—to question the "integrity of the transactions with Player."

But, remember, this was a company controlled by CIA-front Finova. So despite the company's doubts about Player's credibility and integrity, and in spite of Greycas' inability to obtain inspections of the equipment, the company lent Player *another $24 million* in new loans!

Anyone who has ever borrowed money for a car or home must admire the chutzpah of Sheldon Player, whom the business press took to calling an "admitted con artist" though he had no history of financial fraud that we could discover, which took place at the same time officers of a Swiss-based subsidiary of the company were also massively defrauding Greycas, of *another* $120 million, in a (supposedly) unrelated scandal.

"Many borrowers failed to make even the initial monthly payment," court documents stated, about this second scandal. The company's accountants wrote, "…fraudulent and dishonest acts resulted directly in a loss of $119,684,598." Not so, said the company's hapless general counsel, responding weakly that the loss was a mere $72 million.

The double looting was an Iran-Contra 'bust-out' which left hapless shareholders holding the bag. The fraud included checks written as bribes on napkins in Swiss restaurants and then set afire, the reported possibility that one of the participants was blackmailing the company, and angry lawsuits filed by upset shareholders. But the *real* question, which puzzled business reporters were never able to answer, was: why were they were giving money away down at Greyhound during the 1980's?

The criminal trial of Sheldon Player is an illustration of our thesis that being connected means never having to say you're sorry. When Player was sentenced, he received just a five-year sentence. That's just one year for each $13 million he stole. This is clearly a deal that, if offered

to regular Americans, would have them lined up around the Phoenix Federal Courthouse to sign up.

After receiving his 'draconian' sentence, Mr. Player was then given additional time to settle personal affairs before entering prison, which, for Mr. Player, consisted of the Lompoc Camp, a minimum-security facility known as one of the "country club" institutions in operation around the nation, according to Dick Murray of the U.S. Bureau of Prisons.

Even funnier is what happened to the President of hapless Greycas. Robert Bertrand, lucky fellow, never went to prison. Instead he resigned at Greyhound in 1986, and was appointed new president and chief executive officer of Finalco, an equipment finance and brokerage company based in Mclean, Virginia. That's the home of the CIA, folks. Probably just coincidence…

Completing the Barry Seal-to-George W. Bush plane chronology, Merrill Bean sold the plane in May of 1990 to Corporate Wings of Salt Lake City, which flipped it two days later to Gantt Aviation of Georgetown, Texas, which a month later sold it to the State of Texas Aircraft Pool, where it resides today.

Johnny Gantt, President of Gantt Aviation, said he probably knew that the State of Texas had a bid out when he acquired the plane. At the time the Governor of Texas was Bill Clements. His good friend, George W. Bush, was owner of the Texas Rangers.

It was Author Terry Reed who first announced that *a videotape* might surface during the 2000 presidential campaign "showing George W and Jeb arriving at Tamiami airport in 1985 to pick up two kilos of cocaine for a party." Statements in Reed's 1995 book *Compromised* recount how Seal bragged about how he had video of "the Bush boys" doing coke. Other witnesses have refused to go on the record. Are the rumors true? Did the Bush drug sting really happen? We must state honestly: we don't know.

What we do know is that by looking we connected the owners of this one plane to an incredible string of drug and money-related activities, activities carried out, in the normal course of things, by people who are properly called by a name many of them profess to hate.

"Spooks."

CHAPTER TWENTY-EIGHT

SCREAM
A LITTLE SCREAM
WITH ME

WHEN THE DEA CHOSE Screamer as the code name for a massive operation in the early 1980's, the "screamer," a Colombian bird that flies at night, immediately gained a certain immortality in some circles in Miami...

The 18-month investigation was ostensibly designed to penetrate southern Florida's extensive drug trade; prosecutors brought a total of 85 indictments against a mixed bag of pilots, drug financiers and laborers known as "off-loaders."

When the indictments were made public in early 1983, agents busily scooped up defendants in North Carolina, Florida, Colorado, California, Louisiana, Texas and Virginia.

Undercover DEA agents had set up in favorite smuggler hangouts, which were numerous.... Across from Monty's sea-front restaurant, for example, the sprawling bayside eatery/bar/marina in Coconut Grove, sat the rotting hulk of the infamous Mutiny Hotel, the vortex of Miami's cocaine-fueled party in the late Seventies and early Eighties, a favored hangout for drug dealers renowned for its anything-goes-and-everything's-served bashes.

Carlos Lehder made regular pit stops at the Mutiny while passing through Miami, as did conspirators in the $1.5 billion drug-smuggling operation that used Pan Am planes to move cocaine from Brazil to New York's Kennedy Airport in the early Eighties.

It became the favored venue for DEA agents to tape-record meetings with their drug-smuggler prey in the Screamer investigation. The Mutiny, according to Miami Police Detective D.C. Diaz, was where it was at...

"That's where the major narcotics traffickers went, the cocaine cowboys. That was the 'in' place."

In addition to Barry Seal, among its most ardent customers were Willy Falcon and Sal Magluta, acquitted of charges that they imported more than 75 tons of cocaine, valued at more than two billion dollars, over a thirteen-year period.

"Lots of arrests and deals went down there and at Monty Trainer's," recalled one DEA agent involved. "What better place to meet? Dopers would bring their loads in and then they'd celebrate afterward in their boats. They loved that!" Jim Shedd, spokesman for the agency's Miami office, agreed. "They like places on the water. They pull up in their boats, a babe on each arm, and are, like, 'Duuuuuude!'

When agents fanned out to make Operation Screamer's first arrests, Barry Seal was supposed to have been picked up. But spending a lifetime working in intelligence has its advantages: Seal was tipped off, and went on the lam for six weeks before turning himself in ...

The naturally flamboyant Seal's idea of going on the lam differed markedly from that of most 'wanted' men. Seal, for example, sent an underling to land a helicopter in the back yard of his suburban home, pick up his wife and kids on the fly, and spirit them to a secret airfield where a Lear jet waited to fly them out to Vegas to spend Easter gambling at the tables.

Seal's laid-back attitude was hard for others caught in Screamer to adopt. One renowned smuggler, Jimmy Petit, greeted police at his door with a five-gallon can of kerosene, a candle and a handgun, barricaded himself in his home for nearly five hours when police attempted to serve their warrant, and then set his house on fire.

A glance at the people swept up with Seal in Operation Screamer reveals names we've already become familiar with, of people with whom Seal had been 'associating' since the Bay of Pigs...

—Havana mobster Norman "Roughhouse" Rothman, one of Santos Trafficante's close allies, who had run a Havana casino. Barry and the enterprising Mr. Rothman, "the slot-machine king" of Cuba, had both been running guns to Cuba.

—William "Obie" Obront, who newspapers called the Montreal Controni family financier, the family helping out our boy Fidel with those stolen securities back in '57... Obie, then living in Miami Beach, was known as the "the Meyer Lansky of Canadian organized crime."

—And James Boy of Florida Aircraft Leasing, who had provided the DC-4 airplane in the explosives deal in 1972. Boy later will provide cargo planes for many of the illegal weapons flights to the Contras...

Not for the first time, we wondered: could Operation Screamer's true purpose have been to ensure the cooperation of the larger 'smuggling community' in George Bush and Bill Casey's Mena operation?

Recounted in newspapers, books, and movies, the 'official story' of Seal's Screamer bust said Seal became involved with some 'new people' as business partners in Miami; one of them turned him in. A critical mistake had been made in Florida, where Seal had decided to expand operations after Roger Reeves was snared (who disappeared after his indictment).

Seal made a bad mistake, doing business with an informant who worked for Randy Beasley, the agent in charge of Op Screamer. The informant led Beasley right to the hotshot pilot from Louisiana, Seal, willing to fly Quaaludes out of South America.

Agent Beasley called the DEA in Baton Rouge, according to an account in *Kings of Cocaine*. "Hey, I got a guy, he's a pilot, he's from Baton Rouge, and they call him El Gordo," Beasley said, "'the Fat One.'"

"We know who you've got, and if you've got him, we're going to come down and kiss you," replied Charlie Bremer, the agent in Baton Rouge. "We've been working him ten years, and we've never been able to get him."

Based on informant's testimony and wiretapped phone conversations, a federal grand jury in Fort Lauderdale indicted Seal in March of 1983 for smuggling two hundred thousand Quaaludes.

His name and several of his aliases finally made the papers... but in small print, along with eighty-three others. Only Barry was listed twice, though, which might have given him some small satisfaction, as 'Adler (Barry Seal, Bill Elders, Gordo) Seal' and 'Adler (Bill) Seal.' Either way his cover was intact; he was known as Ellis Mackenzie in South America.

Immediately Barry began playing "let's make a deal," approaching Beasley with an offer to "flip," turn informant and go undercover, promising more cocaine than the agents had ever seen.

But he wasn't specific, and he wanted to travel outside the country with very little control by the DEA. What an ego, Beasley thought, related in Leen and Gugliotta's *Kings of Cocaine*.

"He thinks he's untouchable, and even has his own conditions for the government! He wanted the charges dropped against two of his men who had also been caught up in Screamer. All this was said to have made Beasley uneasy, and he turned Seal down flat."

Curiously, Bill Clinton and Barry Seal both shared the same attorney at this time, Richard Ben-Veniste, the former Watergate prosecutor.

Ben-Veniste will do double-duty, first participating in a scandal he will later investigate, when a decade later he will be Democratic co-counsel for the Congressional Whitewater committee. Ben-Veniste reportedly proved helpful in steering the Committee away from the rocky shoals of Clinton's possible involvement in the drug smuggling through Mena into the calmer waters of Presidential blowjobs.

In what follows, one fact must be remembered: Barry Seal was deathly afraid of doing time.

"He was used to flying the wide open spaces. He couldn't stand to be cooped up. He got claustrophobic," his widow Debbie told us. "Going to jail would have meant the end, he thought."

"Had he been willing to do a few years in prison he could have avoided his ultimate demise," concurred Seal's Baton Rouge attorney, Lewis Unglesby.

When his offer to become a DEA informant in exchange for leniency was rejected, Seal made a similar proposal to the U.S. attorney in Baton Rouge, Stan Bardswell, through an intermediary, today a sitting judge in Louisiana. Leo Higginbotham took $25,000 in cash in a brown paper bag for his troubles. No doubt Judge Higginbotham later dutifully reported this bribe as "commission" income on his income taxes.

But this offer was met with a cold shoulder; while both Higginbotham and Bardswell were grade school chums of Barry's, Bardswell was suspicious of Seal's intent.

He knew Seal was also currently under investigation by a state and federal task force in Baton Rouge and New Orleans, and refused to see him, he explained to us, because Seal's request was "too cryptic."

Facing the increasing likelihood of a long prison sentence—the federal judge in whose court he had just been convicted was known as a 'hanging' judge—Seal then went over *everybody's* heads... to Washington, DC.

He had help from his lawyer, Richard Ben-Veniste...

"I did my part by launching him into the arms of Vice President Bush, who embraced him as an undercover operative," Ben-Veniste later told the *Wall Street Journal*.

Barry Seal appeared before George Bush's Vice Presidential Task Force on Drugs in Washington, where he appeared to dazzle 'em with smuggling lore, and how he had made millions in the "trade," as he called it.

But what caught the panel's attention was the bombshell Seal dropped during his closed-door testimony, that the Sandinistas were directly involved in drug trafficking into the United States.

According to Seal, the Medellin Cartel had made a deal with the Sandinistas, awarding them hefty cuts of drug profits in exchange for the use of an airfield in Managua as a trans-shipment point for narcotics.

Presto. Seal had said three magic words, "Commie dope peddler," and faster than you can say 'Being connected means never having to say you're sorry' drug smuggler Barry Seal was transformed overnight from major felon to… star informant.

Neat trick.

Here, then, is the most amazing fact about Barry Seal…

Through the simple expedient of ratting out a country, Nicaragua, with which the Reagan Administration was dying to go to war, he walked away from felony drug convictions for which tens of thousands of American citizens are today doing life in prison.

Under pressure from Bush's Task Force, the DEA now agreed to enlist Seal as an undercover informant with a special emphasis on the "Nicaraguan connection."

Seal then flew his famous Nicaragua sting operation in an acquired C-123 military cargo plane, the famous 'Fat Lady,' which resulted in Ronald Reagan going on television to denounce the Sandinistas as drug smugglers corrupting American youth, waving pictures taken from the back of Barry Seal's plane showing Pablo Escobar helping to load the plane.

The Nicaragua sting led to the indictment of the leadership of the Medellin Cartel, including Jorge Ochoa. In retaliation, Ochoa, or so goes the 'official story,' then had Seal murdered in early 1986, both for revenge and to keep Seal from testifying at his, Ochoa's,

U.S. trial. That Ochoa *never* stood trial in the U.S. is inconvenient knowledge; and it has done nothing to slow the disinformation campaign claiming 'Ochoa did it' that began the night Seal was assassinated, February 19,1986.

What *did* happen?

Start here: in Miami sometime in early '81 a clump of men stood around the trunk of a rented car, opened for inspection of its contents…

A drug deal was about to be consummated in the south Florida sunshine, an event so common as to barely raise eyebrows.

The trunk everyone was peering into was stuffed with hundreds of pounds of Quaaludes. Soon somebody flashed a badge. Two members of Seal's smuggling organization, Calvin Briggs and Gary Seville, were cuffed.

Almost immediately, they began to 'sing.' This is also known as "rolling on your boss."

The man arrested, as Calvin Briggs in Miami in 1981, *wasn't* Briggs—we learned. It had, instead, been Barry Seal's trusted copilot Emile Camp, who gave Brigg's name instead of his own.

But Calvin Briggs *is* the man who later went to jail for the crime. Whether fool or stand-up guy, the important point is Seal trusted Briggs. This, which will be crucial to remember, when we see Brigg's in the next chapter fronting for Seal in a money-laundering dummy corporation.

The 'official story,' of Seal's being caught up in Operation Screamer insists that Barry knew nothing about the secret sealed indictment pending against him, as if he woke up one morning in 1983, two full years after his men got popped, and was shocked (*Shocked!*) to learn that *he* was now about to be arrested for that trunk-full of 'ludes he'd caused to be in a rental car in Miami two years earlier.

This is nonsense, but instructive nonsense, because it conceals, or has until now, what *really* happened when Seal learned that two of his men had gone down in a drug bust in Miami in '81…

Barry Seal shortly thereafter moved his operations to Mena. In criminal parlance, it's called "working off a beef."

"Barry was immediately concerned when Gary Seville and Calvin Briggs were popped with a carload of 'ludes in Miami, then got printed and released less than six hours later," a Seal associate told us…

"The handwriting was on the wall right away."

Seal knew immediately, when his two men were busted, that it was only a matter of time before they would be coming for *him*…

In Seal's world, and the DEA's world, the two-year "secret" sealed indictment naming Barry Seal was no more a secret to Seal than what he had had for breakfast that morning.

When Calvin Briggs and Gary Seville got popped in Miami in the spring of 1981, Barry Seal was as good as gone…to *Mena*.

"Barry got lured into working outside his area," said a Louisiana law enforcement official whose job had been tracking Seal.

"He was just trying to take care of his distribution chain, which needed a constant flow of product, and he got caught."

"Seal probably figured out who the snitch was," this official continued, in a grudging statement of respect for the man he'd hunted…

"Anybody else would have killed the guy. But Barry wasn't violent. We all had to give him that."

We had heard persistent rumors that the *real* objective of Operation Screamer had been to do what the DEA is said to have been set up to do in the first place: reduce free-lance penetration in the lucrative drug trade. But beyond busting the competition, there may have been another covert objective as well: *recruitment.*

"Busting a pilot, and then 'taking care' of the bust for 'services rendered' is standard operating procedure in the Agency," said lawyer and former CIA pilot Gary Eitel.

"It's called being 'compromised.'"

In the official story Seal became a "snitch" and went to work for the DEA only *after* he was convicted in Operation Screamer. But Seal's response to his upcoming indictment can be read by what he did in April of 1982. He moved to Mena. And working off his impending beef was probably just one of the inducements....

For the next two years, based in Mena, he engaged in what *Partners in Power* calls "one of the major crimes of the century."

Neither he nor his accomplices showed the slightest worry about being caught.

"The shadow of official complicity and cover-up was unmistakable in Seal's papers," Denton and Morris wrote.

Those who met Seal in Mena in the fall of 1983 found him at the zenith of his influence, said *Partners in Power*, already a businessman of note in Arkansas, with an address book listing some of the state's well-known names, contacts in Little Rock's banks and brokerage houses, and what a fellow CIA operative called a "night depository" for bags of cash dropped from "green flights" onto the ranch of a politically and financially prominent Arkansas family. A pilot who came to Mena from Louisiana with Seal in 1982 later testified about their first weeks in Arkansas, when they were introduced to pivotal figures in state government and business. "Barry Seal knew them all, and they knew him, the Clinton machine," he remembered. "There was no limit on cooperation by the good ol' boys," a federal agent would say of Seal's Arkansas friends.

Senior law enforcement officials happening onto his tracks in Arkansas were quickly waved off. "Joe [name deleted] works for Seal and cannot be touched because Seal works for the CIA," a customs official noted during an investigation into Arkansas drug trafficking in the early 1980s. "Look, we're told not to touch anything that has Barry Seal's name on it," another ranking federal agent told a colleague, "just to let it go."

"At the zenith of his influence…" is an accurate depiction of Seal in 1983. His records show that he had more smuggling planes in the air that year than any other. He had a *fleet*…. Still, we found it curious. How can a man under indictment on serious felony charges that could put him in prison for the rest of his life be at the same time at the "zenith of his influence?"

Author Rodney Stich hinted at some of the dark secrets of Operation Screamer in his recent book, *Drugging America.*

Navy SEAL Commander Robert Hunt put Stich in contact with CIA operative and State Department employee Michael Maholy, whose primary duty had been monitoring cable traffic at different CIA locations.

"Maholy described his role in Operation Screamer which was a mammoth sting operation aimed at penetrating the network of mercenary pilots that were flying drugs in competition with the CIA," Stich writes.

"On this operation Maholy worked under DEA agent-in-charge Randy Beasley. Maholy described how Seal offered to turn informant, allegedly implicating high federal officials, including former Watergate prosecutor Richard Ben-Veniste."

Barry Seal, Maholy said, had tried to *roll-on* his own attorney, Democratic powerbroker Richard Ben-Veniste!

What a concept. Why? Whatever for? Was this just more conspiracy-mongering balderdash?

Then, in Barry Seal's files, we discovered Maholy had been telling the truth. Correspondence between Seal and Ben-Veniste, which we will shortly quote, will prove Maholy right.

Stich's account said Maholy was a liaison officer for the U.S. Embassy in Panama and worked for the U.S. State Department and CIA for over two decades, and he printed a State Department letter confirming Maholy's employment.

Maholy told Stich he had had frequent contacts with Oliver North, SEAL Commander Hunt, and Barry Seal…

Seal, he stated, had been involved with the Noriega Cartel in a top-secret operation. He described the methods used by Seal's fleet of aircraft hauling drugs, saying they flew mostly at night, with the pilots using night-vision goggles to slip through airspace "windows" when the military radar would ignore the targets.

This was consistent with information received from a long time CIA agent, to whom Seal had once handed the sophisticated portable electronics unit after landing.

Engineered by E-Systems in Houston, Texas, it was a highly classified encoding device to evade air defense and surveillance measures, which allowed Seal to fly with impunity across US borders. The portable device had been far more valuable than the airplane it came off of...

Venezuelan naval officer Lizardo Marquez Perez was in charge of the smuggling operations in Miami, and frequently seen on the CIA oil rigs on which Maholy was stationed, Maholy told Stich...

We knew Marquez as one of the Medellin small-fry lieutenants put in prison by Barry Seal's 'snitch' testimony.

Barry Seal's archives contain information indicating that Seal's relationship with Richard Ben-Veniste was not his only close tie with a top Democratic chieftain...

In a handwritten note in Seal's own hand, he underlines the statement that "Charles Manatt" was the personal attorney for Gene Glick, who, we've seen, was a cutout between Seal and his real bosses.

Charles Manatt, throughout the early and mid-1980's, was the Chairman of the Democratic National Committee.

But the big revelation was in a letter we found in Seal's files from Richard Ben-Veniste to client Barry Seal. In it, Ben-Veniste pointedly states that he has been trying to reach Seal by phone for several weeks, but Seal, then on trial for charges, which could send him to prison for life, won't return his calls...

"I have attempted to reach you by phone... leaving several messages... and have in addition left word with Jon Sale and ███ █████ to pass along my request that you phone me," Ben-Veniste writes. He goes on to complain that there has obviously been a "breakdown in communications" between the two men.

The result of the 'breakdown' quickly becomes clear. Ben-Veniste demands, for what he states is the third or fourth time, that Barry Seal returns "my two briefcases of legal materials which you have been holding."

Why would Barry Seal be holding, and refusing to return, two briefcases of material from Richard Ben-Veniste's office?

One obvious conclusion is that, whatever it was that Barry Seal took from Richard Ben-Veniste's law offices was *exactly* what Seal was attempting to parlay into leniency in sentencing.

And from Ben-Veniste's frantic tone in his letter we can only guess how powerfully incriminating that material must have been.

What could Barry Seal have on Democratic powerbroker Richard Ben-Veniste that he thought would save him from prosecution on major drug felonies?

Were there any *other* indications that Ben-Veniste, an intimate, after all, of the President of the United States, might be linked to the drug trade?

Well... *yes.*

"We (the New York City Police Department) knew Ben-Veniste was a bagman," retired NYPD Detective Jimmy Rothstein told us. "We saw him with known mob associates we were following."

"Barry was going to roll on Ben-Veniste, right," Barry's associate Blackie confirmed.

"He was also offering to turn in Attorney General Ed Meese. There was an IRS agent (William Duncan) who lost his job for asking questions after Barry was dead about the $300,000 bribe Seal paid to Meese."

Blackie's statement is corroborated by numerous accounts of IRS agent William Duncan having been hounded from his career for attempting to present evidence to Congress of a $300,000 bribe Seal allegedly paid to Meese.

Seal's offer to Screamer prosecutors was the ultimate in politically-ecumenical offers, containing incriminating information on the activities of a Republican Attorney General and a Democratic backroom fixer.

But wait a minute, we protested. Hadn't Ben-Veniste been one of the *good* guys in Watergate? One of the bright and idealistic young lawyers who had served the country on the Watergate Committee, even if it was alongside Hillary Rodham Clinton?

Here we recalled to mind our earlier discovery that Richard Nixon had *not* been brought down by the righteous wrath of the American people, but by the CIA.

This places Ben-Veniste's role in Watergate (not to mention Hillary's) in an entirely different light.

Navy Lt. Commander Alexander Martin was an assistant to Major General Richard Secord, and worked closely with Oliver North, Felix Rodriguez, and Jeb Bush, son of then-Vice-President Bush), in Operation Black Eagle, he has stated.

"Take a look at Trinity Energy," Martin advised us. "In 1982 Richard Ben-Veniste incorporated a Trinity Oil or Trinity Energy to launder money for his client Barry Seal."

A cursory glance through newspaper records showed Martin knew something....

In 1995 Barry Seal's partner, Baton Rouge attorney ███ ███,
sold a Trinity Energy Corp and related companies for $22 million to a

shadowy company which we learned was suspected of being controlled by the "old man," Jackson Stephens.

Stephens had been selling the company, in effect, to himself.

"That's how they pay themselves," a Seal associate explained.

Trinity Energy, a Delaware-listed company which dissolved in 1992, had as their listed phone number, in incorporation documents in the Delaware Secretary of State's office, a number which rings at a company called ICF Kaiser International.

It's chairman, a man who had sat on its board for over nine years, was Tony Coelho, a former Democratic Congressman.

When we discovered this information Coelho was running Vice President Al Gore's Presidential campaign.

What did savvy life-long member of "clandestine services" Barry Seal do when he got in to trouble in Miami in 1981? He went looking for someone to 'fix' things.

Enter Richard Ben-Veniste.

But to 'work off his beef' Seal needed a willing partner with the clout to take care of his legal difficulties. And, thanks to Ben-Veniste, he found one in George Bush.

It was time to take a little closer look at Richard Ben-Veniste.

CHAPTER TWENTY-NINE

WHO IS
RICHARD BEN-VENISTE?

"I DID MY PART by launching Barry Seal into the arms of Vice President Bush, who embraced him as an undercover operative," Ben-Veniste had said to reporters who questioned his ethics in sitting as Democratic co-counsel on the Whitewater Commission after being a lawyer-participant in matters being investigated.

Ben-Veniste said he'd 'read' of the Seal-Lasater link," intimating he knew nothing more. But the attorney defending Barry Seal, and later a key figure in the drug angle of the Whitewater probe, surely knew far more than that.

Who *is* Richard Ben-Veniste? He's made, we learned, a career of defending political crooks, specializing in cases that involve drugs and politics. But, in launching the biggest drug smuggler into the arms of George Bush, he may have outdone himself.

The gray-haired lawyer who defended Bill Clinton on the Whitewater Committee first entered the limelight as a Watergate prosecutor in 1973, point man in prosecutions of Nixon aides Mitchell, Haldeman and Erlichman. Displaying total recall of the facts, he led the successful fight to secure the secret Nixon White House tapes.

In the wrangling over Nixon's tapes he worked with Hillary Rodham and Bernard Nussbaum. The three would later find themselves working together again, this time on the defense side, in the Whitewater scandal, where, during Ben-Veniste's tour of duty as minority special counsel to the Senate Whitewater committee, he served up enough disdain, contempt, and indignation to fortify the Democratic contention that the whole investigation was an overblown load of partisan mud-slinging.

But we also discovered *this* curious fact: Ben-Veniste has regularly been referred to in print as "a Mob lawyer," and "Mob figure," and "a very close associate of the notorious Mobster Alvin Malnik..."

These are curious credentials for someone defending the President of the United States. But while Ben-Veniste defended Clinton on the Whitewater panel, the media ignored his Mob connections.

In the early 1980's Ben-Veniste had represented both Barry Seal and Bill Clinton, while, after Clinton was elected for a second term as Governor of Arkansas, Mob money started pouring into Arkansas...

"That was the election when the Mob really came into Arkansas politics, the dog-track and racetrack boys, the payoff people who saw a good thing," a former U.S. attorney told Roger Morris and Sally Denton.

"It wasn't just Bill Clinton, and it went beyond our old Dixie Mafia, which was penny-ante by comparison. This was Eastern and West Coast crime money that noticed the possibilities... just like the legitimate corporations did."

The quintessential Washington lawyer, Ben-Veniste has the huge house, the million-dollar partnership bonuses, the Rolodex with everyone's private number, and the ego to go with it all. He even played a "commentator's" role in the Iran Contra Scandal...

"My feeling is that the American people, within the next six months or so, will have a pretty good idea of what's occurred," he said.

When two former national security officials asserted their Fifth Amendment rights during the hearings he defended their refusal to talk, saying, "In common parlance you would say things might be bad enough without getting hit with your own bat."

When House Speaker Jim Wright (D-Tex.) was caught accepting bribes camouflaged as book sales, he had turned to fixers Clark Clifford and Richard Ben-Veniste.

Clifford himself was later caught up in the BCCI scandal but 'mysteriously' escaped prosecution by the Bush Justice Department.

Ben-Veniste has done more than his share of duty defending people accused of financial scams, a Mob specialty. He represented the central figure in Europe's biggest investment scandal of its time, Thomas Quinn, a lawyer and president of a New York brokerage firm, who was disbarred for involvement in a scheme to promote shares in a company whose assets were all but non-existent.

Later Quinn was charged with pocketing at least $500 million selling worthless stock to thousands of small investors in various European countries.

Ben-Veniste also had defended Charles Gladson, a high-ranking official of the Agency for International Development, often used as a CIA front, and the chief-of-staff to Virginia Governor Doug Wilder in a case that involved the planting of a micro-transmitter listening device, a CIA specialty.

Another client was Truman Arnold, chief moneyman at the Democratic National Committee for a critical five-month period in 1995 when the DNC was deeply in debt and reeling from its historic 1994 defeat at the polls. Arnold also put Webster Hubbell on the payroll between Hubbell's resignation as the Clintons' man at the Justice Department and his subsequent guilty plea to charges that he had defrauded clients and law partners.

Ben-Veniste found himself again at the red-hot center of political controversy at the point at which the Whitewater investigation of independent counsel Kenneth Starr and the unfolding Democratic fund-raising scandal converged.

Ben-Veniste's curiosity about the facts of Whitewater was, as might be expected, highly selective. Said a Democratic staffer who professes admiration for Ben-Veniste's performance in general, "When the administration was on the ropes, he'd throw them a life raft."

He also defended Terry McAuliffe, the wheeler-dealer who slapped down $1.35 million to let the Clintons buy their New York dream house, which some wit dubbed "Dis-Graceland."

Called as a witness in a Teamsters corruption trial, McAuliffe, a Washington lawyer, fixer, and "the top money man for the Democratic Party," was an unnamed player in the indictment of Teamsters political director Bill Hamilton, who prosecutors say illegally schemed with McAuliffe to swap union money for Democratic cash in a money-laundering scheme involving the DNC, the Teamsters, several White House aides and the 1996 Clinton-Gore re-election campaign.

When the chief promoter of a controversial proposal to open an Indian gambling casino in Hudson, Wisconsin told a House committee that President Clinton's top fund-raiser, Terence McAuliffe, had bragged of using political influence to have the project killed by the Interior Department, it was time to call in someone to call off the dogs...

Fred Havenick, head of a Miami company operating dog tracks in three states fingered McAuliffe to the House Government Reform Committee in public hearings on the campaign financing abuses of the 1996 election.

Through his attorney, Richard Ben-Veniste, McAuliffe, predictably, denied everything.

Ben-Veniste had said, "He is acquainted with Mr. Havenick, who apparently was a contributor, but he never had such a conversation with him."

How do "dogtrack guys" get "acquainted" with the leader of the Free World's top fund-raiser?

But all this seemed like small potatoes when we learned more about Ben-Veniste's "close association" with Meyer Lansky's heir as head of the Mob, Alvin Malnik.

How odd, we had thought, when we first heard it, that Barry Seal had offered to roll on his *attorney*...

Rolling on your attorney *is* odd.

But rolling on someone *else* in the criminal organization, slightly higher, like your boss?

That happens all the time.

CHAPTER THIRTY

ALVIN OF ARABIA

IT'S BUGSY SIEGEL who's credited with first envisioning Las Vegas as a gambling Mecca. But Meyer Lansky was the money behind the dream. Bespectacled and known for operating quietly behind the scenes, Lansky took on legendary status in underworld lore, earning a place in books and movies, and even a citation in the Encyclopedia Britannica.

Described in newspaper headlines as "Chairman of the Board" and "Financial Wizard of the Underworld," Lansky opened gambling operations in South Florida after World War II, controlling casinos from Cuba to Vegas. He was even in *The Godfather*. Remember "Hyman Roth?"

Richard Ben-Veniste's 'close associate,' Alvin Malnik, was Meyer Lansky's attorney. When Lansky died in 1983 at age 81, *Reader's Digest* named Malnik his "heir apparent," and the moniker stuck. Malnik has by now been called Meyer Lansky's "heir apparent" so often in print that it must feel like part of his job title.

"It was a known fact among the criminal underworld that dealing with Al Malnik was the same as dealing with Meyer Lansky," said Vincent Teresa, convicted criminal and government witness, to investigators for the New Jersey Gambling Commission.

Alvin Malnik's circle of acquaintances is perfectly illustrated in his role of director of Bank of World Commerce, a Bahamas-based institution involving "some of the nations' top gangsters," the New Jersey report said. "Millions of dollars passed through the door and were reinvested in Syndicate-controlled projects in the United States."

But gangsters weren't all the bank was about…. The Bank of World Commerce was the brainchild of CIA agent Colonel Paul Helliwell. Mob money flowed into its secret numbered accounts by the hundreds of millions—Lansky money, most of it—and then out again to the International Credit Bank of Switzerland before returning to the U.S. for reinvestment.

Paul Helliwell, the "CIA's paymaster at the Bay of Pigs," was also, we were soon to learn, the true owner of Barry Seal's Lear jet.

Malnik had, in the early 1970s, invested in the Cricket Club, a Miami high-rise with 220 condos, and a frequent hangout of Barry Seal's while in Miami, where he also ate often at the Malnik-owned Forge restaurant.

The Club's developer, no doubt by coincidence, had been convicted with Teamster Jimmy Hoffa on fraud and conspiracy charges in 1964.

Blackie had told us one of the Seal organizations' "investors" was the Central State Teamsters Pension Fund. But then, many of the Teamster Fund's borrowers were associates of organized crime… $5.4 million, for example, was loaned to Alvin Malnik.

Malnik had connections to George Bush as well. According to the book *Blue Thunder*, Bush even bought, from Malnik 'associate' Don Aronow, one of his signature 'cigarette' boats, the top choice of offshore smugglers.

After Aronow was murdered, published accounts stated he had been a drug smuggler and money launderer, linked to the Genovese Purple Gang of New York City, within the framework of the Meyer Lansky organized crime syndicate.

Aronow numbered among his friends public figures and celebrities like the head of the "smugglers' airline," Eastern chairman Frank Bormann, Savings and Loan scandal poster boy Charles Keating… and Alvin Malnik, all exalted acquaintances suggestive of intelligence connections as well.

Because Seal's lawyer Richard Ben-Veniste was such a "close associate" of Alvin Malnik's, we wanted to get an idea of what he'd been up to the past several decades. And we didn't have to look very far in newspaper archives to find evidence of his enormous influence.

"The club's location inside the venerable Forge restaurant was meant to recall "old Cuba," and in that it succeeded beyond anyone's wildest dreams," said a Miami New Times profile September 16,1999.

"After all, the Forge *is* owned by Alvin Malnik, a man considered by federal law enforcement officials to be a major organized-crime figure and, as former Miami Beach Police Chief Rocky Pomerance put it: Meyer Lansky's 'fair-haired boy.'"

Richard Ben-Veniste's chum Al Malnik, we discovered, is so powerful that he found a way to legalize loan-sharking. He is 'Mr. Pay Day Loan.' According to the Nashville Tennessean, April 18,1999…

"The shadow of organized crime has descended on Tennessee's political landscape, via campaign contributions from the operator of a string of Georgia-based "auto title" loan companies, The Tennessean has learned."

"The owners of Tennessee companies that loan money at almost 800% annual interest are kept secret from the public under the controversial "payday loan" law passed here earlier this year."

"In Florida, federal investigators have found organized crime figures infected one such Miami-area business, threatening to harm borrowers if they did not repay loans and interest."

The "shadow of organized crime" referred to is Alvin Malnik. And making money off the poor, as anyone who's watched The Soprano's knows, is what Mobsters do…

"According to a federal court indictment, members of the New York-based Gambino crime family found such an opportunity in Deerfield Beach, Fla., at E-Z Check Cashing, a storefront business that extended large short-term loans similar to those made by "payday loan" companies in Tennessee," the *Tennessean* article said, adding, "The last thing needed by consumers who have exhausted all avenues to credit is to turn to businesses that offer loans at triple-digit interest, bankruptcy officials said.

"These are predators," stated one official."

Nine men including John Gotti's successor, were charged with extortion for their E-Z loans, as well as conspiracy to kidnap, murder and commit arson.

"Neither the public nor Tennessee law enforcement authorities have the right to learn who operates similar cash advance companies here," the article concluded. "By law, those records are kept secret at the state Department of Financial Institutions. "I'm just shocked," said state Sen. Roscoe Dixon, D-Memphis.

Senator Roscoe's being "shocked" reminds us of the bit in the movie Casablanca where Lt. Renaud pockets his roulette winnings while simultaneously telling Bogey's Rick that he's "shocked—*shocked!*" that gambling is taking place on the premises.

Several years ago, at the ripe age of 61, Malnik found it necessary to marry a young model 36 years his junior. Theirs became one of the lavish weddings that society columnists like the *Miami Herald's* Joan Fleichmann love to gush about...

"Wedding bells for Alvin Malnik, attorney, millionaire, restaurateur, long-divorced world traveler, wine connoisseur, car collector, fancier of Arabian horses, survivor of assorted federal mob investigations—a guy who really knows his way around. Malnik, 61, will marry Nancy Gresham, 25, a onetime model from Atlanta, in a lavish black-tie bash Saturday night at the private Malnik compound at Boca Raton," she wrote.

The nuptials took place at the Malnik family 'ranch' in Boca Raton, which was, Ms. Fleishmann noted gleefully, "more Hefner mansion than Little House on the Prairie." The 288 guests had cocktails, nibbled on salmon and beluga and "compared wedding notes in the sprawling patio area, which featured a meandering swimming pool, grill center and kitchen, plus cute little fully-stocked townhouses for overnight guests."

The guest list reads like a Who's Who of a certain stratum of American life. Among the invitees were (*but of course!*) Richard Ben-Veniste, as well as F. Lee Bailey, Arnold Schwarzenegger, Debra Winger, designer Nicole Miller; Manhattan real-estate mogul Hank Sopher; LA restaurateur Nicky Blair; *gangsta* rap (*natch*) record producer Russell Simmons; Rebecca Gayheart, co-host of a Steven Spielberg TV show, Carol Connors (who wrote *Gonna Fly Now*, the theme song from *Rocky*); Darien Iacocca, wife No. 3 of former Chrysler chairman Lee Iacocca; Paul Pope, whose dad, the late Generoso Pope, owned *The National Enquirer*; and Mob 'associate' and casino czar Clifford Perlman...

The list, as they say, goes on...

Worth noting was actor Gianni Russo, who, in a bit of unintended irony which the *Miami Herald* reported straight-faced had played Al Pacino's bookie brother-in-law Carlo Rizzi in *The Godfather*.

Also in attendance was Robert Lacey, author of *Little Man: Meyer Lansky and the Gangster Life*, in which the name "Malnik" hadn't even appeared. Presumably Malnik was now returning Lacey's favor by inviting him to the wedding of the year... because although Malnik's yellow Rolls-Royce was once bombed in Miami Beach, he keeps up appearances by denying he even knew Lansky, except for "Once, by chance, in an elevator."

Alvin the groom presented his bride with that ultimate wedding gift of choice, we learned, the 50-carat emerald and diamond necklace. Then we were surprised to read that there had been a table at Malnicks' nuptials reserved for Saudi Arabian sheiks…that St. Louis-born Alvin, who's Jewish, had a son who had changed his name to Shareef and married a woman from the *Saudi* royal family, not previously known, by us at least, as being cozy with Jewish Mobsters.

"They met two years ago at a party and fell in love," said Shareef Malnik, 37, the groom's son and best man. "She's very beautiful."

The story, as we pieced it together, was incredible.

Incredible, but true…

Malnik had befriended a Saudi family in the early '80s, the Al-Fassi Tarek family from Saudi Arabia, various newspaper accounts reported. This set off a dim memory for us, since this family, the Al-Fassi's, had scandalized blasé Beverly Hills while we lived nearby.

After arriving with an entourage of bodyguards, cooks and other servants, the family had purchased a highly visible $2.4 million estate right on Sunset Boulevard in Beverly Hills. They then began "renovating," placing anatomically correct flesh-colored Roman statues on the walls, complete with painted-on black pubic hair. Gawkers were lining up all day.

The house quickly became the talk of the town. Some in the clannish enclave were clearly not amused. The mansion was, in short order, burned down by arsonists.

For those of us living in L.A. at the time, as far as we knew that had been the end of the Saudi scandal. But there was, we now learned with mounting excitement, much more to the story…

When the Al-Fassi's left L.A., they had continued roaming the world, spending spectacular sums of brother-in-law Saudi Royal Prince Turki's money on lavish parties, chartered jets, hotel suites by the floor, automobiles by the fleet, clothing by the rack and jewelry by the tray.

They had soon joined the Prince in Europe, where they became involved with the increasingly ubiquitous Alvin Malnik, settling down for six months at the Intercontinental Hotel in Geneva, where the Prince distributed bundles of cash to his insatiable entourage.

Malnik and Prince Turki, the son of the founder of modern Saudi Arabia, King Abdul Aziz, had grown chummy. As a friend of the Prince told People magazine, "The Prince trusted and respected Al so much that slowly the power shifted to Al. It was Al who controlled the cash, who told the Prince to put money in this business or that business.'"

Then—as if the idea of a Jewish Mobster from Miami controlling the cash of a Saudi Royal Prince isn't bizarre enough—Malnik's son, Mark, a 23-year-old student, 'fell in love' with Sheik Al-Fassi's sister.

"It hardly mattered that a 'Mrs. Mark Malnik' waited for him in Florida," sniffed *People* magazine. "It certainly didn't matter to the Al-Fassi's, whose romantic permutations were already complicated enough to befuddle even the most attentive scorekeeper."

So Alvin Malnik's son Mark, a young Jewish married man, was now in full pursuit of Saudi Prince Turki's sister-in-law... In his new role as adviser and confidante to the Prince, Malnik devised a solution.

"Al came up with a good idea," said *People* mag's anonymous source. "'Come to the U.S.,'" he said. "'I'll take care of everything.'"

Once in Miami, Malnik soon assumed control over the Prince's schedule and contacts. Prince Turki created a two-story apartment in Malnik's North Miami condominium, the Cricket Club, directly below Alvin's penthouse. Soon the entourage was engaging the protective services of half the off-duty police force of nearby Hollywood, Florida.

Under Malnik's tutelage, Prince Turki paid $3 million in cash for the Woodworth estate, one of the most graceful waterfront homes on Florida's Gold Coast. The al Fassi clan also paid an inflated $1.5 million for two waterfront homes between Miami Beach and the city of Miami.

Then, showing that their taste had not improved since leaving Beverly Hills, they demolished the houses to erect what People called "the Xanadu of kitsch," and which one of the contractors described as "the biggest hunk of crap ever built on the face of the earth."

In all, the Al-Fassis would pay $17 million for houses and other properties... and the Malniks, father and son, were now beginning to study Arabic.

Young Mark took to carrying the Koran around with him. Then a devastating blow struck the Saudi Prince and his entourage. Miami police, acting on a complaint that servants were being held as slaves, stormed the Cricket Club sanctuary.

But the cops never got a chance to carry out their search. One of the Princesses' began shouting very unroyal obscenities at them, biting a policewoman deep enough to leave toothmarks for days.

Family bodyguards quickly came to her rescue. A standoff ensued, and startled police were forced to retreat.

As suits and counter-suits began to fly between Saudi Prince Turki and an outraged Florida State Attorney, the U.S. State Department rushed in a former ambassador to Saudi Arabia to serve as intermediary. He secured face-saving diplomatic immunity for the Prince.

Then the Prince's brother-in-law Al-Fassi offered to sell a stolen $1.2 million emerald-and-diamond ring to an undercover FBI agent. He did *not* have diplomatic immunity, and was charged with interstate and international transportation of stolen goods, a felony punishable by a maximum of 10 years in prison and a $10,000 fine.

The lucky Sheik had, at least, a well-connected lawyer: Richard Ben-Veniste.

When all this bad news reached the ear of the Saudi King back in Riyadh, he ordered the Prince to end his long exile and return home. Once at home, the Prince's family circle broadened to include their friends *formerly* named Malnik.

Both father and son were said to have taken Arabic names and converted to Islam.

What pertinence does the story of Attorney Alvin Malnik, heir to Meyer Lansky, converting to Islam and living in Saudi Arabia as an adviser to a member of the Saudi royal family have to the saga of "Barry and 'the boys?'"

In 1982 Barry Seal began flying weapons to the Contras from Mena, Arkansas, which had been paid for with Saudi Royal family money.

CHAPTER THIRTY-ONE

THE CANADIAN 'MEYER LANSKY'

BARRY SEAL'S BUSINESS DEALINGS weren't with only one Meyer Lansky heir. Barry had dealings with two. The Quaaludes he was convicted of conspiracy to distribute came from a man who the Miami Herald called "the Meyer Lansky of Canadian organized crime," William 'Obie' Obront.

A former Montreal meatpacker, 'Obie' was variously described by authorities as 'the financier for a major, major organized crime ring in Canada,' as 'a kind of linchpin among Montreal's criminals,' as 'organized crime's money-mover in Montreal,' 'the Canadian underworld's banker,' an 'underworld figure...' or simply 'Mobster William Obront.'

This is the 'Montreal connection,' prominent since the late '50's for weapons-dealing, securities-stealing, and eventual President-level mayhem. Obie Obront worked for the big boss, Montreal's "Godfather," Vincent Controni, described during the Senate Narcotics Hearings in the early 1980's, as "the head of the largest and most notorious narcotics syndicate on the North American continent."

Obie had a healthy ego, newspaper stories indicated, telling undercover drug agents, "Every Quaalude tablet in South Florida is controlled by me."

Selling Quaaludes, and Quaalude-counterfeiting, was one of the Montreal underworld's most rewarding occupations. It started in the late 1970s, when chemists working in clandestine laboratories outside the city produced millions of tiny diazepam pills—valiums—stamped with the trademark Lemmon 714 of the highly prized Quaalude.

Although the powerful tranquilizers, legally manufactured under the trade name Valium, cost less than five cents a tablet to manufacture, they fetched a street price of $6 each in the US as drug dealers passed them off as real.

When the scam became widely known in the drug world the counterfeit pills were worthless... and anyone with fake Quaaludes had been left holding the bag. Seal associate Bill Bottoms told how he and Barry Seal had had to take dozens of shoeboxes filled with the bogus "'ludes" and dump them in a river near the isolated Seal farm, laughing as they watched the river's water turn foamy.

Operation Screamer had been bad news for Obie, too. He was found guilty on 12 counts of conspiracy, possession, and possession with intent to distribute cocaine and bootleg Quaaludes.

Sentenced to 20 years in prison, stand-up guy Obie chewed gum and clasped his hands behind his back before a U.S. District Judge. His prior convictions, for fraud, forgery, tax evasion, contempt-of-court, and lying about his past to get U.S. citizenship figured in his long sentence... as well as the fact that his associate Marcel Salvail, also convicted and sentenced to nine years in prison, was fingered in an intelligence report as "the No. 3 drug trafficker in the world."

These are the people with whom Barry Seal had been doing business. Organized crime was rampant in Montreal; police recorded 105 meetings between Obront and such Mafia strongmen as Vincent Controni, Paolo Violi and Angelo Lanza. Cotroni and Violi were considered the "godfathers" of the Italian Mafia in town, the two people who controlled most of the criminal activity in the city.

Why does Canada, and Canadian crime figures, play such a large role in CIA-Mob wrongdoing? Probably because the CIA has repeatedly used Canadian firms as 'cut-outs' in everything from ownership of Seal's fleet of smuggling aircraft to money laundering, from the late '50s with the Brockville bank heist and its role in anti-Castro activities to Clay Shaw and Permindex and right up through the cocaine-fueled '80s.

"Montreal was a safe place," Gerry Hemming explained. "When somebody said hey, lets sit down, talk business, its Montreal where they did it..."

"It's all part of the game. When, for example, in a deal, they send the guy to Montreal, its because that's where the money is," he continues, "that's where the guys wheel and deal and can freely *exhibit* the money... *Then* they go down South and 'do the thing.'"

What had been going on in Operation Screamer, we asked him. Was it really, as we'd heard, just a ploy to provide a labor pool for CIA Director Bill Casey's operation out of Mena?

"Ask yourself this," replied Hemming cagily. "Who was so powerful that they can fuck Norman Rothman? Remember, Roughhouse Rothman was one of the people who funded Sturgis all the way back in Cuba. Someone plenty powerful."

No doubt Barry Seal's feelings of immunity stemmed from being in business with such powerful people... There's nothing like walking out of the bank with the bank president's arm around your shoulder to build up your confidence.

So though he was followed constantly after 1982, he calmly accepted the challenge presented by law enforcement. When he bumped into a Louisiana State Police agent on the street in Baton Rouge one time he told him, "You dumb son-of-a-bitch. You'll never catch me."

On stakeouts, agents futilely watched as Seal used two pay phones at a time, working from a little green canvas tote bag full of hundreds of quarters, talking in code to Colombia, transmitting digital messages over the line by computer so the agents couldn't listen in.

State Police narcotics agents laughed as they recalled for us flying surveillance over Seal's Baton Rouge home... only to have Barry appear in the back yard waving a white towel aloft in mock surrender while they circled overhead.

In the summer of 1983, the Associated Press wire service headlines about Operation Screamer trumpeted "Canada-U.S. Drug Connection Broken Up," and "Authorities Say Officials Say Major Florida-Canada Drug Ring Broken Up."

But nothing much has changed, as evidenced in a *Toronto Star* headline fifteen years later: "Montreal Ambush Stirs Fear of Drug Turf War!"

"The gunning down of a reputed member of the Cotroni crime family has police on alert for a drug traffickers' turf war," Montreal newspapers reported. "Paul Cotroni, 42, was shot three times Sunday night as he got out of his Corvette in front of his large suburban home in Repentigny, east of Montreal."

Was the Associated Press back in '83 guilty of mere wishful thinking? Not bothering to re-write DEA handouts? Or was there something more sinister afoot?

In any case, if the Canada-U.S. drug connection *had* been 'broken-up,' it was with laughter.

CHAPTER THIRTY-TWO

TRINTY IS MY NAME

WHAT'S ULTIMATELY MOST interesting about the story of Barry Seal is the question of just where all the money went… and still goes.… The illicit narcotics industry has suffered no discernible dip in sales since Seal's murder; just the opposite: gross revenues in narcotics have risen.

There must be quite a bit of 'discretionary' income in a $300 billion a year business… certainly enough to buy an election, even a Presidential election. Our interest was piqued.

Who gets to pass out all that fresh green?

Who decides who gets what?

By this point in our investigation we were no longer fascinated with stories of pilots skimming mere feet above the waves of the Gulf of Mexico on 'daring' drug runs.

The process of flying narcotics into the United States is no more eventful than driving a bus, unless you're an amateur free-lancer. And there are no longer many of them still around…

What intrigued us now was whether we could, using Seal's own records as a guide, trace any of the money flows up the line.

So we started with the tip we had received about drug money being laundered through a corporation named Trinity Oil or Trinity Energy. In tracking that company we plunged down a rabbit hole which was as deep as any Alice ever saw in Wonderland… before we re-surfaced, we would discover that Seal's organization was linked to the vast criminal enterprise known as "the Company," chronicled in Sally Denton's The Bluegrass Conspiracy."

And to the heart of both this nation's major political parties.

Barry Seal's attorney and partner ██████ ████ ████, re-invented as an international trade consultant in Manhattan, had sold Trinity Energy; a 'front' company we had been told was a drug money laundry vehicle for Seal's operation, in the spring of 1995.

Let's begin with this news release we discovered, from Investment Dealers' Digest's Mergers & Acquisitions Report, indicating that front companies set up by Barry Seal were being traded a decade after his death...

"TARGET: TRINITY ENERGY CORP, Baton Rouge, Louisiana Oil and gas exploration and production. ACQUIROR: INTERNATIONAL REALTY GROUP INC, Miami, Florida Provide real estate agency and appraisal services; own and operate commercial properties."

A second release out of Miami on May 12, 1995 said much the same thing. "INTERNATIONAL REALTY GROUP INC. TO ACQUIRE TRINITY ENERGY CORP."

International Realty Group, Inc. (OTC Bulletin Board: IRGR) had agreed to acquire 100% of "the real estate and energy assets from Trinity Energy Corporation and its affiliates (Trinity), Baton Rouge, Louisiana.

"Under the terms of the agreement, IRGR will acquire from Trinity real estate holdings, located in Baton Rouge, Louisiana, oil and gas rights located in the Port Hudson field in East Baton Rouge, Louisiana, other commercial real estate property and additional working capital in exchange for approximately $21,500,000 in the form of 333,333 shares of IRGR common stock and convertible debentures in the aggregate amount of $21,250,000," the release stated.

"This timely strategic alliance of IRGR and Trinity comes at a time when the growth requirements of energy and real estate related companies need greater access to the capital markets and financial services," said ██████ ████ ████, newly appointed Chairman of the Board of IRGR.

"IRGR and Trinity can help fulfill such needs with full utilization of IRGR's international network developed over 30 years providing valuation and appraisal services from both its Miami (Florida) and Budapest (Hungary) offices."

██████ ████ ████, whose own fumbling smuggling exploits we were to hear about from several sources, was selling Trinity Energy Corporation, located in Barry's hometown of Baton Rouge, for almost $22 million. And ▮▮▮ would end up Chairman of the Board of the buying company.

By the mid-'70s ▮▮▮ was already "deeply involved," as they say in legal parlance, in Barry's activities, an integral part of the smuggling organization.

We heard from several Seal associates accounts of ▮▮▮'s activities upon which the State Bar of Louisiana would presumably frown. Although, Louisiana being Louisiana, one can never be too sure...

There is, for example, the locally famous anecdote in Baton Rouge about ▮▮▮ concerning the time he left a briefcase filled with over $100,000 of drug money sitting on the front car seat of a rental car at Baton Rouge Airport.

▮▮▮, to his subsequent humiliation, had been too afraid to go back to retrieve it.

Another '▮▮▮ sighting' we heard about had occurred near Miami Airport, right after the Screamer indictments were released in March of 1983. Barry Seal, ▮▮▮, and Blackie were attempting to avoid arrest and get out of Florida without being detected...

"Barry was by then already a 'wanted man,' but he wasn't ready yet to turn himself in," Blackie explained. "We were staying at what we had nicknamed the Carpet City Motel, so-called because for some strange reason—which no one ever satisfactorily explained—it had carpeting running halfway up the walls. It was a real cheesy place."

He continued, "But being 'wanted' didn't stop Barry from driving like he always did—a maniac—when we left the motel for the Miami airport to catch a flight back to Baton Rouge. As he was turning onto the highway, instead of stopping at the red light he cut into a service station and out the other side.

"I saw him look in the rear view mirror, and he said something like 'oh shit. Let me do the talking. We're getting pulled over by a cop.'"

Blackie smiled in recollection...

"▮▮▮ and I are going 'shit, Barry, now you've done it!' See, we had a suitcase in the trunk filled with $2 million in cash. In those days we usually carried $2 million, always in cash, around with us in a big soft suitcase, in case we needed anything..."

"And now ▮▮▮ is shitting himself in the back seat, because he's, like, an attorney, right? How is he going to explain sitting in a car with a wanted man and two million dollars? He's thinking, 'disbarred!'"

"So while Barry's standing there arguing with the cop, and ▮▮▮'s shitting himself in the back seat, I get out and pop the trunk of the car, grab the suitcase and say, right in front of the cop, 'Barry, I'm sorry, I'm going to have to split if I'm going to make my flight.'"

"There was a car rental place right there at the corner, and I walked into it with my 'luggage,' then sprinted out the back door and grabbed the first parking lot attendant I saw, peeled off a hundred, and told him to get me to the airport *right now*.

And while I was sitting at the gate waiting for the flight to be called, looking everywhere for cops, Barry and ████ came strolling out to the gate, and Barry, calm as can be, says, 'Blackie, where ya been?'"

Needless to say, none of this flagrantly illegal activity has kept ████ ████ ████ from publicly posing as a pillar-of-the-community. (Why should it... being connected means never having to say you're sorry.) He has hosted a weekly TV segment called "Consumers and the Law," been a grand knight in the Knights of Columbus and pursued avocations like swimming, flying, boating, and tennis.

As we learned more of ████'s career we became more and more incredulous, just at how blatantly he operated... He incorporated, for example, a dummy company called "Crawfish Aviation" in early 1982, which he promptly changed to "California Builders" when Iran Contra 'rep' Gene Glick came on the scene.

When a company sounding like its in the business of hauling seafood, Crawfish Aviation, changes its name to an enterprise, California Builders, which sounds like it builds ranch-style homes... nothing too strictly kosher can be going on.

Then, quite by accident (okay, we eavesdropped!) we overheard someone speaking with ████s ex-wife, asking where the $22 million from the sale of Trinity Energy in 1995 had gone.

The ex-Mrs. ████ was aghast. She and ████ had divorced at the same time, 1995, that the sale supposedly took place...but she said ████ had been so seemingly down on his luck at the time that *she* had had to pay *him* $40,000 to dissolve their union and be done with him.

She knew nothing of any sale for $22 million, she said. She thought ████ had been broke at the time.

Tracking Seal associate ████ ████ ████'s activities into the present revealed how well connected Barry's smuggling associate remains today.

As head of the Millennium Financial Group in New York, he has been instrumental in bringing just two companies public. Both proved fascinating to learn about...

The first, Unique Mobility, receives numerous grants from the Defense Advanced Research Projects Agency (DARPA), the secretive National Security Agency-linked outfit that invented the Internet...

Unique Mobility also cuts lucrative deals with defense industry giants in ways that have business writers sometimes shaking their heads...

"Why would Northrop's electronics arm, which had $ 2.5 billion in revenues and 12,000 employees, see any value in dealing with the small (Unique Mobility) Golden company?" a typical story asked.

Maybe, thought, if it's used for *other* purposes as well.

But it is the *second* company of the two taken public by ████, which led us straight to the 'secret heart of darkness' at the center of the American political process today...

Netivation.com portrays itself as an Internet public policy and political Web site, offering a package of fundraising services to candidates and campaigns, receiving a percentage of the campaign contributions made via the Web.

The name of Netivation's first major congressional endorser, we were stunned to discover, was Arkansas Republican Congressman Asa Hutchinson, who before becoming the marketing "poster boy" for a company Barry Seal's associate ████ ████ had just taken public... was the U.S. Attorney for the Western Judicial District in Arkansas, encompassing Mena.

"We always knew we couldn't prosecute Barry Seal, no matter what we got on him, because of the politics involved in the Western Judicial District," crusty Arkansas State Police Commander Finis Duvall told us.

While Hutchinson made tough-talking speeches to community groups in Arkansas about cleaning up what even *he* had been forced to concede was "a haven for international drug trafficking," at Mena, Barry Seal had blithely continued to operate from an airfield just a few short miles from Hutchinson's office.

Maybe the sound of the C-123's rumbling overhead had scared him, but observers of Hutchinson's lack of performance had grown increasingly skeptical of the boy's fire-eating crime-fighin' credentials.

IRS agent William Duncan had been the first to take his accusations public. In a deposition for the Arkansas Attorney General, he was asked, "Are you stating now under oath that you believe that the investigation in and around the Mena airport of money laundering was covered up by the U.S. Attorney?"

Duncan's reply: "It was covered up."

Hutchinson's serves today, we learned, on the House Speaker's Task Force for a Drug-Free America. (As what? An industry representative?) He was also called on by his fellow Republicans to give a fiery summation in the Clinton Impeachment in the Senate, where he urged "justice" to rain down like mighty waters, presumably on Mr. Clinton.

But were justice to ever *really* rain down, we would urge the Congressman not to wear his good suit that day… because he, along with Bill Clinton, might get awfully wet.

By following a money trail left behind by Barry Seal almost fifteen years ago, we had discovered that members of the drug smuggling organization to which Seal belonged were still paying off favors for the 'boys.'

Next we turned our attention to the company to which ████ had supposedly *sold* his Trinity Energy, International Realty Group.

Would they turn to, to be 'connected,' too? We heard from several well-informed sources that the chief mover of International Realty, Jack Birnholz, was not unknown in 'certain circles.'

"This is a very exciting opportunity for IRGR," Birnholz, chairman and president of International Realty Group, had said in the press release announcing the deal.

But who was Jack Birnholz? The answer, we thought, might provide some leads to where the massive illegal narcotics industry had "gone" when it submerged and became invisible after the spectacular cocaine cowboys like Seal were replaced.

Tracking the financial perambulations of Trinity Energy had soon had immersed us in a netherworld teeming with pirates, sunken galleons, worthless railroad bonds, bogus banks, chicken empires, phony scions of mega-rich American industrial dynasties, Mexican drug czars posing as 'entrepreneurs,' and 3 million acre "cocaine ranches" in the Brazilian rainforest.

CHAPTER THIRTY-THREE

DOING THINGS
CARLITO'S WAY

FOR A MAN WHOSE OSTENSIBLE business is real estate appraisal, Jack Birnholz had a remarkably diverse taste in businesses, we discovered... controlling everything from gold mines to hazardous waste disposal. And his International Realty Group had offices in just two cities, Miami and Budapest, which seems odd...

Had the flourishing trade between Hungary and Florida somehow escaped our attention? No, as it happens... International Realty Company and its Eastern European subsidiary, Stragix, were involved in the conversion of state-owned property to private ownership in Eastern Europe at the same time the boys were said to have been buying up huge chunks of the infrastructure of the disintegrating Soviet empire on the cheap.

Despite their vaunted stagecraft, most of 'the boys' can be recognized by their extraordinarily colorful *curriculum vitaes*. Birnholz is no exception. Among his exotic purchases, he owns a company exploring for gold doubloons. Barry Seal, we knew, was also involved in a gold treasure-hunting venture, with famed Florida adventurer Mel Fisher.

A post-Gulf War *Miami Herald* business story told the tale...
"Jack Birnholz's company has appraised the Mustang Ranch in Nevada a few times. It's also assessed the Drake Hotel in Philadelphia, gold mines in Costa Rica, a telephone company in Hungary, art deco

hotels along Miami Beach and gas stations throughout South Florida. The firm is now up for a $ 50 million contract to evaluate an entire country—Kuwait."

Good thing we won the war.

"Wreckage Found Of Pirate Ship 300 Years Old!" read headlines we discovered about one of Birnholz's companies.

"A local Bayfield diver had been part of a group of underwater explorers who had located the galleon La Trompeuse, a 300 year old privateer, in the U.S. Virgin Islands. The ship had gone down in flames in 1683 after a gun battle with English forces, filled with gold, silver and other plunder," said the Bayfield Wisconsin newspaper.

Thus was born another Birnholz company, Enviro-Recovery, billing itself as "the leading supplier of old growth northern hardwood lumber made from logs that sank in the rivers and lakes of North America during the logging era of the 1800's."

The company salvaged valuable old growth hardwood that had sunk to the bottom of rivers and lakes during logging, said the company's literature, recovering 'antique' quality wood in an environmentally-sound fashion, for use in high end home decor, furniture, instrument manufacture, and premier home building.

Who could be against that?

But what caught our eye was the fact that the company also found it necessary to own a 3.5 million acre "ranch" located in the region of Brazil where the big cocaine labs are—*today*—still located.

"Enviro-Recovery Expands Operations Into South America; Gains Control of Large Underwater Tropical Wood Reserve," read the press release headline...

"Enviro-Recovery plans to substantially increase profits by increasing production, by improving sawing, handling and drying techniques at the mill, and by exporting lumber and finished products made in Brazil."

So...was this just the march of progress? Or were we looking instead at the results of Operation Condor?

Then we discovered another link which we thought at first pointed towards Birnholz being "CIA-involved," since the Agency's ties to the family in question are well-documented...

"Sloan duPont Appointed To Board of Directors of Enviro-Recovery," was the headline of a Sept. 3, 1997 *BusinessWire* release.

"Sloan duPont of the family of duPont (E.I. duPont de Nemours) has been appointed to the Board of Directors of Enviro Recovery, Inc. (OTC Bulletin Board: EVRE)," read the business news release.

"Mr. duPont has been recognized for his good work serving on the board of numerous charitable, public service, public health and philanthropic organizations. Mr. duPont said, "I consider the preservation of America's forests to be of utmost importance and am proud to serve on the Board of Directors of Enviro Recovery. The Company's "zero waste" policy is an important means of maintaining the ecological balance of America's forest and the preservation of its natural beauty."

Bravo, Mr. duPont! Nice to see the scions of weapons manufacturing empires developing a social conscience, especially after all these centuries…

The release continued, "Enviro Recovery's recycling of lost timber submerged under the Great Lakes from an era long past is consistent with Mr. duPont's belief that individuals and corporations should devote their efforts to projects that benefit America."

Birnholz was busting his corporate buttons with pride at attracting such a prominent investor to the tiny concern. As CEO of Enviro Recovery, he intoned, "We are exceptionally pleased to have offered a directorship to Mr. duPont and proud of his acceptance. We look forward to his help and guidance."

Big things must have seemed just around the corner for the company, if you read their press releases. But then we discovered that Birnholz's new director wasn't really a duPont at all.

He was a crook.

In a story about Sloan duPont in the August 14, 1999, *Bath* (England) *Chronicle,* they reported " A SWINDLER, who posed as a member of a mega-rich American industrial dynasty to try and pull off a 6 million pound bank sting, was jailed for three years yesterday."

"As "Sloan Dupont," would-be scion of the duPont fortune, an American named James Rice had tried to pass a bogus $ 9.6 million check at a London bank. DuPpont has been living in London since 1997. Police revealed that extradition procedures were under way in the USA over (an unrelated) $12m fraud."

Poor Jack Birnholz! Here he had appointed "Sloan duPont" to his board, gone to the trouble of sending out press releases to Wall Street broker/dealers about his prestigious new business partner… and the bogus "duPont" was working his charade in London at the exact same time!

Birnholz might have been the innocent victim of a swindler and con man. But we didn't think so. Especially not after we Birnholz had led us to yet-another instance of major financial fraud.

DuPont's appointment, we learned, had been announced at the same time that hapless Enviro-Recovery investors had begun to notice their stock was shrinking to less than a tenth its previous value...

The *Milwaukee Journal Sentinel* reported the bad news: "Enviro-Recovery's president says news reports, red tape have hurt stock value."

The paper reported, "Scott Mitchen, president of Enviro-Recovery Inc., Monday blamed the media, government red tape and reinvestment in equipment for the dramatic decline in the stock value of his company's subsidiary..."

The company's stock had lost 90% of its value in five months, the article said, clearly a horrible toll for the media and government red tape to be exacting...

How the media and government red tape had picked Birnholz's company for such swift economic destruction was left unclear.

What *was* clear, however, was something or someone had just made off with 90% of the worth of a public company... an even more thoroughgoing looting than Greycas had suffered.

The bogus duPont has such colorful news-clippings that he piqued our attention as much as Birnholz's bogus company.

His real name was James Rice, we learned, and his tradecraft must have been impeccable. Even though he had gone from a luxury apartment overlooking a London park directly to jail without passing 'go,' his fiancé, duped and dumped, still believed he was part of the duPont family.

Who was he? Did "James Rice" have the requisite number of interesting connections to be labeled something more than just the financial "soldier of fortune" he was being made to appear?

An AP story on August 14, 1999 provided a clue...

"An international con artist wanted in Oklahoma on fraud charges may not be extradited here until he completes his three-year prison sentence in Britain, officials said. Oklahoma prosecutors allege James Rice also posed as duPont to give credibility to selling shares in old railroad bonds. Rice and others, including three Oklahomans, claimed the bonds were worth millions, but they were actually museum curios, prosecutors allege. Scores of investors as far away as New Zealand lost at least $10 million in the scheme, officials allege."

We were, once again, back in the precincts of major financial crime.

Rice had friends with ambition, who had located some offshore scams right in the heart of Oklahoma, using tribal privileges. The two "businessmen" from Northern California with Rice in the phony railroad bond scheme had also set up a non-chartered bank on an Indian reservation in Oklahoma, which proceeded to defraud unwitting depositors.

Just as with Merrill Bean's Western Thrift in Utah, the deposits turned out to be uninsured.

Located on the Anadarko Indian reservation, the self-described bank offered "Swiss secrecy" to depositors. The Internal Revenue Service, the FBI, the U.S. Postal Service and the Securities & Exchange Commission investigated, and when they executed search warrants found evidence of mail fraud, money laundering and illegal banking stretching from Oklahoma through at least seven other states...

"Depositors lost $8.9 million in the scheme," Assistant U.S. Attorney Hank Hockmeir told us from his office in Oklahoma City.

"The money was not insured, and while we were able to freeze some assets, a lot of regular people are out a lot of money."

A focus of Hockmeir's investigation was "Sloan duPont's" part of the scheme—the sale of 19th century, "gold-backed" railroad bonds that were worthless," he said.

Testimony that the fraudulent sales pitch included an "authentication document" signed by a Gerald A. Dobbins provided some unintended hilarity. Dobbins, claiming to be a "master curator" valued the railroad bonds at $110 million. In person he told a different story.

He admitted doing the bond valuations. But when asked for which state he was "master curator," he confessed, "the state of confusion."

What kind of people are these, we wondered, involved in continuing massive financial fraud that includes things like busting out companies and setting up bogus banks?

They clearly weren't just petty crooks.

Jack Birnholz, for example, operates his companies under the umbrella of a private fund, which he told us is currently valued at over $5 *billion*...

Called Growth Fund Partnership, it styles itself "a diversified asset based trust company with substantial mineral reserves and gold mining claims located in New Mexico and Washington State."

And Trinity Energy isn't the only covert operation we were able to discover in Birnholz's background.

An article in the July 15, 1997 MIAMI DAILY BUSINESS REVIEW revealed that "GROWTH FUND Partnership Inc. said Monday it has agreed with Silverado Milling Corp. of Colorado to purchase mining claims for precious metals in New Mexico in exchange for an undisclosed amount of stock. Growth Fund, a Miami-based corporation, says the mining claims have an estimated appraisal value of $1.5 billion, Jack Birnholz, chairman of Growth Fund Partnership, Inc. (Growth), a private Florida corporation based in Miami, announced.

$1.5 billion is a pretty big deal, isn't it? Could a company this substantial be involved in anything illegal?

The answer came in Birnholz's purchase of a Mexican resort hotel chain for slightly in excess of $100 million on October 17, 1995...

"Miami-based International Realty Group, Inc announced that it received confirmation of an executed agreement with DSC, S.A. de C.V. (DSC), based in Mexico City, to buy a portfolio of real estate properties located throughout Mexico from DSC," read a news story.

The properties are located in major Mexican resort areas including Cancun, Ixtapa, Puerto Vallarta, Baja California Sur, as well as in several mid-sized cities in Mexico.

But what the press release left out was the name of the "Mexican entrepreneur" from whom Birnholz was purchasing the hotel chain.

The "Mexican entrepreneur" is Bernardo Dominguez. He first came to light when he took a run at buying the Westin Hotels chain for more than $ 700 million...

Though the deal fell through, this brash move prompted *New York Times* reporter Anthony DePalma to take a closer look at him...and Dominguez found himself suddenly in the public glare, no longer cruising anonymously aboard his Saberliner 60 jet.

DePalma wrote, in the *Times*, "Bernardo Dominguez Cereceres, head of DSC Ingenieria Inmobiliaria, is regarded as a maverick in Mexico, where culture and tradition rule. The negative opinions about him printed in Mexico City dailies obviously rankle, especially since dignity and reputation count for so much in Mexican culture."

"Education impresses Dominguez, perhaps overly so," DePalma continued. "His curriculum vitae lists a master's degree in administration from the University of Pennsylvania, but there is no record of it there. When confronted he said, "I didn't even know that was on there." He said he took courses at Penn but did not try for a master's. The same goes for the resume listing of a master's degree in finance from the London School of Economics."

Dominguez had fibbed on his resume. Big deal. But that was just the start...

"At the end of the best business day of his life, Bernardo Dominguez Cereceres kicked back in his suite at one of the 74 Westin Hotels he had just agreed to buy for $708 million, punched a few numbers into the pay-per-view television system and ordered the gangster movie "Carlito's Way," wrote DePalma.

"As the violent film unfolded, Dominguez rested peacefully. The touchstone of his quick rise into Mexico's business elite is his addiction to American movies, especially those about good guys who appear to be bad guys."

"Carlito's Way," in which a well-meaning hoodlum tries to go straight but can't, could stand as a metaphor for Dominguez's recent life. In the sophisticated circles of Mexican business, where culture counts and tradition still rules, Dominguez is seen as something of a bad guy, even though he insists he's a model Mexican success story."

"Just 33, he heads a company called DSC Ingenieria Inmobiliaria, which in seven years has grown to 8,000 employees and sales of more than $200 million. Dominguez, with a face like Lou Costello's and a penchant for bright cuff links and big wristwatches, has irritated the business community. His rapid success is viewed suspiciously within the blue-blood Mexico City business community, in which most fortunes are inherited, not made," the *New York Times* article stated.

We tracked down *New York Times-man* Anthony DePalma to ask about the not-so-veiled allusions in his story on Dominguez— the gangster movies, the gold cufflinks etc.—and when we shared with him a few of our suspicions, he said they'd been his as well...

"I had heard rumors that he (Dominguez) was involved in the drug trade," DePalma told us. "That's what had so many people bothered when he tried to take over the Westin chain. Here you have this young rich guy, with no clear explanation of how he had managed to come up with so much money, making a run at a premier hotel chain."

"If you transplanted his rags-to-riches success story to Texas, for example," DePalma said, "I don't think there would have been any questions raised. But, in Mexico, it just doesn't happen that way. The culture just does not allow for that kind of leap-frogging."

"How did you find out about Dominguez?" a shocked and unhappy NSA source demanded when we asked about him.

Was this the "current operations" this man had been warned we were coming close to "compromising?"

Professor Walter Chambliss calls this "state-sponsored fraud." And there aren't a lot of experts in the field, but we found one, who agreed to take a peek at International Realty Group for us...

"You've got the colorful International Realty Group (IRG), with only $500k annual revenues, and less than $200K net profit," she stated briskly. "And this tiny company was going to purchase Trinity Energy for $22 million?"

"These people (Brinholz) feature themselves as specialty international property appraiser and resort developers, developing resorts in Mexico, with projects in the most interesting foreign arenas, involved in real estate, casino development ventures, etc., including plans to develop casinos, through an offshore something called Hemisphere Developments, LTD, for example, based in Geneva, and with Isle of Man offices."

She gazed at us levelly. "Do you know how much goes on through the Channel Islands? Laundering for the cartels?"

What we learned next about Bernardo Dominguez made our suspicions grow immensely...

We found a brief article in Mexico Business Monthly on September 1999, stating that Dominguez was involved in a Spanish consortium paying $261 million for a 15% stake in—and management of—a state-owned Mexican company, Grupo Aeroportuario del Pacifico, which runs 12 airports in western Mexico.

Hmm.

What business "synergies" are there, we wondered, in owning a 3.5 million acre ranch in the cocaine-processing heart of the South American Amazon, as well as effective control of a dozen airports in western Mexico?

Through following the business associations of Seal's smuggling partner ▇▇▇▇▇▇▇ and Trinity energy, we were witnessing, we felt sure, was would reveal itself to be either a simple covert operation... or the "corporatization" of the drug trade.

In either event, they do things "Carlito's Way."

CHAPTER THIRTY-FOUR

TRINITY IS MY NAME TOO

SIFTING THROUGH THE DISCARDED shells of dummy corporations in the musty basement of the Louisiana Secretary of State's office, one can find a treasure trove of conspiracy lore, writ small in the dusty language of incorporation documents.

We came across evidence there, of the sheer effort expended in the gargantuan effort of laundering the proceeds of the drug trade. Clearly, it is an enterprise requiring the services of vast bevies of lawyers… like ███████ ███████ ███████.

We were there seeking to learn more about the multi-million dollar investment of Barry Seal's drug cash that had infused an oil and gas company named Trinity Energy, which ███████ had, in 1995, been selling to his Miami-and-Budapest-based friends.

And there we found records of the incorporation of Trinity Oil and Gas, in September of 1982, the same month that Barry Seal's Mena operation had swung into high gear. The listed officers were Dewey Brister Jr. and trustworthy Calvin Briggs, the Barry Seal employee that didn't mind "doin' the time for another man's crime."

There was, in addition, a "Trinity Securities" with Calvin Briggs name on it as well. Briggs—recall—was the trusted Seal associate who had taken the fall when Emile Camp was busted in Miami with a trunk-full of counterfeit Quaaludes, and had then falsely identified himself as Brigg's.

It made sense that Barry Seal would use as a cutout in a money laundering deal someone like Briggs, whom he knew he could trust.

When we went looking for Calvin Briggs, we learned that he's dead. Louisiana law enforcement authorities said that Briggs was dead, a suicide in the mid-80's. But Barry Seal's widow Debbie told us of bumping into him and having lunch five years after his supposed demise. Go figure…

If Briggs *were* dead, he'd be difficult to locate. But if he had 'switched' identities he'd be impossible to find, we figured…

So we turned our attention to the other listed officer in Trinity, Dewey Brister—today—a financial planner with Paine Webber in Baton Rouge. Needless to say, these are matters Dewey would prefer rested comfortably in the past…

We asked him about the qualifications of his partner in their joint oil-drilling venture.

"Calvin Briggs was dumber than a shit-house brick, heavily-tattooed, your typical biker type with bars and scars," a Louisiana state police source had told us.

Had Brister found Briggs to be a bit unlikely in the role of oil wildcatter?

Brister didn't flinch. But he did grow nervous, stating that he had had no knowledge at all that Calvin Briggs was an associate of notorious drug smuggler Barry Seal, but had just been referred to him by a banker friend of his.

The attorney who'd put together the deal, Andrew Ezell, didn't flinch either. Maybe they'd talked…

"No, it didn't strike me as strange at all when Dewey came into my office with a biker-looking guy and said they were setting up an oil company," Ezell avers. "It's what I do."

"Our first venture raised only $30-40,000. We drilled some in '83," Brister stated, "and hit nothing to speak of. And that was the end of it."

What about Trinity Securities? How had that come about?

"My attorney, Andrew Ezell, was a securities lawyer who told me that incorporating a securities company would help us avoid any SEC problems in limited offerings," Brister said. "I was trying to do everything by the letter of the law, and you needed a guy like Andy Ezell to do it. After I got out of the drilling venture, I gave back the securities company to Ezell."

Andy Ezell had been LSU's quarterback while Seal attorney ██████, ████, Blackie, and Joseph "Beaver" Brantley IV were in law school there, we learned.

When we met him for breakfast one crisp fall New Orleans morning—at what we were told later was a Mob-owned hangout—he was wearing a sleeveless white sweater and the casual air of a Rotarian from someplace where all the news doesn't make the papers.

Like Brister, Ezell seemed eager to deflect attention in other directions, and began positively waxing philosophical when we mentioned the name "Beaver Brantley," who we knew to be involved, with Louisiana Governor Edwin Edwards' son Stephen, in a Texas energy company that came up missing over $100 million...

"Beaver Brantley is the kind of guy who would call around town, during the time we're talking about—the early '80s—and mention breathlessly that he had 300,000 barrels of Arabian light crude, a very desirable grade of oil, sitting on a tanker that he could let you have at a great price if you could do business right away," said Ezell.

Was Brantley "connected?" "Everything in this state is pretty tied in," Ezell said. "Its all of a piece. Who do you think killed Kennedy?"

Brister and Ezell both stated that there was no possible way that the 'Trinity Oil and Gas' and 'Trinity Securities' they had been involved with could have possibly been the company sold by Seal attorney ███████ ████ ████ in 1995 for $22 million.

It wasn't worth a *tenth* of that, they both said.

We went back to the Secretary of State's office for another afternoon in the wading in the big muddy water of Louisiana corporation archives...where before our disbelieving eyes an elaborate charade began to slowly reveal itself. Before we were finished we had discovered a whole 'gaggle' of seemingly connected 'Trinity Oil,' and 'Trinity Energy.'

Which one led back to drug money laundering and Barry Seal? Maybe *all* of them...

"It's the 'name game,'" explained Lois Battuello, a financial investigator in California's Napa Valley, who has been tracking Iran Contra-linked fraud for a decade.

"The name 'Trinity' is code... like wearing a Mason's ring, something which only initiates understand. And—if that's not complicated enough for you already—it's intimately related to *another* code name: 'Triad.' Look in the dictionary...

'TRIAD n. 1. A union or group of three, esp. of three closely related persons, beings, or things; a TRINITY.' "

"Remember Neil Bush and Silverado Savings and Loan?" she continued. "Silverado was a similar code word, which was used by dozens of corporate entities, running, through numerous subsidiaries, the sub-operations of Iran Contra."

Told that Silverado Mining had been purchased by Jack Birnholz's Miami fund, she said, "You have to understand that the name 'Trinity,' like Silverado, was a code name, a variation of Triad, which equals Trinity."

She pointed us to *The Bluegrass Conspiracy* by Sally Denton (1990, Doubleday), where the major smuggler profiled in the book had a horse farm, located just outside of Lexington, Kentucky, named "Triad."

Triad had been owned by a man Drew Thornton, whose body had been found outside of Knoxville, Tenn. He had fallen or jumped from a plane following a chase by DEA planes and his parachute failed to open. On his body was $75 million in cocaine as well as night vision goggles like Barry Seal's pilots used.

Denton wrote, "A sign on the fence surrounding the property reads: Notice-Trespassing on this property may be hazardous to your health. The word 'Triad' was painted on a sign at the entrance to the farm. Other federal agencies had also been enticed by rumors of arms-stockpiling and mercenary training at Triad. "

"U.S. Customs agents in New York, who were monitoring the activities of Adnan Khashoggi, briefly entertained the possibility that Triad was a subsidiary of Khashoggi's Triad America Corporation. The fact that Khashoggi was frequenting Lexington added fuel to the speculation," she wrote, in *The Bluegrass Conspiracy*.

"Coincidentally, Ralph (Ross) had suddenly been receiving complaints about suspicious activity on Triad. Neighbors had reported to state police that a cult of devil worshippers frequented the remote property, and that the constant firing of automatic weapons could be heard. Dozens of people wearing military camouflage uniforms were seen rappelling from the back cliffs of Triad."

"You'll find that these relationships go to Gov. John Y. Brown of Kentucky, and that Bill Clinton was also in this loop, one 'observer' told us...

"And they go to Dan Lasater as well. Since researchers have known for some time that 'Triad' was code, it doesn't surprise me that you're turning up 'Company' fronts named 'Trinity.'"

Drew Thornton had CIA phone numbers in his wallet, too, when he died, just like Barry Seal. And according to *The Bluegrass Conspiracy* Thornton was also a close associate of Jimmy Lambert, the man who gave Arkansas bond daddy and Clinton best friend Dan Lasater his first hit of cocaine.

"Most Trinities and most Triads in the SEC system start out as limited partnerships then become limited liability companies," Lois Battuello told us, "which *then* become investors in *another* company which then goes public…. This is the payoff system of upward "flips" with profits made at each level."

Then we found a "Trinity Energy" which was founded by a man, ████ ████████, who quickly confessed to us having been an "associate" of Company principal and Kingpin Jimmy Lambert…

'Owning' Trinity Energy is only one, we were to discover, of ████████'s claims to fame…

CHAPTER THIRTY-FIVE

DON'T SHOOT!
I'M WITH
TRINITY ENERGY!

AFTER THE RAUCOUS partying on Fat Tuesday, the final day and night of Mardi Gras revelry in New Orleans, the morning after, Ash Wednesday, was a quiet one in popular West Bank (Carlos Marcello country) ██████ *house* ██████ *in the February of 1985…*

A sign on the front door said the restaurant was closed, enraging the steak house's proprietor, 45-year old ████████████████████." ███████ strode angrily across the darkened main dining room.

Accounts vary on what happened next. But all agree that when the smoke had cleared ███████████ had been shot three times at point blank range by his wife ████████

"I went inside and asked someone why the restaurant was closed," ███████ testified at the trial of his wife.

"Then I looked at the bar, and ████ was sitting on a stool. I asked *her* why the restaurant was closed. Then ███ reached in the pocket of her sweater and instantly I *knew* why the restaurant was closed, and the workers had been sent home… I threw my hands up and said, 'uh, don't I ████'"

Being in court the day of ████████'s trial had obviously been great theater…

"I saw the blue flame from the gun," ████████ continued, to a hushed courtroom at Lena's trial for attempted murder…

"I felt the bullet hit me in the jaw. I turned and tried to dive behind the bar. She shot me two more times, in the back. I fell to my knees and crawled toward the bar on my stomach. ███ was hysterical, screaming, pointing the gun at me… but I can't say I heard the trigger clicking anymore."

We found someone who remembered the shooting well…

"I was on the phone with ███ when she shot him," said a longtime business associate of ███████████, Houston restaurateur R███ Kelly.

"When ███ dropped the phone to shoot him I heard the shots and the commotion. When she picked it back up I asked her, "███, did you just shoot ███?"

"'Yeah, I shot the bastard,'" ███ told me. 'But it was a really little gun. He'll live.'"

███ had pumped three .25-caliber slugs into ███████████'s imposing 6-foot-2-inch, 240-pound bulk in the dining room of ███ ███o's restaurant. Just a case of post-Mardi Gras blues?

Not according to the dozen witnesses who testified on ███'s behalf; they characterized steak house owner ███ as a "raging bull" who could go from being calm to violent abusive rages "at the snap of a finger."

Witnesses described numerous occasions on which he had physically abused his wife. Even their only child, ███ told of a reign of family terror as well…

"Once on Father's Day, my mom gave my Dad a pencil sharpener for a present. And he threw it at her in the car, and called her a bitch and a whore, and was driving and hitting her and I held up my arms to separate them all the way from Gulfport (Mississippi) to New Orleans."

In his defense, ███████ had said in a statement to police, that he didn't beat his wife "any more than any other husband."

Ouch!

In a courtroom packed with supporters who cheered the verdict, ███ ███████ was acquitted.

Why is any of this of interest to us? Because the ███████s are listed together as the officers and incorporator's in a company also called Trinity Energy filed in Louisiana during the eventful year of 1981.

Talk about a hall of mirrors.

As the '80s progressed ███████████ became one of America's most successful restaurant entrepreneurs, we learned, eventually selling his ███████ ███ house chain for $22 million in 1995.

Wait a minute, we thought, when we read this: ████████████'s Trinity Energy had also sold for $22 million in 1995!

Was this just more coincidence?

We detected some strong similarities between ███████'s career and that of another fantastically successful steak house chain operator, convicted drug kingpin and Bill Clinton intimate Dan Lasater...

Could steak house chains be a convenient money laundry vehicle? Would we be able to connect the dots, and conclusively prove that Lt. Commander Al Martin had been right about 'Trinity Energy?'

████ and ████'s "Trinity Energy" had first been incorporated, not in Catholic Louisiana, but instead in redneck Baptist Mississippi, where one might expect the theological niceties involved in the concept of a tri-partite deity to be of far less interest than snake handling during Monday night revivals.

███████ denied any secret code involved in naming his oil company Trinity. "I'm just a Catholic boy, and the Trinity is drilled into all Catholics," he protested.

"████████ has never been to church in his life," scoffed sharpshooter ████, his ex-wife...

We found *her* dealing blackjack in a Mississippi Gulf Coast casino.

████ confessed that he had no experience or even *interest* in the oil drilling industry.

Why then, we asked him, had he operated a restaurant chain under the corporate name of an oil company?

███████ asserted that in a free country, one could name one's company anything one damn well pleased.

Driving home Mr. ████████ point, we received a phone call from Mr. ████████'s attorney, Houston Oppenheimer, in Louisville, Kentucky, home of The Company, offering to sue.

Among his achievements, we were to learn, Mr. Oppenheimer represents International Gaming Management Inc., a casino company with ownership links to one of New York's major Mafia families, according to federal affidavits, and a company involved in a major video poker political scandal in Louisiana in the mid-'90's.

Small world.

As might be expected of someone who shot her husband three times (twice in the back), ████████████ today a still-attractive blond in her early 50's, was only too happy to fill us in on the turbulent history of ████████...

██████, she told us, moved to Louisiana with his family while a teenager, from Spokane Washington. Lena remembers receiving early indications that he was, somehow, *connected...*

Like the young Barry Seal, ████████ had somehow excited the interest of the FBI back in the early 1960's in New Orleans.

"While we were still basically newlyweds ███ did something really strange one time," ███ said. "He packed a suitcase with maternity clothes—I was pregnant at the time—and left in a hurry, telling me he was helping the FBI track somebody down."

"Later, when he was arrested for stealing a rental car that same year, 1962, he told me, honey, don't worry, I took the car on orders from the FBI. I thought he was lying until at his trial two men in black suits and skinny ties came over to me in the courtroom, said they were FBI agents, and that everything would be all right."

███ also spent a lot of (early '60's) time at the New Orleans Fairgrounds, ███ told us, as had the Mob's Brothers McLaney, who've we seen are implicated in the Kennedy assassination.

There were rumors that ███ was a bookie, Lena said, which eventually resulted in his being investigated for bookmaking.

We pressed her for more details about this time and place; the early '60's in New Orleans, so important to subsequent American history...

"Once," she offered, "when we broke up for a few weeks, ███ lived in the Town and Country Motel."

Of course, it was Mafia Kingpin Carlos Marcello who had owned the Town and Country; his headquarters was there as well.

██████ called us in a panic one evening after discovering the fact that newsmen (we weren't alone) were nosing into his beginnings. He denied the story completely, and denied, as well, after a long pause, ever knowing Carlos Marcello.

"What was the long pause for?" we asked.

"Because I had to think," he told us. "I did know Carlos' two brothers, both of whom came into the restaurant a lot."

███████ has an interesting background, too, filled with New Orleans Mob connections. One of her uncles had been a lightweight prize fighter, Angelo Conforto, and both he and a second uncle, Jerome Conforto, had both owned "a lot of places" on Bourbon Street, including the famous Papa Joe's, a busy little bar on Bourbon Street that didn't close until 4 or 5 o'clock in the morning, as well as the Silver Slipper, a notorious Marcello hangout.

"I noticed you've been sniffing around the New Orleans Conforte's," wrote a friend who had been following our progress.

"You might be interested in the fact that "Jada" was the stage name of a stripper from New Orleans who was Jack Ruby's girlfriend and whose real name was Janet Conforto."

Janet, or Jada Conforto, we discovered, was ████████'s aunt. And ███'s Aunt Jada had had a *secret...*

On the morning of the Kennedy assassination in Dallas, we learned, Jada Conforto had been in such a panic to leave Dallas that she ran over a pedestrian with her white Cadillac convertible... telling the traffic cop taking a report to please just hurry up and call someone in Ruby's office to fix things, because there was something extremely urgent that she do.

She had to get out of town.

In the days leading up to November 22, 1963, Jack Ruby was handing out 8x10 glossies of Jada to whoever would take one, we learned. There were hundreds of said glossies in the trunk of his car when arrested. Jada was to be the star headliner the weekend Kennedy was murdered.

Dallas police documents clearly indicate that Jada was intent on 'getting the fuck out of Dodge' at the very time she should have been 'opening' at the Carousel.

Can you say "fore-knowledge?" We knew you could...

In a letter to the head of the Dallas Criminal Investigation Division, Assistant Chief of Police Charles Batchelor related how a local man had been hit by a woman fleeing Dallas in a hurry at 10:30 a.m. the morning of the assassination.

Jada Conforto, driving her white Cadillac convertible with Louisiana plates, stopped just long enough to phone for someone in Jack Ruby's office to pick up the slightly-injured pedestrian and take him to a hospital. She told the cop filling out the report, "Let's get this over with. I'm in a hurry to get to New Orleans."

The letter, though basically just an inter-office communication from one cop to another, still gave the appearance of being filled with coded references. Though Jada was a well-known headlining stripper for Jack Ruby, all the letter would say was, "The woman gave the appearance of being in show business."

What the letter states next cannot be mistaken for anything other than studied indifference. "It is unknown if this has any significance in the Oswald case."

Ruby's girlfriend flees Dallas the day of the assassination, and it didn't even make the papers.

A young student working at a Dallas health spa had told police both that he had seen Ruby with Lee Harvey Oswald and that he had been given cards advertising Jada's appearance. But the cops pooh-poohed the report, stating that the student "wasn't as busy as he says he is."

Two days before the assassination Ruby was passing out cards hawking Jada's appearance at the Dallas D.A.'s office. There, he introduced himself to assistant Dallas DA Ben Ellis, telling him, "You probably don't know me now, but you will."

Telling, in a recently released analysis the FBI still characterizes Ruby as a small-time operator who was "never able to cultivate" friendships with important figures or organized crime.

You never rat out your friends.

We phoned ████████████to ask if she could get us an interview with 'Aunt' Jada.

"Jada's dead," ████ told us. "She was killed during the (House Select Committee) Kennedy assassination investigation in a motorcycle accident. My sister in Kenner told me a few years later that Jada had been murdered because she knew too much."

On a whim, we asked her where she and ████████████ had been when Kennedy was killed…

After all, everyone remembers where he or she was when Kennedy was killed. Except George Bush, Richard Nixon, Howard Hunt, and Felix Rodriguez…

"We were on our way to a big party that night," ████ said. "I was on a streetcar on Canal Street, shopping for a new dress to wear to the party, when I heard the news. I turned around and went home, and didn't have the heart to go to the party. ████ went, though."

Had this been the big post-acquittal bash Carlos Marcello held after being found "not guilty" of federal charges that same day?

Too much time has passed, ████ said. She couldn't remember. Once again we were reminded of John Kennedy Jr.'s quote: "Time is the great enemy of the truth."

Jada was a stripper, but her niece ████ will own an oil company, and, even if it was used for money-laundering, that is the very definition of American upward mobility.

Details of ████'s life with ████████ included frequent moves—they lived in 20 different houses in their time together, and strange skills: after he had broken into a safe at his place of employment, ████ boasted to ▇▇ that he knew how to beat a lie detector test, should investigators come calling.

The ▇▇▇▇ grew increasingly affluent in the 1970s, owning a plush spread called Oak Lawn Plantation outside Pass Christian, Mississippi, where ▇▇▇, supposedly, plugged away as an insurance agent.

Then the ▇▇▇▇▇'s divorced, in 1978, for several years. During the interim ▇▇▇ left the country, sailing to Dutch Guyana in South America for a year on a shrimping vessel called the *Nuthin' Special.*

When he returned he had discovered his true calling in life, he said. "I'm going into the restaurant business! It's my destiny!"

Had Mr. ▇▇▇▇▇'s "destiny" been sealed by something that occurred during his "shrimping" sojourn in South America?

He denied it. "I had a crazy idea that a lot of folks in New Orleans had—of going to South America and striking it rich," he said. "We took a special 35-foot shrimp boat that Halter Marine had developed down to Pareibo, Dutch Guyana, and the very first time we dropped a line the boat went underwater and I ended up selling it to some Dutchman down there for 50 $100 bills, which I used to open my first restaurant when we got back."

Contradicting this story is the fact that the *Nuthin' Fancy* sits at anchor today in Biloxi, Mississippi, in a marina outside of the Grand Casino.

And ▇▇▇▇▇'s voice carried such sincerity that we didn't have the heart to tell him that we already knew that Halter Marine had been, and was still, owned by a company called (Can you guess?) Trinity Marine Group, itself owned by the huge Dallas Bass-brothers-controlled Trinity Industries.

Could this be recent secret history? Offshore supply vessels *are* a favored method of bringing drugs to shore, according to law enforcement authorities. And while the 1980s oil bust had devastated most of the Gulf offshore supply vessel business, the Trinity Marine Group had grown fat, buying up the mom-and-pops going under all around them at fire sale prices.

They were also big beneficiaries of Louisiana's new laws authorizing riverboat gambling, designing and building huge 3,000-passenger sternwheeler gambling riverboats—like the $30 million, 350-foot-long Queen of New Orleans—to carry roulette wheels and blackjack tables on the Big Muddy.

At the same time this was happening the lucky company's military business grew by leaps and bounds, with some $100 million in military contracts coming to account for 70-75 per cent of its activities.

Huh! Imagine that!

██████'s first I██████'s ██████house opened in 1980, in Louisville, Kentucky, home of "the Company" and Jimmy Lambert…

"The money all went to Louisville," longtime ██████ associate Resa Kelly told us. "It went to a man named Innes Mather, from the famous Mather family up there in horse country. They're like the Cornelius's, or the Whitney's or the Vanderbilt's."

"Innes Mather was my CPA," ██████ retorted angrily. "All I know about him is that he has a son who's a first-rate tennis player there in Louisville."

Like Arkansas Chicken King Don Tyson, there have long been 'rumors' in law enforcement that Popeye's chicken founder Al Copeland had made himself a 'killing' in the drug trade, at the exact *same time* Barry Seal was creating, for somebody, enormous wealth.

In addition to Popeye's Chicken, Copeland was, perhaps unsurprisingly, the proud owner of the fastest offshore powerboat in the known world, berthed, naturally, in Miami.

And ██████, we discovered, had been 'in' the 'restaurant' business with Al Copeland.

██████ owned the franchise for Popeye's restaurants on the Mississippi Gulf coast," said ██████. "But his very first Popeye's was in Louisville."

██████ admitted this was true.

"But all Al Copeland taught me was the meaning of the word 'leverage,'" he said hotly. "That he was involved in any way with drug smuggling is ridiculous."

Later, the former head of intelligence for the Louisiana State Police told us of the folder they had kept on the Copeland brothers, Al and Will, and their suspicions that the explosive growth of that fast food chain had indeed been prompted by secret ingredients… not all of which were spices.

We'd already learned enough to permanently label Mr. ██████ as 'colorful' even before we discovered the *Dallas Morning News* had printed his claims to being "D. B. Cooper," skyjacker extraordinaire, who parachuted from an airliner over Washington state with $200,000, and whose real name and fate today remain—almost thirty years later—unknown.

"The letterhead of Mr. ██████'s stationary reads "██████ f/k/a (formerly known as) I██████ n/k/a (now known as) D.B. (Bob) Cooper," the Dallas paper reported.

"This time around, he's doing business as "Capt. Bob Cooper" or "D.B. Cooper"—hybrid personae of an adventurous North Texas trading-post pioneer and the skyjacker who absconded with $200,000 by parachuting out over Washington State in 1971."

██████████, a history buff who made off like a bandit by pocketing the lion's share of $ 23 million from the sale of ████████ ████████ ████████████, says draw your own conclusions. "My friends call me Coop," he adds."

Our interest in ████████████was strictly in his possible role in drug money laundering through a corporation he owned, which, though he was in the restaurant business, had been named Trinity Energy...

And thanks to ████████s participation in what ABC's 20/20 called "The Great Steak Wars," we finally got some answers.

It all started when the famous Ruth's Chris ████████e chain was bumped off the list of America's Top 10 ████████ Both Ruth's ██████e and ████ had flourished in that bastion of seafood, New Orleans, until 1985 when ████████'s wife shot him, and ████████'s restaurant closed.

Ruth Fertel, owner of Ruth's Chris, told ████████ now ex-wife, "By the way, ████ I got to tell you, I'm going to have to give you shooting lessons—anyone who shoots at someone five times and doesn't get him *needs* shooting lessons!"

This didn't help relations with ████████ who had left New Orleans to open a ████████s in Dallas. Weeks later his new restaurant made its debut on the newly created Knife and Fork Club's America's Top 10 ████████ and Ruth's Chris ████████publicly charged its longtime rival with bogus advertising, a charge ████████hotly denied.

Ruth Fertel began her crusade to expose the annual list as a fraud. It became, quite literally, a federal case...

Fertel, with 42 s████████ nationwide, contended the list was bought and paid for by her nemesis, ████████ owner by then of the ████ ████████████████House in Dallas, and sued.

Fighting back, ████████ ████████k House filed suit as well, accusing Ruth's Chris of misleading advertising, libel, and slander.

Prime beef became a tender subject in Dallas. In the sizzling culmination of their ongoing feud, the two steakhouses made ready to grill each other in state district court...

Then the feud got *really* "up close and personal."

Ruth Chris' spokesman slammed the Knife and Fork Club, theorizing that its "unethical rating system" was nothing but a front for ████████, saying he "welcomed the chance to expose ████████"that creep in Dallas."

According to Ruth's Chris attorney, he forced ███████ to acknowledge the connection between the restaurant and publicity firm during a deposition. "I hammered away at it until I got the answer," he said, of the deposition. "It was not a pretty sight."

A settlement was reached when ████████ admitted that his public relations man had dreamed up the list.

"All my life, I've had a hard time getting along with myself, let alone anybody else," said ███████

Though both sides claimed victory, ███████'s ██████████ E███████████ was crowing louder, noting that they were now almost $23 million richer since the settlement. ███████ said the libel suit had been holding up the sale of his chain to l██████████ & Saloon Inc. of Wichita, Kansas.

Right after settling its suit against Ruth's Chris, ███████'s closed the sale to Lone Star. Unknown to observers, ███████'s chain had been owned by Trinity energy.

We had now discovered a *second* Trinity Energy, one that had *also* sold for the *exact s*ame amount, $22 million, and in the *exact* same year, 1995, as Seal associate ███████ reported Trinity Energy sale.

We were befuddled and amazed. We asked ourselves, somewhat numbly: what's up with *that?*

During depositions, the accounting practices of ████████ steak house chain were revealed for the first time. And they are so unusual that after reviewing them we were certain we were looking at something only an elite deviant class like the CIA, or the Mob, or both, could have dreamt up...

ITEM: The land and building of the chain's headquarters was not owned by the company, but by Mr. ███████ wife, Colleen Keating.

ITEM: The restaurant was leased to something called the "Irwin J. ███████ Foundation, Inc.," a nonprofit organization. Mr. ███████ was president of the foundation, technically the owner of the restaurant, and which held a private club license from the Texas Alcoholic Beverage Commission.

Who were the members of the ███████ Foundation? Anyone, it turned out, who had ever purchased an alcoholic beverage at ███████'s restaurant.

ITEM: "The ███████ foundation" employed the 110 people who worked in the restaurant's kitchen and dining rooms. Mr. ███████ received only a salary of $ 35,000 a year from the foundation.

ITEM: The management contract for ███████'s chain was held by an entity called Beefsteak Ltd. Mr. ███████ owned 99 percent of the stock in the limited partnership, registered with the Texas Secretary of State's office. He said he received 10 percent of the restaurant's gross revenue and a management incentive bonus.

ITEM: Brass Balls Inc., of which ████████ is sole owner, had previously had the management contract for ████████'s, holding the remaining 1 percent of stock in Beefsteak Ltd., and was listed as the general partner.

ITEM: Manessah Management Co., was the advertising agency for the restaurant. ████████'s wife Colleen was the president. In his deposition, Mr. ████████ said the restaurant transferred $20,000 a month to Manessah to cover its advertising costs…

Irwin J. ████████ is "just a name he made up," Mr. ████████ said in a phone interview. "It is just like if you have a child, you name it Billy Joe or Mary Ann,' he said. "Irwin J. ████████ is the entity in the steakhouse; I was just giving birth to a child.'

This is, we realized, the "elite deviant" approach to following the rule of law.

So we just kept digging into ████████ and his operations…

When ████████ sold ████████████████████ House to Lone Star, the Dallas restaurant alone was grossing nearly $1 million a month. And the buying entity, Lone Star, was itself fabulously profitable, with operating margins among the highest in the industry, averaging 25% before tax and 13.7% net after tax. (Compare that to rival Outback ████████, which averages just under 8.1% net after tax.)

Could laundering drug money help account for such incredible profitability? A too-brief look at Lone Star reveals that its chairman, Jamie Coulter, handles all accounting and administrative functions for this publicly traded company through a private company—which *he* controls.

When asked about the unusual arrangement Coulter explained, "The reason Coulter Enterprises does administrative and financial services for Lone Star is that no one else can turn around a financial statement in six days as cheaply as we can."

Sure.

And this may also be the only steak house chain in the known world to have not *one*… not *two*… but *three* Learjets. They exist to, the company says, "facilitate a mobile staff."

Sure.

With seats for 850, ████████'s current ████████ casts a big shadow in the outsized town of Dallas. It's the biggest restaurant in the state of Texas. Atop the restaurant's roof, a 24-karat gold-leaf dome glistens, rising 55 feet above ground as a gilded beacon to his new III Forks restaurant. Inside, the restaurant boasts a staircase out of Gone With the Wind, while stained glass, hand-crafted in France, glows above a foyer.

Greeting guests is a former fiddle-playing Miss Texas who has been the marketing director for Caesar's Palace casinos in Las Vegas, the same casino from whom Kentucky Fried Chicken magnate and later Kentucky Governor John Brown bought the Lum's chain... the same casino linked to drug money laundering in a major DEA investigation of the drug smuggling Chagra brothers... the same casino whose ownership had come under SEC scrutiny for connections to Meyer Lansky and organized crime.

Could ███████████ Baton Rouge millionaire drug smuggler Barry Seal, and Arkansas bond daddy Dan Lasater all belonged to the same organization?

█████████ and Lasater were both in thoroughbred horse racing at the same time, we learned. Both had horses run in the Kentucky Derby, and both kept racing stables at infamous Oak Lawn Race Track in Hot Springs, Arkansas.

████████s trainer, from Bay St. Louis, Mississippi, was a man dubbed "Jake the Snake," Jake Morreale. In the same year that ████████'s estranged ex-wife says ████ had to leave the country, Morreale was convicted of race fixing in Illinois.

So what *were* we looking at here?

A ██████████ chain owned by a "Trinity Energy," sold to Lone Star ██████████ during exactly the same time (in 1995) and for exactly the same price ($22 million) as the "Trinity Energy" owned by Barry Seal's smuggling partner ███████████████.

We had received a tip that the Trinity Energy we *really* wanted had been incorporated in Delaware. ██████████ answered evasively, vaguely recalling that Trinity Energy was registered in that state.

This 'Delaware' Trinity is, in 1992, gobbled up by a company called ICF Kaiser, composed of former Defense Department officials, on whose Board and whose soon-to-be-Chairman is former Congressman Tony Coelho.

Coelho's numerous distinctions included having been linked in print to the drug smuggling organization "The Company" while still a congressman from California... being the political protégé of the personal lawyer for Seal associate Gene Glick, Democratic National Committee Chairman Charles Manatt... and being forced to resign in disgrace from the House of Representatives in 1989 to thwart a growing investigation into his fund-raising activities for the Democratic Party.

Of course, his most *recent* claim to fame was as Al Gore's campaign chairman.

CHAPTER THIRTY-SIX

PAUL HELLIWELL, THE 'COMPANY,' AND MENA

THE DETAILS OF BARRY Seal's very public fall from favor during his last two years are well known.... Seal spent his last days on earth testifying at the trials of small fry in the narcotics industry, as well as fending off law enforcement in Baton Rouge, Louisiana. As his star went into eclipse, we wondered if we could catch a glimpse of the shadowy organization behind him, hovering in the background...

And as we had pursued our investigation into where the money goes in what we had come to see as the "covertly nationalized" illegal narcotics industry, we came to understand the words of a courageous U.S. Attorney, Joe Cage, who had eventually won conviction of the man known as Carlos Marcello's banker, Herman Beebe, after painstakingly unraveling Beebe's deliberately-tangled affairs for a grand jury.

"We'd have say, 10 issues, trying to get them resolved with the grand jury," he remembered. "And in solving those 10, another 15 would come up. It was like trying to nail jelly to the wall."

'Nailing jelly to the wall" was an apt characterization for our pursuit of Trinity Energy, until we'd discovered the Tony Coelho ICF-Kaiser connection. At that point we found ourselves shocked at the appalling lack of tradecraft displayed by people who think themselves 'masters of the universe.'

Then again, maybe these people felt safe because nobody has been looking very hard into anything much beyond discussions of the differing 'campaign styles' of this year's Presidential contenders in America's media for some time now…

The result was that Trinity Energy had ended its utility as a money-laundering vehicle in the arms of a Washington D.C. company that we learned was filled with former Pentagon officials.

And its chairman was Democratic fund-raiser and power broker Tony Coelho, known as Charles Manatt's political protégé.

And Manatt, according to the note in Barry Seal's own handwriting we had discovered, had been Gene Glick's attorney.

Was Glick the cutout between Seal, Manatt, and the Agency? Or was former DNC chairman, who author and activist Michael Ruppert pointed out; is today the current US Ambassador to one of the biggest Caribbean conduits for narcotics into the US, the Dominican Republic, a CIA asset or agent all along?

Based on the evidence developed so far, we believe it is fair to ask if Manatt's 'duties' in the Dominican Republic include things like overseeing the smooth and effective functioning of the narcotics apparatus.

██████'s story offered one clue. He had connections to 'Company' principal Jimmy Lambert, and roots in the Louisville, Kentucky setting of many of "The Company's" activities.

██████ had also numbered among his long-time associates a man, Al Copeland, founder of the Popeye's chicken chain, whose meteoric business success was suspected, the head of Intelligence for the Louisiana State Police had told us, of having been aided by 'contact' with associates of Barry Seal.

Who or what was behind the organization with the same name, the Company, as the nickname of the CIA?

"The Company" was a drug smuggling organization whose tentacles reached into the statehouses of numerous Southern states, we'd learned from Sally Denton excellent "Bluegrass Conspiracy."

The man who had had dinner with Barry Seal the night before he died, a long-time 'business' associate, was, we learned, a good friend of a 'Company' figure, Colonel Jim Atwood, referred to in 'The Bluegrass Conspiracy' as a "shadowy spook" who controlled several companies used for international gun deals… including one which turned out the popular lightweight SM-90 machine gun, which we were told were manufactured at two locations in Bolivia, and then ferried over the Andes by Seal to buyers in Honduras, Columbia, and Panama.

The gun was especially popular, according to Denton, with gunrunners and drug smugglers. Had Seal, Atwood et al, working under the supervision of the shadowy National Security Agency, armed both the Colombian drug cartels, as well as the supposedly Communist rebel groups?

The preponderance of evidence says yes.

Denton demonstrated Colonel Atwood's links to "The Company;" Seal's NSA contact in Bolivia had also been involved with the cocaine trade, as drug lord Roberto Suarez' "handler," after having married a close relative of Suarez.

Reputed "Company" head Robert Nichols had deep ties to the NSA; in his own testimony in a lawsuit against the Justice Department filed by INSLAW Corp…

"Robert Nichols told… about an incident in the early 1980's when a colonel from the NSA Headquarters at Fort Meade, Maryland, allegedly flew out to the Cabazon Reservation for the day for the single purpose of assuring that FBI agents investigating a triple homicide of the Vice Chairman of the Cabazon Tribe and two associates did not attempt to probe the classified U.S. government work being performed under the auspices of the Wackenhut-Cabazon Joint Venture."

Why, we wondered, and not for the first time, was there murder around these guys all the time?

Let's indulge in a little conspiracy theorizing…

Could it be that the *NSA*—and not the CIA, as is commonly thought—is the 'secret team' responsible for the explosion in the cocaine trade during Barry Seal's tenure during the 1980's?

Might that—the NSA's rumored license-to-kill—be the reason that the scandals of Iran Contra and Whitewater were never truly exposed?

Atwood, to be sure, was an integral part of what became known as Iran Contra, and the focus of a congressional investigation into arms dealing.

"Retired Maj. Gen. Richard V. Secord and his partner, working with a shadowy former Army colonel who later helped them sell arms to the CIA, last year tapped an Iran-bank account in Switzerland to invest at least $60,000 in a venture to sell submachine guns to the contras and others, reliable sources said Friday," the L.A. Times reported on December 31, 1987.

"Retired Army Col. James P. Atwood of Savannah, GA successfully brokered the CIA purchase from the Enterprise after another middleman's effort had failed. At the time, investigators discovered, Atwood was helping set up a private arms business for the son of a CIA covert procurement official who approved the deal as part of a "highly unusual" scheme to generate a multimillion-dollar surplus for companies secretly owned by the CIA, sources have told the *Times*."

"Moreover, a series of congressional depositions of CIA employees and others revealed that Atwood had curried favor with CIA covert procurement officials in the past with personal gifts varying from watches and buckets of shrimp to rare chrome-barreled Chinese AK-47 rifles. At least one covert procurement official quietly returned a desk pen set to Atwood in a brown paper sack. More often, however, the gifts were not returned," the paper said.

The financial details uncovered by Iran-Contra investigators about Atwood were compared by one official close to the probe to an organized crime money-laundering scheme.

"The mob is probably better at it than anyone else, but these guys weren't bad," said a source familiar with the scheme. "It's a textbook example of how things could go south" without proper management controls.

The arms deal was investigated by independent counsel Lawrence Walsh, and although officials said they believed it could yield new evidence of the financial and personal ties linking the CIA, North and his army of private operatives in the Iran-contra scandal, it quietly died.

As the French say, *'Quelle surprise.'* What a surprise.

Then came a revelation from an unexpected source. We heard from the daughter of a friend who had begun work as a bank teller in Louisiana. During a training course for tellers they had shown a training film on money laundering laws, using footage of Barry Seal to make the point...

When Barry's face had flashed across the TV monitor, one teller trainee exclaimed, "I know that man! He worked with my father!"

After class our young friend met her new co-worker, and heard her story...

Her father was a native Colombian who moved to Barry Seal's hometown of Baton Rouge, Louisiana in 1975. There he owned a seafood market/ restaurant named (for his wife) Laura's Restaurant and Oyster Bar.

Less than a week before Barry Seal's murder, he received a visit from a group of FBI agents at his home, his daughter said, called his family together, told them he loved them, and vanished forever.

Years later his family learned that he had moved to Costa Rica, where he had a second wife and owned several prosperous businesses.

Weeks later, we met the daughter of this 'vanished' Seal associate, and were surprised to learn that this man's new wife in Costa Rica is a Russian translator. More 'mere coincidence?' Or had this man—along with Seal and the others—had some connection to the federal agency called "shadowy" so often it should be in its title, the (shadowy) NSA... the same agency so clearly behind the drug smuggling organization calling itself "The Company?"

How America had first learned of the existence of "The Company" bears retelling. A man with a dark mustache, wiry build and incredibly bad timing walked into the Acapulco Mexican Restaurant in Fort Lauderdale one night, at the tail end of a raucous party.

An FBI party, one of the agents recognized the man ordering a margarita as perhaps the most wanted drug fugitive in America...

And that's how the FBI, investigative pit-bulls that they are, captured Richard Dial Thorpe, the chairman of the board of the biggest made-in-America drug ring ever uncovered.

Headquartered in the heartland outside St. Louis, birthplace of Alvin Malnik, "The Company" launched in 1976 and grew into an enterprise with over 350 employees, with separate executives in charge of buying airports, leasing warehouses and even giving polygraph tests to new employees. There was even a $2 million fund for bail. In just two years The Company had acquired 33 airplanes, 3 airports, warehouses in 7 states, and profits of $48 million.

1976 was also the year, according to Barry's widow Deborah, when Barry Seal's smuggling career began...

Where had the expertise come from to create such an elaborate organization? Vietnam, apparently: Thorpe had gotten used to taking risks as a door-gunner on a U.S. Army helicopter. He also got well acquainted with drugs.

Just how "connected" was—or maybe *is*—"The Company?"

When a Colombian army unit caught a Company pilot and crew in smuggler's alley—the Guajira Peninsula, "The Company" promptly paid $200,000 to arrange a jail break, while bribing the local power company to turn out the lights, as an army colonel and the local police chief walked the prisoners out of jail.

The local Colombian press blamed the CIA.

Another example occurred in the steamy climes of South Carolina, where to weed out informants The Company had hired a local security chief, a South Carolina man who had once worked as a lie detector examiner for the congressional subcommittee investigating the assassination of John F. Kennedy.

Later, when a Company member, a prominent lawyer and congressional candidate in South Carolina, violated protocol and recruited someone who had *not* taken the requisite lie detector test, retribution was swift.

Charleston County Deputy Sheriff G. Lloyd Woodbury, former employee of the state Disaster Preparedness Agency, who provided internal security for "The Company," threatened and intimidated former Darlington County Democratic Party Chairman John R. Etheridge into pleading guilty to state and federal charges.

That's clout.

Soon the Company's pilots—seasoned commercial fliers and at least one Vietnam War hero—were flying 10-ton loads of high-grade Colombian marijuana into Missouri, Georgia and South Carolina.

On Thorp's 31st birthday "The Company" threw a party at a private country club in Ft. Lauderdale, where 300 celebrants arrived by Lear jet and limousine, dined on smoked salmon, caviar and round of beef, and sampled Dom Perignon and their own wares to keep things festive.

During a two-year investigation by the DEA—which determined "The Company" owned marijuana valued at a *billion* dollars-agents watching the huge smuggling ring learned that the Company was peering right back at *them*. When they began busting the ring they discovered how sophisticated that scrutiny had been…

"They had the secret (radio) frequencies of federal, state and local authorities," a DEA spokesman said. "They had mechanical programmers and night-viewing devices. They had air-to-ground radios so sophisticated we don't even have them on our own planes. They had electronic geniuses in their employ capable of making their own equipment or modifying it to meet their own designs."

"The defendants would employ the services of skilled electronics experts using counter-intelligence equipment to identify and remove electronic tracking devices from aircraft used in smuggling operations," according to the indictment.

Prominent Company members included Drew Thornton, who died in 1985 trying to parachute into Knoxville, Tenn. with a load of cocaine that he had flown in from Colombia; drug smuggler and convicted weapons dealer Bradley Bryant; Henry S. Vance, a former Kentucky gubernatorial and legislative aide convicted of supplying the gun used to murder a Florida prosecutor; Harold Brown, disgraced DEA regional director in Louisville who died an apparent suicide; and Jimmy Lambert, drug supplier to Lexington's horsy set, close friend of former Gov. John Y. Brown Jr., and buddy, as we've heard, of ████████████.

Sally Denton's *Bluegrass Conspiracy* said that "The Company" members played central roles at the highest levels of the international narcotics trade, corrupted top officials of Kentucky government and of federal and state law-enforcement agencies, had access to U. S. military installations, supplied arms to Central America and perhaps Libya, and had shadowy connections to the Central Intelligence Agency and the DEA.

Our NSA informant, who'd had dinner with Barry the night before his murder, had visited Libya several times, he told us casually in conversation, most often with Reagan's Ambassador to the Vatican, William Wilson. This turned out to be the truth; Wilson was forced to resign from his Ambassadorship when newspapers revealed his secret trip to Libya in 1986.

"The Company" was said to have trained a private army on a farm named Triad, and to have been responsible for the murders of informants, prosecutors, a federal judge, and numerous drug couriers and other criminal associates.

Denton's unspoken but unwavering conviction seemed to be that Kentucky Gov. John Brown was part of this large criminal enterprise; that he and his Administration had protected criminals and interfered with honest law-enforcement officials, and that Brown had presidential aspirations that attracted strong underworld backing.

But Kentucky Governor Brown was only one of a number of Southern Governor being corrupted by the drug trade. An eyewitness told us Louisiana Governor Edwin Edwards received so much cash from Barry Seal that it required three separate flights in a private King Air 200 to get all the money safely out of the country.

"The Company's" reach was national in scope. Brian Leighton, an assistant U.S. Attorney in California, prosecuted several top members in Fresno for stealing specialized military equipment, infrared sniper-scopes, television cameras capable of taking pictures in darkness, tracer ammunition for night combat, a remote control helicopter, and other even-more 'secret' components like the radar unit of a Sidewinder guided missile from the U.S. Naval Weapons Station at China Lake in the Mojave Desert.

"Story of Spies, Stolen Arms and Drugs," read the headline in the *San Francisco Chronicle* on April 28, 1982...

"The Company consisted of about 300 members, many of them former military men or ex-police officers with nearly $30 million worth of assets, including planes, ships and real estate," the article stated.

"Here was a group of over 300 people, most of them ex-law enforcement and ex-military, ex-intelligence people, involved in a major drug and smuggling operation."

Federal agents said the stolen equipment was to be used to make electronic equipment for drug smugglers and drug suppliers in Columbia.

Twenty-nine members of the Company were indicted by a Fresno federal grand jury in 1981, among them Andrew "Drew" Thornton, 40, the former narcotics officer who had set his plane on automatic pilot before parachuting to his death with 77 pounds of cocaine.

The *Los Angeles Times* published a story on Thornton's death called "Former Narcotics Officer Parachutes Out of Plane, Dies with 77 Pounds of Cocaine." Assistant US Attorney Leighton told them, "I'm glad his parachute didn't open. I hope he got a hell of a high out of that."

'These people were smuggling large amounts of drugs into the United States," Leighton said.

He stated his office investigated Thornton for the theft of military equipment from China Lake Naval Weapons Center, and that Company member (and close friend of Colonel Atwood) Bradley Bryant was offered a contract to kill U.S. District Judge John Wood of San Antonio. Although Bryant turned the contract down, he did work for the man eventually convicted of killing Wood in 1978, Jimmy Chagra.

One well-placed source had told us that "The Company" developed out of a CIA 'Old Boy' network involved in illegal gun and drug trade as far back as WWII. This dovetailed perfectly with reports we had received about meetings setting up the Mena Arkansas drug and weapons pipeline having been held on Congressman John Hammerschmidt's ranch. Attendees, reportedly, included Barry Seal, National Security Advisor Brent Scowcroft, and Congressman Hammerschmidt...

Hammerschmidt was, of course, the congressman from the district encompassing Mena. There sat the Mena airport, looking like an ordinary, normal airport, save for the row upon row of hangars housing aircraft refitting facilities, an industry in demand by just two principal paying customers, the CIA, and drug smugglers.

A search through Hammerschmidt's bio for clues to why he might have been called on to play such a role reveals his previously hidden connections. He had been, in 1966, part of a large GOP freshman class, where he quickly became close friends with another freshman from Houston, George Bush.

John Paul Hammerschmidt, in fact, is one of George Bush's very closest friends, and the Arkansas Presidential Campaign Manager for both the Bush's campaign in '76 and again in 1980.

Hammerschmidt was also, we learned, a much-decorated pilot in the China-Burma-India Theater of World War II.

And that's when we said *"bingo;"* OSS/CIA agent Paul Helliwell, the man who got the CIA into the drug business after watching the British trade opium, was prominent in Burma during World War II, where, the *Wall Street Journal* had reported, he often paid for information with "three sticky bars of opium."

Paul Helliwell, as we will see in the next chapter, was the ultimate "owner," for the Agency, of Barry's Seal's most prized possession, his Learjet.

We were looking at the secret group that ran the largest operation ever to smuggle narcotics into America.

When we reached Hammerschmidt by phone to ask him about the meeting in Harrison and his association with Helliwell, he would say only, "I knew a lot of people during World War II. Helliwell may have been one of them."

Like then-US Attorney Asa Hutchinson, Hammerschmidt 'turned a blind eye' to the activities at Mena.

During the height of the smuggling through the airport, a deputy sheriff in Mena sent Hammerschmidt a moving appeal, beseeching him to help get an investigation going into the crimes being committed right in his district...

John Paul Hammerschmidt—Congressman, Contra supporter and close friend of George Bush—never replied.

CHAPTER THIRTY-SEVEN

IT'S A SMALL WORLD AFTER ALL

BY 1985, THE UNITED STATES was well on the way to be coming the first narco-democracy in North America... 'The boys' were now making so much money so fast that tradecraft flew out the window. Cockiness ruled the day. So when the first serious attempt was made to kill Barry Seal, on February 20, 1985, almost a year to the day from when he was finally assassinated, it was poorly disguised... because on that very same day they also repossessed Barry Seal's most prized possession, his Lear jet.

They gave themselves away, not to Seal, who well knew who his adversaries were, but to *us*... Americans interested in our own suppressed and secret history.

The reason they gave themselves away has much to do with boys and their toys. They thought Seal was dead; and they wanted their Lear back. It was a CIA plane all along, we are about to learn, and had never really been Seal's, except in a paper sense.

Now they were anxious to avoid the plane going through probate after Seal's death.

Because 'the boys' wanted their Lear back so badly, in their eagerness to get back the jet they left a trail of bread crumbs that—fifteen years later—can be used to track up the Nile to a place near the "headwaters" of the drug trade...

Seal, we discovered, had signed a series of promissory notes on the Lear jet in 1982 totaling $1.8 million—*twice* what the plane was worth. This puzzled us until we learned, from former CIA pilot Morgan Hetrick, that this was Standard Operating Procedure, allowing "the boys" to express their displeasure by taking away your toys at will.

"Barry called me on the morning the Lear jet disappeared," says Seal's longtime friend, Houston flight controller Charlie Montgomery...

"He asked me, 'What do you know? What happened?' So I checked with the Flight Center. The Lear would have shown up on our radar, and we'd have a record of it.... But the tapes for that morning weren't available for some reason."

By 1985, evidence was everywhere that *something* had spun wildly out of control *for some reason*...

—The number of cocaine users in the United States had risen to six million, ten times the number of heroin addicts... And here came crack... by chemically converting cocaine powder to a granular base state suitable for smoking, a readily-usable, cheap narcotic was created selling for as little as $10 a dose; use spread to a generation of younger users unable to afford the high price of pure cocaine or heroin.

—A woman beachcombing near "Millionaire's Row," a ritzy area of Palm Beach, noticed green duffel bags strewn along the water's edge, which contained 1,076 pounds of cocaine, nearly $200 million worth of "powdered money."

—Proposals about what to do included one from Florida Sen. Paula Hawkins, clearly no brain surgeon, seeking to outlaw the $100 bill, so drug smugglers would have a tougher time laundering their money. The local sheriff replied, gently, that this wouldn't work, outlaws would "just get bigger bags."

—When police pulled up to a disabled truck on the side of Interstate 95 outside Miami to offer assistance; the worried driver offered without prompting, "I don't know anything about the stuff in the back of the truck." Inside, they found millions of dollars worth of coke.

—The currency in Florida was found to be tainted with traces of cocaine. The *Miami Herald* had an expert analyze $20 bills from a dozen prominent Floridians. Who was 'holding?' Everybody, from the archbishop to the Dade County state's attorney to the Dade County chairman of the Republican Party to a former Miss America.

— "Every time Berri [sic] Seal flies a load of dope for the U.S. Govt.," one law enforcement officer noted resignedly in a log in the summer of 1985, "he flies two for himself."

The bargain was plain even then...

"Seal was flying weapons to Central and South America," an agent noted, recording what "was believed" within the DEA.

"In return he is allowed to smuggle what he wants back into the United States."

—A secretary to an executive of "The Company," then the nation's largest drug-smuggling outfit, testified she made at least six trips a year to the Caymans to deposit all the loot.

—And Emile Camp, one of Barry Seal's most expert pilots, as well as the only witness to his transactions with both Sandinista "drug lords" and US intelligence agents, and a member of the Marcello Family to boot... was murdered when his elaborately-equipped Mena-bound Piper Seneca unaccountably ran out of gas on a routine approach and slammed into a mountain.

Camp and Seal, as we've seen, met while in prison in Honduras, and Camp became Seal's co-pilot.

"Emile and Barry worked really closely," Seal's secretary Dandra Seale said, "They were together at all times."

That the plane had been rigged to go down had been the suspicion of more than one observer, including Arkansas criminal investigator Russell Welch. The technique, we learned, is simple: an inflated balloon inside a gas tank causes false readings, both when fueling and in-flight.

And we know why: Barry Seal was supposed to have been on it. Here's what happened...

It started as a simple marital spat. Emile Camp and his wife of many years, Carol, were not getting along. To show her displeasure Carol packed up their youngest and headed off without telling Emile.

Ironically, she headed for Disney World...

CIA agent Col. Paul Helliwell—to whom Seal's Lear jet is about to return—was also the man to whom Walt Disney had turned, back in 1964. Disney asked Helliwell, because of his unparalleled facility in setting up dummy companies, to quietly buy up Orlando for the creation of the new theme park.

Carol Camp's act of defiance was uncharacteristic; and when she was ready to return several days later she was leery of her fiery husband's reaction...

She called Barry from her Orlando hotel, explained the circumstances, and asked Seal to send Emile away on a job so she could return to an empty home, providing them both an additional couple of days to cool off.

Barry's response was characteristically, understanding. "Consider it done," he told Carol.

The next morning of February 20, Seal assigned Camp the task of flying up to Mena in the twin-engine Piper Seneca, while he himself flew commercial down to Miami...

The sad result came three days later, when Polk County authorities recovered the body of Emile Camp from the wreckage of his plane.

The Piper Seneca Camp was flying was reported missing about 3:30 p.m. that same afternoon, but authorities searched unsuccessfully for the missing aircraft for several days.

Then Seal and his brother Ben arrived with two helicopters, joined the search, and found the wreck on Fourche Mountain about 10 miles north of Mena.

"Barry said he had a feeling that he knew where Emile had crashed," his secretary told reporters.

Authorities said the plane apparently was flying a level course, with power in both engines, when it hit the mountain about 500 feet below the crest. The Mena area, they explained, in the heart of the Ouachita Mountains, had been the site of a number of airplane crashes, and is marked as a "high fatality area" on aviation charts because of the steep rise of area mountains.

There was no mention by the 'authorities' of the fact that the plane was out of gas....

The cover-up had begun.

The National Transportation Safety Board ruled that pilot error was the cause of the crash. Still, the unanswered questions—many with national security implications—began almost immediately...

FAA records confirmed that the downed plane had been previously owned by CIA proprietary Air America. It carried the original logs of one of Seal's other planes, a Vietnam-era-123K Seal had christened the Fat Lady; they were missing when the wreckage was discovered.

Rudy Furr, the Mena airport manager (and former business manager of Rich Mountain Aviation) said Camp was bringing records to Mena for review by a Federal Aviation Administration inspector, records revealing that Seal was converting a Coast Guard C-131 for civilian use.

The big question was why had the Seneca, as well-equipped as anything out of James Bond—pocket-sized digital encryption devices to send coded telephone messages, Loran-C radar altimeters, beacon interrogating digital radar—*still* slammed into a mountain?

A. L. Hadaway, also a pilot and former Mena sheriff, said he was surprised to learn that Camp, an experienced pilot, had crashed. "He could find this airport at night and land without lights; I've seen him do it."

Camp's associates believed his plane had been sabotaged, pointing out that he was one of the few to witness many of Seal's activities for the CIA and DEA.

Then their suspicions were given credence when it was discovered that although Emile Camp had topped off his plane with fuel before leaving Baton Rouge, there was no evidence of any fire on the mountainside where it was found. The fuel gauges read 'empty.'

According to Terry Reed's *Compromised* Emile Camp had also worked with Reed, whose job was to create a remote Arkansas air base to upgrade the skills of Contra pilots and teach them techniques for aerial re-supply inside Nicaragua, reminiscent of the training given to Cuban exiles before the Bay of Pigs.

Barry Seal was profoundly shaken by the crash. He holed up at Mena for a week after Camp's body was recovered. Observers noted that though still cocky, he was now increasingly anxious about his *own* safety.

Camp was an integral part of Seal's organization... when Seal was cleared for his first DEA-sanctioned cocaine run, he had taken along longtime copilot Emile, bound for Colombia in Seal's retooled Lockheed Lodestar jet.

There, in a scene made famous by Dennis Hopper's movie *Doublecrossed,* they arrived at a small airstrip in the mountains outside Medellin in a driving rainstorm that had turned the dirt runway into a strip of mud, nearly wrecking the plane on landing by sliding off the runway into a ditch.

Senior cartel executive Carlos Lehder—today 'inexplicably' free after being set loose by the Clinton Administration from his "100 year" prison sentence—was at the airstrip to meet the plane. From astride a white Arabian stallion, Lehder had supervised a team of Indians who loaded the Titan with more than a ton of cocaine, then forced the two men to take off against their better judgment, brandishing an Uzi to make his point.

Had any of this really happened? One of the two participants was now gone.

Unfortunately for 'the boys.' it was the *wrong* one.

A careful perusal of FAA records of Barry Seal's Lear jet revealed what we'd suspected all along: the plane was never really *his.* Through a series of ingeniously connected Paul Helliwell-designed fronts, like Intercontinental Holding, it had belonged all along to the CIA.

We wondered, who had 'owned' the Lear just before Barry Seal? And the answer was revealing... two drug-smuggling brothers, Reggie and Bill Whittington.

The Whittington brothers—like Mob front man Allen Glick—had raced sports cars in the United States and Europe in the '70s and '80s, winning the 24-hour Le Mans in France and coming in sixth in one Indianapolis 500.

Authorities said they financed their racing operation with drug profits. When they got into trouble in late 1981, their bosses took their biggest toy—the Lear—away from them, and gave it to... Barry Seal.

Four years later they pled guilty to charges in federal court in Florida of importing 400,000 pounds of marijuana into the US and evading taxes on $73 million.

In an amusing postscript, after being released from prison one of the brothers dug up 220 pounds of gold they had stashed away before going to prison. He took it to be cashed-in at a Delaware bank. The government, notified of the transaction as a routine process, a DEA spokesmen said (yeah, right) leapt into action the way they only do when money is involved, and seized the gold.

And though the brothers were outraged enough to file a lawsuit, of course (*What were they, dreaming?*), they never got it back.

Satisfied as to the Lear jet's thoroughbred lineage, we next turned to the question of whom the plane had been registered to while Barry Seal flew it...

The answer took us straight into the heart of darkness, which we discovered is apparently located in the sun-splashed Cayman Islands of the Caribbean.

Isles of sun, surf and secrecy, where the water sparkled, the beaches were pristine white, and the cash that left its banks was crisp and clean... The Caymans were awash, we learned, in wary money, and widely known as the international laundromat for soiled cash. They conjure up such strong images of discreet banking transactions that they were the perfect place to shoot part of *The Firm*, a movie that touched on the mob, lawyers and money laundering.

Even though the three islands (Grand Cayman, Cayman Brac and Little Cayman) are a holiday paradise with exquisite scuba diving, their reputation is tarred by scandal... With more than $500 billion in banking assets and more than $100 billion in mutual funds, a conduit for drug money laundering and a magnet for tax evaders, the British colony has always attracted critics.

Why? Because, although the Caymans are just a tiny slip of sand and coconuts 20 miles long, natives boast they have the third largest banking community in the world.

It's, apparently, a great place to stash your money.... And when its high noon and the sun beats hot on the dark suits of businessmen who walk between the banks that crowd Georgetown's dusty streets, they may look comical, stuffy and out of place among the tans and the swimsuits of snorkelers moving from hotel to beach... but they're the reason its here.

The Caymans is where the Bank of Credit and Commerce International scandal took root and festered, Panamanian and Colombian drug cartels wash their dirty money, and where OSS/CIA agent Paul Helliwell established banks and front companies like a New York sidewalk hustler playing three-card Monte with the tourists (us)...

The Contras banked here too. After the stunning Sandinista attack at the Masaya military barracks outside Managua in October of 1977, worried members of Nicaragua's upper classes began looking for ways to transfer assets out of the country, and set up a secret financial network which was used to receive and distribute tens of millions of dollars in 'donations.'

A Cayman account was used to conceal the millions in 'donations' from Saudi Arabia... and Barry Seal, Louisiana law enforcement authorities told us, was involved in this effort, setting up dummy companies there and elsewhere around the Caribbean.

The Caymans' bank laws promoted a culture of secrecy running deeper than money, an AP wire story reported...

"Lounging with young girls on the white beaches are ex-U.S. Air Force pilots with deep tans. When asked about their pasts, they admit only to running "some contract stuff" during the 1980s with a certain air cargo company that made regular flights to rural Honduras, where the U.S.-backed contra rebels were based."

Had Barry Seal lived, he might today be one of these men.

Here, beyond the reach of U.S. courts, is where we found the paper "owner" of the Lear jet repossessed from Barry Seal on the day the Company thought he died.

His name is Gordon Aiton, and like almost everyone else in the Seal saga, he too, we learned, was involved in some of the most monumental fraud ever perpetrated on long-suffering taxpayers...

To the relief of American taxpayers, he pulled *his* big fraud in Toronto.

And even before that he had been involved with the biggest financial brouhaha of the 1970's, the Castle Bank scandal that featured—front and center—CIA agent Col. Paul Helliwell.

The Castle Bank Scandal broke, and the Cayman's closed-mouth policy was tested, because of a sexual encounter featuring a nosy girl reporter and a Cayman-based banker visiting the Bahamas carrying a briefcase full of information on some of his clients.

"A female reporter from America got friendly with the banker in a hotel room," a Cayman banking official testified later. "When he dozed off, she copied the names of his clients and later wrote some stories. There was a big inquiry."

It became known as the Castle Bank scandal. Castle was an offshore bank used as an illegal tax dodge for the wealthy, and a money laundry for the underworld where the CIA and the Mob commingled assets to their mutual advantage.

Colonel Paul Helliwell, known then only as a Miami lawyer, was its President and founder.

Newsweek was the first to report that investigators believed the dominant figures in the Nassau bank's operation were Burton Kanter of Chicago and Paul Helliwell of Miami, both of them well-known lawyers with impressive client lists.

Chicago's Burton Kanter is a lawyer who helped Cleveland racketeers set up Rancho La Costa in La Jolla, California, with Teamsters funds, the same fund playing a role in financing Barry Seal's operations. La Jolla also nurtures crooks like former California Governor Jerry Brown's long-time chief of staff John Silberman, who was laundering money for Barry Seal associate Carlos Bustamonte from Miami.

Like many of the shadowy figures in our story—Barry Seal's New Orleans CIA handler Dave Dixon comes to mind—Kantor too was associated with the NFL, even taking a run at buying the Miami Dolphins in the early '90's.

But even business-friendly *U.S. News & World Report*, though they treated Helliwell with kid gloves, looked askance at Castle Bank. "One of those apparently best informed about Castle is Paul L. E. Helliwell, a Miami lawyer and a bank president whose firm represents Castle in this country and who has a long history of association with the American intelligence community. Although he would not comment on his rumored relationship with the Central Intelligence Agency, Mr. Helliwell spoke openly about his early career as an intelligence officer as he talked with an editor. He said that in 1944, he was a 29-year-old major in U.S. Army intelligence in the Middle East and Africa. He then moved to China, with the Office of Strategic Services."

With the Castle Bank investigation the IRS tried to cut through the bank secrecy laws, and get a look at the records of the Castle Bank on Grand Cayman Island...

But a banking official from the Cayman Islands threw a monkey wrench into the investigation, and received credit for having saved Paul Helliwell.

As the Castle Bank manager in the Cayman Islands was preparing to return voluntarily to Miami to testify, he got a threatening letter from the government inspector of banks in the Caymans, warning that if he testified it "would be treated with the utmost gravity" and "pursued to the fullest extent of the law."

Who was the Cayman government banking official making this threat? Who saved Paul Helliwell's bacon?

Gordon Aiton, the same man whom, a decade later, lays claims to be the true owner of Barry Seal's Lear.

A federal judge eventually cleared the (presumably grateful) Central Intelligence Agency of running Castle Bank, because further IRS probing would have brought to light information deemed embarrassing to CIA operations.

The investigation was terminated, said an April 18, 1980 *Wall Street Journal* article, because the bank was "the conduit for millions of dollars earmarked by the CIA for clandestine operations against Cuba and other countries in Latin America and the Far East."

Helliwell and Miami were made for each other... Miami became the home town of Helliwell CIA fronts like Sea Supply, Double-Chek, Zenith Technical Enterprises, Gibraltar Steamship, and Vanguard Service, as well as the site of famous Mob meetings at the Fontainebleau Hotel between Santo Trafficante, Sam Giancana, John Roselli, Robert Maheu, William Harvey, and Meyer Lansky.

Did the one have anything to do with the other? Of course it did... Among his business 'associates' was Louis Chesler, a Florida real estate developer who had dealings with Meyer Lansky. And Helliwell also served as legal counsel to a Panamanian holding company that controlled a Bahamian gambling casino connected with Lansky.

Helliwell, the CIA paymaster at the Bay of Pigs, was a master of conspiracy. According to Miami *New Times*, "The building that once stood at 600 Brickell housed the offices of Paul Helliwell, a prominent Miami attorney and veteran of the OSS, the CIA's World War II predecessor. Helliwell's place of business was also where the phone rang if anyone dialed the number for Red Sunset Enterprises, an Agency front company set up to recruit frogmen and other boom-and-bang experts for Operation Mongoose. Red Sunset was typical of the more than 50 dummy corporations created by the CIA in Dade to conceal its anti-Castro activities.

"What the CIA did, in many cases, they would cut a deal with an attorney who would essentially serve as a point to receive phone calls and also mail drops," said *Soldier of Fortune* magazine editor Robert K. Brown, a sardonic observer of South Florida's early-Sixties cloak-and-dagger scene. "If some of their personnel got in trouble, there was an address they could give, and there would be a dedicated phone line so that if you called in on this number, the number would be answered with the corporate name of the cover."

Brown recounted how in the early 60's he and a friend had walked into Helliwell's posh office suite without calling ahead. They announced that they were former members of a navy underwater demolition team looking for work. Without batting an eye, the receptionist handed them employment applications.

Helliwell's true claim to fame long predated the Bay of Pigs. He is cited as having the distinction of linking the CIA to the international heroin traffic. In *The Politics of Heroin in Southeast Asia* Alfred McCoy showed that during World War II Luciano and Lansky secretly worked with the CIA's forerunner, the Office of Strategic Services when OSS agents in China became deeply involved in the heroin-funded politics of Gen. Chiang Kai-shek. After the war and Chiang's defeat by the Communists, opium production shifted to Southeast Asia, and several of the most important agents who had collaborated with the generalissimo moved to Miami.

One of those agents was Miami banker and lawyer Paul Helliwell, who had served as chief of special intelligence in China. When the O.S.S. was reorganized as the CIA, he was in on the ground floor.

He was Colonel Helliwell in those days, and E. Howard Hunt was one of his agents. According to the *Wall Street Journal*, "CIA sources told The *Wall Street Journal* that in Asia, Helliwell frequently bought information with five-pound lots of opium ("three sticky brown bars"). After the war he returned to his native Florida, where he helped set up and run Sea

Supply Inc., a CIA front in Miami. Sea Supply shipped arms to Thai opium producers and to members of the Nationalist Chinese Army who had fled to Burma and were engaged in opium smuggling.

Among his business associates was Louis Chesler, a Florida real estate developer who had dealings with Meyer Lansky. Helliwell also served as legal counsel to a Panamanian holding company that controlled a Bahamian gambling casino connected with Lansky.

We had discovered how small a world it is when you're connected... Take Seal associate ███ ███ ███, trying to sell Trinity Energy to Miami-based International Realty Group. International Realty, we learned, had previously been known as Bosco Resources Corp, incorporated in Delaware, operated until 1973, when its assets were nationalized without compensation, by the *Libyan* Government.

The man who headed Bosco, Clarence Holden, is deceased. When *his* widow died, her obit said, "She married Clarence Holden, afterwards accompanying him in his work to live in Shanghai, China, Manila, and Hawaii. During World War II she moved to New York City where she still enjoyed oriental art and history through coursework at Columbia."

Like Helliwell and Mena Congressman Hammerschmidt, Holden was another China hand.

Gordon Aiton, in addition to fronting for Helliwell and the CIA in the ownership of Seal's Lear, was also involved in a case described by Canadian police as the largest fraud in Canadian history...

It began in late 1982 when the giant Cadillac Fairview Corp. sold 10,931 apartments to Greymac Credit for $270 million. Greymac "flipped" the apartments, and, supposedly, re-sold them for $500 million to what turned out to be non-existent Arab investors... using Gordon Aiton's Cayman bank.

Documents showed the sale never occurred, and that the announced $109 million down payment—allegedly placed in Aiton's Cayman Island bank—was never made. Aiton, managing director of Bank Intercontinental Ltd., said the bank was paid $136,000 to stage a paper arrangement that made it appear the down payment from supposed Saudi Arabian investors had been made.

Nor was this Agent Aiton's only problem with the law.... He was also arrested on charges he stole 987 gold Krugerands worth more than $500,000 from a client of his bank.

This, then, is Gordon Aiton, who, acting as an agent for a Cayman secrecy-shrouded principal, his associate Paul Helliwell, repossessed

Barry Seal's Lear jet on the day they knew in advance Seal had been scheduled to die…

A final irony: the financial mastermind behind the "biggest financial fraud in Canadian history," in which Gordon Aiton had participated, was financier Leonard Rosenberg.

One knowledgeable Canadian source told us, about Rosenberg, "I came across a blip about two Canadian pilots being busted in Havana in 1963 for importing C4 plastique. The putty was in cans marked 'food.' Castro charged them as CIA spies. The man who sponsored the C4 plastique run, and chartered the plane to Cuba, was Leonard Rosenberg."

"One of the pilots on this '63 plastic explosives run was Ron Lippert, who re-emerges two decades later in Iran-Contra."

"There he flew a desperate CIA agent, wanted for murder and drug smuggling in Costa Rica, safely out of that country to Haiti. The 'saved' agent's name?"

"John Hull, famous from the Iran Contra scandal for running a 'refueling ranch' for drug smugglers in Costa Rica."

Small world.

CHAPTER THIRTY-EIGHT

THE KILLING OF
BARRY SEAL

THE WHITE UNMARKED POLICE car carrying Louisiana State Police Lt. Robert Thommasson, head of a special 21 man narcotics unit tasked solely with stopping Barry Seal, rolled slowly out of New Orleans in the hazy twilight.... After another long day Thommasson was going home; his car inched through traffic onto the 24-mile long Causeway across Lake Pontchartrain, which connects New Orleans with its leafy northern suburbs.

Though Thommasson was tired, fatigue has not dulled his vivid recollections of what happened next.... A call crackled over his police radio. "1018. Repeat: 1018. Immediately call headquarters," ordered a grim dispatcher's voice.

A cop who had learned a grudging respect for his elusive quarry, Thommasson heard the news in disbelief...

"What's white-and-brown-and-red and rolling around in Baton Rouge?" asked the dispatcher in the mirthless tone cops use to distance themselves from bloody events. "Barry Seal. They just gutted him."

As he heard the news, in the distance he was still listening to his cruiser's tires rolling over the causeway's grating.

Thump... Thump... Thump...

A $500,000 Medellin cartel murder contract had hung over Seal's head, upped to a cool $1 million if he was brought alive to Columbia....

Still, the chilling brutal and clinical efficiency with which the 'renegade' agent had been dispatched was breath taking... especially given that Seal himself, a man with the most impeccable intelligence sources, had not felt threatened. He certainly hadn't availed himself of the Federal Witness Protection program when it was offered to him.

The dispatcher asked, "Hey, bud, where you at?"

Thump...

"Middle of the causeway," Thommasson replied numbly.

"Good," came the curt rejoinder. "Get a bridge ticket on your way back into town, stamped with date and time."

"See, how volatile the whole Seal thing was," says Thommasson today, "is that they wanted me to have proof of exactly where I had been when Seal was killed, to remove any suspicion that *we* had played any role in it. It felt very much like 'where were you when Kennedy was shot?' It was *that* big—at least in Louisiana it was—especially since tensions had been running so high since Barry was convicted."

In retrospect, Thommasson says, the murder was a shock, but no surprise; Seal had seemingly fallen from favor with whoever had been protecting him. He'd been on a well-documented downward spiral for over a year, losing status, possessions and immunity from prosecution he had once taken for granted as a member of a 'protected' class.

Even in defeat, Seal's sense of play, almost of camaraderie, with the law enforcement people charged with the thankless task of tracking his movements, remained intact, said long-time DEA pilot Dave "Chicken" Gorman. "Chicken" had flown B-52's and C130's in Southeast Asia, and then flew out of New Orleans for 17 years. Seal had plied his trade in the same regions.

So he had known Barry for a long time, Gorman told us. He recalled running into him one time at Hurlburt Field in Panama City, "in the company of civilian Israeli's who had left the military and Mossad, supposedly, and were now supervising training of the PDF (Panama Defense Forces.)

This was not the first time we'd heard of American involvement with Israeli intelligence in the South American drug trade. A former Mossad agent told us that Seal had been running a big operation with their service right up until the time of his death.

Chicken Gorman explained the complexity of his relationship with Seal by means of an anecdote that occurred on one of Barry Seal's last days on Earth...

"Jake Jacobsen (Seal's supposed DEA 'handler') sent me out to confiscate a plane of Barry's at Ryan Field in Baton Rouge sometime in late '85. And while I'm poking around looking for it Barry came right over to me."

"'Chicken are you looking for my plane?' Barry asked.

"Yeah, Barry, I got orders to re-possess it, man" I told him.

'Well, its over here," Barry said. And then he took me to it, and it was like, 'no hard feelings,'" Chicken stated. "Barry was like that, a good guy, mostly."

Dark machinations surrounded the months preceding Seal's assassination. DEA pilot Gorman offered us a glimpse into the players, and the intrigue, swirling around Seal and the Central American operation...

"I was working in Belize out of Amberguey Cay. And we had been there for a month, flying ops around the Caribbean, when someone out at the airport decided to 'squeeze' us.... They hit us up for a huge bribe to continue operations."

"So we made a few calls. We heard back from the CIA station chief in Guatemala, who said, 'I understand you're having problems. Speak to them. Tell them you talked to me. Everything will be fine.'"

Gorman continues, "So I walked over to the tower to this guy's office that had been trying to make us pay. And now this guy is almost weeping with fear, cowering behind his desk, saying, 'Please don't kill me! Please don't kill me! They told me you would kill me if we didn't leave you alone!'"

"Then in late '85 I got another call from the same guy who had fixed things for us earlier, the CIA station head in Guatemala. He told me, 'Barry's wife just flew in. She landed in a private plane in Honduras, then took off and flew to San Jose in Costa Rica, where at this very moment she's depositing $7 million in a bank there.'"

Barry's wife Debbie has never been to Costa Rica. So, when she heard this, she was understandably curious about this money and drug courier who had been using her name.

She pressed Chicken Gorman on the point. "Who was this person in Guatemala who told you this?"

"Just a 'leg'" he replied, shrugging. "A field agent, a soldier, nothing more."

Piecing the story together took time. But even this small anecdote helped, another tiny piece of the puzzle...

From an eyewitness we heard that several weeks before his murder, Seal was frantically phoning associates—screaming at them —to stop two women from boarding a plane to fly to Central America who were on their way to 'clean out' his offshore bank accounts.

One of them, Barbara, was a teenage Cuban drug courier with whom Seal had been carrying on an affair; the other, Theresa, was the daughter of his Colombian associate, Stephen Planta.

What had happened? When word got out that Barry Seal's 'sanction' had been removed, it became open season on him and his assets, we were told.

The IRS seizure of all of his property had been a signal that his assets had become fair game.

The feeding frenzy now began...

Was Seal's downfall the same as John Gotti's? Arrogance, growing notoriety, a refusal to take a fall—however slight—to protect those higher up on the food chain?

Someone who had known Seal all his life, childhood friend John Prevost, had never seen Barry so full of himself, so arrogant, acting like a character out of one of Seal's favorite movies, the Al Pacino remake of *Scarface*, he said. Prevost watched Barry change in his last desperate months...

"I was a Dodge dealer, and Barry bought cars from us regularly, always paying cash, always bringing in just under $10,000. All my managers would stand around and just snicker... you know?"

"Then I remember seeing him just before he died. He pulled up in a Mercedes, and he was on a 'high' from the 300K-ransom business, talking loud, boastful. And he had a gun under his seat. It wasn't the Barry I knew."

Seal's assassination had a morality play dimension, Prevost felt. The results of the cocaine epidemic had begun to hit home.

"I had bumped into Barry's ex-wife (Linda) in a restaurant in Baton Rouge, and she waved and I went over and said to her, "'I've got two boys who are drug dependent. You tell Barry if he's dealing drugs, he needs to die in a flaming car wreck.'

Little acts of private desperation tell the tale... While briefly in Witness Protection as he testified in a trial a few months before he died, Seal let a record producer from New York sell him his 'foolproof' formula for playing roulette for the price of the gold Rolex Barry was wearing on his wrist... a sucker's bet, uncharacteristic for someone whose seeming recklessness had always camouflaged a shrewd capacity to calculate the odds.

Seal had been double-crossed, he felt, by the difficulties leading up to sentencing in Baton Rouge.

Why did Seal refuse to enter the federal witness protection program, which would have allowed him to assume a new identity in a secret location with the help of federal officials?

Incredibly, because Barry thought he could *walk*...

His attorney, Lewis Unglesby, had argued that U.S. Judge Frank Polozola should follow the lead of a federal judge in Miami, who had rewarded Seal for his 'work' as an 'informant' by approving a plea agreement on drug charges, letting him go free without serving time. He was already free of all of his Miami legal problems.

One need look no further than this for major scandal.... The biggest drug smuggler in American history, after being caught in multiple jurisdictions, was able, in Miami, to walk.

Convictions on multiple serious felonies resulted in nothing more than probation... and even *it* had now been vacated. He had, in fact, spent only one night in jail, after being convicted of charges for which convicts in every state in the US today are serving life without parole.

What's up with that? Had he *really* just been too valuable an informant? Or, was Barry Seal just too good an "earner" to spend more than a day in jail? The answer is in the non-identity in the drug world hierarchy of the 'pip-squeaks' whom Seal was, ostensibly, sprung from prison to send to jail.

None of them were ever a tiny fraction of the threat to society that Seal himself was. Today the 'drug dealing' Sandinistas are a fading memory.

But the drug business is as pervasive as ever.

Federal Judge Frank Polozola in Baton Rouge refused to follow the script in Seal's Louisiana sentencing. Instead of giving him 'time served' on his two drug felony convictions there, he sentenced Seal to six months in a Baton Rouge halfway house.

"I don't see any reason for coddling him," Polozola said during the sentencing hearing. "In my opinion, people like you ought to be in prison."

This begs, of course, the question of how it can be considered "coddling" to send someone convicted of major class A drug felonies to six months in a halfway house.... Most people in prison today for drug felonies would take that deal in a heartbeat.

But even that was an affront to the arrogant Seal, who, in his defense, has been used to having arrests "fixed" for him ever since he was a teenager caught flying weapons to Castro in Long View, Texas.

The idea of someone as "connected" as Barry Seal ever going to jail is even today preposterous. Speculation has always centered on who had 'got' to Judge Polozola… from one 'deep background' intelligence source, we heard that Polozola had a deep but hidden connection to Bill Casey.

Be that as it may, Polozola didn't do to Seal anything more than the IRS already had…. When they seize all of your assets, including children's' toys, if you were Seal—when you look at the suddenly empty house around you—you've got an inkling that the good times may be over.

"They *had* Judge Polozola, I mean they'd put the mark of the beast on him," said drug pilot Clarence Harp, about the federal judge's inexplicable action of placing Seal in a Salvation Army halfway house…

What did *that* mean?

"I was trailing Barry at the time he was killed, shadowing him for the Agency, just to find out who he was talking to…asked to by Bill Casey, who was a friend of mine," Harp told us.

"We didn't know how much the 'outside government' knew. I was told not to make contact. You know, Barry had a way of playing both ends against the middle. And he didn't have a whole lot of friends when he died."

A former NSA agent, who'd done a lot of "Bolivian duty," told us, "When Barry was killed a massive operation in Puerto Rico was closed down at the same time…. And $23 million washed up on the beach of this one tiny village which operated right next to this DEA operation, which operated right next to a massive smuggling op with which Barry Seal was associated."

The Puerto Rican op—we heard—was run by another drug smuggling legend, pilot Billy Lane. Lane also trained contra pilots before they moved on to the Mena, Arkansas portion of their training… in the 'sure-busy-for-a-tiny-town' of Long View, Texas, where Barry was nabbed by the FBI thirty years earlier and had the arrest 'straightened out' with the help of an accommodating local judge.

Why—we wondered—had the DEA situated itself right beside a smuggling operation in Puerto Rico? Our informant smiled…

"Pilots from the two different ops would see each other every morning at breakfast. A DEA pilot might ask, 'which way you going?' If the 'smuggler' pilot answered, 'South,' the DEA guy would say, 'Well, I'll head north then.'"

Just before Seal was murdered, his associate Russ Eakin had been attempting to help Barry transition back into the "straight" world, he told us…

"Barry called me the night before he was shot. He wanted out. I had already 'converted,' and he wanted to know how he could make that transition, too. And that's what I do; I'm very good at moving money around. He wanted to resume a normal life, but, as it happened, wasn't able to."

"I was waiting in a restaurant across the street from him when he was killed," Eakin told us. "I saw Barry get killed from the window of the Belmont hotel coffee shop. The killers were both out of the car, one on either side, but I only saw one shoot, cause Barry saw it coming and just put his head down on the steering column."

Seal's old friend Bill Maux had saw Barry Seal for the last time several days before he died.

"We lived right off Airline Highway, where the murder took place. Barry stopped by two days before it happened. He said they had him in a box. I told him to 'pull up a suitcase' and give it to Benjie (his brother) to hide for future needs. He said he was afraid that would tip off somebody. Two days later, when it happened, it tore me up. I was sick."

"As long as he could go and come as he pleased it was okay," Maux continued. "Because they weren't about to come to his house to kill him. Before that, he didn't have a schedule. But the Judge's order left him with a schedule on the outside, to keep from 6:00 AM to 6:00 PM."

There had been others en route to kill Seal at the same time as the hit squad was preparing to swing into action, we discovered. Bill Maux, with a pipeline into the world of the Mob, had heard 'something was coming,' and then moved to forestall it…

"I told Barry, when I saw him two days before he was murdered, that I had got word that a certain 'Chickie' Phillici out of Pittsburgh was coming down. Chickie was an explosive man. Barry took this to the DEA; they assured him that Chickie had been killed in a gun fight a few years before."

"But what they didn't know, or I should say pretended they didn't know," Maux continues, "Is that Chickie had a son that went by the same name… Donald Phillici, 24 years old. I heard through the grapevine he was the guy after somebody in Louisiana. It came back that they were gonna hit a guy named Seal…

"So I sent word back to Uncle Sal," said Maux, "saying, keep your trash in Pittsburgh."

We heard anecdotal evidence that a CIA agent had acted as 'paymaster' for the Seal hit…

Colonel Al Carone, who died in 1990, was a CIA paymaster and Mafia-connected money launderer who also held the rank of full Colonel in Army Intelligence. His daughter Dee told us that her father had even been sent to Dallas to pay off Jack Ruby before the Kennedy assassination.

Thirty-three years later, she said, he performed the same function for the Seal 'hit.' This proved impossible for us to verify; but one military intelligence source, who had known Seal since the 60's, admitted that he knew a "depressing number" of "Big Al's" confirmed 'close associates'…

"Big Al" had, clearly, been one of 'the boys.'

As Oliver North's bagman, Carone couriered large amounts of cash in and out of the country, according to former FAA investigator Rod Stich, "Carone was a member of the Gambino family, had connections to other crime groups in the eastern part of the United States, a member of the military, a CIA operative, and a detective and 'bag man' in the NYPD, collecting money that was distributed to captains and inspectors as payoffs for 'looking the other way' where drugs were involved."

Like Seal's, Carone's connections covered the waterfront.

Most who knew Barry Seal were saddened at his execution, but not surprised. His secretary Dandra Seale (no relation) was typical…

"The day Barry was killed, when he came back from lunch…" she began, and then stopped, her throat catching.

"See, he *knew* that day that they were killing him. Yes he did. Good lord. And he took it calmly, and continued with what he'd been doing, which was trying to get the Playboy Channel into the Salvation Army, so that he and the rest of the men could watch it while he was locked up there at night."

Not surprisingly, Dandra blames the 'government' for Seal's murder, and *not* the Medellin Cartel 'tar baby' of the official version of events…

"The CIA people here allowed it to happen. He had a chart, he had dirt on anybody and everybody."

Bob Thommasson, now a federal drug enforcement official teaching interdiction techniques to state and local police officers, recalled what happened when the state Police learned that Barry Seal had been murdered…

"I immediately put out troops in Baton Rouge. Now, keep in mind, we are the *State* Police. The murder jurisdiction was in the city/parish.

State police go in only when they're *called* in, all right? Then I put the crime lab on standby."

"The city cops took one look at Seal's bloody body, realized what they had, and requested the state police at the scene. So I immediately put the New Orleans office on standby," he continued.

"At that time we had no idea yet that these guys—the shooters—were like rabbits spreading out in a wildfire. None whatsoever. Thirty-five minutes after the shooting, I had dispatch call the Baton Rouge office of the FBI, and the New Orleans office of the FBI, to give a notification, just because its the right thing to do…. You know, we've got a major smuggler murdered, da-da-da-da-da."

We interrupted him…

"We discovered that one of the killers actually took pictures of the murder-in-progress, but that the FBI agent who nabbed this guy at New Orleans International Airport as he was trying to flee the country that night *exposed the film*, rendering it useless as evidence."

Thommasson chooses his words carefully. "What you get, when you call the FBI at night," he explains, "is a *duty agent*, okay? He's just a kid, usually, just out of the FBI Academy, his standing orders are, 'Make No Decisions Under Any Circumstances.'"

"What you *don't* get at that time of night is a seasoned agent or a SAC (Special Agent in Charge). You don't get anybody important. So the apprehension at the airport was made by a kid.

"It went like this: my headquarters called the New Orleans FBI office. As soon as that phone call was received, the two 'baby' agents that had watch that night—they're called 'watch supes'—went out to cover the airport."

"Now, never in a thousand years would this ever happen again, but these two lucky guys park their car at the airport, and head into the terminal *at the exact same time* as this shooter, and they've got a physical description over their radio that exactly matches the guy they're seeing. That's the only way that guy got caught."

"So… if you're asking me, did they deliberately expose that film at the airport? I gotta say: look at who these two FBI guys were. Rookies. These are *not* the Men in Black."

"Why was there so much suspicion of the CIA?" we asked.

From his grimace we surmise he feels we're pushing. He pauses, straightens in his chair, and then fixes us with a stare felt before, no doubt, by innumerable Southern miscreants.

"Tell me why you're doing this," Thommasson demands.

From the way he says "this," we know exactly what he means…. And after we tell him he sits, thinking hard. And then without another word of comment, while staring fixedly out a 12th story window of a hotel room in Daytona Beach, Florida at the blue-green Atlantic, turning now a deeper blue as the sun slowly sets somewhere a million miles away, he starts to talk…. And the words at first come slowly, but soon enough are pouring out in torrents.

"This gets really black, okay, and it gets black for a *lot* of people…. But I'll give you a sequence of events: The FBI appears, shows up, *on* site, *at* the shooting, okay?"

"And I go, hmmm… it happens… its not *too* fucking extraordinary, but still…. And then the contents of the car, the trunk, were seized."

"But they can't just seize material evidence in a capital crime!" we protested. "Isn't it illegal for anyone but the investigating officers to remove evidence from a crime scene?"

"I told you," he continued, "this gets really black. But some of the contents of the trunk, anyway, made it to my lab…our Louisiana State Police lab, which is definitely *not* a mom and pop shop—they've got 60-80 highly-trained employees…"

"Here's the police procedural: if its *my* case and I call the lab, I *own* the lab, okay? They take orders only from *me*. It would be the same procedure if a sheriff from Podunk called—*they* would then own the lab, the lab would work only for them. Understand?"

"Now, it would be *beyond* a breach of ethics, it would be *criminal*…if, say, I called the lab, and said, hey, I hear the city police submitted a report on Joe Schmo, I'm coming by to pick it up. Its called "tampering with evidence." We're into criminal acts here."

"The evidence that went into that lab on Barry Seal went to a guy that won't talk to you, so don't ask me for his name or phone number. This has caused a lot of stress in his life. He's a long-time friend, and a top gun in forensics. And he gets the contents of Barry Seal's briefcase, and some other contents of the car as lab exhibits. And he brings it into the lab. Our lab had worked the scene, and so had then brought the trunk's contents back to the lab," he continued.

We can't help ourselves, and blurt out the 'Big Question.' "What was in the trunk of the Cadillac?"

"I'm not trying to be evasive…," Thommasson answers somberly. "But, I want to make it *very clear*… I only have third-hand reports. *Okay?*"

"Seal's trunk contained compelling and—*again, from 3rd hand data*—very very compelling documents and tapes. Several briefcases, boxes—wherever Seal's Cadillac was, that was where Barry's instant records were."

From the way he stressed '3rd hand' we knew he was speaking for the record. Later, we discovered that this man's family dog was decapitated and left floating in their backyard pool as a warning... fully three months *after* Seal's assassination...

"See, Barry taped his calls. Barry taped *all* of his calls, including all his calls to his controllers. I suspect that were you to have seen the contents of the trunk, it would certainly validate for whom he was employed, and what his mission was."

"Okay, who has heard those tapes that I could talk to?"

The tension in the room rises. When he speaks his voice is soft, barely above a whisper.

"That's living?" he asks. "No one. I told you: this gets really black."

Barry Seal, who didn't show any nervousness or anxiety about being assassinated by the Medellin cartel, had explicitly denied that he had anything to fear from them. In a television interview with TV reporter John Camp, he shrugged it off..., "If it's to come, it will come."

John Camp is the pseudo-journalist who disgraced himself and his profession by producing an hour-long documentary apologia for Seal called "Uncle Sam Wants You."

No drug smuggler in history has ever received better publicity. We heard, but were unable to confirm, that the owner of the Baton Rouge station for which Camp produced this psy-ops piece had been personally asked to 'help out' by a figure who has already played a role in our drama, Democratic National Chairman Charles Manatt.

"Charles Manatt put Camp's bosses up to it," emphatically stated this source, who, for this piece of explosive information at least, insisted on strict anonymity.

Good doggies get tossed a few bones... and John Camp went from being just another small-market TV reporter with a bad toupee, to heading a "special investigations unit" at CNN.

Lily Tomlin put it best: "No matter how cynical I get, I just can't keep up."

If Seal was right in being unafraid of Medellin cartel retaliation, then who then *was* responsible for his murder?

There is no better source for this critical information than the three Colombians convicted of the killing, sentenced to life in prison without parole.

We interviewed Richard Sharpstein, a prominent Miami criminal defense attorney, and the lawyer for one of the three convicted assassins, who casually revealed the explosive truth about who ordered Barry Seal killed—and why.

"I represented Miguel Velez for the Barry Seal homicide, which was one of the most incredible experiences I have ever been through," Sharpstein began.

"It was an amazing experience. Nobody wanted to think about what any of this meant back in 1986. The implications were just too big. And I'm only speaking with you now because some of this has leaked out."

"All three of the Colombians who went on trial always told us— their lawyers—that they were being directed, after they got into this country, on what to do and where to go by an 'anonymous gringo,' a United States Military officer, who they quickly figured out was Oliver North," Sharpstein says.

"Say that again?" we asked. We were sure we'd heard it right the first time; we just needed confirmation...

"Once they rendezvoused together in the States," explained Sharpstein, "they, the Colombians, were being directed, by phone, by a man who insisted on remaining anonymous, but who did identify himself as being an officer in the American military..."

"They were put in touch with this officer through Rafa (a Colombian smuggler) who was the guy my client worked for. And they all believed that it was Oliver North."

What corroborative indications are there to justify the charge of murder against Lt. Col. Oliver North?

North, numerous sources stated without prompting, had been running an assassination squad right out of his White House office. So the extra-judicial execution of Barry Seal wouldn't have made him blink an eye. There are even allegations that he had been tasked with drawing up plans to suspend the US Constitution and declare martial law, in the event the massive drug smuggling taking place ever came to public light.

In *Guts and Glory: The Rise and Fall of Oliver North*, author Ben Bradlee, Jr., writes..."North's work for FEMA from 1982 to the spring of 1984 was highly classified, and some would say bizarre. He was involved in helping to draft a sweeping contingency plan to impose martial law in the event of a nuclear war or less serious national crises such as widespread internal dissent or opposition to an American military invasion abroad."

But the popular mythology of Seal's assassination is—not just *wrong*—but active disinformation.

When we began to examine Seal's assassination more closely, we saw that even basic facts, like how many killers there were, was stated wrong to slant the story. In the official version of events recounted in newspapers the killers were always described as a "three man hit team of Colombian nationals."

Even a cursory reading of the headlines revealed, to our amazement, there weren't hadn't been three men involved... there had been *eight*.

Three men may be a hit 'team. Eight is a hit *'squad.'*

So this is clearly active disinformation; even newspaper reporters can count to ten... *unaided.*

Six men had been arrested at various stages of attempting to flee the scene. A seventh, Rafa Cardona, who had dispatched the team, was safely ensconced in Colombia... at least for a while. He was charged in absentia for planning the hit, but was himself mowed down, in a spray of automatic gunfire inside his antique car dealership, in Colombia later that year.

Then there was the "eight man," Miami CIA 'asset' Jose Coutin, who had supplied the machine gun. More on him in a moment...

Richard Sharpstein's client, Miguel Velez, *aka* 'Cumbamba,' has been described as a "CIA hit man" in the New York press, where he was wanted for murder.

It was a total fluke that he was caught. He was done in by a deer. Earlier, Velez had been spotted, questioned, and then released at the airport, by those sharp dressers at the FBI.

After escaping the feeble clutches of the FBI at the airport, Velez had hired a cab to *drive* him from New Orleans to Miami.

In the middle of the night, in Meridian Mississippi, the cab hit a deer at a lonely gas station on the interstate. While waiting for repairs, a highway patrolman happened by, and noticed that the surgical outfit worn by the cab's passenger fit the description released by Baton Rouge police of one of the triggermen.

Officers immediately put Velez in handcuffs. The cabbie, irate at losing such a big fare, professed to the cops that he couldn't understand why the police were making such a fuss over a dead deer...

Police then raided two "safe" houses in Algiers, a seamy suburb of New Orleans, and nabbed Bernardo Vasquez and Louis Quintero-Cruz, the other two men later convicted, as well as John Cardona, brother of the man fingered as at the trial, Rafa Cardona Salazar.

Eliberto Sanchez was caught trying to flee at the New Orleans International Airport. Jose Renteria was nabbed the next day while waiting to board a plane in Miami.

The "eighth man" in the assassination is Jose Coutin, who had supplied the weapons for the hit. He is thus, by law, guilty of murder; or, at the very least, of conspiracy to murder.

But being connected means never having to say you're sorry...

Coutin was never even charged with a crime. He went on to testify before the Kerry Committee, saying, no doubt, anything his 'benefactors' wanted him to say.

Coutin was the proprietor of the Broadway Boutique, a Miami fashion shop with a unique inventory: ladies clothing in the front, and military gear in the back. According to Lesley Cockburn in "Out of Control," he was a well-known CIA asset, FBI informant, and Contra weapons supplier.

Why Sanchez and Cardona were simply deported and never charged with murder has never, unsurprisingly, been satisfactorily explained...

But what happened to Jose Renteria is revealing. Testimony at the trial of the three accused of killing Seal revealed that Renteria had been the cut-out between Coutin, known to be linked to Oliver North, and the shooters, to whom he delivered the weapons from Coutin.... So Jose Renteria's case was severed from the trial of the other three.

"It was the strangest thing," says attorney Sharpstein. "He was severed on some odd theory that he wasn't at the murder scene. What really happened, is he had indicated that he might—in exchange for a deal— be willing to talk..."

"Someone on the government side was clearly not very eager for that to happen."

According to trial testimony, it was Renteria who took pictures of the murder. When his camera was confiscated by an FBI agent at the New Orleans airport, it was opened and the film inside exposed.

Renteria was sent to Miami to face (minor) pending charges. His bosses must have felt that his had been a job well done.

"They cut him a deal, they made a fast plea and he was in and out, serving a bit of time and then being deported," states Sharp-stein.

"The result was we never got to hear the story he was ready to sing at the trial."

And Coutin?

"Same thing," Sharpstein said. "They made a deal with him; he testified at the trial, and then later before the Kerry hearings in Washington. I was the lawyer who brought up his CIA and Contra connections in the trial, because I felt that there were *lots* of reasons why the CIA might want to murder Barry…"

"And Coutin went crazy on the stand when I did. You'd have thought he'd been zapped with a ray gun."

Had the Colombians discussed motive with their lawyers?

"They were just soldiers," Sharpstein stated. "They did what they were told. But in testimony at the trial given by one of Seal's attorneys, Lewis Unglesby, we *did* finally hear about motive…"

Lewis Unglesby is today a prominent and *very* well connected Louisiana lawyer. At the time his name was daily on the front page of the state's newspapers, defending his long-time client and associate, Governor Edwin Edwards.

Unglesby had told *us* about a confrontation he had with Barry over the fact that Seal was keeping him in the dark about matters Unglesby considered crucial to defending him…

"Barry pushed the phone across the desk to me and said, 'You wanna know what's going on? Here. Dial this number. Tell 'em you're me,'" Unglesby related.

"When I did what he requested," he continued, "A female voice answered the phone, sayin', 'Vice President Bush's office, may I help you?'"

"I said, 'This is Barry Seal.' She asked me to wait while she transferred the call, which was immediately picked up by a man who identified himself as Admiral somebody or other, who said to me 'Barry! Where you been?'"

"That's when I told him that I wasn't Barry Seal, I was his lawyer," said Unglesby. "Immediately he slammed down the phone."

"So why was Barry Seal murdered?" we asked Sharpstein.

"Unglesby said he had been with Seal when the IRS came and seized all his property," Sharpstein related. "The IRS man said, 'You owe us $30 million for the money you made in drug dealing.'"

"Hey, I work for you," was Seal's reply. "We work for the same people."

"You don't work for us," the IRS agent stated. "We're the IRS."

"Unglesby was with Seal when he retired to a back room," Sharpstein stated. "He watched as Seal placed a call to George Bush. He heard Barry Seal tell Bush, 'If you don't get these IRS assholes off my back I'm going to blow the whistle on the Contra scheme.'"

Sharpstein spoke solemnly, aware of the gravity of his words..., "'That's why he's dead,' is what Unglesby said."

One week after the phone conversation between Barry Seal and George Bush, Seal was sentenced to a halfway house. Two weeks later he was dead.

"Barry Seal, you mean that agent that went *'bad?'*" Gordon Novel had casually inquired, when we'd posed the question of his associations with Seal.

An agent that 'goes bad,' as we understand intelligence industry trade jargon, is one who contemplates *talking.*

"Seal was gunned down, supposedly by those Colombians," says Sharpstein. "But they were fed information by the assholes in our government who wanted him dead."

The assassination of Barry Seal was very likely even not the first attempt on Seal's life by North, we were told by CIA electronics expert Red Hall, on the ground in Nicaragua with Seal on the Sandinista drug sting...

"The only thing I knew was the CIA had to do a lot with it (Barry's murder.) The killers were being directed by Oliver North at the time. It was the same thing Oliver North pulled on us down in Nicaragua."

"Then, I didn't know yet that Oliver North had it for Barry Seal, because he was working with Oliver at that particular point. We was undercover, and we were still down there (Nicaragua), when Oliver North blew the whistle on us."

Chip Tatum, another covert operative who had known Seal and shared confidences with him, listened with amusement the first time we breathlessly relayed what we'd discovered: that Oliver North is guilty in the assassination of Barry Seal...

"No shit, Sherlock," he replied, laughing. "It ain't exactly the secret of the century, I can tell you."

Barry Seal had threatened George Bush over the IRS trouble he was having. Why couldn't Bush have 'taken care' of the IRS?

Perhaps he could have. But there were other Seal 'problems' as well, like state police so disgusted they were threatening to go to the media with damning evidence of official corruption in Seal's case, should the biggest drug smuggler any of them had ever seen receive no 'time' at all.

"Al Capone killed over five hundred people. What did he go to prison for?" asked one former state police official.

We remembered. "Tax evasion?"

"Exactly. Tax evasion. Get the picture? I beat on desktops in IRS offices all across the United States to find somebody that would take the case, till I found a criminal investigator for the IRS named Earl Buck Holmes, willing to come down and set up a war -room in my office."

Some 'wised-up' local and state cops had figured out that Barry Seal had been too valuable to certain people in the federal government of the United States of America to ever go to prison for his crimes...

Knowing this, local law enforcement had done an end-around on them, and taken their case to the IRS, where they hatched a plan to at least strip Seal of some of his ill-gotten goods.

Remarkably, in the court proceedings in neither Miami nor Baton Rouge had Seal's organizational assets—like his fleet of planes—been confiscated, although this is standard operating procedure in drug cases?

Why not? Because they were still being *used...*

Local and state cops, we found, to our amazement, had tracked a shipment of cocaine to one of Seal's ocean-going vessels, the Captain Wonderful, just weeks before Seals' murder. There they were met—and dissuaded from boarding—by DEA and CIA agents.

State and local cops in the South often appear to know the score... When we told one Louisiana law enforcement source what we had learned from Miami attorney Richard Sharpstein, about how the hit team had been getting orders from Oliver North, he said simply, "That doesn't surprise me at all."

Then we discovered why Seal had been so unconcerned about being killed by the Medellin cartel...

'I asked Barry why he wasn't worried about the Colombians killing him," stated close associate, Mob pilot Rene Martin. "He said he had told the Colombians he was going to pull a fast one, and testify for Ochoa *against* the US government."

Two weeks before he died, Barry Seal had hired a private investigator in Miami, Steve Dinerstein, to run FAA title searches on 15 different airplanes he had used in his smuggling Enterprise....

Seal was getting ready to talk about who had owned his smuggling fleet fifteen years ago.

Barry Seal was assassinated because he was getting ready to *talk*.... He had even contacted a Paramount Studios production vice president about making a movie.

While the killers approached Barry Seal's Cadillac in the Baton Rouge twilight, Seal had been on his car phone with a CIA aircraft procurement executive in Arizona, Bill Lambeth, who will himself be murdered in Phoenix seven years later.

Suddenly cut off, and fearing the worst, Lambeth frantically dialed Barry's home phone, where his wife Debbie answered. "I think something's wrong with Barry," Lambeth said ominously.

Debbie—unable to reach her husband—bundled her three small children into the car and frantically headed for the Salvation Army halfway house where he had been sentenced to sleep for six months. On the way she stopped at a pay phone to make another attempt to reach her husband, and learned he was now 'unreachable.'

"He's not going to the hospital," she remembers being told. "He's dead. Don't come here Debbie. Don't."

As she returned to her car she could see through her tears, her three small children's heads barely peeking over the car seats. And though Barry Seal is anything *but* blameless, his three small children were... they symbolize the millions of lives ruined by a phony drug war whose only purpose is to line-still-more the pockets of a crew of elite deviants who took over our country.

"All I could think of was my poor little babies... my poor babies," Debbie Seal told us, choking back tears. "I didn't know how I was going to tell them that their Daddy was dead."

We were to make one final discovery.

After Barry Seal had threatened to roll on Richard Ben-Veniste, and while he was still in possession of those "two briefcases" filled with incriminating information he had 'liberated' from Ben-Veniste's office, Ben-Veniste had interceded for Seal and set up a meeting with the then-Vice President of the United States, George Bush.

We learned that Seal had not attended this meeting.

Instead, he sent the Attorney General for the state of Louisiana, William J. Guste, Jr., to argue on his behalf. The Vice President of the United States, George Bush, sat down and cut a deal with the Attorney General of the State of Louisiana—in what amounted to state-to-state-negotiations—about the fate of a Louisiana native CIA agent with a 'little problem,' Barry Seal.

The result, which we already knew, was that Seal had moved his operation to Mena in the spring of 1982, and went to work for Oliver North.

But who was William Guste? Why had Seal placed such faith in him?

And the answer, when we found it, brought our story of Barry and 'the boys' full circle…

William Guste, Jr., in addition to involvement with Edwin Edwards in shady casino deals—standard Louisiana fare—had been, way back in 1956 and '57, when our story began, the head of the New Orleans Metropolitan Crime Commission, where he had been instrumental in bringing to town Guy Banister, the agent who had helmed the entire New Orleans operation from its inception.

Small world.

At the Baton Rouge funeral home where mourners gathered for Barry Seal's wake, the newly-widowed Debbie Seal's oldest childhood friend noticed with curiosity an entire line of men in sleek dark suits hovering at the back of the room.

"Who are they?" she asked Debbie.

"They're with the government," Debbie replied. "They've come to make sure that he's dead."

This has been the story of Barry Seal, the biggest drug smuggler in American history, who died in a hail of bullets with George Bush's private phone number in his wallet.

APPENDIX

"Boy's Life. . ." With friends (Barry in middle)

A mother's card to a young man going off to war.

Postcards from the Edge. . .
On March 29 1961, two days before the Bay of Pigs Invasion, 22 year old Barry Seal wrote home from Guatemala, "I am probably going to stay at this picture (of the volcano overlooking Lake Atitlan) a couple of days…"

The Brigette Bardot card was from a friend who introduced Barry to Elvis Presley…

Sixteen year-old Baton Rouge Civil Air Patrol cadet Barry Seal boards a US Air Force plane on July 23, 1955 to fly to a two week training camp at Barksdale AFB in Shreveport, Louisiana where he will meet fellow cadet Lee Harvey Oswald from New Orleans and both will fall under the sway of CIA agent and pedophile Capt. David Ferrie

BOYS INVOLVED IN JEFF INQUIRY

Metairie Man Booked in Indecency Case

A Jefferson parish man was being investigated Friday in connection with alleged indecent acts against juveniles at his Metairie home.

New Orleans police juvenile bureau officers and Jefferson parish deputies said the 43-year-old airline pilot apparently used alcohol, hypnotism, and the adventure of flying to lure the juveniles—mostly 15- and 16-year-olds — into committing indecent acts.

Capt. David Ferrie, 331 Atherton dr., Metairie, has been booked in Jefferson parish with committing a crime against nature on a 15-year-old boy and indecent behavior with three juvenile boys, including the 15-year-old.

REPORT STUDIED

The Orleans parish district attorney's office Friday was studying a report on Ferrie's alleged contributing to the delinquency of juveniles.

New Orleans juvenile bureau officers Roland Fournier and Charles Jonau worked on the case with Jefferson parish sheriff's office Sgt. Richard Thompson and Ptn. Fred Roth.

According to the New Orleans officers, runaway boys are involved.

Ferrie allegedly assisted and encouraged two juveniles to run away from home, one in August 1960 and another this August, police said.

Officers said Ferrie, as well as being an airline pilot, was a former Civil Air Patrol squadron commander.

After he was "quietly dismissed" from his CAP unit about a year ago, he formed his own unit, "The Metairie Falcon Squadron," officers said.

CAP officials in New Orleans told police that CAP national headquarters in Houston had no record of a "Metairie Falcon Squadron" charter and these officials expressed the opinion that the charter shown to parents by Ferrie was a forgery.

TELL OF STAY

New Orleans officers said they took a number of statements from juveniles who reside in New Orleans. These statements tell how a number of the teenagers stayed at Ferrie's home in Metairie on different occasions, police continued.

Ferrie is listed in the telephone book as "Dr." and officers said they understand he is a doctor of philosophy.

Patrolmen Fournier and Jonau said they entered the case when a New Orleans family contacted officers that their 15-year-old son was missing from home earlier this month.

Officers said the family told them the youth disappeared several days before they called police but another member of the squadron told them he knew the boy was at Ferrie's home and could get him back.

The missing youth returned home but left a day or so later, police said.

He telephoned from Houston and said he would return home if the parents agreed not to prosecute Ferrie.

Officers said the parents followed instructions and signed a notarized statement that they would not prefer charges against Ferrie.

Upon the boy's return to New Orleans, he was questioned by juvenile bureau officers but he refused to accuse Ferrie of anything.

AIRPLANE FLIGHTS

Other boys gave police statements that Ferrie took them on airline flights to Houston and Corpus Christi on different occasions.

Ferrie encouraged the boys to stay at his home on various occasions "so they could get an early start working on a plane," one boy told New Orleans officers.

The plane was being constructed at an airline hwy. tourist court, officers added.

New Orleans officers working with Jefferson parish authorities obtained a search warrant and went through Ferrie's home earlier this week.

They reported they discovered seven or eight World War I rifles with a quantity of ammunition. Many maps of Cuba were found at Ferrie's home, police added.

One of the juveniles told officers he had flown to Cuba with Ferrie on different occasions. Ferrie asked another teen-ager to drive a Cuban citizen to Miami, police said.

Ferrie would lend the youths his automobile when he was flying, according to officers.

PILOT ACCUSED OF TAMPERING

Intimidation Charged in Jefferson Case

Charges of intimidation of a witness were filed Monday against an airline pilot by the Orleans parish district attorney's office.

Charged was Capt. David Ferrie, 43, 331 Atherton Dr., Metairie.

He was booked last week in Jefferson parish with committing a crime against nature, and indecent behavior with juveniles.

New Orleans police juvenile bureau patrolmen Ronald Fournier and Charles Jonau said

signed a paper that he not prefer charges against Ferrie. The juvenile had previously made a statement to that led to Ferrie being in Jefferson parish with crime-against-nature charge.

The youth, according to officers, said Ferrie told him that "a Cuban friend" he did not sign.

Officers said the juvenile them he signed out a Ferrie promised to give a motor hike if he signed youth told officers.

Officers said they had looking for Ferrie for few days.

A $750 bond was recorded.

A trade association in Richmond, Va., wanting to better image for its r Ferrie visited a 16-year-old boy used the advertising pag

CIA agent David Ferrie, Pedophile

PARISH SETS FIRST OF VARIETY SHOWS

The first of two summer variety show performances at Our Lady of Good Counsel parish will be held Saturday at 7:30 p. m. on the parish grounds, Louisiana and Chestnut.

More than 20 musical numbers, skits, and dance routines have been prepared by parishioners and special guests, according to the Rev. Harold Menard, director, who said the second performance will be held Sunday at 7:30 p. m.

Times-Picayune

and partly cloudy with variable winds five to 12 miles an hour is the weather bureau forecast. Highest Wednesday 91, lowest 76; highest expected Thursday 88-92, lowest 72-76. Weather map, details, Sec. 1, Page 18.

NEW ORLEANS, THURSDAY MORNING, AUGUST 1, 1963   Entered N. O. Post Office as Second-Class Matter Under Act of March 3, 1879   SINGLE COPY 5 CENTS

Photo by C. Bennette Moore
W. O. TURNER

TURNER NAMED TO SPAN BOARD

Replaces Robertson on Bridge Authority

Gov. Jimmie H. Davis announced Wednesday the appointment of William O. Turner to the Mississippi River Bridge Authority. He replaces Willard E. Robertson.

Turner, chairman of the board and chief executive officer of the Louisiana Power and Light Co., was an original member of the authority, first appointed in July 1952. Since that time he has served through three different appointments, his last term expiring in September, 1962, when he was vice-chairman.

Robertson, friend and supporter of Mayor Victor H. Schiro, was appointed by the governor in March 1962. At the time Robertson's appointment filled the vacancy of the unexpired term of the mill supply company in New Orleans. Simpson's five-year term would have expired July 2, 1962.

RED-INFLUENCE CHARGES MADE

New Englander, Mississippian Dispute RFK

(Times-Picayune Washington Bureau)

WASHINGTON — A New England newspaper publisher joined southern leaders Wednesday in leveling new charges of communism in the civil rights controversy.

From the North and South came attacks on a statement by Atty. Gen. Robert F. Kennedy saying there is no evidence of Communist involvement in racial demonstrations around the country.

The Northern voice was William Loeb, publisher of the Manchester, N. H., Union Leader. He said, "Communists definitely are a factor in the civil rights agitation." He branded Robert F. Kennedy's statement "entirely unbelievable" and entitled to no credibility whatsoever."

'COVER UP JOB'

Loeb's testimony against President Kennedy's civil rights package came in the wake of a charge by Mississippi state Sen. John C. McLaurin that Atty. Gen. Kennedy is guilty of "the most brazen cover-up job ever perpetrated on the American people."

McLaurin, a candidate for state attorney general, made the charge in Tuesday's Democratic primary, declared:

"When he (Kennedy) says there is no evidence that Martin Luther King, or any of the top leaders of the major civil rights groups are Communists or Communist-controlled, then he has either deliberately misstated the facts or is the most ignorant attorney general. Kennedy is not an ignorant man."

CACHE OF MATERIAL FOR BOMBS SEIZED

Probe of St. Tammany Case Continues

EXAMINING BOMB CASINGS is a Federal Bureau of Investigation agent. The cluster of casings are part of 20 seized Wednesday in a frame house near Mandeville. More than a ton of explosives, which investigators said could be used to make the casings deadly, were also found in the home. The FBI said the explosives were to be used against a country "with which the United States is at peace."

Another Picture in Sec. 1, Page 3

More than a ton of dynamite, 20 bomb casings three-feet long, napalm (fire-bomb) material and other devices were seized Wednesday by Federal Bureau of Investigation agents in a resort area in St. Tammany Parish, between Mandeville and Lacombe.

H. G. Maynor, special agent-in-charge of the New Orleans FBI office, in making the announcement, said the dynamite, bomb casings and other materials were seized in connection with an investigation of an effort to carry out a military operation against a country with which the United States is at peace." This is in violation of Title 18, Section 960, of the U.S. Code.

Maynor said the FBI has been investigating this matter for several days and seized the following material under a search warrant obtained Wednesday, authorized by U.S. Attorney Louis C. LaCour, and issued by U.S. Commissioner Fritz Windhorst Jr.:

1. 20 empty 100-pound bombs, blue in color.
2. 25 fuses.
3. 26 striker assemblies for the above fuses.
4. 18 locking nuts, which lock fuses in place.
5. 24 firing devices, which fit on nose end of bombs.
6. One pair of non-sparking crimping pliers.
7. 1/25 pieces of primer cord, each about two feet long.
8. 21 commercial type percussion blasting caps.
9. A 20-pound container of Nuo...

Work on Michoud Jobs Resumed Despite Dispute

Non-Union Electricians Reported Hired

Construction jobs at Michoud resumed progress Wednesday despite a month-long dispute which has threatened to halt production at the rocket plant.

Informed sources reported that substitute non-union electricians...

MARRERO BOY, 5, SHOT TO DEATH

Children Discharge Gun While Playing

A five-year-old Negro boy was killed instantly at 8:45 p. m...

The raid on the renegade CIA camp in Lacombe; when the assassins-in-training were released without being booked, it was clear that President Kennedy's 'sanction' had been removed.

RECEIVED
NOV. 14 1969

explosive services incorporated

Post Office Box 6327

New Orleans, Louisiana 70114 • U.S.A.

Area Code 504 362-8222 • Cable: EXPLOSERV

Mr. Barry Seal, President
Helicopter Airways, Inc.
International Trade Mart Garage
100 Poydras Street
New Orleans, La. 70130

November 10, 1969

Dear Barry:

If you concur with this letter, please sign both copies and
return to me for Mr. Richardson's signature upon his return.
At that point a fully executed copy will be returned to you.

Enjoyed working with you last week and look forward to
joining you again in Houston Wednesday or Thursday.

Sincerely,
EXPLOSIVE SERVICES INCORPORATED

Haven Emerson

HE:br.
Enclosures

Buying Explosives in 1969. . . Operation Condor required a lot of 'boom
boom' Note Seal's business address in Clay Shaw's International Trade Mart.
where he undoubtedly got a 'trade' discount on his office rent.

11-27-73 *Statement of A B Seal*

On or about October, 1969 I had just recently started the
HAD
helicopter company. We have several helicopters working in
the Gulf of Mexico and oil industry flying passengers and
cargo. We were also located offices in the international
during
trademark building in New Orleans, Louisiana. Always looking
first
for new business we didn't notice the great interest in the
Trans Alaska pipeline which was large developing at that time
The pipeline of course had to be serviced for both workmen
logistics
and material. The majistics of this was to provide great
problems for everyone. At that time we did contact people
in charge of the pipeline in Houston, Texas, Associated
Pipeline, Inc., and found out that probably the greatest
logistic problem at first would be to carry the explosives
up and down the pipeline to blow the hole that the pipe
would be laying in. We then got in contact with a company
operating in the New Orleans area, Explosives Services, Inc.
and They were located on General DeGaulle Boulevard. Their
partn parent corporation was a large corporation and in
Delaware, I believe. After they many meetings with Explosives
Services, Inc., Their company president was named Mr. John
Richardson . Im' sure of the last name. I'm not sure of the
first name. At that particular point at which time I had
met Mr. John Charpentier who at that time was a explosives
employee of Explosives Services, Inc. I'll mention him just
a little bit later on. Also I have several documents here,
letters from Explosives Services, Inc. expressing the joint
participation in the Trans-Alaskan Pipeline project with
myself and I say myself, I mean Helicopter Airways, Inc.
and Explosives Services, Inc.

"The dog ate my homework…" After his arrest for attempting to export 7 tons of plastic explosive, Barry Seal gave a statement to police that revealed that he was not as fast on his feet as he may have thought.

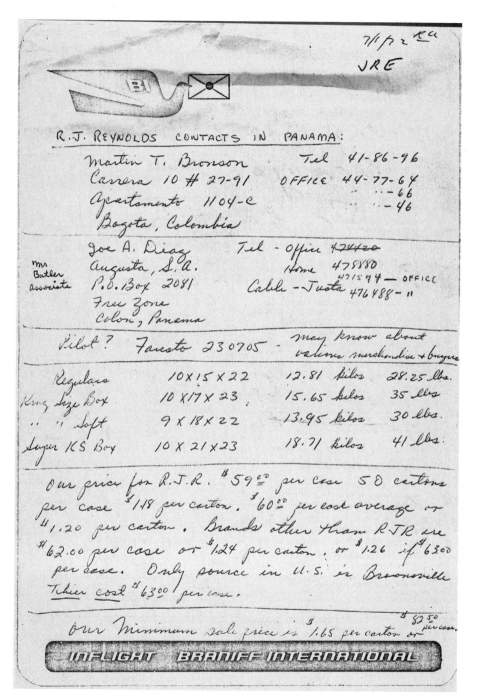

"Carlo Gambino, meet Jesse Helms." RJ Reynolds' executives in Central America assisted Barry Seal in smuggling contraband into the US, as well as in the CIA's planned 'move' against Castro in 1972.

	1. LAST NAME - FIRST NAME - MIDDLE NAME	2. SERVICE NUMBER	3a. GRADE, RATE OR RANK	b. DATE OF RANK (Day, Month, Year)
PERSONAL	SEAL, ADLER BERRIMAN	NG 25 511 721	Pvt (P) E-2	31 Dec 61
	4. DEPARTMENT, COMPONENT AND BRANCH OR CLASS	5. PLACE OF BIRTH (City and State or Country)		DATE OF BIRTH: DAY 16 MONTH Jul YEAR 39
	ARMY NGUS CE	Baton Rouge, La.		
	7a. RACE Caucasian	b. SEX Male	c. COLOR HAIR Brown / d. COLOR EYES Green	e. HEIGHT 5'11" / f. WEIGHT 212 / 8. U.S. CITIZEN ☐YES ☐NO X	9. MARITAL STATUS Single
	10a. HIGHEST CIVILIAN EDUCATION LEVEL ATTAINED 1 Year College College	b. MAJOR COURSE OR FIELD Aero Engr		

TRANSFER OR DISCHARGE DATA	11a. TYPE OF TRANSFER OR DISCHARGE Reld to ARNG of La, (See 32)	b. STATION OR INSTALLATION AT WHICH EFFECTED Fort Benning, Ga.
	c. REASON AND AUTHORITY AR 635-205 SPN 21L & DA Cir 612-1 6 Jun 62 Sep for Christmas Holidays	d. EFFECTIVE DATE: DAY 14 MONTH Dec YEAR 62
	12. LAST DUTY ASSIGNMENT AND MAJOR COMMAND H & S Co, (Abn), 4th Stu Bn, The Stu Bde	13a. CHARACTER OF SERVICE HONORABLE / b. TYPE OF CERTIFICATE ISSUED None

SELECTIVE SERVICE DATA	14. SELECTIVE SERVICE NUMBER 16 98 39 135	15. SELECTIVE SERVICE LOCAL BOARD NUMBER, CITY, COUNTY AND STATE LB #98, Baton Rouge (East Baton Rouge) La.	16. DATE INDUCTED: DAY NA MONTH YEAR
	17. DISTRICT OR AREA COMMAND TO WHICH RESERVIST TRANSFERRED Revert to ARNG of La.		

SERVICE DATA	18. TERMINAL DATE OF RESERVE OBLIGATION: DAY 30 MONTH Aug YEAR 67	19. CURRENT ACTIVE SERVICE OTHER THAN BY INDUCTION a. SOURCE OF ENTRY ☐ ENLISTED (First Enlistment) ☐ ENLISTED (Prior Service) ☐ REENLISTED ☑ OTHER: Ord to 6 Mos ACDUTRA	b. TERM OF SERVICE (Years) NA	c. DATE OF ENTRY: DAY 20 MONTH Jun YEAR 62

20. PRIOR REGULAR ENLISTMENTS None	21. GRADE, RATE OR RANK AT TIME OF ENTRY INTO CURRENT ACTIVE SERVICE	22. PLACE OF ENTRY INTO CURRENT ACTIVE SERVICE (City and State) Baton Rouge, La.

23. HOME OF RECORD AT TIME OF ENTRY INTO ACTIVE SERVICE	24. STATEMENT OF SERVICE		YEARS	MONTHS	DAYS
315 Lovers Lane Baton Rouge (East Baton Rouge) La.	CREDITABLE FOR BASIC PAY PURPOSES	(1) NET SERVICE THIS PERIOD	0	5	25
		(2) OTHER SERVICE	0	9	19
		(3) TOTAL (Line (1) + line (2))	3	3	14
25a. SPECIALTY NUMBER AND 120.00 Pioneer	b. RELATED CIVILIAN OCCUPATION AND D.O.T. NUMBER Equip Oper	c. TOTAL ACTIVE SERVICE	0	5	25
		d. FOREIGN AND/OR SEA SERVICE	0	0	0

26. DECORATIONS, MEDALS, BADGES, COMMENDATIONS, CITATIONS AND CAMPAIGN RIBBONS AWARDED OR AUTHORIZED
Expert (Rifle)
Parachutist Badge

27. WOUNDS RECEIVED AS A RESULT OF ACTION WITH ENEMY FORCES (Place and date, if known)
None

28. SERVICE SCHOOLS OR COLLEGES, COLLEGE TRAINING COURSES AND/OR POST-GRADUATE COURSES SUCCESSFULLY COMPLETED			29. OTHER SERVICE TRAINING COURSES SUCCESSFULLY COMPLETED
SCHOOL OR COURSE	DATES (From - To)	MAJOR COURSES	
None	NA	NA	ATP 21-114 Code of Cond Mil Justice Geneva Conv

VA DATA	30a. GOVERNMENT LIFE INSURANCE IN FORCE ☐YES ☑NO	b. AMOUNT OF ALLOTMENT NA	c. MONTH ALLOTMENT DISCONTINUED NA
	31a. VA BENEFITS PREVIOUSLY APPLIED FOR (Specify type) None	b. VA CLAIM NUMBER C- NA

32. REMARKS
Blood Group "O"   SSAN: 436 56 3353
RFA 55, 6 Mos ACDUTRA
Item 11A: Reld from AD & Ret to ARNG of La. to Complete remaining Svc
       obligation of 1 yr and 9 mos.
Lump sum payment made for 2 days accrued leave.

AUTHENTICATION	33. PERMANENT ADDRESS FOR MAILING PURPOSES AFTER TRANSFER OR DISCHARGE (Street, RFD, City, County and State) (See 23)	34. SIGNATURE OF PERSON BEING TRANSFERRED OR DISCHARGED
	35a. TYPED NAME, GRADE AND TITLE OF AUTHORIZING OFFICER AMOS J. ROGERS, Capt. Inf. Pers Off	b. SIGNATURE OF OFFICER AUTHORIZED TO SIGN

DD FORM 1 NOV 55 214   REPLACES EDITION OF 1 JUL 52, WHICH IS OBSOLETE.   ARMED FORCES OF THE UNITED STATES REPORT OF TRANSFER OR DISCHARGE   8

Barry Seal's military records

Just thought you would like to see my bunch. I'm on the 3rd or rather middle row, last man down.

Love

Barry

Secret Agent Man… Suave and debonair was how the image of the spy was marketed, through the James Bond movies; Barry acted accordingly.

Barry Seal's fortress-like CIA safe house in Baton Rouge

"**Where to, Jefe?**" With New Orleans' Jackson Square in the background, Seal waits for Mayor Victor Schiro and a still-unidentified man with the well-fed look of a Teamsters' union boss.

"**Known associates…**" Carlos Marcello lieutenant and Mob smuggling pilot Rene Martin.

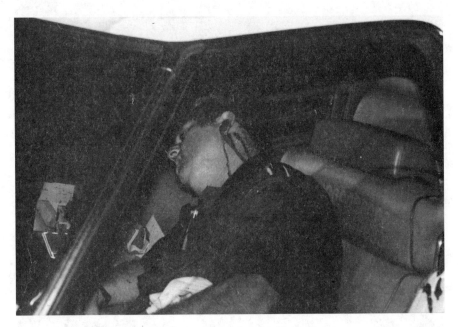

Seal's death, while brutal, was mercifully swift. Eyewitnesses said he saw it coming and put his head down on the steering wheel.

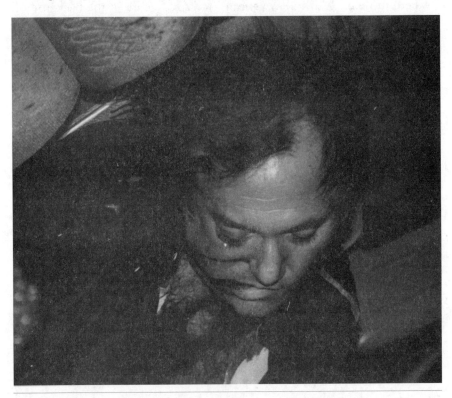

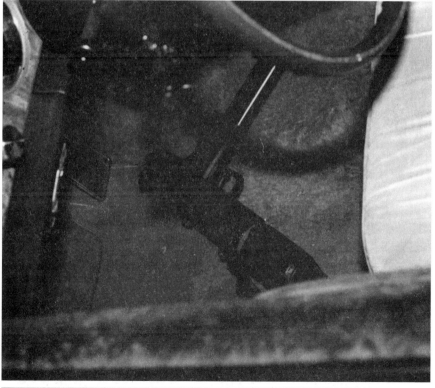

Barry at home.

STATE TIMES

FOUNDED 1842

143RD YEAR, NO. 44
BATON ROUGE, LA.
60 PAGES

T H U R S D A Y

FEB. 20, 1986
FINAL
25 CENTS

Seal's manner, flamboyance was rare in smugglers

His new life at Salvation Army was far cry from former lifestyle

By Edward Pratt/
State-Times writer

Three suspects in Seal murder are in custody

Confessed smuggler is gunned down at Salvation Army

By Steve Wheeler
and Edward Pratt/
State-Times writers

Three people are in custody today in Louisiana, Mississippi and Florida in connection with the machine gun killing of confessed drug smuggler Adler "Barry" Seal at the Salvation Army Center on Airline Highway Wednesday night, an FBI spokesman said.

FBI spokesman Ed Grimsley said one man is being held by authorities in Meridian, Miss., and another suspect is being held in Miami and one in New Orleans.

Seal's death was front page news all over the Southeast

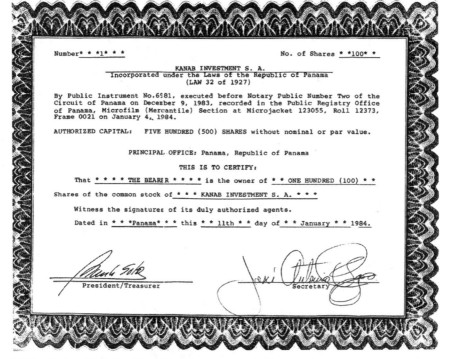

"Where they hide it all. . . in Panama, one of Seal's companies.

December 27, 1971

Mr. A. B. Seal
Box 64801
Baton Rouge, La. 70806

Dear Mr. Seal:

This will confirm our conversation in my office on December 23, 1971.

On December 20, 1971, you were assigned and accepted standby duty. You did not, however, make yourself available in accordance with standby duty. For that reason you will not be credited with standby pay or credit for that 48 hour period. Your assurance that this will not again occur is accepted.

As discussed, I must remind you that you are not to bring discredit to TWA through involvement in your personal affairs. I will expect confirmation of your handling of the other items discussed.

Very truly yours,

B. N. Williams
Manager – Pilots
JFK

cc: O. W. Elsner
C. M. Horstman

CERTIFIED MAIL – Return Receipt Requested

AROUND THE WORLD   U.S.A. • EUROPE • AFRICA • ASIA • PACIFIC

Strange TWA letter to its employee Seal in 1971.

August 10, 1977

AeroAmerica
777 Perimeter Road
Seattle, Washingtin 98108

Dear Sir:

I am holder of ATP Certificate Number 1351550 rating including
720 - 707, all models 747, most pilot-in-command in 707s, extensive
overwater experience in doppler, loran and inertial navigation.
Additionally, I am flight engineer qualified on all models of
707s and rated flight engineer on turbo jet and reciprocating
engines. I have flown extensively worldwide for TWA for approximately ten years but am not now employed. I have accummulated
over 15,000 accident-free hours with no violations.

I am 38 years old, in excellent health (overweight but am dieting)
with a current Class I physical; no smoking and no drinking and
am a current member in good standing with A.L.P.A. I am
married and have two children, college educated and business minded.
I have flown everything from J-3s to 747s and have 1500 hours in
helicopters.

I enjoy sky diving, hunting and jogging. I received an honorable
discharge from the 82nd Airborne Green Berets with a secret
clearance from the Department of Defense.

If you could send or call with general information on the basics;
salary range and type of flying, I will send a detailed resume.
I am only interested in pilot-in-command position please. Full
or parttime employment is acceptable and I am willing to relocate.

Sincerely,

ADLER B. SEAL
Post Office Box 64801
Baton Rouge, Louisiana 70816
Phone: (504) 389-0811 (24 hours)

Another day, another dummy front company... Note Seal's clearance.

ENTIN, SCHWARTZ, DION & SCLAFANI
ATTORNEYS AND COUNSELORS AT LAW

ESS PROFESSIONAL BUILDING
1500 NORTHEAST 162nd STREET
NORTH MIAMI BEACH, FLORIDA 33162
DADE. (305) 944 6556
BROWARD. (305) 921 6556

ALVIN E. ENTIN
SHELDON R. SCHWARTZ*
RONALD A. DION
THOMAS D. SCLAFANI**
JONATHAN B. BLECHER

OF COUNSEL
JOHN M. SPOTTSWOOD, JR.

Also admitted to the Bar of
*Washington, D.C.
**New York

REPLY TO
NORTH MIAMI BEACH OFFICE

October 11, 1984

416 FLEMING ST.
KEY WEST, FLORIDA 33040

2738 S. UNIVERSITY DRIVE
SUITE 15C
DAVIE, FLORIDA 33328

1105 HAYS STREET
TALLAHASSEE, FLORIDA 3230

Stanford O. Bardwell, Jr., Esquire
United States Attorney
Middle District of Louisiana
352 Florida Street, Second Floor
Baton Rouge, Louisiana 70801

EXPRESS MAIL

URGENT

Re: Adler Barry Seal

Dear Mr. Bardwell:

I have been advised by my client, Barry Seal, that he is being followed by federal and local law enforcement personnel at your direction. Aside from the harrassment that he is experiencing, Mr. Seal was yesterday placed in an apparent life-threatening situation because of the actions of one of your agents. It seems that Mr. Seal's secretary was followed to a local hotel in Baton Rouge and that one of your police officers was pointing an object that, from a distance, looked like a rifle toward the window of my client's hotel room. This is especially problematical given the fact that there is a $350,000.00 contract out on my client's life, which contract you have been made aware of weeks ago through our prior conversations.

As a result of these actions, my client, who lives in fear of his life, has today hired an armed licensed Louisiana private investigator to be with him at all times and to be with his family at those times when he is not home. The purpose of this letter is to put you and your agents on notice of this situation and to urgently request that you tell your agents and local police to refrain from harrassing my client, especially since either he or his bodyguard could very easily mistake one of your agents for a person seeking to execute the contract on Barry's life. The last thing my client needs is to be involved in a tragic incident.

Very truly yours,

THOMAS D. SCLAFANI

TDS/le

Smugglers blues…" Police surveillance of a convicted smuggler might be considered cost of doing business

Internal Revenue Service　　　　　　Department of the Treasury

District　　　　　　　　　　　　Address any reply to District
Director　　　　　　　　　　　　Director at office No. __2/Rm309D__

　　　　　　　　　　　　　　　　Person to Contact:
Mr. Adler B. Seal　　　　　　　Richard M. Kapouch
P. O. Box 64801　　　　　　　　Telephone Number:
Baton Rouge, LA 70896　　　　305-527-7034
　　　　　　　　　　　　　　　　Refer Reply to:
　　　　　　　　　　　　　　　　910
　　　　　　　　　　　　　　　　Date:
　　　　　　　　　　　　　　　　May 23, 1985

Dear Mr. Seal:

This office is currently assisting a Federal grand jury in their
investigation of Reginald Donald Whittington and William M. Whittington.
It has come to the grand jury's attention that you purchased a Lear jet
aircraft from General Credit Corporation, a Whittington company.

Kindly research your records and provide this office with photocopies of
any and all documents relating to this transaction, as well as any other
financial transactions you may have had with the Whittingtons or their
related companies. These records should include, but are not limited to,
sales contracts, bills of sale, correspondence and record of monies
received from or paid to the Whittingtons.

Your cooperation in this matter is greatly appreciated. If you have any
questions, do not hesitate to contact me at the above listed telephone
number or at the address indicated in Item 2 below.

　　　　　　　　　　　　　　Sincerely yours,

　　　　　　　　　　　　　　Richard M. Kapouch
　　　　　　　　　　　　　　Special Agent
　　　　　　　　　　　　　　Criminal Investigation Division

"**Our Lear jets go to those who need them…**" The previous 'owners' of the
Lear Seal later flew were two race-car drivers, the Whittington bothers, who
no longer needed the plane after they'd been caught

STATE OF ALABAMA

MOBILE COUNTY

Affidavit of Ernst Jacobsen

I am Special Agent Ernst Jacobsen. I personally participated in investigations involving Barry Seal and others when I was employed as a Special Agent with the Drug Enforcement Administration. I personally debriefed Seal after he decided to cooperate with the Government. I received no information from Seal which indicated that Ellis McKenzie was a drug smuggler. Seal told me that he had a business in McKenzie's name which owned a boat. He told me that McKenzie was a boat captain who did "go-fer" work for him. McKenzie took care of Seal's boats. Seal said he met McKenzie in Tegucigalpa in about 1981. Seal was involved in air-smuggling. Seal flew 35 to 50 loads by airplane. Seal did not utilize vessels for smuggling. Seal was attempting to establish a "sea lane" at the time he elected to cooperate with the Government, but this plan was not brought to fruition.

I met McKenzie twice in Cancun in about 1984 or 1985 through Seal. McKenzie knew I was a Government Agent at that time. I talked with McKenzie in Miami after Seal was killed. I told McKenzie I was moving to Alabama, and wanted him to work as an informant. I asked him to advise me of any contacts made to him by drug smugglers in Honduras. I instructed McKenzie that he could not violate any laws of the United States in making cases. I told him he could not "entrap" anybody. I explained to him that he could not put it in their minds to engage in illegal activity; he had to let them come to him. I did not conduct an initial debriefing of McKenzie. He did not have a contract with Customs or DEA; rather, he provided information on a case by case basis.

I do not recall any conversation in which McKenzie told me that he used drugs. Because Seal did not tolerate drug abuse by people around him, I did not believe that McKenzie would be a drug abuser, at least during the time he was associated with Seal. I have received information relating to McKenzie's alleged involvement with marijuana on two occasions. One was in 1987 when he loaned an M-16 rifle to someone. Another person was apparently killed and Honduran authorities searched for this weapon at McKenzie's residence. Honduran authorities allegedly found marijuana there and took McKenzie into custody for a short while. The other incident in which McKenzie was taken into custody involved a stop of his vehicle, when a gun and a small quantity of marijuana was allegedly recovered. To the best of my knowledge, McKenzie was not convicted of any offense in Honduras relating to either of these incidences.

The foregoing is true and correct to the best of my knowledge, information, and belief.

Ernst Jacobsen

Sworn to and subscribed before me this 31ˢᵗ day of August 1990

Notary

Universally considered by narcotics cops to have been operating on some other agenda, Seal's supposed DEA handler Jake Jacobsen stated—under oath—how little he knew of a man he'd vacationed with in Cancun.

Translation:

ARMED FORCES OF HONDURAS

11/20/89

TO: Mister
        Chief/4th Battalion; Infantry
        Colonel of Infantry DEM
        Sr. Erick Sanchez Sandoval
        His Office

RE: Report

1. This is to advise ? (superior) re. intelligence matters provided by one of our collaborators detailed as follows.

    a) VILORIO BARDALES (distributor of cocaine and mary). Cocaine provider ELLY McKENSY (dangerous), date case commenced 9/4/89 small quantities were purchased to establish relations.

       9/8/89. Lunch at "Captain Oso" rest. and negotiated for 1K of cocaine at 35,000.00 lps per K, leaving 5 days to confirm delivery in Roatan.

       9/16/89. Only 1/2 K confirmed. Delivery postponed for non-arrival from SPS.

       9/25/89. Dinner at the "Palace" rest. 1K of cocaine is again negotiated to be delivered 10/21/89. This is not accomplished because it doesn't arrive personally from SPS and because there is no contact with the bosses.

       10/27/89. Provider travels to U.S.A. and returns the week of 11/12. Product is found in provider's house. Relations with provider continue and have progressed with reference to confidence (trust).

       10/28/89. Trip to Sambo Creek with VILORIO BARDALES to family party (gathering).

       11/1/90. Trip to Trujillo with VILORIO BARDALES to meet friends* and arrive at agreement (reach agreement) to make one delivery.

       *to meet for the first time.

    b) RAMON CABRERA — Works in Dept. of Propaganda of Honduras Brewery. Cocaine distributor and basketball trainer.

    c) ANDRES CACERES — Ex-Chief of Security of HONDUTEL, has friendships with DNI agents, distributor of cocaine, was previously detained for selling cocaine. Presently distributor of cocaine, father is army official.

Ellias McKenzie was well known to the Honduran Army. .

~~~~~~

..t is unknown at this time if SCHOLER is involved with the operation in White Castle.

Barry and Wendell SEAL's plan of operation is the same as previously stated in the other MOIRs, only Barry and Wendell know when they are going to move large shipments of contraband by air. Barry will do the flying, and Wendell will set up ground operation by running counter-surveillance in the area where Barry would land his aircraft.

They have several airstrips available to themselves. These airstrips are located in Mississippi, Ryan Field in Baton Rouge, French Settlement (See MOIR NOZZDI1L0039), and White Castle. Barry is also looking to build another airstrip somewhere north of Baton Rouge.

Barry SEAL's Rent-A-Sign business has been closed since November 1981, but he maintains two employees that live in his office building and two secretaries. Although Barry does not do any business out of this office, he spends several hours a day there. Wendell drops by the office approximately once a week for a few hours.

Wendell and Barry have a camp on Lake Salvador, LA, where people have reported seeing helicopters landing in the back of the camp and seaplanes landing on the lake. Both Barry and R. T. LEBLANC have licenses to operate a seaplane.

It is believed that Wendell and Barry, with the aid of LEBLANC, will attempt to move a large shipment of contraband in southern Louisiana in the near future. The exact time and location is not known at this time. Additional information will follow when it becomes available.

<u>ACTION TAKEN:</u> Notified Air Support Branch, NOLA and briefed Customs Air Officer Clyde McCoy on the situation. CF 4621 initiated.

<u>INVESTIGATION REQUESTED:</u> DEA, OI and ASB are requested to supply any available information. Ongoing Patrol Case.

<u>OFFICE INDICES QUERIED:</u> Positive

<u>ACTION TO BE TAKEN BY OES/TECS:</u> None. Update will be made by this officer.

<u>RELIABILITY OF SOURCE:</u> Generally Reliable.

<u>INFORMATION EVALUATION:</u> Plausible

<u>IDENTIFYING DATA/TECS QUERY:</u>

SEAL/Berriman/Adler   ALLEGED C-9   SYSIDNO: 137951
W/M, DPOB: 071639/Baton Rouge, LAUS
5'10", 190 lbs
HAIR: BR, EYES: GR
ADD: 1. 1201 W. Foster Drive Apt 2181/Baton Rouge/LAUS
     2. 2100 College Apt. 200/Baton Rouge/LAUS
L: LAUS/221828
SN: 436-56-3533
PH NO: (504) 287-3369, (504) 927-9300, (504) 377-3889, (504) 377-6453-Pager

Sample law enforcement report on Seal's smuggling in the early 1980's reveals what an open secret his activities were.

BRITISH ≡ CONSULATE
APARTADO NUM. 89
MERIDA, YUC., MEXICO

T O W H M   I T   M A Y   C O N C E R N
==

     This is to certify that on the 24th of November
1984, a MR. ELLIS McKENSIE came to see me personally at
this Consulate, to say that he was the Capt. of the
M.V "CAPT WONDERFULL", Registered at GRAND CAIMAN No
702488, which was under repair in the Port of Yucalpeten
Progreso; and to complain that the Delegado Regional del
Registro Federal de Vehiculos in Merida, wasd imposing
a fine of $10,000.00 U.S. Dollars for alleged violations
to their regulations; and that he had been threattenned
with the search of the vessel for carrying illegal cargo,
implicating drugs, and that it would be better for all
concerned for him to pay the fine.

     I did not see Mr. McKensie again, as apparently
he had been thoroughly frightened and left Mexico.

     Given on the 3rd of ~~May~~ JUNE 1985 at the request of
MR. ALFRED D MCDANIEL and MR. PETER EVERSON, representatives
of the M.V. "CAPT. WONDERFULL" this day.

Alfred Dutton
Hon. British Consul.

Records like this reveal a huge operation underway by mid-1984
using bases in Mexico's Yucatan.

QUAN.	PARTS	PRICE	
1	Attennuator Str. crewsdoor+ earp. door	100 00	
2	volt amp meter	370 00	
	Aeroshell oil	1219 82	
12	A-8008-1-331 pool lights	201 00	
1	Null unit	210 00	
1	35-5011-1 VOR Antenna	354 85	
4	Assemb+ arm light Grimes	110 40	
	Angles M. Lambert + B. Hall Limetree Inn	302 43	
1	RMI Converter		
1	Battery box contactor	126 00	

RMA
RICH MOUNTAIN AVIATION
FRED L. HAMPTON
STAR ROUTE 9, BOX 6C · (501) 394-3124
MENA, ARKANSAS 71953
REPAIR STATION 206-35

Insurance Co.

Date 12-3-84

Name Seala

Phone Number

Address

N-Number N-6518

City

Make & Model

Repair Description: Labor to repair aircraft 77.37 hours @ $28.00 an hour.

Work Order N? 228

		Amount
	Total Parts	2964 50

#	OUTSIDE WORK	AMOUNT
1	RMI Convertor - sent out to be repaired	180 00
1	RMI Indicator - sent out to be repaired	↓
1	X-Ray wings + travel time	1,274 50
	TOTAL OUTSIDE WORK	1,454 50

Total Labor	2,166 36
Total Parts	2964 50
Outside Work	1,454 50
Freight	89 72
Gas & Oil	
Tax	
Total Amount	6,675 08

A sample of the thousands of aircraft maintenance receipts in CIA
aircraft procurement executive Seal's files.

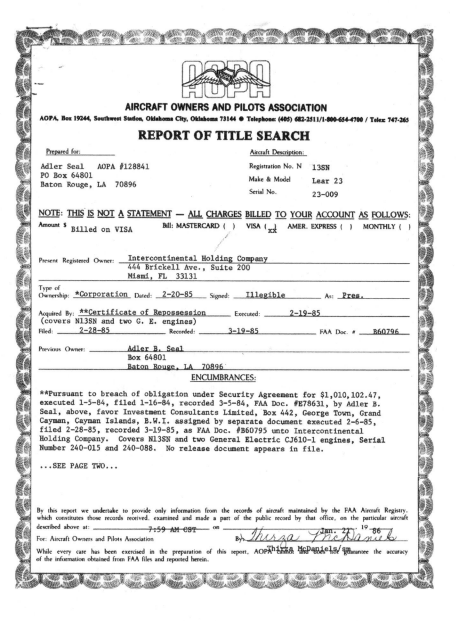

AIRCRAFT OWNERS AND PILOTS ASSOCIATION

AOPA, Box 19244, Southwest Station, Oklahoma City, Oklahoma 73144 ● Telephone: (405) 682-2511/1-800-654-4700 / Telex: 747-265

REPORT OF TITLE SEARCH

Prepared for:

Adler Seal   AOPA #128841
PO Box 64801
Baton Rouge, LA 70896

Aircraft Description:

Registration No. N 13SN

Make & Model Lear 23

Serial No. 23-009

NOTE: THIS IS NOT A STATEMENT — ALL CHARGES BILLED TO YOUR ACCOUNT AS FOLLOWS:

Amount $ Billed on VISA   Bill: MASTERCARD ( ) VISA (xx) AMER. EXPRESS ( ) MONTHLY ( )

Present Registered Owner: Intercontinental Holding Company
444 Brickell Ave., Suite 200
Miami, FL 33131

Type of
Ownership: *Corporation Dated: 2-20-85 Signed: Illegible As: Pres.

Acquired By: **Certificate of Repossession Executed: 2-19-85
(covers N13SN and two G. E. engines)
Filed: 2-28-85 Recorded: 3-19-85 FAA Doc. # B60796

Previous Owner: Adler B. Seal
Box 64801
Baton Rouge, LA 70896

ENCUMBRANCES:

**Pursuant to breach of obligation under Security Agreement for $1,010,102.47,
executed 1-5-84, filed 1-16-84, recorded 3-5-84, FAA Doc. #E78631, by Adler B.
Seal, above, favor Investment Consultants Limited, Box 442, George Town, Grand
Cayman, Cayman Islands, B.W.I. assigned by separate document executed 2-6-85,
filed 2-28-85, recorded 3-19-85, as FAA Doc. #B60795 unto Intercontinental
Holding Company. Covers N13SN and two General Electric CJ610-1 engines, Serial
Number 240-015 and 240-088. No release document appears in file.

...SEE PAGE TWO...

By this report we undertake to provide only information from the records of aircraft maintained by the FAA Aircraft Registry.
which constitutes those records received. examined and made a part of the public record by that office, on the particular aircraft
described above at: 7:59 AM CST on Jan. 22, 19 86
For: Aircraft Owners and Pilots Association By Thirza McDaniel
While every care has been exercised in the preparation of this report, AOPA cannot and does not guarantee the accuracy
of the information obtained from FAA files and reported herein. Thirza McDaniel/sm

Barry Seal's CIA Lear-jet was repossessed by a Paul Helliwell front company.

JENNINGS, STROUSS & SALMON
COUNSELLORS AND ATTORNEYS AT LAW
III WEST MONROE
PHOENIX, ARIZONA 85003
TELEPHONE (602) 262-5911

CHARLES L. STROUSS (1891-1958)
RINEY B. SALMON (1902-1970)
IRVING A. JENNINGS (1899-1972)

CLARENCE J. DUNCAN
OF COUNSEL

May 5, 1981

WRITER'S DIRECT LINE

262-5852

ARIZONA CORPORATION COMMISSION
Incorporating Division
1210 West Washington
Phoenix, Arizona 85007

1 0 2 3 6 7 7 - 6

Re: Continental Desert Properties, an
Arizona corporation

Gentlemen:

I, LEE E. ESCH, having been designated to act as Statutory
Agent, hereby consent to act in that capacity until renewal or
resignation is submitted in accordance with the Arizona Revised
Statutes.

Lee E. Esch

LEE:bw

Current Arizona Senator John Kyl was a partner in the politically-connected law firm which helped put together dummy companies used in massive drug smuggling

OPCA-20 (12-3-96)

XXXXXX
XXXXXX
XXXXXX

FEDERAL BUREAU OF INVESTIGATION
FOIPA
DELETED PAGE INFORMATION SHEET

_4_ Page(s) withheld entirely at this location in the file. One or more of the following statements, where indicated, explain this deletion.

☒ Deletions were made pursuant to the exemptions indicated below with no segregable material available for release to you.

Section 552		Section 552a
☒ (b)(1)	☐ (b)(7)(A)	☐ (d)(5)
☐ (b)(2)	☐ (b)(7)(B)	☐ (j)(2)
☒ (b)(3)	☐ (b)(7)(C)	☐ (k)(1)
National Security Act of	☐ (b)(7)(D)	☐ (k)(2)
1947 and CIA Act of	☐ (b)(7)(E)	☐ (k)(3)
_1949._	☐ (b)(7)(F)	☐ (k)(4)
☐ (b)(4)	☐ (b)(8)	☐ (k)(5)
☐ (b)(5)	☐ (b)(9)	☐ (k)(6)
☐ (b)(6)		☐ (k)(7)

☐ Information pertained only to a third party with no reference to the subject of your request or the subject of your request is listed in the title only.

☐ Documents originated with another Government agency(ies). These documents were referred to that agency(ies) for review and direct response to you.

_____ Pages contain information furnished by another Government agency(ies). You will be advised by the FBI as to the releasability of this information following our consultation with the other agency(ies).

_____ Page(s) withheld inasmuch as a final release determination has not been made. You will be advised as to the disposition at a later date.

_____ Pages were not considered for release as they are duplicative of _____

_____ Page(s) withheld for the following reason(s): _per letter of 1|11|99._

☒ The following number is to be used for reference regarding these pages:
_245-76-128 X_

XXXXXXXXXXXXXXXX
X   Deleted Page(s)   X
X   No Duplication Fee   X
X   for this page   X
XXXXXXXXXXXXXXXX

XXXXXX
XXXXXX
XXXXXX

FBI/DOJ

Last page of Nazi Klaus Barbie's Freedom of Information Act files, indicating pages were being withheld... **by the DEA.**

INVESTIGATION REPORT

NEW ORLEANS, LOUISIANA   ACCESS COI

TITLE	DATE OF REPORT	FILE NUMBER
GUY PENILTON OWEN ETAL	031883	NOGPDO3(
	CUSTOMS DISTRICT	
N90201	South Central Region	
	PERIOD OF INVESTIGATION	
	May 9, 1983 to Present	
	DATE OF ASSIGNMENT	CASE STATUS
	May 9, 1983	☒ OPEN ☐
	VIOLATION	
	21 USC 952	

CHARACTER OF INVESTIGATION

Narcotics Smuggling Alleged

OFFICES OF ORIGINATION AND RELATED FILE NUMBER(s)

MOAADT3M0035 - MIZZDI6f0084 - COJUDS1L0052 - JXAWDS1L0158
TAZZDI260216 - SVEWDS9L2521 - MS32BR994017 - NOBODS1L0197

SYNOPSIS

On 050883 Aircraft N90201 arrived at the Mobil, Alabama Airpor
where it cleared Customs and proceeded to Jackson, Mississipp

Subsequent investigation by the reporting officer has revealed
that Aircraft N90201 is part of a large narcotics smuggling
organization operating in the United States, Honduras, Costa I
and Colombia.

PROPERTY OF THE U. S. CUSTOMS SERVICE

This document is for the confidential and exclusive
use of law enforcement agencies. It is loaned to you
by and remains the property of the U.S. Customs Service
It contains neither recommendations nor conclusions of
U. S. Customs. Neither it nor its contents is to be
distributed outside the agency to which it is loaned.

DISTRIBUTION		SIGNATURE of officer
RDP/NOLA AOB/HDQ ALL/AOB		
SECTOR V INTEL AI/NOLA		Luis A. Nunez CAO
		Floyd Lacewell ASCAO

Office of ...   South Central Region

1983 US Customs report revealed Seal was smuggling in partnership with
CIA asset Juan Matta Ballesteros

285

- 7 -

Case # NOGBDQ3000036
Guy OWEN ETAL

4. Darrell Reynolds has been under investigation by the
    Customs Service for narcotics smuggling in Missouri
    and New Orleans.

on interviewing U. S. Customs Intelligence Officer Harvey
.es of the New Orleans office it was found that on 112181
uy Owen arrived at the New Orleans International Airport from
;an Pedro Sula, Honduras on board a Beech SNB-5 aircraft bearing
FAA registration N222EL. A customs search of the aircraft was
conducted with the aid of a narcotic detector dog. During the
inspection, the dog had a positive reaction indicating that
narcotic substances had recently been present in the plane.

Officer Hues further advised the investigating officer that the
Customs Intelligence Unit had received information from Captain
Michael Bryan of the Louisiana State Police Intelligence Division
in New Orleans also implicating Guy Owen with narcotics smuggling.

On 051883 at 1130 hours, the investigating officer contacted Captain
Michael Bryan who stated that on September of 1982, he had received
information from a highly reliable source that N90201 had been
purchased by Atlas Aviation and was in route to La Ceiba,. Honduras
where it would be outfitted with auxiliary tanks. Upon completion
of the alterations, the aircraft would be utilized to smuggle narcotics into the United States. Captain Bryan further added that
according to the informant arrangements had been made to airdrop
large quantities of marijuana and cocaine at an isolated farm near
Baton Rouge, Louisiana. The farm's address Rt. 6, Box 282E in
East Baton Rouge, Louisiana belonging to Adler.B. Seal and
Wendell K. Seal both allegedly major narcotic smugglers and distri-
butors throughout the eastern and southern United States.

The investigating officer was able to obtain copies of Guy
Penilton Owen telephone tolls for the year of 1981 through the
Mississippi Bureau of Narcotics Agent Norton. The tolls were
submitted through TELAN (Telephone Analysis) and revealed that
Guy Owen had called 912-638-3191 which is listed to Bill Walker
and Associates, address of 2606 Frederica Rd., St. Simons, GA.
William Qualy Walker is a well documented narcotics smuggler.

On 051583 the reporting officer met with Agent Dick Boyles of th
Drug Enforcement Administration in Jackson, Mississippi who state
that his office had previously received information from various
sources indicating that Jim Hankins and Guy Owen were involved in
narcotics smuggling by aircraft. Agent Boyles added that survei-
'--ce cameras had been installed at Hankins Aviation by Hankins

Some of the many 'front' companies with which Barry Seal did business. Many had 'cute' names with inside-the-Agency allusions.

AIRCRAFT
OWNERS
AND
PILOTS
ASSOCIATION

REPLY TO: AOPA, Box 19244, Southwest Station,
Oklahoma City, Oklahoma 73144
Telephone: (405) 682-2511 / Telex: 747-265
or: 1-800-654-4700

January 21, 1986

Adler Seal
PO Box 64801
Baton Rouge, LA 70896

RE: N13SN
     Lear 23
     SN: 23-009
     Partial Chain of Lien - 1980 - 1985

Dear Mr. Seal:

A review of the FAA records, as those records pertain to that certain
aircraft described above, revealed as of 7:59 AM CST on January 21, 1986,
the state of the records is as follows:

Conditional Sale Contract for $604,000.00 executed 9-12-78, filed 10-23-78
recorded 11-3-78, FAA Doc. #X067854, by E.C.E. Corporation, 130 Sowers St.,
State College, PA 16801, favor Sana Air, Inc., PO Box 726, Toms River, NJ
08753. (Covers N13SN and two General Electric engines).

Release of Doc. #X067854 by Sana Air Inc., executed 9-29-81, filed 2-24-83,
recorded 4-20-83, FAA Doc. #U69425.

Security Agreement for $1,010,102.47, executed 1-5-84, filed 1-16-84,
recorded 3-5-84, FAA Doc. #E78631, by Adler B. Seal, PO Box 64801, Baton
Rouge, LA 70896, favor Investment Consultants Limited, PO Box 442, George
Town, Grand Cayman, Cayman Islands, B.W.I. Assigned under separate document
unto Intercontinental Holding Company, executed 2-6-85, filed 2-28-85,
recorded 3-19-85, FAA Doc. #B60795. (Covers N13SN and two General Electric
Engines).

Certificate of Repossession of Doc. #E78631 by Investment Consultants
Ltd. executed 2-19-85, filed 2-28-85, recorded 5-19-85, FAA Doc. #B60796.

"Biggie's Getting Set to Talk." One of the many plane ownership records
requested by Seal... just before his killing.

mb

INVOICE

PLEASE SHOW THIS
INVOICE NUMBER 44868
WHEN REMITTING.

ElectroSonics Division of AiRadio Corporation
PORT COLUMBUS INTERNATIONAL AIRPORT
Box 19767, Columbus, Ohio 43219

Telephone:
(614) 236-8531

NOT PLANES

SOLD TO	SHIP TO

Carlo Medina
Lima, Peru

DC 5/18

SHIP VIA	YOUR ORDER NO.	SALESMEN HALL	TERMS COD	DATE 4/29/82

☐ 90 DAY WARR. ☐ LIFETIME INSTALL. WARR. ☐ ONE YEAR INSTALL. WARR.   PLEASE SEE REVERSE SIDE FOR FINANCE CHARGES AND WARRANTY

QUAN.	PART NO.	DESCRIPTION	UNIT PRICE	AMOUNT
		Line Service – Navajo N7409L	$145.21	
		Line Service – Navajo N7409L	82.59	
		Line Service – Seneca N8658E	171.12	
		Line Service – Seneca N8658E	176.53	
		Line Service – Seneca N8658E	146.89	
		Total Line Service	$722.34	

☐ DEALER SALE ☐ SHIP OUT SALE ☐ OFF AIRPORT DELIVERY ☐ AIRPORT TAXABLE SALE
Ownership of the above delivered property, exclusive of repaired items and repaired parts, remains with ElectroSonics until fully paid for.

FAA REPAIR STATION 1009

The War of '82. When the boys went to war in Central America in April, 1982, Seal spent millions in cash on planes

R I C H · M O U N T A I N · A V I A T I O N, I N C.
FRED L. HAMPTON, PRESIDENT

BARRY SEAL

STATEMENT OF ACCOUNT

AS OF 1/28/86

WORK ORDERS	DOLLARS
442	(403.01)
523	443.59
524	229.78
525	226.85
531	180.78
543	2,252.70
551	195.40
565	187.40
570	161.22
574	787.09
579	194.20
584	379.63
534	12,018.52
598	465.92
599	817.88
TOTAL	18,137.95
Less payment of 1/18/86	5,000.00
BALANCE DUE AS OF THIS DATE	$13,137.95
Less payment for fuel billed on wo 534	982.08
BALANCE DUE AS OF 1/29/86	$12,155.87

INTERMOUNTAIN REGIONAL AIRPORT · ROUTE 1, BOX 294M · MENA, ARKANSAS 71953 · (501) 394-3124
AIRCRAFT REPAIR AND MODIFICATION · FAA REPAIR STATION #206-35

Active to the Bitter End. Law enforcement noticed no cessation or even slowing down of Seal's smuggling organization in the months before he died.

BEN-VENISTE & SHERNOFF

ATTORNEYS AT LAW

SUITE 400
4801 MASSACHUSETTS AVENUE, N. W.
WASHINGTON, D. C. 20016

(202) 966-6000

RICHARD BEN-VENISTE*
WILLIAM M. SHERNOFF**

———

PETER D. ISAKOFF*

———

*ALSO ADMITTED IN NEW YORK
**ADMITTED IN CALIFORNIA ONLY

April 23, 1984

EXPRESS MAIL

Mr. Barry Seal
Post Office Box 64801
Baton Rouge, Louisiana   70896

Dear Barry:

I have attempted to reach you by telephone over the last two weeks, leaving several messages, and have in addition left word with both Jon Sale and ████████ to pass along my request that you phone me. Obviously, there has been some breakdown in communications.

As matters stand, sentencing before Judge Roettger has been continued until May 3, 1984, at 2:00 p.m. While we did not discuss this adjournment personally, I have been advised by both Jon Sale and ████████ that it was a priority request on your part to get this adjournment, even though I advised Jon and ███ that I may well be unable to represent you at sentencing on May 3 inasmuch as depositions in California have been set up for that week. Jon Sale advised me that you were aware of this time conflict on my part but still wished to get the continuance until May 3, even though it might mean that Jon or ███ would represent you at sentencing instead of me.

Both ███ and Jon have discussed with me certain matters in your pre-sentence report that require correction. I am advised that ███ and Jon will handle that matter directly, either by motion, letter or oral presentation at the time of sentencing. I have mentioned to you both after your conviction and from time to time thereafter that it would be helpful to you to have various persons -- preferably clergymen or other respected members of your community -- write to Judge Roettger on your behalf in connection with sentencing. To date, I have not been advised that any such letters have been sent. I repeat that it would be a good idea to have such letters, if they could be obtained, delivered to the Court prior to sentencing.

I have mentioned several times that I would appreciate your returning my two briefcases of legal materials which you have been holding as soon as possible. These materials may be

Mr. Barry Seal
April 23, 1984
Page 2

important in connection with my providing legal assistance to you
or any lawyers who you should subsequently retain in connection
with any aspect of the trial before Judge Roettger.

Please give me a call as soon as possible so that we
may discuss these and other matters and insure that all your
legal needs are served as best as can be.

Best regards,

Very truly yours,

Richard Ben-Veniste

RB:cr

cc: Jon Sale, Esquire
     ███████, Esquire

The real secret history. Barry Seal and Democratic powerbroker and Mob
lawyer Richard Ben-Veniste fencing over who will 'go down' first.

Rollins Burdick Hunter of Kansas, Inc.
Mid-Continent Airport, P. O. Box 9210, Wichita, Kansas 67277
Telephone 800 835-2677 or (Kansas) 316 943-9331
Cable Airsure, Telex 417407

Formerly   Don Flower Associates, Inc.

Mr. Adler B. Seal
P.O. Box 64801
Baton Rouge, LA   70896

March 30, 1983

Reference: Policy 97GW-53309
             1982 King Air 200, N-1860B
             1982 King Air 200, N-6308F

Dear Barry:

We are now pleased to enclose your insurance policy covering
the above aircraft which replaces the temporary evidence of
coverage previously forwarded. Please read it carefully to
be certain the coverage is exactly as desired. Pay particular attention to the sections regarding approved pilots and
uses to be sure they meet the necessary requirements.

Appropriate Certificates of Insurance have been forwarded to
Baton Rouge Aircraft, Greycas Inc., Beechcraft Acceptance
Corporation, Continental Desert Properties, and Greyhound
Leasing Inc. for their records.

In the event the policy is not correct in every detail,
please notify us at once. We appreciate this opportunity
to again be of service.

Sincerely yours,

B. Don Wineinger
/sb

Enclosure

P.S.   Please find attached our credit memorandum in the amount
of $76.00 which we ask you to subtract from the balance out-
standing of $21,265.00. This credit represents a correction
in premium respects the addition of Charter Use.

Two Operation Seaspray King Air's were operated by Seal's organization.

Baton Rouge Aircraft, Inc.

BATON ROUGE METROPOLITAN AIRPORT
AT RYAN FIELD
BATON ROUGE, LOUISIANA 70807-4084
TEL: (504) 357-6471

AIRCRAFT LEASE - SHARED USAGE

THIS LEASE is entered into this __21st__ day of __March__ ,19__83__ , between__ Continental Desert Properties, Inc.__ ,hereinafter called "Lessor", and __Baton Rouge Aircraft, Inc.__ , hereinafter called "Lessee".

The parties hereto, in consideration of the mutal promises and conditions expressed herein, agree as follows:

1. AIRPLANE. Lessor does hereby lease unto Lessee, and Lessee does hereby lease from Lessor, the following described airplane:

Manufacturer of Airplane: Beech Aircraft Corporation
Model:__ 200__ Serial No:__BB-1014__ Reg.No:__N6308F__
Engine Make: __PT6A-42__
Equipment and Accessories therein

hereinafter called "the Airplane".

2. TERM. The term of this lease shall begin at 12:01 O'Clock AM C.S.T. on the __21st__ day of __March__ ,19__83__ , and end at 11:59 O'Clock PM on the __21st__ day of__ March__ ,19__84__ or at an earlier date as provided herein. Either party may terminate this lease by giving the other party __30__ days written notice.

3. RENT. Lessee shall pay to Lessor as rent for the Airplane $ __500.00__ for each hour flown by Lessee or its sublessees as recorded on a Hobbs hourmeter or the tachometer if there is no Hobbs hourmeter installed on the Airplane. The rent shall be paid by the 20th of each month for the hours flown in the month prior. Lessor agrees that there is no minimum monthly rent, that Lessee has not represented an amount of rent to be expected from this lease.

4. OPERATION.

4.1 The Airplane will be permanently based at__ ✓ __ __Ryan Airport__ and will be returned to Lessor by Lessee at such airport

4.2 Lessee shall have complete use of the Airplane except as set forth in Section 4.5 and except that Lessee will not use, operate, maintain or store the Airplane unsafely, improperly, carelessly, or in violation of this Lease or of any applicable law or regulation, Federal or State.

4.3 The Airplane will not be operated any place beyond the continental limits of the United States of America.

4.4 Lessee agrees that Lessee is leasing the Airplane for the purpose of:

(a) Subleasing to others
xxxxxxxxxxxxxxxxxxxxx
(c) Charter
(d) Demonstration
xxxxxxxxxx

Records of a famous plane. . . Seal's King Air 200

Enter the hall of mirrors… Systems Marketing Inc. is itself a front for a company called Military Electronics.

DEPARTMENT OF TRANSPORTATION
FEDERAL AVIATION ADMINISTRATION

FORM APPROVED
OMB NO. 2120-00XX
EXP. DATE 6/30/89

THIS FORM SERVES TWO PURPOSES
PART I acknowledges the recording of a security conveyance covering the collateral shown.
PART II is a suggested form of release which may be used to release the collateral from the terms of the conveyance.

PART I – CONVEYANCE RECORDATION NOTICE

NAME (last name first) OF DEBTOR

merrill BeanChevrolet Inc

NAME and ADDRESS OF SECURED PARTY/ASSIGNEE

General Electric Credit Corp.
2260 S. Xanadu Way Suite 330
Aurora, Colo

NAME OF SECURED PARTY'S ASSIGNOR (if assigned)

X I I 3 0 0 6

CONVEYANCE RECORDED

MAY I 0 21 AM 90

FEDERAL AVIATION ADMINISTRATION

Do Not Write In This Block
FOR FAA USE ONLY

FAA REGISTRA-TION NUMBER	AIRCRAFT SERIAL NUMBER	AIRCRAFT MFR. (BUILDER) and MODEL
6308F	*BB-1014*	*Beech B200*

ENGINE MFR. and MODEL	ENGINE SERIAL NUMBER(S)
Pratt + Whitney PT6A-42	*93363* *93364*

PROPELLER MFR. and MODEL	PROPELLER SERIAL NUMBER(S)

SEE RECORDED CONVEYANCE
NUMBER *K 5731/2*
FICHE # *B-4* PAGE # *15-15*

THE SECURITY CONVEYANCE DATED *6-14-84* COVERING THE ABOVE COLLATERAL WAS RECORDED BY THE FAA AIRCRA
ISTRY ON *7-10-84* AS CONVEYANCE NUMBER *K 57312*

Bresley Crum
FAA CONVEYANCE EXAMINER

PART II – RELEASE – (This suggested release form may be executed by the secured party and returned to the FAA Aircraft Regist terms of the conveyance have been satisfied. See below for additional information.)

THE UNDERSIGNED HEREBY CERTIFIES AND ACKNOWLEDGES THAT HE IS THE TRUE AND LAWFUL HOLDER C NOTE OR OTHER EVIDENCE OF INDEBTEDNESS SECURED BY THE CONVEYANCE REFERRED TO HEREIN ON THE DESCRIBED COLLATERAL AND THAT THE SAME COLLATERAL IS HEREBY RELEASED FROM THE TERMS O CONVEYANCE. ANY TITLE RETAINED IN THE COLLATERAL BY THE CONVEYANCE IS HEREBY SOLD, GRANTED, FERRED, AND ASSIGNED TO THE PARTY WHO EXECUTED THE CONVEYANCE, OR TO THE ASSIGNEE OF SAID IF THE CONVEYANCE SHALL HAVE BEEN ASSIGNED; PROVIDED, THAT NO EXPRESS WARRANTY IS GIVEN NOR IN BY REASON OF EXECUTION OR DELIVERY OF THIS RELEASE.

This form is only intended to be a suggested form of release, which meets the recording requirements of the Federal Aviation Act of 1958, and the regulations issued thereunder. In addition to these requirements, the form used by the security holder should be drafted in accordance with the pertinent provisions of local statutes and other applicable federal statutes. This form may be reproduced. There is no fee for recording a release. Send to FAA Aircraft Registry, P.O. Box 25504, Oklahoma City, Oklahoma 73125.

ACKNOWLEDGEMENT (If Required By Applicable Local Law)

DATE OF RELEASE: *10-3-89*

General Electric Credit Corporation
(Name of security holder)

SIGNATURE (in ink) *Cheryl A. Falk*

TITLE *Mgr. Acct. Admin*

(A person signing for a corporation must be a corporate office hold a managerial position and must show his title. A person sig for another should see Parts 47 and 49 of the Federal Aviation F lations (14 CFR).

AC Form 8050-11 (7-83)

U.S. GOVERNMENT PRINTING OFFICE: 1983-678-9

King air 'cutout' and paper owner Merrill Bean was also part of Iran Contra financial fraud.

CERTIFICATE OF INSURANCE

Date __October 11, 1983__

This is to certify to: __Daniel and Robin Click__
P. O. Box 571
Palm Desert, California 92261

That the following policies have been issued to: __S. F. O. Helicopters, Inc.__
P. O. Box 6789
Oakland, California 94603

ITEM 1. Aircraft Liability Policy No. __AV987-3279__ of the __National Union Fire Insurance Company__
Policy Period: from __August 5, 1983__ to __August 5, 1984__

Coverage		Limits of Liability	
Bodily Injury (Excluding Passengers)	$_____	Each Person $_____	Each Occurrence
Passenger Bodily Injury	$_____	Each Person $_____	Each Occurrence
Property Damage		$_____	Each Occurrence

Single Limit Bodily Injury and Property Damage
☐ Excluding Passengers
☒ Including Passengers $ 20,000,000.00   Each Occurrence

ITEM 2. Airport Liability Policy No. _____ of the _____
Policy Period: from _____ to _____

Coverage		Limits of Liability	
Bodily Injury	$_____	Each Person $_____	Each Occurrence
Property Damage		$_____	Each Occurrence
Single Limit Bodily Injury and Property Damage		$_____	Each Occurrence

ITEM 3. Workmen's Compensation Policy No. _____ of the _____
Policy Period: from _____ to _____
Limits of Liability: Statutory
Coverage B — Employers' Liability: _____

ITEM 4. OTHER INSURANCE AS DESCRIBED: Owner/Lessor is included as an additional insured.
Aircraft: 1976 Bell 206B III, N1219W
Insured Value: $200,000.00
Amount of Lien: $125,000.00
Deductibles: $500.00 Rotors Not In Motion/$10,000.00 Rotors In Motion

This Certificate of Insurance neither affirmatively nor negatively amends, alters or extends the coverage(s) afforded by the policy(ies) described above.

The Aviation Managers have made provision for prompt notice to you in the event of cancellation of the above described policies but, except as otherwise stated in this certificate, the Aviation Managers assume no legal responsibility for any failure to do so.
*30 days (10 days for non payment)

JG:at

☐ Southeastern Aviation Underwriters, Inc.
☒ Southeastern Aviation (California) Insurance Services
  Division of Southeastern Aviation Underwriters, Inc.
☐ Southeastern Aviation (Texas), Inc.
☐ Southeastern Aviation (Illinois) Corp.

(SPECIAL CONDITIONS, if any, on reverse)

AV-37 (1-80)

By _____
Authorized Representative

Some of Seal's helicopters were 'converted' into paying assets.

INVESTMENT CONSULTANTS LIMITED

TELEPHONE: (809) 94 94316
CABLES: CONSULGRAM
TELEX: CP 4351 ANSWERBACK CONSUL

P. O. BOX 442
KIRK FREEPORT BUILDING
CARDINAL AVENUE
GEORGE TOWN, GRAND CAYMAN
CAYMAN ISLANDS, B.W.I.

January 25th 1984.

Mr. A. B. Seal,
P. O. Box 64801,
Baton Rouge,
La. 70896,
U. S. A.

Dear Sir,

Further to telephoned request enclosed for your records are copies of the following documents:-

1. Aircraft registration application ref N 13 S N (Lear) and dated December 15th 1983.

2. Aircraft bills of sale dated 1st December 1982 and 1st September, 1982.

3. Cancelled note (ref FL8210) dated October 18th 1982.

4. Replacement notes, three in number (references FL8401, FL8401A, FL8401B) and dated January 5th 1984.

The personal insurance coverage discussed required a premium of US$4,644.00 (Policy # ETL - 811223-9) and look forward to receiving your check by return.

I would also take this opportunity to remind you that the monthly payments must be paid expeditiously allowing time for clearance and subsequent credit. You will appreciate our position in this matter.

A separate statement of the out of pocket expenses etc., will be forwarded under separate cover.

Yours faithfully,

G. H. Aiton.
Director.

CIA legend Paul Helliwell, using Gordon Aiton as his cutout and Cayman Island minion, was the true owner of Seal's Lear jet.

Seal handwritten notes on a huge California operation importing tons of cocaine through Newport Beach and an airport near Edwards Air Force Base.

The Smoking Gun? Note in Seal's own handwriting linking Democratic National Committee Chairman Charles Manatt with Iran Contra 'cutout' Gene Glick.

October 23, 1985

Mr. Barry Seals
2391 North Street
Baton Rouge, Louisiana   70802

Dear Barry:

Enclosed please find chart of the Cocos Islands that I copied
off the master chart here in the office. I have many more maps,
one in particular map #21030 Central America Pacific Coast Cabo
Velas to Punta Mala. You may obtain this map through the Director
of Defense Mapping Agency, Hydrographic/Topographic Center, Washington,
D.C. 20315, Attention: Code PRH. This map shows the Cocos Islands
is on a heading of 208 degrees approximately 289 nautical miles
from the outer buoy at Puntarenas. If you would like me to order
this map, please let me know as it shows Puntarenas and Golfito in
the Bay of Gulfodulce. I will be very happy to order these charts
for you.

I would like very much to talk to you about this amphibious
venture of yours as I have spent the last five years researching
all of the legalities of this country. I think a firm understanding
of the way Costa Rica rules its country needs to be acknowledged
as these people are very innovative in their ideas of promoting
Costa Rica and yet very protective of this particular area of
operation (Cocos). Our office here in Las Vegas is well-equipped
to handle the problems that you may face in Costa Rica as all of
the research on the cruise ship side has been painstakingly
completed. If you need any further investigations into this
project, please let me know and I will personally make personal
contact with the proper people in high government.

"Cover for the Condor…" Seal purchased a minesweeper for use as a floating
platform 'offshore Central America.'

David J. Seymour, Ltd.

NAVAL ARCHITECTS — MARINE CONSULTANTS

851 Traeger Avenue, Suite 320
San Bruno, CA 94066
Telephone (415) 872-2760
Cable Address: SEAMOR SBNO
Telex: 171548

June 17, 1983
File No. 979

Moroto Investment Company Limited
c/o Cayman Management Services Ltd.
Kirk Freeport Building
P.O. Box 1569
Grand Cayman, B.W.I.

Attention: Mr. I.G. Hutchinson

SUBJECT: M/V "CONDOR' (ex R/V EAGLE, ex USS TANAGER)
         REACTIVATION CONTRACT PLANS & SPECIFICATIONS

Encl. 1) Reactivation Specifications M.V. CONDOR
      2) Contract Guidance Plans M.V. CONDOR

Gentlemen:

As your design agent we are pleased to advise that we have completed subject
reactivation and conversion specifications and forward copies under
Encls. 1) and 2) for your information and file.

We await your approval action on the specifications either by your authorized
agent, appointed vessel operator or Mr. Barry Seal, prior to soliciting bids
from shipyards in the San Francisco bay area to undertake such work.

In addition we will require issuance of Panama Registry before commencing
any reactivation work, since Panama Bureau of Shipping surveyors will not
inspect the vessel until her valid registration is issued. We understand
that all Panama papers are ready awaiting payment of fees.

Regarding economic evaluation of your project, (reactivating costs,
operating costs, revenue estimates, profit) we would be pleased to assist in
this area. We have experience in marine operation cost studies and analysis
utilizing our computer programs.

Looking forward to hearing from you or Mr. Seal regarding approval action,
I remain,

Very truly yours,

David J. Seymour

DJS/rb
cc: Barry Seal

…Two months after being charged with major drug felonies Barry Seal
purchased a US minesweeper, envisioned as a floating offshore the "Central
American conflict.

DELTA SIERRA SERVICES

(415) 331-6426
CABLE: DELTA

147 La Perdiz Court
San Rafael, CA 94903

TELEX: 176021
ANSWBK: DELTA SIERRA

April 20, 1984

Mr. Walter Bowden, Chief Wharfinger
Port of San Francisco
Ferry Building
San Francisco, Ca. 94111

Dear Mr. Bowden:

Re: Moroto Investment Company
MV CONDOR (ex Eagle)

On October 5, 1983 the above vessel was moved from Pier 24 to Pacific Drydock & Repair Co. at Oakland, such move having been precipitated by the takeover of Pier 24 by Southwest Marine.

Monthly, the Port continues to send to us a statement of past due items, adding a service charge thereto. This charge is for electrical power originally billed under billing number 239070 in the amount of $412.21. As per statement of 3/31/84 this amount is now billed as $450.05 as a result of adding monthly service charge since originally billed.

As you may recall, the Port's dredge was connected to the power source of the then "Eagle" for a considerable period of time; also it is possible that American Navigation did use some of that power, although they have denied it to us for the month in question.

In any case, the crux of the matter is that the "Eagle" had in continous use ten 40 watt and four 100 watt bulbs at the beginning of August. At times, these burned out and were not replaced. However, the vessel could not have used more than 576 kilowatt hours, which at our present rate of .09 per KWH at Pacific Drydock is equal to $51.84.

I also comment that the vessel now has heaters going constantly in the engine room, an engineer liveing aboard with electric cooking, washer/dryer, etc. and heat in his living quarters; with all this, our most recent bill to Pacific Drydock was $372 as compared to the $412 charge of the Port of San Francisco. It is not an equitable charge and we do not intend to pay it; we will, however, in the interest of getting no monthly bill, pay $51.84 for the 800 watts per day we used.

Your assistance in cleaning this old chestnut from both our books will be greatly appreciated.

Sincerely,

Daniel J. Seid, President

cc: D. J. Seymour
    Adler B. Seal

Transportation Consultants -------- Ship Agents -------- Equipment Leasing

The 'business' of a CIA agent... Standard correspondence concerning the US minesweeper USS Condor, one of Seal's busy fleet of airplanes and oceangoing ships.

CITIBANK

3828076740116128060256000

For Investment Savings Information see reverse side.
For Change of Address or Phone Number: please
print new address or phone number below.

( )   ( )
New Home Phone   New Business Phone

Payment Due Date		Statement Date
12/18/85		11/25/85
▼ Enter Amount Enclosed		New Balance
		$ 6128.06
		Minimum Amount Due
		$ 256.00

0485 2 00 A1

DEBORAH D SEAL
            DR
BATON ROUGE LA
70810-

Account Number

Please save your charge receipts.
Payment Coupon: Please tear along perforation and return this portion with your payment. Make check payable in U.S. dollars
on a U.S. bank to Citibank Visa. Include account number on check or money order. No cash please.

Citibank Preferred Visa

For Customer Service call anytime or write:
800-645-9565   P.O.BOX 6062, SIOUX FALLS, SD 57117

Account Number	Cash Advance Limit*	Total Credit Line	Statement Date	Payment Due Date
	$3000	$10000	11/25/85	12/18/85

Sale Date	Post Date	Reference Number	Activity Since Last Statement			Amount
	1108	02691133	PAYMENT THANK YOU			-461606
	1120	T9946144	PAYMENT THANK YOU			-300000
1030	1030	3024041146	ALL AMERICAN SPTS	BATON ROUGE	LA	-5345
1105	1105	31143260	THE SLEEP SHOP	BATON ROUGE	LA	-8731
1017	1026	18631033	PEOPLE EXPRESS AIRLINE	NEWARK	NJ	17700
1017	1026	JEL01NK1	NEW YORK AIRLINES	KENNER	LA	5900
1018	1026	94501237	EXXON	BATON ROUGE	LA	3000
1021	1026	3P4BX7JL	DELTA - ATA	KENNER	LA	30000
1021	1026	17300558	CONTINENTAL AIRLINES	KENNER	LA	6000
1021	1026	17300559	CONTINENTAL AIRLINES	KENNER	LA	15000
1022	1026	46338647	AEROMEXICO	MIAMI	FL	20300
1024	1026	99818791	PATS OF HENDERSON INC	BATON ROUGE	LA	6810
1025	1026	14541724	ALL AMERICAN SPTS	BATON ROUGE	LA	8309
1027	1027	99819323	MIKE ANDERSON'S	BATON ROUGE	LA	20115
1028	1028	20441793		BATON ROUGE	LA	6000
1028	1028	T1023014	CHAMPS #125	BATON ROUGE	LA	9628

Account Summary If payment of the New Balance for Purchases is received on or before the Payment Due Date, there will be no additional Finance Charge for Purchases.

	Previous Balance	Purchases & Advances	Payments	Credits (+)	Finance Charge	Late Charges	New Balance	Payment Due
Purchases	159328	774099	309328	14076			610023	22817
Advances	302278	150000	452278		2783		2783	2783
Total	461606	924099	761606	14076	2783		612806	25600

	Purchases	Advances	Number of Days This Billing Period		
Balance Subject to Finance Charge		165544		Amount Over Credit Line ▶	
Periodic Rate	1.65%	.05424%		Unpaid Fees ▶	
Nominal Annual Percentage Rate	19.80%	19.80%	31	Past Due ▶	
Annual Percentage Rate	19.80%	19.80%		Minimum Amount Due ▶	25600

Send Payments to: P.O. Box 6001, Sioux Falls, S.D. 57188-6001   If you have an amount in dispute, please see reverse side.

Citibank Investment Savings

	Amount	Annual Interest Rate

TAKE ADVANTAGE OF OUR CURRENT HIGH CD RATES.
THEY'RE COMPETITIVE, COMPOUNDED DAILY FOR A HIGHER YIELD
AND OFFER THE SECURITY OF FDIC INSURANCE.
SO TAKE ADVANTAGE, OPEN AN ACCOUNT TODAY.

FOR INVESTMENT INFORMATION ONLY, CALL
YOUR CITIBANK PREFERRED VISA ACCOUNT EXECUTIVE
TOLL-FREE, MONDAY-FRIDAY 8AM-11PM, E.T.: 800-645-9181.SL02

Purchase Date	Annual Interest Rate/Yield	Certificate Numbers	Amount Invested	Interest to Date	Projected Interest

*Cash Advance Limit Is A Portion of Your Total Credit Line.   Citibank (South Dakota), N.A. Member F.D.I.C.
NOTICE: See Reverse Side for Important Information.

A splatter of Barry Seal's blood marks his last credit card bill...

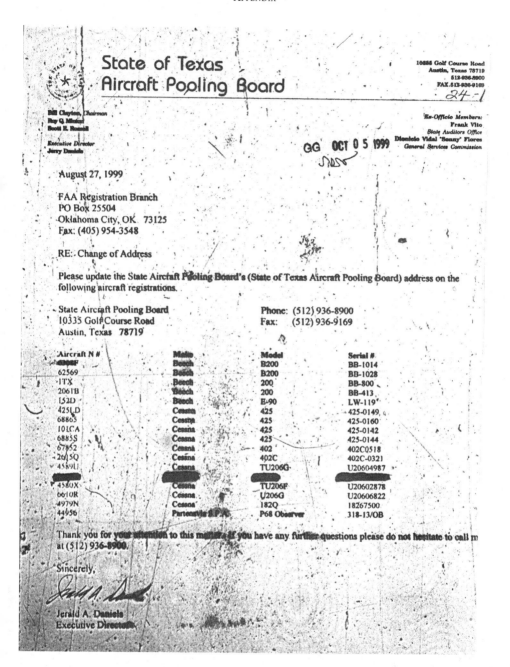

State of Texas
Aircraft Pooling Board

10333 Golf Course Road
Austin, Texas 78719
512-936-8900
FAX.512-936-9169

Bill Clayton, Chairman
Ray Q. Minter
Scott E. Russell

Executive Director
Jerry Daniels

Ex-Officio Members:
Frank Vito
State Auditors Office
Dionisio Vidal "Sonny" Flores
General Services Commission

GG OCT 0 5 1999

August 27, 1999

FAA Registration Branch
PO Box 25504
Oklahoma City, OK 73125
Fax: (405) 954-3548

RE: Change of Address

Please update the State Aircraft Pooling Board's (State of Texas Aircraft Pooling Board) address on the following aircraft registrations.

State Aircraft Pooling Board   Phone: (512) 936-8900
10335 Golf Course Road   Fax: (512) 936-9169
Austin, Texas 78719

Aircraft N #	Make	Model	Serial #
	Beech	B200	BB-1014
62569	Beech	B200	BB-1028
1TX	Beech	200	BB-800
2061B	Beech	200	BB-413
152D	Beech	E-90	LW-119
425LD	Cessna	425	425-0149
68865	Cessna	425	425-0160
101CA	Cessna	425	425-0142
6885S	Cessna	425	425-0144
67852	Cessna	402	402C0518
20JSQ	Cessna	402C	402C-0321
4589U	Cessna	TU206G	U20604987
458OX	Cessna	TU206F	U20602878
6610R	Cessna	U206G	U20606822
4979N	Cessna	182Q	18267500
44956	Partenavia S.P.A.	P68 Observer	318-13/OB

Thank you for your attention to this matter. If you have any further questions please do not hesitate to call me at (512) 936-8900.

Sincerely,

Jerald A. Daniels
Executive Director

A "late scratch…" The 'N' number of the plane used by both Barry Seal and George W. Bush appears to have been hastily scratched off (top plane in list) off this list of the State of Texas' planes.

phone bill 10/15 at 12:12 from St. Augustine.
~~Do not pay~~ Operator did not say collect. minutes.

10/9	Honduras	2:19 thru 2:24	Me		5
10/9	Mexico	9:49 thru 9:56	Gary?		7
10/10	Honduras	806 — 818	Gary		12
10/10	Mexico	8:36 — 8:39	Gary		3
10/11	mexico	4:10 — 4:22	Gary		12
10/15	Honduras	7:00 38 — 7:03 3-16	Gary		3 min
10/17	Honduras	6:29–637	Gary		8 min
10/12	Golfito Costa Rico		Gary		15 min
10/19	mexico — Boat captain —	1:16 – 1:22	Gary		6 min
10/21	Honduras —		Gary		5 min
10/21	Costa Rico —		Gary		20 min
10/22	~~Caracas~~ Grand Turk 1:21 —		Gary	~~10 min~~ 4 min
10-22	Costa Rica		Gary		10 min
10-23	Honduras		Gary		8 min
10-23	mexico		Gary		7 min

Handwritten logs of Seal's phone conversations, while in protective custody in Nevada, reveal that "the most important informant in DEA history" was still doing big business in Central America.

March 30, 1977

Captain Wiley McCormick
Troop Commander, Troop A
Louisiana State Police Headquarters
11117 Airline Highway
Baton Rouge, Louisiana 70816

  re: Formal Complaint Against Sgt. Cook

Dear Captain McCormick:

On Wednesday, March 16, 1977 at approximately 8:00 P.M., I was
travelling in my automobile in the Parish of East Baton Rouge west
on Goodwood Boulevard between Airline Highway and Jefferson Highway
when I stopped for a red light signal on the corner of Lobdell and
Goodwood, being the second car in a flow of traffic directly behind
a white state police vehicle equipped with red lights on the roof
and bearing a Troop A state police plate. As the light turned green,
I proceeded in the normal traffic flow behind the state policeman
westbound toward Jefferson Highway. I was surprised to see my speed-
ometer rapidly approaching and passing through the published 35 mile-
per-hour speed limit. To my amazement I found myself following this
state police vehicle to a speed in excess of 65 miles-per hour. As
we approached Jefferson Highway the light turned red and he was
forced to stop still showing no signs of emergency procedures, i.e.
flashing lights, sirens, etc. I felt at this point that if he had
time to stop for a red light, he was in no condition of emergency.
At this point I pulled along beside him, motioning him to roll his
window down. I advised that he was speeding and going at speeds in
excess of 65 miles-per-hour in a 35 mile-per-hour zone, and I felt
that he was breaking the law. At that point he immediately advised
me that my safety sticker was expired and I then suggested that we
both pull over into the closed Exxon Service Station and discuss the
matter. Upon getting out of the vehicle, he advised that I could
not under any circumstances stop a state policeman for speeding and
that he was the shift supervisor at Troop A and he was responding
to another trooper's call for help at the Rodeway Inn on a hit-and-
run case, at which point I immediately said, "Please don't waste anymore time with me; if another trooper is in need of help, please
proceed immediately about your business." At this point he advised
that it was not of much urgency and then said, "Don't I know you?"
I said, "Yes you do, you were the shift supervisor on duty when my
attorney and myself had gone to Troop A to secure a release on an
impounded vehicle." At this point he acknowledged recognition and
again said, "Mr Seal, I don't want any trouble with you but you can't

The Price of Arrogance... Barry Seal attempted to give a uniformed Louisiana
State Trooper a ticket for speeding.

Florida Aircraft Leasing Corp.
GENERAL DECLARATION
(Outward/Inward)
AGRICULTURE, CUSTOMS, IMMIGRATION, AND PUBLIC HEALTH
Florida Aircraft Leasing Corp.

Owner or Operator: Florida Aircraft Leasing Corp.

Marks of Nationality and Registration: 1) U.S. N 4826C   Flight No. Special   Date March 6, 1985

Departure from Fort Lauderdale, Flordia   Arrival at Illopango, San Salvador
(Place)   (Place)

FLIGHT ROUTING
(*Place Column always to list origin, every en route stop and dest.)

PLACE	TOTAL NUMBER OF CREW 1)		NUMBER OF PASSENGERS ON THIS STAGE 2)
Fort Lauderdale, Florida	Ronald Roy	Captain	Incomplete
Illopango, San Salvador	Danny Vasquez	First Officer	Departure Place: 0 Embarking
	Robert Joe Thompson	Agent	
	Steven Carr	Agent	Through on same flight 0
	Robert Corvo	Agent	
			Arrival Place: 0 Disembarking
			Through on same flight 0

Declaration of Health

Persons on board known to be suffering from illness other than airsickness or the effects of accidents, as well as those cases of illness disembarked during the flight: NONE

Any other condition on board which may lead to the spread of disease: NONE

Details of each disinfecting or sanitary treatment (place, date, time, method) during the flight. If no disinfecting has been carried out during the flight give details of most recent disinfecting: Sprayed prior to alighting.

Signed if required ....
Crew member concerned

For Official Use Only

Dec/6R

0058
EC32

U.S. CUSTOMS LOG NO.

I declare that all statements and particulars contained in this General Declaration, and in any supplementary forms required to be presented with this General Declaration are complete, Exact and true to the best of my knoledge and that all through passengers will continue/have continued on the flight.

The Kerry Commission heard testimony that Florida Aircraft Leasing flew numerous illegal flights for the Contras. Barry Seal had ties with this company and its owner, James Boy, going back to 1972, when he was arrested with 7 tons of plastic explosives loaded into one of their planes.

November 13, 1984

Mr. Jack Lamb
Chief Operating Officer
NUNASI Central Airlines
Hangor T-139
626 Ferry Road
Winnepeg, Man. Canada   R3HOT7

Dear Mr. Lamb:

Regarding our telephone conversation of 11-13-84, we will
do everything possible to support your effort to import
the Fairchild C123K Provider into Canada. We will contact
the Department of Transportation, Canada, to determine
ways of expediting the licensing process.

If you have any questions regarding the aircraft, or if
you would like to schedule a flight demo, please don't
hesitate to call.

Very truly yours,

Bill Lambeth

BL:mk

1930 S. Alma School Rd, Suite A114, Mesa, AZ 85202 ● Telephone: (602) 897-8049 ● Telex: 852-832

LAMBETH AIRCRAFT CORPORATION. Transport Aircraft Marketing ● W. R. LAMBETH AND ASSOCIATES. Airline Consultants ● LAMBETH AERONAUTICAL PUBLISHING. Air Operations Manuals

Arizona-based CIA aircraft executive Bill Lambeth was speaking with Seal
on his cell-phone when Seal died. Lambeth was himself murdered seven
years later.

Caribbean Management Ltd.

Formerly Centre Management Caribbean Limited

INTERNATIONAL FINANCIAL & MANAGEMENT CONSULTANTS

P.O. Box 856, 3rd Floor, West Wind Building, Grand Cayman, Cayman Islands, B.W.I.
Telephone 9-4907/9-4891 From UK & Canada 809-94-94907/94891 Telex 4418 CENTRE

Directors
A. Smith
E.M. Pierson
J.B. Smith

your ref   our ref   date

Received from Capt. McKenzie US$3000 (three thousand cash) in partial settlement of outstanding fees. In regard to various companies of which he is to beneficial owner

A Smith

19/2/86

Representative Offices in Jersey, Guernsey, Holland, Italy, Nigeria, U.K., Switzerland, U.S.A.

Rendering Unto Caesar... The same day Barry Seal was assassinated, his assets--planes and ships--were repossessed by their true owner, the Central Intelligence Agency, in a coordinated operation throughout the Caribbean.

HARVEY JONES VESSEL AGENTS, INC.

2613 Marais Street
New Orleans, LA 70117
[504] 945-7204

February 20, 1986

U.S. Customs Service
Baton Rouge
Louisiana

RE: MV CAPTAIN WONDERFUL
    Vessel documents

Gentlemen:

We, Harvey Jones Vessel Agents, Inc., as agents for the MV CAPTAIN WONDERFUL would like you at this time to release the vessel's documents to Mr. Dan D. Chaneville, Attorney-at-Law, who will send the documents to the Vessel Registry Office in the Cayman Islands to amend the documentation to reflect a change in the corporate name of the owner of the vessel and then return the documents to U.S. Customs.

In so doing we hold the U.S. Customs Service blameless for any events or expenses which may occur.

Regards,
HARVEY JONES VESSEL AGENTS, INC.

Harvey Jones

Baton Rouge, La. FEB 5 1986

I certify that the within is a true
copy of the original ... at this
office. ...

Form No. 9

CERTIFICATE OF BRITISH REGISTRY

PARTICULARS OF SHIP

Official Number	Name of Ship	No., Year and Port of Registry	No., Year and Port of previous Registry (if any)
702488	CAPTAIN WONDERFUL	NO. 55 IN 1983 GEORGE TOWN CAYMAN ISLANDS	541495 U.S.A.

Whether a Sailing, Steam or Motor Ship; if Steam or Motor, how propelled	Where Built	When Built	Name and Address of Builders
MOTOR TRAWLER SINGLE SCREW	FLORIDA	1972	BUILDERS UNKNOWN TRAPON SPRINGS FLORIDA

			FEET	TENTHS
Number of Decks ONE	Length from fore-part of stem, to the aft side of the head of the stern post / fore side of the rudder stock		60	6
Number of Masts ONE	Main breadth to outside of plating		17	6
Rigged NOT	Depth in hold from tonnage deck to ceiling amidships		7	8
Stem RAKED	Depth in hold from upper deck to ceiling amidships, in the case of two decks and upwards			
Stern ROUND	Depth from top of upper deck at side amidships to bottom of keel			
Build CARVEL	Round of beam on upper deck		0	3
Framework and description of vessel STEEL FISH TRAWLER	Length of engine-room (if any)		19	5
Number of Bulkheads FOUR				

PARTICULARS OF PROPELLING ENGINES, &C. (IF ANY), as supplied by Builders, Owners, or Engine Makers.

No. of sets of Engines	Description of Engines	When made	Name and Address of Makers	Reciprocating Engines		Rotary Engines	B.H.P. Estimated Speed of Ship
				No. of cylinders in each set	Diameter of cylinders	No. of cylinders of each set	
TWO		Engines 1972	Engines MURPHY DIESEL COMPANY	FOUR	5.5"		149 (EACH) 298 (TOTAL)
	MURPHY DIESEL MODEL 452M	Boilers	MILWAUKEE, WISCONSIN 53219	Length of Stroke			
	Particulars of Boilers		Boilers				
	Description						
	Number						
TWO	Loaded pressure						

"**Offshore Kind of Guys…**" Seal's Agency assets, like this smugglers' vessel formerly named "Big Rock Candy Mountain," were registered in 'safe havens' in the Caribbean like the Cayman Islands

January 22, 1963, Mexico City… Only extant photo of CIA assassination squad Operation 40. Barry Seal, third from left. Porter Goss is sitting on Barry's right with his hand on Felix Rodriguez, front left. William Houston Seymour, front right. To Seymour's left, hiding his face, is Frank Sturgis.

Imagine our surprise when an astute reader informed us that the man who had just been picked to head the CIA, Porter Goss, was seated next to Barry Seal in the famous Mexico City picture from 1963

Barry Seal's death hardly ended the history of CIA drug running. These two DC9's, whose list of owners will be familiar to readrs of this book, were painted to look like U. S. Dept of Homeland Security planes. One of them was caught carrying 5.5 TONS of cocaine in Mexico in April 2006.

Greyhound Leasing owned Barry Seal's favorite plane, Tex. Gov George W. Bush's favorite plane... and a DC9 which passed between CIA front companies for 20 years.

Ramy El-Batrawi, a longt-ime lieutentant of Adnan Khashoggi, was the president of the airline that flew Olivwer North's TOW missiles to Iran in the Iran Contra Scandal. One of Barry Seal's attorney's incorporated a company for him in 1988. Small world.

443

```
0  0  0  0  UNITED STATES OF AMERICA 3              FORM APPROVED
                                                    OMB NO. 2120-0042
U.S. DEPARTMENT OF TRANSPORTATION FEDERAL AVIATION ADMINISTRATION   Q Q 0 2 7 6 2 7

              AIRCRAFT BILL OF SALE
```

FOR AND IN CONSIDERATION OF $10.00+OVC THE UNDERSIGNED OWNER(S) OF THE FULL LEGAL AND BENEFICIAL TITLE OF THE AIRCRAFT DESCRIBED AS FOLLOWS:

UNITED STATES REGISTRATION NUMBER **N 120NE**

CONVEYANCE RECORDED

AIRCRAFT MANUFACTURER & MODEL
McDonnell Douglas DC9-15

AIRCRAFT SERIAL No.
45731

2003 AUG 21 PM 12 16

DOES THIS 2nd DAY OF July 2003 HEREBY SELL, GRANT, TRANSFER AND DELIVER ALL RIGHTS, TITLE, AND INTERESTS IN AND TO SUCH AIRCRAFT UNTO:

FEDERAL AVIATION ADMINISTRATION
Do Not Write In This Block
FOR FAA USE ONLY

NAME AND ADDRESS (IF INDIVIDUAL(S), GIVE LAST NAME, FIRST NAME, AND MIDDLE INITIAL.)

PURCHASER

FINOVA Capital Corporation
4800 N. Scottsdale Road
Scottsdale, Arizona 85251

DEALER CERTIFICATE NUMBER

AND TO **its successors,** EXECUTORS, ADMINISTRATORS, AND ASSIGNS TO HAVE AND TO HOLD SINGULARLY THE SAID AIRCRAFT FOREVER, AND WARRANTS THE TITLE THEREOF.

IN TESTIMONY WHEREOF I HAVE SET my HAND AND SEAL THIS 2nd DAY OF July 2003

NAME (S) OF SELLER (TYPED OR PRINTED)	SIGNATURE (S) (IN INK) (IF EXECUTED FOR CO-OWNERSHIP, ALL MUST SIGN.)	TITLE (TYPED OR PRINTED)
Genesis Aviation, Inc.	Dough E Jacobs	CFO

CERTIFIED COPY
TO BE RECORDED BY FAA

ACKNOWLEDGMENT (NOT REQUIRED FOR PURPOSES OF FAA RECORDING: HOWEVER, MAY BE REQUIRED BY LOCAL LAW FOR VALIDITY OF THE INSTRUMENT.)

ORIGINAL: TO FAA

AC Form 8050-2 (9/92) (NSN 0052-00-629-0003) Supersedes Previous Edition

Orig ret'd to m+T

When the dust settles from the Iran Contra Scandal, the plane that began it all, the C130 that Barry Seal flew to pick up cocaine from the Sandinistas that later went down in Nicaragua with Eugene Hasenfus onboard, was discoverd to belong to Finova, a company exposedf as a CIA front in Toronto. Finova also "owned" one of the CIA's DC9's. Small world.

UNITED STATES OF AMERICA
U.S. DEPARTMENT OF TRANSPORTATION FEDERAL AVIATION ADMINISTRATION

AIRCRAFT BILL OF SALE

FORM APPROVED
OMB NO. 2120-0042

FOR AND IN CONSIDERATION OF $ _1,00C_ THE
UNDERSIGNED OWNER(S) OF THE FULL LEGAL
AND BENEFICIAL TITLE OF THE AIRCRAFT DES-
CRIBED AS FOLLOWS:

P 0 2 9 1 4 8

UNITED STATES
REGISTRATION NUMBER N *120NE*

AIRCRAFT MANUFACTURER & MODEL *DC-9-15 McDonnell Douglas*

AIRCRAFT SERIAL No. *45731*

CONVEYANCE RECORDED

DOES THIS *13* DAY OF *January* *2005* 2005 AUG 15 PM 3 34
HEREBY SELL, GRANT, TRANSFER AND
DELIVER ALL RIGHTS, TITLE, AND INTERESTS
IN AND TO SUCH AIRCRAFT UNTO:

FEDERAL AVIATION
ADMINISTRATION

Do Not Write In This Block
FOR FAA USE ONLY

NAME AND ADDRESS
(IF INDIVIDUAL(S), GIVE LAST NAME, FIRST NAME, AND MIDDLE INITIAL.)

PURCHASER

Royal Sons Inc.
15875 - Fairchild Dr.
CLW, FL 33762

DEALER CERTIFICATE NUMBER

AND TO EXECUTORS, ADMINISTRATORS, AND ASSIGNS TO HAVE AND TO HOLD
SINGULARLY THE SAID AIRCRAFT FOREVER, AND WARRANTS THE TITLE THEREOF.

IN TESTIMONY WHEREOF HAVE SET HAND AND SEAL THIS DAY OF 19

SELLER

NAME (S) OF SELLER (TYPED OR PRINTED)	SIGNATURE (S) (IN INK) (IF EXECUTED FOR CO-OWNERSHIP, ALL MUST SIGN.)	TITLE (TYPED OR PRINTED)
Royal Sons Inc		CO-owner
Skyway Comm Holding Corp.	*James Hansen Vice President*	CO-OWNER

ACKNOWLEDGMENT (NOT REQUIRED FOR PURPOSES OF FAA RECORDING; HOWEVER, MAY BE REQUIRED
BY LOCAL LAW FOR VALIDITY OF THE INSTRUMENT.)

ORIGINAL: TO FAA

08/12/2005 $5.00

Skyway Aircraft was also the name of an international airline owned by a
Texas backer of George W. Bush, James Bath, which had one of its planes
busted in Paris with a Saudi Prince and several thousand pounds of cocaine
onboard.

Index

Welcome to Terrorland
Mohamed Atta & the 9-11 Cover-up in Florida

Meet Mohamed Atta's American girlfriend, with whom he lived for two months in Venice, FL., and who was intimidated into silence by the FBI after the attack...

Venice, Florida, where three of the four terrorist pilots learned to fly, is the biggest September 11 crime scene that wasn't reduced to rubble. Yet it has until now received no serious scrutiny for what it might reveal about the nature of the 9/11 attack. Investigative journalist Daniel Hopsicker went searching for evidence that Mohamed Atta and his Hamburg cadre received outside help while they were in the U.S., as authorities initially stated, from a shadowy 'global network,' or even from foreign governments.

What he found was a massive cover-up-in-progress in Florida designed to conceal the true story of what was going while Mohamed Atta and his Hamburg cadre conspirators made Venice, Florida their 'home away from home' base for a year and a half.